The Craft of Historical Research

Isaac Land

The Craft of Historical Research

A Practical Guide from Start to Finish

Isaac Land
Indiana State University
Terre Haute, IN, USA

ISBN 978-3-031-68456-2   ISBN 978-3-031-68457-9 (eBook)
https://doi.org/10.1007/978-3-031-68457-9

© The Editor(s) (if applicable) and The Author(s), under exclusive license to Springer Nature Switzerland AG 2024

This work is subject to copyright. All rights are solely and exclusively licensed by the Publisher, whether the whole or part of the material is concerned, specifically the rights of translation, reprinting, reuse of illustrations, recitation, broadcasting, reproduction on microfilms or in any other physical way, and transmission or information storage and retrieval, electronic adaptation, computer software, or by similar or dissimilar methodology now known or hereafter developed.
The use of general descriptive names, registered names, trademarks, service marks, etc. in this publication does not imply, even in the absence of a specific statement, that such names are exempt from the relevant protective laws and regulations and therefore free for general use.
The publisher, the authors and the editors are safe to assume that the advice and information in this book are believed to be true and accurate at the date of publication. Neither the publisher nor the authors or the editors give a warranty, expressed or implied, with respect to the material contained herein or for any errors or omissions that may have been made. The publisher remains neutral with regard to jurisdictional claims in published maps and institutional affiliations.

This Palgrave Macmillan imprint is published by the registered company Springer Nature Switzerland AG.
The registered company address is: Gewerbestrasse 11, 6330 Cham, Switzerland

If disposing of this product, please recycle the paper.

*To the memory of
Stephen Hum, Sarah Bandes, and Don LaCosse
my graduate school classmates
gone too soon*

Acknowledgments

The first book about method that I ever encountered was Norton Juster's children's classic, *The Phantom Tollbooth*. Long before I knew anything about rhetoric or higher intellectual pursuits, his book exposed me to little unforgettable parables about wisdom and folly, purpose and futility. It encouraged my fondness for whimsy, but above all, *Phantom Tollbooth* showed me that it's possible to express big truths in simple language.

I'm still out there searching for Rhyme and Reason in a confounding world, but all of us need companions in the quest. Cathy Pearce immediately understood the value of this project and read chapters with an eye toward how it would go over with her own students. Anna Pilz suggested that I needed a whole chapter on revision. I cannot imagine the book without it now. Sean Fraga and Taylor Easum offered valuable suggestions on the parts of this book that were furthest from my own research and writing experience.

More than any other single person, Julia Leikin influenced the shape of the book, prodding me to think hard about where the advisor fit into the picture, and urging me to engage more with the promise and pitfalls of student projects that relied primarily, or exclusively, on digitized materials.

My little valiant band of student readers helped get this project over the finish line. After completing their BA, Holly Crowley and Tony Wilson stuck with me over a period of sixteen months, asking for updates and reading every single chapter until it was all written. (Then they asked for updates on whether I'd heard back from the peer reviewers yet!) Their loyalty made all the difference. Helena Jancosek and Catherine O'Brien read the book as they were completing their own Master's degrees and offered thoughts from that perspective. Rowan Eggert has the distinction of being the first reader to hold a complete, printed out copy of the entire manuscript. He immediately read some chapters out of order, and the book did not explode, so I guess it is safe to do that if you insist on giving it a try. Charlotte Olsen was the last of my student readers. Fittingly, it is a conversation with her that inspired what is now the last paragraph of the final chapter.

Holli Moseman's team at the Inter-Library Loan office fielded even more requests than usual from me, without complaint. Katherine Black brought library books directly to my office on many occasions.

This project, more than most, has been long in the making. During a sabbatical from Indiana State University in the Spring of 2013, I did extensive background reading and completed a rough draft of many portions of the manuscript. Other developments in my professional life meant that I had to set this entire project aside for almost a decade, although I continued to add notes when I saw something that reminded me of a particular theme or subsection. Aside from some subsequent fine-tuning, the version of the book you hold in your hands is the result of a writing (and rewriting) process from May 2021 to September 2023. I have no conflicts of interest to declare.

Although I tried to keep track over a period of more than ten years, it is likely that there are careless omissions in the list below. With the necessary caveat that any shortcomings and errors are mine alone, I certainly must thank:

Ruth Ahnert, Kimberly Alexander, Simon Appleford, Andrea Arrington, Aaron Benanay, Heather Coombes, Dan Clark, Elsa Devienne, Carlos Dimas, Sydney Feldhake, Anne Foster, Joana Gaspar de Freitas, Gabriel Gee, Romain Grancher, Melissa Gustafson, John Handel, Mandy Haggith, Yasir Ibrahim, Kit Kincade, Thanasis Kinias, Deidre Lynch, Rivkah Mentzner, Amy Milne-Smith, Chris Olsen, Ezra Pennington, Sara Spike, Steve Stofferahn, Jay Stull, Johnathan Thayer, Brooke Truax, Chris Weber, Katy Werlin, Victoria Woolcott, and Ash Wright.

At Palgrave Macmillan, Carly Silver, Emily Russell, and Eliana Rangel were staunch and patient advocates. Thanks also to the three anonymous peer reviewers who took the time to offer their insights and support.

My heart is full, my debts are great. For many years, this book was never far from my thoughts. It was all worth it, though, because finally it is in your hands.

Contents

1	**Introduction**	1
Part I	**Articulating Your Vision**	13
2	**Getting Your Bearings**	17
	A Browser's Manifesto	18
	Browsing Historiography	20
	Browsing the Unbrowsable	25
	Rambles, Detours, and Short Cuts	27
	Conclusion	32
	Further Reading	33
3	**Encountering the Experts**	35
	The Skeptic's Credo	36
	Your Cousins, Evil Twins, Frenemies, Soul Mates, and Role Models	39
	A Trip to the Anti-library	42
	A Word About Interdisciplinary Projects	44
	Conclusion	47
	Further Reading	48
4	**Questioning Primary Sources**	49
	The Past Has No Voice	50
	When Is a Source Not a Source?	51
	The Educated Source	56
	Conclusion	61
	Further Reading	61

5	**Finding a Place to Stand**	63
	The World of Incremental Scholarship	64
	The Bold and Lonely Path	66
	That's Obvious… That's Interesting… That's Absurd	69
	Conclusion	72
	Further Reading	73
	Checking in with Your Advisor: Part One Worksheet (The "Vision" Checklist)	73

Part II Selecting Your Focus   75

6	**Planning for Success in the Archives**	79
	Thinking Critically About Archives	80
	A "Dry Run" Exercise	85
	A Different Kind of Reading	87
	The Human Element	90
	Practical Strategies	93
	Conclusion	98
	Further Reading	99
7	**Planning for Success in the Digital Realm**	101
	Thinking Critically About Digitization and Digitized Materials	102
	The Zigzag Path	104
	Is a "Big Data" Approach Right for Me?	109
	Taking Your Database for a Test Drive	111
	Conclusion	113
	Further Reading	115
8	**Designing Your Project**	117
	The Art of Changing Your Topic	119
	Compared to What?	123
	From When to When?	125
	What's Your Sample?	128
	From Research Question to Research Prospectus	130
	Conclusion	134
	Further Reading	136
	Checking in with Your Advisor: Part Two Worksheet (The "Focus" Checklist)	136

Part III Developing and Supporting Your Thesis — 139

9 Imagining Claims and Counterclaims — 143
- *What Do Historians Think About Truth?* — 146
- *Avoiding Common Errors* — 149
- *Drafting a Provisional Thesis Statement* — 156
- *Writing About Causation, Contingency, and Change over Time* — 158
- *The Art of Changing Your Mind* — 162
- *Conclusion* — 166
- *Further Reading* — 167

10 Supporting Claims with Evidence — 169
- *Verbal Warrants* — 170
- *Numerical Warrants* — 177
- *Visual Warrants* — 182
- *Spatial Warrants* — 189
- *Conclusion* — 193
- *Further Reading* — 195
- *Checking in with Your Advisor: Part III Worksheet* — 195

Part IV Writing Up — 199

11 Structuring Your Paper — 201
- *Are We Storytellers First?* — 202
- *From Writer's Block to Building Blocks* — 205
- *How Much Background Should I Give?* — 208
- *Ordering the Parts* — 212
- *Beginnings and Endings* — 217
- *Conclusion* — 221
- *Further Reading* — 221

12 Crafting Your Exposition — 223
- *Thinking Critically About Quotation* — 224
- *The Artful Footnote* — 231
- *Visual Explanations* — 234
- *Adopting the Right Tone* — 239
- *Conclusion* — 245
- *Further Reading* — 245

13	**Working with Feedback**	247
	The Art of Revision	248
	Reappraise, Rework, Rebalance	251
	Settling Your Intellectual Debts	253
	Titles and Abstracts	256
	The Defense	258
	Further Reading	264
Part V	**Looking Ahead**	265
14	**Joining a Community of Scholars**	267
	Networking and Academic Small Talk	268
	Giving Your First Conference Paper	271
	Submitting Your Work for Publication	275
	Conclusion	281
	Further Reading	282
15	**Exploring Alternatives**	283
	Academic-Adjacent Jobs	285
	Public-Facing History	288
	Looking Further Afield	291
	What Goes on Your Resume?	293
	Conclusion	295
	Further Reading	296
Index		297

About the Author

Isaac Land (PhD, University of Michigan, 1999) has published extensively on the history of sailors, port towns, and islands. His "Coastal History Blog" sought to bring together scholarship on the range of people, themes, and topics that are often overlooked because they do not fit neatly into oceanic or terrestrial categories. Later, he helped to establish the interdisciplinary journal *Coastal Studies & Society*. After twenty-five years of teaching, he recently retired from Indiana State University, closing out a career in which he worked primarily with first-generation college students. His email Isaac.Land@indstate.edu remains active, and he would welcome messages about this book, how you have used it, what works well, and what could be improved if there is a second edition at some point in the future.

List of Figures

Fig. 1.1	The project that is never done. Diagram by Isaac Land	3
Fig. 1.2	The project that has found its natural center. Diagram by Isaac Land	4
Fig. 10.1	Ages of foreign correspondents, 1995. (Graph by Isaac Land)	180
Fig. 10.2	"Plaque with Scenes from the Life of the Buddha," twelfth century (India: Bihar or West Bengal). (Metropolitan Museum of Art, New York. Open Access image, Accession Number: 1982.233)	184
Fig. 10.3	Thomas Rowlandson, "The Contrast" (1792). (Metropolitan Museum of Art, New York. Open Access image)	185
Fig. 10.4	Honoré Daumier, "Dernier conseil des ex-ministres," March 9, 1848. (National Gallery of Art (U.S.A.), Corcoran Collection, gift of Dr. Armand Hammer. Open Access image)	186
Fig. 10.5	Honoré Daumier, "Rue Transnonain, le 15 avril 1834." (Metropolitan Museum of Art, New York. Open Access image)	187
Fig. 10.6	Telephone ownership. (Graph by Isaac Land)	190
Fig. 11.1	What's knowable; what you know; what the reader needs to know. (Diagram by Isaac Land)	208
Fig. 11.2	William Henry Goodyear, "Mosque of Suleiman I," Istanbul, Turkey, 1903. (Brooklyn Museum Archives, Goodyear Archival Collection (S03_06_01_003 image 1711) via Wikimedia Commons)	214
Fig. 12.1	David Octavius Hill and Robert Adamson, "Willie Liston redding the line," 1843–1847. (Metropolitan Museum of Art, New York. Open Access image under the title "Newhaven Fisherman")	235

CHAPTER 1

Introduction

Here's the problem with instructions: They are written by experts. The artist Paul Klee opened his *Pedagogical Sketchbook* with a suggestion that art could be as simple as "taking a line for a walk."[1] Or consider this tip from hockey star Wayne Gretzsky: "I skate to where the puck is going to be, not to where it has been."[2] There may be some breathtaking insight behind expressions like this, but good luck trying to make use of it without already possessing an accomplished eye.

The Craft of Historical Research is a book of practical advice and practical solutions. It's the book that I wish had existed when I undertook an undergraduate Honors thesis and in the following years, as I moved on to graduate school in a combined Master's/PhD program. You are about to begin what is, for everyone, a difficult period of transition and questioning. Most students are surprised by how little structure and how little feedback there is at this level. With that in mind, this book is designed to gently help students help themselves.

You could read it quickly at the outset of your project and return it to later as needed. Perhaps, if it's assigned as part of a methods course, you could ration it out over several weeks and months. Ideally, though, I envision it as a supplement and facilitator to an ongoing series of conversations with your advisor. Even if your meetings with them are infrequent, the worksheets at the end of Parts One, Two, and Three will offer you talking points. Discussing your jottings at each stage will help *you* help your advisor to be a better ally. Beyond that, what I've written is the 2:00 AM book when doubts or worries arise, and there is no one on hand to answer.

---

[1] Laura U. Marks, "Taking a Line for a Walk: From the Abbasid Caliphate to Vector Graphics," *Third Text* 23, no. 3 (May 2009): 229–240, see 230.
[2] Jason Kirby, "Why businesspeople won't stop using that Gretzsky quote," *Maclean's*, September 24, 2014.

© The Author(s), under exclusive license to Springer Nature Switzerland AG 2024
I. Land, *The Craft of Historical Research*,
https://doi.org/10.1007/978-3-031-68457-9_1

There are many short manuals covering elementary concepts, how to cite sources, and an introduction to basic library skills. After this, though, budding historians are transitioned abruptly to roundups of schools of thought and trendy new approaches. These don't speak to many students where they are and offer little advice about the challenges involved with designing one's own project and seeing it through to completion. In contrast, social scientists in training can consult practical books with titles like "research design."

Perhaps to our credit, when we serve as mentors and project advisors, historians do not demand "mini-me" projects that fit neatly under the umbrella of our own preferred research interests and source materials. This does set up possibilities for friction or misunderstanding when a student and an advisor work on quite different things. The proliferation of specialized short manuals (history of emotions, women's history, quantitative history) is a mixed blessing; they help to make that situation more viable, but also sidestep some of the central issues involved with what supervision should look like *across* the boundaries of specialization.

At the other extreme, there are the generic books on academic writing. These, necessarily, focus on the problems that face writers in *all* disciplines. I acknowledge their insights when appropriate; excellence, however, is discipline-specific. To the extent that generic manuals hint at what would distinguish great work from merely adequate work, they lean too far to the norms of the social sciences, or of literary criticism. Many of the most basic concerns that arise for History students go unmentioned.

Hence the need for something that targets History students in particular. In keeping with its mission as a nonspecialized guide, this book takes a firmly agnostic stance on topic choice. In a similar spirit, although I could not hint at every possibility, I sought out illustrative examples from around the world, and from many different time periods. The types of sources mentioned range from hagiographies of Buddhist nuns to the personnel files of Africans who served as police officers under French colonial rule. Political cartoons make an appearance in this book. So do emails. So do cuneiform tablets.

While academic values—as well as the underpinnings of academic research and writing—transcend national boundaries, the *vocabulary* referring to students, student projects, and faculty does vary quite a bit from one country to another. For example, readers in the United States would expect a dissertation to be the product of a PhD candidate, while readers in the UK might well associate that word with undergraduate research. I have sought to use generic language ("your paper"; "your project") to avoid confusion.

I've written this book for the student undertaking their first major independent research project, or who otherwise find themselves caught in a daunting transition. For example, graduate school expectations may come as a shock—or just seem worryingly unclear—to the person who excelled as an undergraduate. Other readers may have simply developed enough self-awareness that research and writing no longer seems quite so simple and straightforward. Don't be too alarmed by those sensations. It's wise to remember the humility of the published and the proficient, who are prone to say things like "we may write three novels before we write a good one."[3] While this is a textbook aimed at students, the truth is that a newcomer writing their first long paper and a senior scholar writing their fifth book have to reckon with many of the same classic issues and decision points. Over a lifetime in the profession, we revisit and refine our grasp of these fundamentals.

This book, then, is appropriate for the student undertaking an ambitious undergraduate paper, *or* making the transition to a Master's program, *or* venturing on the first steps toward a doctorate. It's not unusual for the best undergraduate research papers to evoke comparisons to what we see at the Master's level, and so on. As Jonathan Grix has observed, perhaps the key difference between the undergraduate, MA, and PhD levels—beyond the obvious increase in the length of the final paper—is in how much independence the student has in devising and executing their project.[4] In all three situations, the core expectation is that you will produce something that "adds to knowledge on [the] topic either by generating new knowledge or clarifying or furthering existing work."[5]

Whether at the bachelor's, master's, or doctoral level, academic writing involves projects that must be executed on a small scale. Most are shorter (sometimes considerably shorter!) than a book-length work. A completion time is also limited; for many student projects, it might even be expressible in weeks or months. There's a need, then, to right-size *both* the research question *and* the scale of the undertaking. Two simple diagrams (Figs. 1.1 and 1.2) may help you visualize the choice here:

Fig. 1.1 The project that is never done. Diagram by Isaac Land

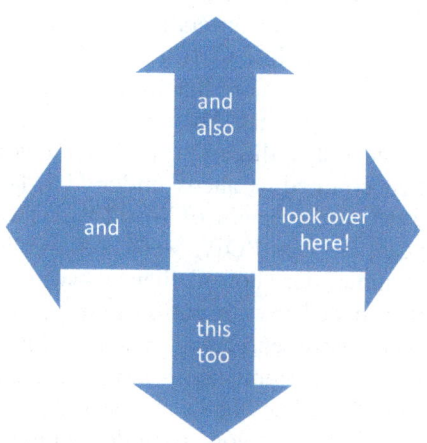

---

[3] Natalie Goldberg, *Writing Down the Bones: Freeing the Writer Within* (Boulder: Shambhala, 2016), 135.
[4] Jonathan Grix, *Foundations of Research*, 3rd ed. (London: Red Globe Press, 2019), 10–11.
[5] Grix, *Foundations,* 10.

Fig. 1.2 The project that has found its natural center. Diagram by Isaac Land

One reason that these diagrams are a necessary warning is that History is a book-centered discipline. Often, the work that's assigned to students—or otherwise held up as iconic, definitive, and admirable—is book-length. This means that students often approach their first major independent project without an appropriate role model in mind.

For instance, Mae M. Ngai's *Impossible Subjects: Illegal Aliens and the Making of Modern America* examines the treatment of four different groups: Filipinos, the Japanese, the Chinese, and Braceros (guest workers from Mexico).[6] It is bracketed at one end by a chapter considering an immigration law from 1924, and at the other by a similar treatment of a law from 1965. Ngai draws on a wide range of primary sources, from court cases and bureaucratic papers to letters to the editor from small town newspapers. Her book comes in at close to 400 pages.

For you, a more helpful reference point would be a 30-page article from an academic journal. An article about similar issues by Barbara Schmitter Heisler covers only a three-year period and contrasts the treatment of just two groups that counted as aliens under U.S. law—Braceros, and German prisoners of war.[7] At the height of World War Two, when hostility to Germany was at its peak, German POWs were periodically granted leave from their camps; some communities allowed them to swim in municipal pools.[8] Braceros, although they hailed from a nation that was not at war with the U.S., experienced a much more segregated existence. This small but telling comparison establishes something significant—and memorable. One day, perhaps, you will write something like Ngai's magisterial book. But Heisler's article is a much better model for what you are undertaking now.

---

[6] Princeton, NJ: Princeton University Press, 2014.

[7] "The 'Other Braceros': Temporary Labor and German Prisoners of War in the United States, 1943-1946," *Social Science History* 31, no. 2 (Summer 2007): 239–271.

[8] Heisler, "'Other Braceros,'" 256.

Selection is key, of course. *Which* small, self-contained body of primary sources would help you establish something noteworthy? Drilling down to *what* particular geographical location, or considering *which* brief interval of time, would prompt your readers to think in a new and productive way about something that matters? Archimedes once said that given a place to stand and a lever long enough, he could move the whole world. I'm suggesting that you, too, can find your Archimedean Point.

This should come as good news to you. It suggests that brute force methods (a ridiculous number of hours spent, a gargantuan number of sources consulted) are not necessary after all. Doing a great job at this doesn't require torturing yourself.[9]

A glance at the Table of Contents will give you a quick sense of the overall plan of this book. While the topics covered are—for the most part—conventional elements addressed in a conventional order, I would like to draw attention to some important choices I made, and the ways in which this book differs from others.

Almost half of this book—Parts One and Two—is devoted to helping students proactively make the right choices, or at least better choices, *early on* in the research process. The seeds of unsuccessful projects are sown early; so are the seeds of dissatisfaction with your own project. It's understandable if you feel eager to please your advisor. If you rush to commit a prospectus to paper, though, the risk is that you're setting yourself up for spending a great deal of time reading primary sources that bore you, while seeking to make the evidence conform to a theoretical framework that you don't agree with, all in the service of contributing to a debate that never interested you much in the first place. You don't want to be that student.

It is unusual to emphasize the early stages so much. What's the point of investing so much time and discussion into planning now, when it is possible you'll rethink things midway through the project? An insight from economics is pertinent here. Old factories or infrastructure might look different (and perform better) if they were rebuilt from scratch. In practice, that rarely happens, because what's already laid down is a "sunk cost." For similar reasons, you are likely to find yourself finishing the project you started, with some small modifications. It's best to exercise your nimble side now, at the blueprint stage, before all that heavy machinery gets trucked in and bolted to the floor.

The expectation for any serious student research project is that it will do more than just demonstrate competence; it will, in some meaningful (if small) way, add to our knowledge. There is a standard template for the expectations here. Your project needs to be *original* and make a discernible contribution. Nevertheless, it must be *grounded* in the existing scholarship. You should locate

---

[9] For a different perspective on what is at stake in articulating a manageable set of goals for this process, see Travis Chi Wing Lau, "Slowness, Disability, and Academic Productivity: The Need to Rethink Academic Culture," in *Disability and the University: A Disabled Students' Manifesto*, ed. Christopher McMaster and Benjamin Whitburn (New York: Peter Lang, 2019), 11–20.

and work with a *substantive* body of source material that speaks to your research question.

Until you've gotten your bearings, you won't have a way to assess which versions of a possible project come close to meeting these criteria. Part One, "Articulating Your Vision," is your companion as you sort through the relevant historiography, primary sources, and theory—or, indeed, as you try to determine *which* materials are relevant to your interests. It also provides some advice about common trouble spots in the earliest stages of a project. I conclude Part One with an entire chapter just about originality, a topic that often worries students and receives too little systematic attention in books about academic writing.

Historians respect an ambitious vision, but *vision tempered by focus* is the ideal. Often, the presence of just one, but not the other, holds a project back; the presence of both, in the right circumstances, can look like genius. Part Two, "Selecting Your Focus," will help you move from general ideas for a project to the Archimedean Point. This is the circumscribed research space that will give you a shot at excellence, but that is also aligned with the arithmetic of completion. Of course, this means you'll really have to think through what Julia Laite has called the "age-old question of how to link small stories to a wider context."[10] By the end of Part Two, you'll be ready to formulate, in one or two sentences, a research plan that nods to the historiography, indicates the direction you'll take, and connects the dots: To get at *this*, I will look at *that*.

Arriving at a workable *that* to complete the sentence will, of course, require you to test your hopes and ambitions against the reality of what you can actually access. There are two separate chapters on the search for materials. One deals with archives. The other is centered squarely on the digital realm.

Perhaps you are skeptical that there is any need to go to a physical archive. I concede that *at what point* in your research you would go, and possibly even *whether* you will do so, are more complicated and debatable questions today than they ever were for past generations of historians. It is also true that where health, mobility, travel, and money issues come into play, the existence of online material offers an inviting alternative path.[11] However, the fact is that even now, most primary source material is not digitized. The cyberattack on the British Library in October 2023 should remind us that access to digital resources—at exactly the time that you would need them—is not a certainty, either. With this in mind, the typical reader of this book will have reason to look both at the digital realm chapter, *and* at the archives chapter.

Part Three, "Developing Your Thesis," rejoins you as you complete your research. Now it will be time to sort out the relationship between all that work

---

[10] Julia Laite, "The Emmet's Inch: Small History in a Digital Age," *Journal of Social History* 53, no. 4 (Summer 2020): 963–989, see 975.

[11] Barbara Weinstein, "Historians and the Mobility Question," *AHA Perspectives* (2007) https://www.historians.org/publications-and-directories/perspectives-on-history/february-2007/historians-and-the-mobility-question, accessed 9/28/2022.

you did, and the conclusions you hope to draw from it. This is the point where you'll transition from saying "it could well mean…" to "*it does mean…*" and from "it would be nice to look at…" to "*when we look at it in this way, here's what we see.*"

Advancing a thesis statement means anticipating objections. I supply exercises and examples to help you formulate at least a draft of a thesis statement, but I also help you get into the habit of asking yourself the hard questions about your choice of evidence, and the logic of your argument. You can expect quibbles. Does *this* evidence prove *that* point? Is the amount of evidence adequate for the scale of the claims made? Were alternative interpretations by other historians addressed, or not? If you don't raise these questions as you develop your argument, you can expect that someone else will raise them for you.

While Part Three encourages you to boil down your argument to the bare essentials (a thesis statement; a few representative examples of your best evidence for it), Part Four, "Writing Up," explores your choices as you develop your entire manuscript, beginning with a chapter on structure and overall organization. Working with students over the years, I have noticed that their past education emphasized the start and the finish of a paper, with tremendous emphasis on title pages, "works cited" pages, introductions and conclusions. Even in the best-case scenario, this is a sandwich with bread but no filling! What goes in the middle is the most important part, of course. It's no accident that the filling is usually what gives the sandwich its very name.

What constitutes good academic writing—or is that a contradiction in terms? Richard J. Evans has remarked that "Most history books are hopelessly unreadable."[12] One might dispute this, on many grounds. Let me suggest that there's a specific *kind* of eloquence that distinguishes academic writing. Roy Porter wrote of *Decline and Fall of the Roman Empire*:

> Gibbon's "great work" reads like a chorus of voices. The contemporaries speak; Gibbon's sources comment on them; Gibbon adds his glosses, often scolding away in the footnotes; and the reader is invited to listen and participate in the intellectual symposium.[13]

Here, we are not in the presence of the same eloquence that you'd see in an elegant poem, or in a descriptive, suspenseful novel. It's also not quite what we'd expect from a skillful editorial or opinion piece in a newspaper. If we insist on applying those standards inappropriately, then academic writing will always come out designated as "bad" writing.

In an eagerness to distance the profession from reductionist or narrowly empirical stances, historians sometimes offer guidance that's ambiguous, or less than useful. Anthony Grafton has stated that "footnotes have never supported,

---

[12] Richard J. Evans, *In Defense of History* (New York: W.W. Norton, 1999), 59.
[13] Roy Porter, *Gibbon: Making History* (London: Palgrave Macmillan, 1988), 163.

and can never support, every statement of fact in a given work."[14] Arlette Farge has remarked that "a quotation is never proof," yet in the same book she praised a historian who offered "a convincing interpretation."[15] One might legitimately wonder when and how all this convincing took place! The minute we admit words such as "convincing," we tacitly concede that we still seek evidence, we care about logic, and statements unaccompanied by any form of proof will be met with irritation.[16]

Rather than downplaying what they can accomplish, the chapter on exposition explains that there is a craft to deploying footnotes, quotations, and other supporting materials effectively and clearly. This gives you a chance to anticipate and fix shortcomings in those areas *before* your advisor spots them. Part Four concludes with a chapter about your encounter with feedback. Revision is an inescapable part of the academic writing process, but it throws up some emotional and intellectual challenges, and I offer solace and guidance there. For students facing a formal defense, a section offers advice on navigating that experience.

This book does *not* end at the moment that you complete your final round of revisions. Part Five, "Looking Ahead," begins with a chapter about more advanced academic activities. It's common to wonder: Could I present a paper at a conference? What about submitting to an academic journal? What would that be like? Traditionally, books like this one have left those activities only hinted at, or left them altogether unmentioned. Yet that is a missed opportunity, because there is a great deal of continuity here. If you plan to share your work in a larger professional setting, many of the problems you puzzled over in Parts Three and Four of this book will return, in a slightly more refined yet perfectly recognizable form. I also consider what makes this stage look and feel different (networking with strangers; coping with peer reviewers) and offer tips about navigating some predictable difficulties that arise.

Even as you are embroiled in completing your degree, it's only human to wonder about where you'll be in five or ten years. Perhaps you are happy to defer those worries for now, but friends, family, and loved ones persist in asking about it. It's a fact that most people who receive degrees in History today will not wind up in a job that corresponds—in some uncomplicated way—to what they studied in school. For the times when that sense of uncertainty is making it hard to concentrate on your project, the final chapter of this book explores a range of possible paths, and even some things you can do now to put yourself in a stronger position.

When liberal arts graduates contemplate the job market, too often they have only one destination or role in mind; every other future scenario, by

---

[14] Anthony Grafton, *The Footnote: A Curious History* (Cambridge, MA: Harvard University Press, 1999), 233. Grafton offers a more nuanced assessment in his article "The Footnote from De Thou to Ranke," *History and Theory* 33, no. 4 (December 1994): 53–76, see in particular 54–57.

[15] Arlette Farge, *The Allure of the Archives* (New Haven: Yale University Press, 2013), 74 and 99.

[16] As argued in Joyce Appleby et al., *Telling the Truth about History* (New York: Norton, 1995), 255, 259, 261.

implication, looks unfulfilling. It's helpful to learn (or remind yourself) that the very same skills, attitudes, and instincts you're developing as you work your way through this book make you a desirable candidate for many different kinds of employment. Knowing the general contours of what is (loosely) known as the "alternative" job market may allow you to loosen your grip on Plan A, in the realization that there are Plan B and even Plan C scenarios where you would be valued, proud of your contributions, and thriving. I made a deliberate choice to end the book on that note.

There are some things that this book *doesn't* do. My aim was not to duplicate what was already available. For example, time management and writer's block are classic problems, but others have addressed them well in short, user-friendly works.[17] There are standard guidebooks on the art of framing a well-crafted sentence.[18] I also do not include a tutorial on the basics of avoiding plagiarism, although I address issues around originality and academic integrity that rarely make an appearance in introductory works.[19]

Explaining potential legal hazards is also outside my scope (or, indeed, my expertise). Particularly if you are working on the history of recent decades, you may find that with some source material—such as records pertaining to minors—there are considerations around privacy and confidentiality. Even if your research is not for publication, you may find that your access is restricted in some way.[20] If you might conduct interviews as part of your project, your first step should be to familiarize yourself with statements on ethics and best practices in the area of oral history.[21] Next, consult with your advisor, who may direct you to the relevant committee or review board at your university; research on human subjects often requires a preapproved plan. Depending on

---

[17] Eviatar Zerubavel, *The Clockwork Muse: A Practical Guide to Writing Theses, Dissertations, and Books* (Cambridge, MA: Harvard University Press, 1999); Paul J. Silvia, *How to Write a Lot: A Practical Guide to Productive Academic Writing* (Washington, D.C.: American Psychological Association, 2007); see also Peter Elbow's superb *Writing with Power: Techniques for Mastering the Writing Process* (New York: Oxford University Press, 1981).

[18] Joseph M. Williams, *Style: Ten Lessons in Clarity and Grace*, 8th ed. (New York: Pearson Longman, 2005).

[19] Charles Lipson, *Doing Honest Work in College: How to Prepare Citations, Avoid Plagiarism, and Achieve Real Academic Success*, third edition (Chicago: University of Chicago Press, 2018).

[20] Susan C. Lawrence, *Privacy and the Past: Research, Law, Archives, Ethics* (New Brunswick, NJ: Rutgers University Press, 2016); Laura Farley and Eric Willey, "Wisconsin School for Girls Inmate Record Books: A Case Study of Redacted Digitization," *The American Archivist* 78, no. 2 (Fall/Winter 2015): 452–469; Christine Anne George, "Archives Beyond the Pale: Negotiating Legal and Ethical Entanglements after the Belfast Project," *The American Archivist* 76, no. 1 (Spring/Summer 2013): 47–67.

[21] "OHA Statement on Ethics," https://oralhistory.org/oha-statement-on-ethics/, accessed 8/18/2023; Alan Christy et al., *Doing Recent History: On Privacy, Copyright, Video Games, Institutional Review Boards, Activist Scholarship, and History That Talks Back* (Athens: University of Georgia Press, 2012). Journals like *Oral History* are an amazing resource both to learn about what works and also to alert yourself to possible pitfalls and quandaries; for example, David W. Jones, "Distressing Histories and Unhappy Interviewing," *Oral History* 26, no. 2 (Summer/Fall 1998): 49–56.

exactly what part of the world you are researching, it is also worth cultivating some awareness about which subject matter is considered sensitive, and what the laws about defamation and libel look like *in that country*. In some places, even a social media post or an offhand remark to a journalist about your research could get you in trouble.[22]

There are also no software tutorials in this book. Some books on academic writing which attempt this are obsolete almost from the moment that they are published. I have kept references to social media apps and specific software confined to the footnotes. In the appropriate chapters, there is also some guidance in the "Further Reading" sections.

A different concern about technology, of course, is the advent of artificial intelligence software that can churn out pages of plausible-seeming prose in minutes. For a long time, research papers were the gold standard for academic achievement. Perhaps the risk of AI ghostwriting will prompt universities to move away from that particular format. For History students, I predict that a written paper will remain part of the process. However, some form of in-person defense will become more common at all academic levels. Where defenses are already present, they may carry more weight than in the past.

Such an oral exam would be similar to the poster sessions that are standard practice in many of the sciences. Typical questions might be: What was your research question? How did you settle on a proper scope for your inquiry? Where does your project sit in relation to the existing scholarship? How did you navigate finding aids and inventories, and sort through the dense array of primary sources? Why these sources? Why this time? Why this place? What is the relevant context? Why are some comparisons appropriate, and others not? What are your conclusions? Can you connect the dots between the conclusions you reached and the evidence that you actually can produce? How do you react to counter-examples, or in the face of ambiguous evidence? How would you respond to some of the likely objections to your line of reasoning? In this book, I proceed as if a research paper were the definitive final output. However, a high-stakes defense, perhaps accompanied by a slideshow or a showcase of supporting "exhibits," would center on the very same issues that this book returns to again and again.

That said, nothing in this book is meant to distract you from any detailed guidelines provided by your university for the type of project you are undertaking. Consult these early on, and check with your advisor if you are unclear on anything connected with them.

In the course of researching and writing this book, I found myself strangely intimate with many authors, some long dead. Before me, they struggled with many of the same themes that I explore in these pages. My footnotes—and,

---

[22] Antoon de Baets, "Defamation Cases against Historians," *History and Theory* 41, no. 3 (October 2002): 346–366; Paweł Machcewicz, "When History Matters Too Much: Historians and the Politics of History in Poland," *Contemporary European History* 32, no. 1 (2023): 15–20.

sometimes, direct quotations—preserve some traces of that underlying reading. You can see that I had the privilege of keeping some excellent company.

Nearly two thousand years ago, Quintilian told his rhetoric students that they shouldn't be "contented with the slow progress of those who walk on ropes," putting one foot gingerly ahead of the other as if the only way forward was in a straight line.[23] Why proceed this way, he asked, if you could be a trapeze artist, reacting to obstacles by going over, going under, swinging, seizing, or leaping?

Quintilian's words struck a chord with me. Like him, I'd noticed that it was all about the pivots—pivots taken, pivots missed, opportunities to pivot that just went unnoticed—that set the best work apart from the might-have-beens. It's no accident that I have section headings like "The art of changing your topic" and "The art of changing your mind." You'll also come across special "Pivot Point" features throughout the book. We aren't all acrobats, but a readiness to spot alternatives and act on opportunities—the nimble mindset—is the way to take something good and make it great.

This book is also informed by my observations from a quarter century of teaching at the college level. It has left me with an enormous respect for the variation in personalities and learning styles. All the classic activities—from note taking to brainstorming to generating a first draft—are experienced *differently*, in the context of that diversity.

Have you noticed that sometimes a manual seems to prescribe something mainly because it worked for the author? In a less digitized era, Eviatar Zerubavel recounted how he organized his notes by anticipating the whole structure of the manuscript in advance:

> working on a book that has seven chapters subdivided into twenty-six sections, for example, I arrange on my desk a set of twenty-six such intellectual containers unambiguously organized in seven distinctly color-coded clusters.[24]

I promise you, not everyone works (or thinks) like this! Indeed, readers who prefer to "make a mess, and then make a plan" may find themselves making use of my Chapter Twelve, which is about writing at the paragraph level, *before* they spend much time with Chapter Eleven, which deals with how to settle on an overall architecture for the paper's parts.[25]

I'll occasionally mention what works for me. More often, you'll find me discussing two or three different ways of conceptualizing a problem—or six ways of addressing it—rather than stipulating just one as the correct or obvious approach. My hope is that diverse readers will, *each in their own way*, find something useful as a result. For example, some of us are mavericks—the

---

[23] Quintilian, *Institutes of Oratory*, chapter 13.
[24] Zerubavel, *Clockwork*, 92.
[25] John Bean, *Engaging Ideas: The Professor's Guide to Integrating Writing, Critical Thinking, and Active Learning in the Classroom* (San Francisco: Jossey-Bass Publishers, 1996), 16–17.

proverbial square peg in the round hole—while others agonize over their (apparent) inability to have a single original thought. Imposter syndrome is a real issue, but so is overconfidence. A one-size-fits-all approach will miss that every time.

Likewise, not everyone approaches these educational milestones at the same phase of life. You may have young children at home. You may have a demanding day job. You may have responsibilities for an aging parent. It's possible that you have all three of those at once. You're becoming an author, but authors have lives. We are friends, lovers, neighbors, citizens. We have ailments, imperfections, vulnerabilities. This makes us more human and more connected, but it also means that crisis can erupt on any front at any time. I cannot show you how to navigate all of those challenges, but here's what I know for sure: You will be living with this project for some time. A cluttered project will, in turn, clutter your life. Designing *a project that knows when it is finished,* and understanding just a little better what to expect at all the various stages of this undertaking, just might leave you that much steadier, and that much freer, to look after *all* the things that matter.

Let's get started.

PART I

Articulating Your Vision

Are you preparing for your first substantive conversation with your advisor about your project? Is that conversation already behind you, and you're about to start drafting your prospectus? In either case, this part of the book is aimed squarely at you.

Perhaps because they are so short, it is common to throw together a research prospectus rather quickly. However, your writing decisions will only be as good as your reading decisions were earlier. This sounds daunting, yet articulating the reading choices is the moment when a project acquires individuality and starts generating a momentum of its own.

Chapter 2, "Getting Your Bearings," approaches browsing as an integral part of the research process. It articulates two concepts, "browsing *for*..." and "reading with accomplishment," which are applicable to historiography, but also to primary sources and even to looking at theory. Conducting this preliminary survey of what you *might* look at is a prelude to looking at *some* things very carefully.

Chapter 3, "Encountering the Experts," concerns an activity that is often discussed under the heading of "literature review." Establishing a relationship with the scholarship closest to your own is crucial, yet it also requires a complex settling-in process as you adjust to your new neighbors, differ from them, and learn from them. The chapter concludes with some advice on interdisciplinary projects.

Chapter 4, "Questioning Primary Sources," helps you think through your relationship to the raw material you hope to use in your research. Primary sources are more slippery and self-interested than most students realize, and the search for an "unbiased" source is a quixotic quest. You must become an expert on your sources before becoming an expert on your topic. The good news is that many successful History projects focus squarely *on* the trickier aspects of the source material.

Chapter 5, "Finding a Place to Stand," coaches you as you search for a "generative" location that draws energy from others' work without being purely derivative. I also include a list of strategies for students hoping to make their project a bit more creative. The chapter concludes with a discussion of the balancing act between originality, and the hazards of positioning your project so far on the academic fringe that it won't interest many people.

Part I concludes with a one-page checklist or worksheet. It encourages you to jot down a line or two about where you are at that time with each element of the project. Some advisors may not articulate any special expectation that you will submit a prospectus to them. They assume that the parts of your project will fall into place, or naturally emerge, as you go. While this avoids the problem of prematurely locking in poor choices, it also misses a terrific opportunity to think and plan and daydream and strategize.

Skipping the prospectus stage also creates some risks. I would encourage you to draw up a short prospectus on your own, and run it by your advisor anyway. This will minimize surprises for both of you down the road. You can simply offer it as "my plan for the project." Or use it as a set of talking points, and have a conversation with them about firming up your next steps.

When will you have the elements of a discussible draft prospectus? If you are meeting regularly with your advisor and you feel comfortable thinking out loud together, Part I should offer you many suggestions for conversation topics. If contact is only occasional and brief, you might consider completing both Part I and Part II of this book before sharing a polished proposal.

In this book, I take the unusual approach of encouraging students to draft notes for not one prospectus, but two. Part I is concerned with an overall vision for the project, and the worksheet at the end puts you well on your way to having a readable Vision Prospectus. In Part II, which is entitled "Articulating Your Focus," you will learn how to refine that promising research topic into a fully developed research question, with an accompanying plan for consulting primary sources. At the end of Part II is a second worksheet that sketches out the elements of the Focus Prospectus. These two worksheets could be simply for your own use, *or* notes for discussion with your advisor, *or* something close to a rough draft of a formal, written document, if your program requires one.

If two prospectuses mean two consultations with your advisor, the project will be better off for it. Remember that a prospectus is a list of preliminary *decisions*, each of which will shape (or limit) your final product. Talk to your advisor about those decisions—it's much easier to take on feedback or make corrections at this stage.

Before you go any further, have you looked at actual examples of whatever it is that you are going to write and defend? Make it local, and make it recent. Your advisor may be able to suggest examples, including some that they supervised. If you are aware of only one example from your department, perhaps one that won a prize or otherwise came to your attention, recognize that this may not be a representative sample at all. Skim a *range* of examples. This is the way to make sure your expectations about length, sophistication, and archival legwork are lined up with reality.

While you may, possibly, encounter one or two theses that set a dauntingly high standard in some respect, you should also find plenty of examples of work that leave you feeling somewhere on the spectrum of "okay, not as challenging as writing a monograph" or simply, "I could do better than *this*."

The most daunting black box is the one that remains unopened, because you can populate it with your worst fears. Once you've had a look, you'll be ready to turn the page and start Chap. 2.

CHAPTER 2

Getting Your Bearings

Most likely, at this stage, your advisor is offering a few general suggestions and nothing more. There are different reasons why the guidance is so thin. Many students choose research topics that are simply not aligned to the advisor's area of greatest expertise. Even if the match is a close one, though, most advisors would hesitate before offering a ready-made kit for a student's project. After all, telling a student "read these classics in the field, examine this set of sources, and consider it through this theoretical lens" is very nearly designing the project for them.

Adjusting to a low-guidance environment is a big transition for students accustomed to structured syllabi. By all means, take any input seriously, yet take joy in your new freedom—devising your own reading lists is an academic rite of passage. There are no more assignments. You are the one who determines what is the best way to spend your time. As a student in a classroom, you received the equivalent of a packed lunch, someone's idea of a balanced meal; in contrast, undertaking your first major independent project can feel more like foraging for nourishment in the wild.

A good general principle is that if something interests you, it has already interested others. If a published article exists entitled "Crossing the Road in Britain, 1931-1976"—and it does—then I'm inclined to believe there's something out there for you, too.[1] Perhaps your example or instance hasn't found its historian yet, but close analogues to it in a different time period or a different location *have* received attention. Don't underestimate the value of that scholarship! Suppose what interests you is how new ideas in child psychology drove changes in the design of playground equipment. A study of the debates around playground design in Meiji Japan, or the early Soviet Union, won't speak directly to your particular focus—say, the issues at stake for a municipal

---

[1] Joe Moran, "Crossing the Road in Britain, 1931–1976," *Historical Journal* 49 (2006): 477–96.

© The Author(s), under exclusive license to Springer Nature Switzerland AG 2024
I. Land, *The Craft of Historical Research*,
https://doi.org/10.1007/978-3-031-68457-9_2

park in a small California town in the 1960s—but spending time with this scholarship could be an enormous step forward. You'd learn what sort of primary source material comes in handy in such an inquiry. You'd find out what themes, concerns, or debates crop up when historians ask the tough questions about this kind of subject matter.

It's possible that you have a clear idea of what your topic *is*, but you don't yet have a firm grasp of what it's *called*. Perhaps the challenges of bringing the Khmer Rouge to justice interest you. Looking for "post-conflict societies" or "transitional justice" would unlock a rich vein of scholarship, but without some alert browsing first, most of us would never think to type those particular terms into a search box. Once you have that first bibliographic nibble, exploit it fully. Who does it cite, who has cited it, what terms do *they* use for the subject matter?

It's one thing to urge you to narrow your search terms, read the article abstracts, or use the finding aids and subject headings. This will get you in the neighborhood, perhaps, but it does not come close to addressing *knowing what you need to read*, which requires a different kind of thinking: strategic, discipline-based, and subject-matter-specific.

You may come across a helpful librarian who procures for you what appears, at first, to be *too much* for you to read. Here, again, you face a challenge that does not regularly occur in classrooms. Perhaps one semester you felt overwhelmed by assignments that felt like hundreds of pages more than you could handle, but in the unstructured environment you have entered now, there is no theoretical upper limit. Adding in sprawling databases of academic articles and digitized primary source resources, you could easily wind up wondering what you are supposed to do with 20,000 pages of potential reading material.

Advice on time management tends to focus on mastering the time itself: Pomodoro technique, minimizing distractions, using a daily and weekly planner. This perhaps misses the highest level of time management, which is really about deciding how to *use* the available time. To select an arbitrary number as a reference point, think of the time it takes for you to read 1000 pages as a budget; if you had $1000 to spend, you could do so in various ways, some wiser than others. Perversely, it appears—at first glance—that the only way to know if any given 1000 pages are worth reading is to have already read them. There's a way around this paradox: a particular kind of purposeful browsing.

A Browser's Manifesto

Every historian will look at, or look though, far more pages of material for a project than they will use *in* the project. How to approach this task? You will browse.

A rather ugly colloquialism that is popular among academics is the expression that one "guts" books and articles. You probably have some experience with this kind of reading-as-dissection, if you were challenged in class to spot the thesis in an article, or comment on a historian's use of evidence. What school of thought does the piece belong to? What sorts of sources does it draw upon? What does it emphasize or single out for interpretation? What is the main takeaway message that it suggests? The practiced eye is accustomed to looking for these things.

There are people who say they can "gut" an entire academic book in a matter of minutes.[2] Perhaps they should not be quite so proud of this, because it means that they are glancing through for things they expect to find, rather than keeping an open mind about what they might learn. A more humble stance would emphasize that learning how to efficiently process large amounts of prose will help you generate a small, manageable pile of material that deserves a slower, more patient reading.

It's not your fault if this all sounds unfamiliar. Browsing is perhaps the least written-about form of reading. It is the reading activity in which we reflect in an open-ended way on possible purposes for reading, and the possible benefits of pursuing one direction or another, remaining open to selection or rejection. In the context of your project, what you are *browsing for* is a set of readings that is right-sized for the task, and that would leave you with a sense of accomplishment at the end.

Have you noticed how your reading slows down when you encounter a new author, a new genre, or a new subfield? Perhaps someone suggested that you just pick up the latest journal in your field and read it cover to cover. If you did it, you made many troublesome transitions—each article forced you to re-orient anew. The jargon, the priorities, the themes were probably a little different each time, to say nothing of the location, the personalities, and the immediate historical context that each article (or book review) addressed. This is an example of a discontinuous, non-sequential set of readings. Likewise, you could read the last ten years' worth of winners of a particular book prize, and they will have excellence in common, but not much else. If you are looking at a lot of unrelated material, whatever you estimate your reading speed is, you probably need to calculate *as if you were slower.*

Understanding the reasons for slow reading suggests a path to fast reading. Design your browsing projects so that you'll be plowing through material that is in some sense "of a type," or part of the same conversation. You may have had this experience already, perhaps in a particularly well-designed course. Your reading speed at the beginning was slow and unremarkable, yet as you got oriented (e.g., to the language and priorities of historians who study colonialism), you went faster and faster. You can deliberately replicate that experience, which we might call r*eading with accomplishment.* Find a block of readings with an identifiable beginning and end, whose completion leaves you feeling that you've got one major aspect of your project squared away—at least for the purposes of this early stage. The good news is that you can apply this approach

---

[2] Oscar Wilde quipped about never spending more than ten minutes on a book: Pierre Bayard, *How to Talk about Books You Haven't Read*, trans. Jeffrey Mehlman (London: Bloomsbury, 2007), 170–171.

to *all* of the types of reading that you will do: primary sources, historiography, even theory.

In order to read really fast, it may also be necessary to break some deep, ingrained habits. A couple tricks I have developed for powering through a book: reading every other page, or reading the whole book backward. In either method, you must keep the pages turning—the point is not to get stuck wondering what you might be missing.

If you have trouble doing this, the trouble is probably not with your eyes or your nervous system—it may be with your guilty conscience. Anxious browsers might consider the words of the sociologist C. Wright Mills. He expressed the activity this way: It's what happens when a scholar reads "parts of many books from the point of view of some particular theme or topic in which you are interested," with the result that "you will take notes which do not fairly represent the books you read" because instead of replicating their structure and their priorities in your notes, what's going on is that you are "*using* this particular idea, this particular fact, for the realization of your own projects."[3] Mills is letting us off the hook; he knows we have anxiety and hesitancy about any kind of reading that's less than complete. One way to capture the activity he describes is to call it *browsing for*. You are *browsing for* opportunities, *browsing for* openings, *browsing for* useful tips and tricks, perhaps even *browsing for* a strategic overview of the competition.

Browsing Historiography

Are you doing a study of a red-light district? Read a dozen journal articles, each of which investigates a different red-light district. You'll still have questions, but "what does a study of a red-light district look like?" will no longer be one of them.

Not everyone's project is quite this crisply defined at the beginning, though. You may be feeling your way forward. It is not yet evident which body of scholarship would have the most to say about your interests. Your previous coursework brought you up to speed on certain debates between historians, they familiarized you with certain luminaries and Big Names, but not on those who specialize in the time, and place, and themes that you plan to focus on now.

Perhaps you started with a general interest in municipal corruption, or in poverty and policing, or in the options available to working-class women in big cities. Your next logical move might be to assemble a reading list on urban history. This may not be your advisor's specialty. Plundering the footnotes of a recent journal article is one path forward. You may be able to access recommended reading lists online, or graduate syllabi, once again selecting those that are most recent. These are rich, dense fields of information, yet they may lack a visible structure, or any commentary on the relationships between the pieces

---

[3] C. Wright Mills, *The Sociological Imagination* (New York: Oxford University Press, 1959), 199; see also Bayard, *How to Talk*, 177.

of scholarship that they contain. Therefore, it is unclear where to begin, what is essential, or which readings best complement each other.

Often, the only way to set priorities is to sort things out for yourself. This forces us back to a fundamental question, though: When you make your first approach to an academic literature, what are you sorting *for*, exactly? Some manuals on research skills offer advice that's a bit too elementary. For instance, encouraging students to dutifully jot down the fact that so-and-so has a doctorate in the field doesn't really help us when it's the people with doctorates who are disagreeing with one another! Other research skills manuals tip you abruptly into difficult territory, pushing you to ask such questions as "can you tell why the book was written" or "can you figure out what the target audience was." This presumes a sense of the field that you may not possess quite yet. Other questions, such as "is the information accurate for when it was written" or "has the author looked at the material objectively," not to mention, "has it been well researched," really are only answerable late in a research process, not in these initial phases.[4]

There's a different way to sort out your problems with sorting. Try starting here: Can you spot who's quoted, who's cited, whose names are dropped and in what spirit? We might substitute "ethnographic reading" for that old expression "gutting."[5] Just as an ethnographer arrives at a place that is unfamiliar to them and patiently observes the norms, habits, and customs, a good working definition of ethnographic reading in an academic context would be "an analytic process of working out the nature of the community, its histories, debates, genres, conventions, cherished truths and current hot topics."[6]

Mark Gaipa, a professor of literature, challenges his students with this scenario: You, the student, are about to enter a ballroom at a major convention in his field. All the famous scholars the class has been reading are in the ballroom together. He asks the class to draw a cartoon with stick figures showing who is hanging out together, who's shunning who, and who's the eccentric off in the corner.[7] It's a charming exercise, but it's also a reminder that knowing your way around these cliques and coteries is a necessary prelude to so many key moves in academic research and writing.

However, Gaipa had already taught his students about those odd little cliques. He was just asking them to visualize the cliques distributed across a ballroom. You, on the other hand, can't even populate the ballroom until

---

[4] Joanna Burkhardt et al., *Teaching Information Literacy: 50 Standards-Based Exercises for College Students* (Chicago: American Library Association, 2010), see, for example, 22–23 and 58.

[5] I have adopted the term "ethnography" from an oblique remark in Sara Efrat Efron and Ruth Ravid, *Writing the Literature Review: A Practical Guide* (New York: Guilford Press, 2019), 191, but developed it differently here.

[6] Pat Thomson and Barbara Kamler, *Writing for Peer Reviewed Journals: Strategies for Getting Published* (London: Routledge, 2013), 37; Bayard, *How to Talk*, 11, 12, 73, 140, discusses a book's "location" in the "collective library" very much in this spirit.

[7] Mark Gaipa, "Breaking into the Conversation: How Students Can Acquire Authority for Their Writing," *Pedagogy* 4, no. 3 (2004): 419–437.

you've oriented yourself by a regime of reading. To accomplish this efficiently, you will have to retrain your eye. All those things you are in the habit of skipping or only half-reading now take center stage. You are reading for affiliations, to obtain a quick overview of the state of the field, or more precisely a *dramatis personae* of the field.

Here's an example of exactly the sort of paragraph that can supply the quick orientation that you need. Simo Laakkonen gets right down to business:

> What on earth does a fascist dictatorship have in common with nature conservation and environmental protection? Historian Milan Hauner aroused discussion on the theme by claiming that the National Socialists were the first rulers in the world to be radical environmentalists, an assertion that sparked intense academic debate ... Environmental historian Thomas Lekan sees researchers as having concentrated overly on the National Socialist worldview and ignoring military-political consequences. Others like Joachim Radkau and Franz Uekötter have argued that the National Socialist period did not signify increasingly environmentally friendly policies, but rather intensified industrialization and destruction of nature.[8]

This is enormously helpful to someone unfamiliar with those reference points, but writing a brief, clear overview like this is hard work, and not everyone takes the trouble to catch the reader up in this way. In fact, openly expressing your own verdict on the historiography, or summarizing someone in a way that annoys them, can seem like picking a fight when it's not strictly necessary. As a result, the information that's on offer is sometimes enigmatic.

One way to pick up on more subtle signals is to notice which scholars are named and discussed in the *body* of the text of a book or article. Usually, this is a small subset of those cited, so if someone is named, it suggests they are important. Are they featuring here as an inspiration, a nemesis, a friendly rival, an ally? Or simply as a comparison or contrast? Check the endorsements on the back cover of a book, paying attention to the content of the statements, but also noticing the names of those who wrote them.

The introductions to edited volumes usually offer businesslike summaries of where the field's been, where it is now, and where it's going. These introductions bristle with useful footnotes. Therefore, locating one or more recent edited volumes that are close to your interests should be high on your to-do list. For the same reasons, finding a special issue of a journal dedicated to a theme that interests you is often a very productive browsing experience. Occasionally, books are reissued for a twentieth or twenty-fifth anniversary edition, and the author offers an insightful new foreword or afterword, rich in

---

[8] Simo Laakkonen, "Environmental Policies of the Third Reich," in *The Long Shadows: Toward a Global Environmental History of the Second World War*, ed. Simo Laakkonen, Richard P Tucker, and Timo Vuorisalo (Corvallis: Oregon State University Press, 2017), 55–74, quoted 55.

citations of important newer scholarship and critique.[9] These retrospective editions, though, are ordinarily reserved for that rare book that became an instant classic.[10]

For less renowned scholarship, review essays perform some of the same functions. These vary in length, though they are much longer than a stand-alone book review. They are usually organized around the task of comparing and contrasting several new books on closely related topics. Often, they also flag subtopics or themes that have attracted little attention, but really deserve more. That, in itself, could amount to a handy to-do list, or at least suggestions, for your own project. There are a few journals (*Reviews in American History; History Compass; Kritika*) that are composed of nothing but review essays, or that feature them heavily. Other journals may feature them on occasion; check with your advisor for tips about where to look, given your interests.

If you're starting to discern a clique, school, or coterie of scholars, look for their "home base" or headquarters. Is there a particular journal where a lot of these people hang out? If they are in the habit of citing a journal a lot, and publishing in it as well, it might be a good idea to backtrack to the debut issue of that journal. First issues sometimes contain manifestos or state-of-the-field pieces; after all, the journal had to justify its existence in the first place. If that doesn't pan out, try celebratory anniversary issues, which often venture into that territory as well. If the journal seems like a really good fit for your project, you can conduct a mini-ethnography just of the journal itself, noting its most popular articles ("most cited," "most accessed").

Through all of this browsing, be sure to scan for keywords, buzzwords, and priorities. Learn the secret handshake. Which labels, concepts, or methods come up again and again? Is there a favorite theorist? Using these techniques, you'll get good at spotting something from the same "school" with remarkable rapidity. Bear in mind that like other research processes, it is iterative or circular; once you know the preferred vocabulary, you'll have new ideas about how to search online for others writing in the same vein.

Negative buzzwords, and antagonistic name-dropping, demarcate the shape of a "school" or academic clique in another way, showing off the contrast with rival scholars or different approaches. There is something deeply human about one clique's need to demarcate itself from other cliques. Set out to familiarize yourself with one, and you may actually become pretty conversant in the ways of two or three. It's best to take disparaging remarks with a grain of salt. In fact, if you notice that a scholar who doesn't thrill you keeps complaining

---

[9] Excellent examples of this genre are the afterword to the reissue of Christopher R. Browning, *Ordinary Men: Reserve Police Battalion 101 and the Final Solution in Poland* (New York: Harper Perennial, 2017) and the preface to the new edition of George Chauncey's *Gay New York: Gender, Urban Culture, and the Making of the Gay Male World, 1890–1940* (New York: Basic Books, 2019).

[10] Retrospective pieces written by someone other than the original author are also enormously valuable: Jan Machielsen and Michelle Pfeffer, "A Work out of Time: *Religion and the Decline of Magic* at Fifty," *Past & Present* 261, no. 1 (November 2023): 259–296.

about so-and-so, maybe that's your hint to go take a close look at the rival school.

With this general orientation behind you, you are ready to craft a selected reading list in a much more purposeful way. *Reading with accomplishment*, in the context of historiography, would mean you should identify a body of scholarship that is self-referential, even if it is an uneasy succession of challenges across the generations (such as E.P. Thompson, his allies, and his critics).[11] If all you read are scholars who talk past each other, it is difficult, if not impossible, to learn how scholarly debate works. It may seem counter-intuitive, but the best debates happen *within* a school of thought, rather than between two or more of them.

One of the experiences that every student should have early in their education is of reading an exchange between historians who are concerned with substantially the same issues, and share some things in common (roughly the same body of evidence, roughly the same or kindred methodologies). See the claims and counterclaims fly. How are individual bits of evidence handled? What is the role of debates over definition? When are comparisons accepted as valid, and when are they rejected?

It can be revelatory to watch exactly what happens when you try to prove something in the face of opposition, and what sort of academic conversation follows. *Browse for* a substantive and recent debate on, or around, the subject matter you'll be writing about in your own project. Even a tangentially relevant debate could work. To return to the hypothetical student who will eventually narrow down their project to red-light districts, they could benefit from studying a debate about zoning; about redlining; about policing; about the politics surrounding "urban blight" and "urban renewal." While none of these center on red-light districts, they could supply a solid education in the themes, concerns, and techniques of urban historians.

For now, you are suspending belief (and disbelief); you do not know yet for sure whether you are going to affiliate with this group of historians, and it is not necessary to reach a decision at this time. Instead, in that ethnographer's spirit, you are going to observe their ways, understand what is important to them, and learn how they perceive the subject matter that also interests you.

Examining the actual deployment of evidence to support particular claims, or exploring the more subtle aspects of a historian's thesis, will require you to shift to a much slower, more attentive style of reading. I will have more advice on those matters in Chapter Three.

---

[11] Antoinette Burton and Stephanie Fortado, eds., *Histories of a Radical Book: E. P. Thompson and the Making of the English Working Class* (New York: Berghahn Books, 2020).

Browsing the Unbrowsable

There is no robust, clearly articulated tradition of browsing archival material that corresponds to "gutting" secondary sources. Indeed, the emphasis on selectiveness and speed seems to evaporate at the archive's door. Here, for example, is a truly depressing statement about research:

> Scholars must not only be capable of hard, often totally fruitless work—they must actually relish it ... boxfuls of fragile and half-illegible holograph letters to be examined in quest of a single clue; volumes upon volumes of dull reminiscences to be scanned for the appearance of a single name.[12]

If this were truly the ratio of hours spent to useful material found, most student projects would be doomed. You'd probably have to be a well-established academic, or be independently wealthy, to pursue research at all.

A different, and somewhat more cheerful, type of workflow narrative involves immersing yourself until something gels, and inspiration strikes. Geoffrey Parker relates his experience:

> One wet March afternoon in 1967, as I gathered material in the Belgian royal archives for my thesis on how Spain failed to suppress the Dutch revolt in the sixteenth century, I ordered a volume of documents listed in the inventory as "Military Papers." ... All historians at some point in their professional careers feel their hair stand on end, as I did just then, when they suddenly make sense of documents that had baffled others.[13]

What should worry you about both of these quotations is that there is no sense of a strategy, and no plan or process; the archive is just where you show up and do the work, whether the method is waiting for the thunderbolt of genius to strike from the heavens, or hammering away like a battering ram.

Before applying such drastic tactics, make a circuit of the entire castle wall and look for multiple points of entry. Ask yourself about the possible benefits of looking at the files of Office X, rather than those of Office Y, or Office Z. Lara Putnam has coined the term "side glancing" to describe this kind of activity in a transnational context, noting how

> digitized secondary and tertiary sources allow quick eyeballing of the bigger picture or of doings next door: a sideways glance that can uncover connections or commonalities worth exploring. Where were those exports going, anyway? What

---

[12] Richard D. Altick and John J. Fenstermaker, *The Art of Literary Research*, 4th ed. (New York: Norton, 1993), 18.

[13] Geoffrey Parker, "Foreword," in *Rebellion, Repression, Reinvention: Mutiny in Comparative Perspective*, ed. Jane Hathaway (Westport, CT: Praeger, 2001), vii–ix, see vii and viii.

was going on there? Why was that place sending missionaries (or migrants, or movies) over here to begin with?[14]

After this quick look around, you can make an informed decision about where your efforts will be rewarded. Don't prematurely commit yourself to slogging through 10, 30, or 100 boxes of material just because they are there, and it would make you look productive and purposeful. I will have much more to say about how to undertake that sifting and selection process in later chapters.

There isn't a standard name for secondary scholarship that is intended more or less solely to shed light on the potential uses of a single type of primary source, but for historians, this is an important category in its own right. For example, there's a notable difference between finding a piece of scholarship on some aspect of the lumber industry, versus a deep dive specifically into what we can do with the scribbled logbooks kept by the "timber cruisers" who appraised sections of forest.[15] Likewise, a fine article on same-sex desire in eighteenth-century England is not the same as one that focuses solely on the weirdly lurid (and ambiguous) category of "keyhole testimony" from those who heard suspicious noises, caught a glimpse of something, and then reported it.[16]

Browse for these. Coming across even one such article, if it is aligned with your area of interest, can accelerate your progress overnight. You might learn what to do with a source type you've already encountered. Or, it might motivate you to branch out and make use of something that you'd not considered. An article could alert you that a particular—seemingly unique—item you'd found belongs to a whole family or genre of evidence.[17] This could suggest a new vein of inquiry, as you seek to understand how your instance of it fits into that bigger picture.

Finally, I would urge students to browse even where browsing dare not speak its name: in the area of theory. Most of us first encountered theory as something that was inflicted *on* us; we dutifully, or not so dutifully, read the theorists that someone assigned, or the names dropped in a portentous-sounding public lecture by a visiting speaker. Surveying *all* the theorists until you find the one that's a nice fit for your needs is not only a skill that isn't taught; it's actually a bit scandalous to even suggest it.

However, it is a fairly safe bet that for every project, there is a body of what might be called "friendly theory" that shares enough of its priorities and concerns to be relevant and useful. This is what you are *browsing for* here. It won't

---

[14] Lara Putnam, "The Transnational and the Text-Searchable: Digitized Sources and the Shadows They Cast," *American Historical Review* 121, no. 2 (April 2016): 377–402, see 383.

[15] Craig William Kinnear, "Cruising for Pinelands: Knowledge Work in the Wisconsin Lumber Industry, 1870–1900," *Environmental History* 21, no. 1 (January 2016): 76–99.

[16] George E. Haggerty, "Keyhole Testimony: Witnessing Sodomy in the Eighteenth Century," *The Eighteenth Century* 44, no. 2–3 (2003): 167–182.

[17] Heide Fehrenbach and Davide Rodogno, "'A Horrific Photo of a Drowned Syrian Child': Humanitarian Photography and NGO Media Strategies in Historical Perspective," *International Review of the Red Cross* 97, no. 900 (2015): 1121–1155.

necessarily give you the green light to carry on just as you have, but its challenges will be more profound and more urgent because you and the theorist have at least one or two priorities in common. Theories are often easier to understand when you see them applied, so have a look: What have social scientists with kindred interests done with the concepts, definitions, and research questions that caught your eye? What about scholars in the various disciplines of the humanities? Have any historians tried it out?

The theory that is friendly to your project may not be the prevailing trendy and ubiquitous theory. If so, you will have more explaining to do, but that should not dissuade you. If you are writing about more-than-human histories, then referring to assemblages might be appropriate. A study of networks would have good reason to consider eigenvector centrality. If you are struggling to describe a certain kind of change over time, punctuated equilibrium might be a useful concept.[18] However, seizing upon one theorist simply because they are getting a lot of attention at the moment may be the equivalent of grabbing a wrench, when what you needed for your task was a screwdriver.

It is helpful to return, once again, to Gaipa's analogy of the crowded ballroom. If all the theorists you're hearing about leave you unimpressed, maybe that's a sign that you, and your project, belong in a different corner of the ballroom. I will have more to say about theory and interdisciplinary projects in the next chapter, but you won't find that body of friendly theory if you don't look for it.

Rambles, Detours, and Short Cuts

Many breakthroughs (large and small) in scholarship begin simply in the *noticing*. There is often a substantial time lag between the act of noticing and the act of explaining; yet the *noticed* material puzzles you, bothers you, suggests the need for explanations, prods you to look in places you'd otherwise not considered. As Arlette Farge remarks, research requires an odd mix of single-minded diligence and remaining "sufficiently open" that you are capable of seizing upon the unexpected when it flits across your view.[19]

One place where you should keep your options open, if you can manage it, is in the reading order itself. There is no intellectually grounded reason why we must read intensively in historiography, and follow that with an equally intense, and single-minded, phase in which you are steeped only in primary sources. What often determines the rhythm for researchers is the logistical realities (you won a grant to go to the archive; you can only be away from work or family commitments for so long). Without that constraint—for example, if you are doing a local history project, or if most of your source material is digitized online—the iterative nature of the research process could well lead you in a

---

[18] John Lewis Gaddis, *The Landscape of History: How Historians Map the Past* (New York: Oxford University Press, 2004), 98.
[19] Farge, *Allure*, 69.

series of tight loops, as archival material suggests new points of dialogue with the historiography, or vice versa.

Yet there is a fine line between noticing something new, and being distracted by something extraneous. What counts as a legitimate detour? An afternoon with a database of historical newspapers might prompt you to consult the local police records. Unless budget constraints or apartment leases completely lock you in, there is no reason why a week in one archive should not send you to a month in another, perhaps wholly unanticipated, archive that turns out to hold related material.[20] Although most scholarship is not accompanied by a detailed narrative drawing the reader's attention to the fact, it is common for ambitious projects—especially book-length works, but many journal articles as well—to thread together materials from several different locations and databases.

Yet a productive zigzag from one archive to the next is only one of the possible forms that a detour could take. It is, by now, a familiar exhortation that a good researcher wouldn't simply come to rest where their first keyword search left them. Yet, as a profession, we probably could do more to urge students to consider sometimes stepping away from the keyboard, the library, and the archive altogether. A story goes that R.H. Tawney once sat through a conference paper entitled "The Open Field," but then rose to his feet and announced: "What historians need is not more documents but stronger boots."[21]

In an award-winning work, *Wisdom Sits in Places,* the anthropologist Keith Basso considered how Apache methods of narration differed from "history of the Anglo-American variety," which seems "geographically adrift" with "few spatial anchors."[22] In contrast, in Apache storytelling, "The location of an event is an integral aspect of the event itself ... placeless stories simply do not get told" and the place-names themselves are often long, detailed, and eloquent.[23] Of course, if an outsider ever learns these names, that comes only at the end of a process, a process that requires patience, commitment, and hard-earned trust.

Lara Putnam, a US-based historian of Costa Rica, has remarked on the disappearance of "real-world friction" if historians conduct most of their research online, or make a hasty visit from the global North to photograph thousands of documents, and then depart. "When historians research far from home but don't stay around long enough to be inconvenienced, insulted, or instructed," she notes,

---

[20] The growing interest in "linked archival metadata" may soon make it easier to make these connections through an internet search.

[21] Ross Terrill, *R. H. Tawney and His Times: Socialism as Fellowship* (Cambridge, MA: Harvard University Press, 1973), 7.

[22] Keith H. Basso, *Wisdom Sits in Places: Landscape and Language among the Western Apache* (Albuquerque: University of New Mexico Press, 1996), 33.

[23] Basso, *Wisdom,* 87.

the quality of their analysis suffers. Again, the forced contextualization that made traditional historical research inefficient looks, on reflection, like a significant contributor to knowledge production in our discipline.[24]

While travel is the classic method of arriving at this kind of productive disruption, even the right regime of reading could help you here. Epeli Hauʻofa has remarked that while "those who hail from continents" may imagine that "people in most of Oceania live in tiny confined spaces," an examination of the legends and the oral tradition shows that

> Their universe comprised not only land surfaces, but the surrounding ocean as far as they could traverse and exploit it, the underworld with its fire-controlling and earth-shaking denizens, and the heavens above with their hierarchies of powerful gods and named stars and constellations that people could count on to guide their ways across the seas. Their world was anything but tiny. They thought big and recounted their deeds in epic proportions.[25]

One corrective that should be standard practice: If you write about a part of the world that you do not hail from yourself, make it a top priority to familiarize yourself with scholarship and critical essays from people who do.[26]

If you can manage to have a physical encounter with the subject matter at an early stage of your project, jump at the chance. I can say from experience that even a single day in an English cathedral town will make you think differently about late medieval piety and the complex sequences of reforms and iconoclasm that followed. While one would reach a point of diminishing returns eventually, an excellent reading list *coupled* with visits to a dozen or two cathedrals and parish churches surviving from that period would be invaluable. While you are welcome to take pleasure in the activity, what you would be engaged in there is something well beyond tourism.

A direct encounter with objects can also prompt a decisive rethink. Christopher de Hamel's observation that "No photographic reproduction yet invented has the weight, texture, uneven surface, indented ruling, thickness, smell, the tactile quality and patina of time of an actual medieval book" is, perhaps, in line with our expectations.[27] However, scholars in a range of subfields are learning to respect what immersive, sensory exploration adds to our awareness. In the course of Karin Dannehl's research for her PhD thesis on eighteenth-century metal cooking vessels, she conducted in-depth interviews

---

[24] Putnam, "Transnational," 380, 396.

[25] Epeli Hauʻofa, "Our Sea of Islands," *The Contemporary Pacific* 6, no. 1 (Spring 1994): 147–161, see 152.

[26] Like superheroes, every scholar has their own origin story. Sometimes the challenge is that you are an outsider, but there are also special burdens imposed on those who are considered, in some sense, insiders: Azra Hromadžić, "On Being Too Close to It," *Genealogy* 7, no. 4 (2023), 76: https://www.mdpi.com/2313-5778/7/4/76, accessed 3/30/2024.

[27] Christopher De Hamel, *Meetings with Remarkable Manuscripts: Twelve Journeys into the Medieval World* (New York: Penguin Press, 2017), 2.

with re-enactors in Odessa, Delaware, about their embodied experiences, including the sensation of heat while cooking with cast-iron replicas over open flames. The actions of "lifting, moving, pulling, and pushing" heavy cookware filled with food forced the re-enactors to recruit "their entire skeletal and muscular structures" to complete the tasks without losing their balance, or spilling the contents on the floor![28]

I will not dwell at length on learning a new foreign language here, because many student projects have built-in time constraints. Don't assume, though, that there is a wise, well-funded committee behind the scenes somewhere that makes sure all the "best" things get translated into English.[29] Meanwhile, a round-up assessing the state of the field twenty-five years after the publication of Keith Thomas' classic, *Religion and the Decline of Magic*, remarked that the book was scarcely cited by witchcraft scholars on the European continent, and hadn't been translated into French or German.[30] This should be twice humbling to Anglophone readers. First, just because a work looms large for us doesn't guarantee that it's read elsewhere. Second, what historiography is shaping their ideas that remains invisible to us?

There is no shame in conducting a quick reconnaissance using apps, translation software, English-language abstracts, or even the assistance of a friend to assess whether a major investment in a new language (or upgrading your skills in an "old" one) is really appropriate for your project. When it comes time to settle down to the serious reading, though, you will need a more proficient grasp of grammar and nuance to avoid misunderstandings. Even in the era of translation apps—*especially* in the era of translation apps—it is important to be mindful of the honest toil inherent in actually learning a language, and through this, developing a deeper, more respectful, relationship with a literature, a location, a culture.

If you have an opportunity to take an intensive summer language course, seize the opportunity. A well-known program in the United States is the Foreign Language and Area Studies (FLAS) fellowships. Some other entities, like Alliance Française, have an international presence, but sprang from an initiative on the part of the country where the language originated. Many large universities routinely offer "reading for research" language courses which focus on the needs of students (at any level) who need an accelerated introduction. This would open up the secondary literature to you, and some primary sources as well. A reading course won't prepare you for ordering food in a restaurant or bantering with strangers, but it might serve your present needs perfectly.

---

[28] Karin Dannehl, "Object Biographies: From Production to Consumption," in *History and Material Culture: A Student's Guide to Approaching Alternative Sources*, ed. Karen Harvey (London: Routledge, 2009), 123–138, see 130.

[29] Lawrence Venuti, *The Translator's Invisibility: A History of Translation*, second edition (London: Routledge, 2008).

[30] Jonathan Barry, "Introduction: Keith Thomas and the Problem of Witchcraft," in *Witchcraft in Early Modern Europe: Studies in Culture and Belief*, ed. Jonathan Barry, Marianne Hester, and Gareth Roberts (Cambridge: Cambridge University Press, 1996), 1–45, see 17.

Many historians work extensively with handwritten primary source documents. Past generations sometimes experienced a bit of a shock when they finally made it to an archive and ran into a script that seemed impenetrably strange, but the internet has made it easier to hunt down some samples of what this material might look like. There are seminars, workshops, and even some web tutorials devoted to getting newcomers up to speed on certain forms of paleography, so don't assume that you are totally on your own here. Ask around in advance about what options are available.

Tertiary sources can speak very effectively to a common problem: You're interested in a source *type* that is unfamiliar to you. Even the most accomplished advisor probably isn't a true jack-of-all-trades; those who are proficient with census data are rarely comfortable working with old newsreels, and vice versa. Two very helpful book series that cover a variety of source types are the Routledge Guides to Historical Sources, and the Bloomsbury Research Skills for History. Like other detours, this may sound like spreading your attention too thinly. Consider, though, in how many ways primary, secondary, and tertiary sources can support each other, working like a lattice or scaffolding to support a more ambitious set of insights.

It may be necessary to assemble your own little kit of supporting materials. When Matthew Craske was writing a book about the elaborate monumental sculptures that loom over the tombs of famous eighteenth-century figures in Westminster Abbey, he came to realize that he needed to come to terms with the reference points that mattered most to their creators. Many didn't correspond to what we imagine, today, belongs to the category of "sculpture." Craske found himself engaging with erudite tracts such as Joseph Addison's *Dialogues upon the Usefulness of Ancient Medals,* and thumbing through reference works so that he could distinguish between the meaning of an "escutcheon" and a "device" in heraldry.[31]

This seems straightforward enough when you see it in a finished, well-regarded work of scholarship. Yet in your own project, you may come to a crossroads where the choice of *which* additional reading you ought to pursue is, for the moment, unclear. If you are finding yourself thinking hard about how to interpret the use of a photo in an ad that appeared in a glossy magazine from the 1950s, should you reach for a collection entitled *Classic Essays on Photography,* with musings from Alfred Stieglitz, Siegfried Kracauer, and Roland Barthes?[32] Or should you be looking for a monograph about that particular magazine? Or is the really smart move to consult a textbook from the 1950s on *Practical Advertising,* which discusses layout, offers tips, and catalogues the standard practices of the trade?

A reference librarian could help you find any, or all, of those materials. Yet the decision about whether or not to pursue them belongs only to you. Each

---

[31] Matthew Craske, *The Silent Rhetoric of the Body: A History of Monumental Sculpture and Commemorative Art in England, 1720–1770* (New Haven: Yale University Press, 2008), 1, 101.
[32] Alan Trachtenberg, ed., *Classic Essays on Photography* (New Haven: Leete's Island Books, 1980).

of these choices could take your project in a different direction. It is a series of reading decisions like this that give a research project its own unique stamp. Acknowledging that these *are* decisions is the first step toward making the best ones for your needs.

In "Axioms for Reading the Landscape," a classic essay in the study of popular culture, Peirce K. Lewis urged scholars to read the trade journals: "If, for example, you want to know why your local franchised hamburger joint looks the way it does, try browsing through the pages of the journal *Fast Food*."[33] In addition to offering unsentimental advice about what works and what doesn't, trade journals often feature columns about upcoming legislation, the impact of a particular lawsuit, and so forth.

The student who's convinced that the only serious work is archival might feel guilty about spending a week reading that trade journal. Yet for the right project, it could set you up to interpret the archival material successfully, or view it in the correct context—in short, the kind of detour that's really the straightest line toward your goals.

It is possible to use Lewis' suggestion as the basis for a more general principle about research. Some sources are sufficient unto themselves. The moment you first see them, you know what you will do with them, or what they will accomplish for you. Other sources are valuable, but only in tandem with something else. Often, arriving at the right pairing of source materials is the decisive moment when a History project really comes to life.

Conclusion

If browsing still sounds too superficial, think of it as reconnaissance. Set aside a whole week for it. This may feel like postponing really getting to work. Yet it is on the basis of your browsing that you will decide what you must settle down to read with meticulous care. You will be making reading decisions almost from the first moment of your research. Therefore, it is not far-fetched to argue that it is the browsing that makes everything else possible.

This chapter has been an extended look at the practice of reading quickly and incompletely. Chapters Three and Four, in contrast, are about reading slowly, thoughtfully, and skeptically. Visualize a packed shelf of materials, or perhaps two shelves. This is what you are assembling now. Some of the contents of that "shelf" may be in hard copy, but of course, others will exist only digitally. These are the materials—historiography, primary sources, perhaps some theoretical or interdisciplinary reading—that seem, so far, to be the closest and best match for your interests. In Chapter Three, we'll direct some

---

[33] Peirce K. Lewis, "Axioms for Reading the Landscape: Some Guides to the American Scene," in *The Interpretation of Ordinary Landscapes, ed.* Donald W. Meinig (Oxford: Oxford University Press, 1979), 11–32, see 20.

concentrated attention to a few carefully selected books and articles that are close enough to your project to almost count as its cousins. Really coming to terms with this scholarship is the best thing you can do right now, as you try to get a sense of the shape and priorities of your own project.

Further Reading

Pierre Bayard, *How to Talk about Books You Haven't Read*, trans. Jeffrey Mehlman (London: Bloomsbury, 2007).

Alberto Manguel, *The Library at Night* (New Haven: Yale University Press, 2006).

Lawrence Venuti, *The Translator's Invisibility: A History of Translation,* second edition (London: Routledge, 2008).

K.T. Ewing, "Fugitive Archives: Black Women, Domestic Repositories, and Hoarding as Informal Archival Practice," *The Black Scholar* 52, no. 4 (2022): 43–52.

It's not too early to think about taking accurate notes, especially when you are working with scholarship that resembles your own interests and approach. Charles Lipson, *Doing Honest Work in College: How to Prepare Citations, Avoid Plagiarism, and Achieve Real Academic Success*, 3rd ed. (Chicago: University of Chicago Press, 2018) has a system that he calls "Q quotes" which will help you avoid careless errors.

CHAPTER 3

Encountering the Experts

If you are unaware of the relevant scholarship, you will be playing chess on an empty board. Any move to any square will appear to have the same effect—none at all. This is why the literature review, even if it remains primarily in the form of notes to yourself, is an indispensable part of any serious academic project. It's so integral to our work that scholars have coined an affectionate nickname: It is universally known as the "lit review." The practical benefits of a thorough lit review extend even down to the level of composing individual paragraphs. For example, when should you dwell on a point, or multiply examples in support of it? The only way to know how to use your space (and the reader's time) efficiently is to anticipate how likely your reader may be to concede the point in question.

The most important benefit of the lit review is that you will find some productive ways to interact with the existing scholarship. This could take many forms. You might discover that you're a member of a club that you didn't even know existed, and feel that finally you've come across some true kindred spirits. Or you may see how your project is in a kind of friendly rivalry with theirs. You may get really mad at someone who engaged with your topic, but bungled it. Any one of these experiences can be like rocket fuel for your own work. A successful lit review, then, can leave you empowered, energized, and street smart.

The experience of creating a lit review can also be revelatory and disconcerting. Some approaches (or concepts, or information) are genuinely new. Others—to be blunt—were just new to you. After you've surveyed the best and most current scholarship, it may be time to adjust your tone—and your appraisal of your own project's novelty—accordingly. It is common to discover that *you* were the one who was a bit out of date. If you expected to write about an episode that unfolded during the Industrial Revolution, and it's increasingly clear to you that there's a hot dispute about whether there even *was* an

Industrial Revolution, then this could be a time to reappraise some things. Let the lit review unsettle your plans. Your project will be more interesting as a result.

Margaret Walshaw suggests that we consider a lit review as "a story about what has already been found"; in other words, it has a plot.[1] She's got a point. Most lit reviews—even quite dry ones—follow a narrative structure. There's often an origin story of some kind. There are important characters—the key scholars—often operating at cross-purposes to each other. There's something important at stake. While events in the non-academic world sometimes make an appearance, the publication of a few particularly influential or controversial pieces of scholarship supplies most of the plot twists. Another book on academic writing even suggests that you end on a cliffhanger: "The research story so far is not yet complete."[2] In other words, you can use the lit review to develop intellectual suspense: How will your project, themes, or approach save the day? You can't set this up without an intimate familiarity with the strengths and weaknesses of what's gone before.

In that spirit, although Chapter Two sang the praises of browsing, the focus of this chapter—and the one that follows—is on slow, thoughtful, skeptical reading. Skeptics are not cynics; they are not impossible to convince. They do, however, expect to see a clear chain of reasoning and evidence before they are willing to accept anything.

I haven't met your advisor, but I'm pretty confident that they are a skeptic. It goes with the territory. What's the best way to learn how to *write* for skeptics? Start *reading* like one yourself.

THE SKEPTIC'S CREDO

How does a skeptic operate? Let's consider this first through a contrast with the opposite approach, which we might call the "magisterial" style. Encyclopedias—the classic example of a magisterial work—present entries without drawing any attention to the author's name. Documentaries feature a disembodied, god-like narrator who makes pronouncements that stand without interruption or critical interjections. Textbooks generally have no footnotes, on the assumption that the reader would not need—or care—to delve deeper.

If you expect a skeptic to defer to the verdict of vaguely defined "experts," you'll be disappointed. They want to inspect and crosscheck each individual claim. Much of what we refer to as "scholarly apparatus" (footnotes and bibliography, but also the conventions of academic prose) exists to fulfill the

---

[1] Margaret Walshaw, *Getting to Grips with Doctoral Research* (New York: Palgrave Macmillan, 2012), 40.
[2] John M. Swales and Christine B. Feak, *Academic Writing for Graduate Students: Essential Tasks and Skills*, 3rd ed. (Ann Arbor: University of Michigan Press, 2012), 348.

skeptic's need to pin all this down. "I went to the archives" does not satisfy the skeptic; they need a citation attached to each invocation of an archival source so that if necessary, they could go to that archive, order that document, and read the relevant portion for themselves.

This much, I expect, is familiar to you. Yet the skepticism does not end there. It is applied to any scholar's logic and analogies, to their definitions of key terms and concepts, and to any conclusions they may draw at the end. Above all, though, skepticism zeroes in on warrants, the muscle, and sinew of persuasive academic argument. Oscar Handlin once wrote a book entitled *Truth in History*, scolding his fellow scholars, with chapters sarcastically entitled "How to Count a Number" and "How to Read a Word."[3] Handlin's status as a Pulitzer Prize winner and a member of the Harvard faculty did not exempt this book from receiving, in turn, its own skeptical reception.[4]

Skeptical does not need to mean sour or dismissive. Consider the title of H.S. Versnel's short piece, "Did the Greeks Believe in Their Gods?"[5] Such formulations are an invitation to an intelligent conversation. One of the primal forms of skeptical inquiry is a close examination of names and categories. If an academic journal published a whole stand-alone article just on a dispute over how a term is defined and used, that's a sign to sit up and take notice. I have seen historians tie themselves in knots over the term "working class."[6] The debate over who counts as a Muslim—and whether there is one Islam or multiple Islams—is also rich, complex, and not fully resolved. The *Huijiao ren* (回教人) acknowledge their descent from Chinese Muslims, but allow the consumption of pork. Does their act of self-identification settle the question, or not?[7]

Speaking with a constant awareness of contradictory possibilities and propositions takes some practice. Once you're in the habit, though, you may find it seeps into your offhand remarks about almost any historical topic. István Deák's students recalled his teaching style; he was "famous for offering all kinds of counter-arguments to his own statements, effectively exhausting the field of possible critical engagement right before our eyes."[8] I'll let you in on a

---

[3] Oscar Handlin, *Truth in History* (Cambridge, MA: Harvard University Press, 1979).

[4] See, for example, the review by Bruce Kuklick in *Social Science History* 5, no. 2 (Spring 1981): 238–239.

[5] H. S. Versnel, *Coping With the Gods: Wayward Readings in Greek Theology* (Leiden: Brill, 2011), 539–559.

[6] Robert Gray, "The Deconstructing of the English Working Class," *Social History* 11, no. 3 (October 1986): 363–373; Geoff Eley and Keith Nield, "Farewell to the Working Class?" *International Labor and Working-Class History* no. 57 (Spring 2000): 1–30.

[7] Rian Thum, "What Is Islamic History?" *History and Theory* 58, no. 4 (December 2019): 7–19.

[8] Holly Case, "On History and Human Experience: In Memory of István Deák," in *H-Diplo Forum: Tribute to the Scholarship and Legacy of István Deák*, ed. Diane Labrosse (June 2023), 13–19, see 18. https://issforum.org/ISSF/PDF/jt1.pdf, accessed 3/29/2024; for a taste of how this informed Deák's own writing style, see István Deák and Norman M. Naimark, *Europe on Trial: The Story of Collaboration, Resistance, and Retribution During World War II* (London: Taylor & Francis, 2013), 4–9.

secret: The people who get really good at this are also the ones who, in the end, know how to frame their own arguments in the most compelling ways.

Review essays are one of the best ways to see an entire, perhaps decade-long, debate boiled down to just a few incisive pages. Some journals specialize in review essays, while others offer them only occasionally. Some titles are as bland as "New Work in …." Others recapitulate the turmoil they seek to distill: "The Russian Revolution as Continuum and Context and Yes,—as Revolution."[9] For students unfamiliar with the genre, review essays can feel like a mixture of navel-gazing and backbiting, if that is anatomically possible at the same time. Some of the best review essays, though, sketch out a path forward, or suggest a synthesis that incorporates some of the best in both sides of an argument.

Facing what looks like an infinite regress of claim and counterclaim, the response of many students peering over this abyss for the first time is to step back from the edge. Does the existence of debate block us from making reasonably sturdy claims? Consensus does emerge, on most things, for a while at least. Social scientists have offered four hundred different definitions of the term "personality," yet undergraduate psychology textbooks are still published, even if they will need revision every few years.[10] As you know, the same thing occurs with history textbooks.

You will have no trouble imagining that we accumulate extra knowledge over time. You should also observe how our individual imbalances and shortcomings add up to collective strength. Even Marc Bloch, a strong advocate of big-picture thinking, assumed that most scholars would specialize to some degree, notice some things, and miss others. He likened the combined result to a "play of converging searchlights whose beams continually intermingle and interpenetrate each other."[11]

Through the messy process of revisions and rebuttals, a richer, more complex, and more nuanced picture emerges than any one of us flawed mortals could produce on our own.[12] One day, you, too, can add to the picture. Reaching that point does involve engaging with, and sooner or later differing from, some established scholarly position. As Christina Maranci put it, "A good critique begins with *allowing yourself the freedom to disagree*."[13]

---

[9] Peter Holquist in *Cahiers du monde russe* 58, no. 1&2 (2017): 79–94.

[10] Kenneth Hoover and Todd Donovan, *Elements of Social Scientific Thinking*, 9th ed. (New York: Wadsworth, 2008), 18.

[11] Marc Bloch, *The Historian's Craft*, trans. Peter Putnam (New York: Alfred A. Knopf, 1962), 150.

[12] Appleby et al. *Telling*, 229, 247, 281, 283, 285, 309.

[13] Christina Maranci, *A Survival Guide for Art History Students* (New York: Pearson Prentice Hall, 2005), 124.

Your Cousins, Evil Twins, Frenemies, Soul Mates, and Role Models

It's time to turn that skeptical eye on the scholarship that's the closest match to your own interests. Approaching this portion of the lit review is something of a personality test. For some, there is the pleasure and challenge of measuring oneself and one's ideas against the best writing and thinking on the topic. For others, prone to eye rolls and irritated outbursts, you need to take a deep breath and try not to overreact. For still another group, already apprehensive about how "everything has already been said," it can feel like an invitation to confirm their worst fears, in detail and at length.

Yet riches await here. I am not even referring to the potential for footnote plundering, and the treasure trove of new keywords and search terms that you'll find in this scholarship. What I need you to focus on is the larger intellectual opportunity presented by these "cousins" to your own project. While they may look like rivals at first glance, finding these close neighbors is an encouraging moment; it suggests that your interests are aligned with those of others whose work was deemed significant and publishable. Moreover, it is very nearly a law of physics that academic writing goes nowhere without something to leverage off of, or work against. This goes by various names, including "generativity" and "leapfrogging."[14] It is also inherent in popular templates such as Steven Posusta's "Instant Thesis" formula, which asks you to insert language to complete this sentence: "although ... nevertheless ... because."[15] Don't shy away from productive critical friction with the scholarship that shares some of your priorities. It will accelerate the development and maturation of own project.

In what follows, I will continue to refer to this little constellation of works as your cousins, without quotation marks. It is a term of convenience and (I hope) goes some way toward demystifying what's involved here, but since the usage is unique to this book, you'll probably have to explain it to people if it creeps into your conversation.

Even before you have a clear idea of what the working title for your own project will be, the decision to list particular works as cousins can be a powerful way to assert what interests you most and how you hope to approach it. Kate Briggs captures the intense, uneasy energy here in her statement: "I write because I have read."[16] With admirable candor, she describes the reader's envy, fascination, and ambivalence. There is a half-articulated impulse to rewrite it and insert yourself in some way—but how?[17] Really reflecting on everything your cousins have to teach you, and clarifying your relationship to them, isn't

---

[14] David N. Boote and Penny Beile, "Scholars before Researchers: On the Centrality of the Dissertation Literature Review in Research Preparation," *Educational Researcher* 34, no. 6 (Aug-Sept 2005): 3–15, see 3; Gaipa, "Breaking."

[15] Steven Posusta, *Don't Panic! The Procrastinator's Guide to Writing an Effective Term Paper* (San Diego: Bandanna Books, 1996), 12–13.

[16] Kate Briggs, *This Little Art* (London: Fitzcarraldo Editions, 2018), 99.

[17] Briggs, *This Little Art*, 115–117, 271.

a process that will neatly resolve itself overnight. It may be an ongoing dialogue throughout your entire project.

Still, it's time to get organized. Print out a slim binder's worth of articles that seem closest to your concerns and interests. Prop it up on your shelf next to a couple books that also fit this description. Set yourself some time (several days? a week?) to re-read this set of materials, making detailed notes.

I have written the last few paragraphs as if *who* your cousins are is a straightforward matter. Perhaps, for some students, this exercise will be helpful in a different way—choosing your cousins is forcing you to grapple with aspects of the definition, character, and boundaries of your project. One way to brainstorm your way through that is to jot down some *alternative* cousins' lists, play around with those for a bit, take a break, and give yourself time to reflect and make choices.

Sometimes half the battle is figuring out where your cousins would publish. The good news is that often finding where one publishes will turn up others in the same place. Assessing the prestige, scope, and focus of a publisher is sometimes hard to judge just from their name. The *Virginia Magazine of History and Biography* isn't for hobbyists; it's a weighty academic journal dating back to 1893. The *William and Mary Quarterly* isn't an alumni magazine. The *Austrian History Yearbook*, despite its name, covers the history of all the former Hapsburg territories. It's not surprising that McGill-Queens University Press publishes lots of fine Canadian history, but would you guess that Northern Illinois University Press is a go-to publisher for Russian history? Pay attention to any tips down these lines, follow up on leads, and do the requisite browsing.

Once you are ready to settle down with your preferred set of cousins, approach each individual piece of scholarship with all of the components of the skeptical toolkit at your fingertips. Jot down the distinctive traits of each scholar. Which one is strong on definitions and concepts? When it comes to primary sources, who made unusual and interesting choices? Inevitably, some of your cousins will focus on your chosen topic, but in a slightly different setting or time period than the one you hope to pursue. Keep track of any positive role models, bearing in mind that you'll probably borrow just one aspect, such as the use of sources or a theoretical framework. You'll find negative role models as well. You've already spotted an opportunity that they missed, perhaps, or their conclusions aren't the ones you'd have drawn from the same evidence.

You are also at the stage where you can sum up, in a few lines, the state of the field. Collectively, how are your cousins describing the problem (do they really all see the problem in the same way)? What are the key terms and concepts; how are they defined; is there agreement on the definition and usage? Are there fundamentally different ways to interpret what went on, and which scholars are on each side of that debate? What are the typical primary sources used to approach this topic? What are the most common methods? What are the important ideas, themes, or conclusions that turn up repeatedly—or is there an implicit disagreement here as well? Overall, what feels like it's been done exceptionally well, and what feels missing?

It is possible that some of the works you have selected as your cousins are not yet on speaking terms. You came looking for something that would have generative energy with your project, and what you're noticing is two or more works that have generative energy *with each other*. This opportunity to combine the strengths of multiple strands of scholarship can be as jarring and momentous a discovery as any other, and it may suggest a way forward for your own project.

Among the cousins, I can almost guarantee that you will find one or two pieces that leave you with a strong feeling that you could do better, or at least that there is a visible flaw or omission that cries out for redress. If you have doubts about your own adequacy for the task ahead, this experience is one of the best cures available.

Yet you will encounter other cousins that leave you unsettled because they come so close to the goals you have set for your own project. You will have an urge to emulate, repudiate, associate yourself, and differentiate yourself—sometimes more or less all at once. This is stressful to think about, so let's adopt some playful terms for discussing the on-again, off-again feelings that you will have about your closest academic counterparts.[18] One or two are your role models or soul mates. Another looks more like your evil twin. Maybe a couple are best described as your frenemies.

One reaction deserves special attention here: "This is so good, and so close, *how* do I distinguish myself?" Let's remember the lesson that all skeptical readers learn before long: Asymmetrical excellence—or to be more colloquial, lopsided excellence—is not unusual; it is typical. An individual scholar possesses just one or two great strengths, which double as weaknesses. In Chap. 5, I will have more suggestions on how to approach the task of finding a new angle that others have missed. But for now, take some time and reflect on just where that fearsome rival of yours is shining their spotlight, and you may surprise yourself with some ideas about what that spotlight doesn't touch.

What you have compiled in your cousins' list is a kind of small, personal library tailored to your project. Like cousins, you may be looking at a number of scholars whose work bears the marks of a family resemblance. Several probably do cite each other. You are finding that your reading speed is going up, because you can predict a point before it is made, you no longer need to wonder about the definition of the concepts that are deployed, and so on.

You can pat yourself on the back. This means that now you are well grounded in *a* literature. As the economist Nassim Nicholas Taleb observed in his book *The Black Swan*, this would be a perfect time to start wondering about *other*

---

[18] Irene L. Clark, *Writing the Successful Thesis and Dissertation: Entering the Conversation* (Upper Saddle River, NJ: Prentice Hall, 2007), 98, develops a very similar concept, but she refers to them blandly as "text-partners."

literatures, *other* academic voices, *other* debates. Taleb wrote: "The more you know, the larger the rows of unread books."[19] He calls this the "anti-library."

A Trip to the Anti-library

Suggesting a trip to the anti-library sounds like a bit of a joke, or an incident from the children's classic *The Phantom Tollbooth*. Yet in a way, the anti-library has a physical location, because it is firmly located *elsewhere*. What you are looking for is a genuinely different point of view, which nonetheless speaks in a meaningful way to what interests you.

For many years in my undergraduate methods class, I assigned an article about Vietnam War vets who suffered from post-traumatic stress syndrome, felt misunderstood and overlooked, and wrote about their memories, as well as their difficulty integrating back into society. The twist was that these alienated vets were women, the force they served in was North Vietnam's Youth Shock Brigades (Thanh Niên Xung Phong), they were teenagers—not adults—when they fought, and the challenges they faced included several gender-specific issues, including learning that an amputated limb impacted their eligibility for marriage.[20]

Behind the decision to write an article about the veterans of the Youth Shock Brigades lies a whole series of insights brought about, in the first instance, by an ability to grapple with the numerous sources written in Vietnamese about the conflict, most of which will never be translated into English. Yet what is going on here is more profound and complex than simply a historian who has an "extra" skill, the ability to read a particular language. The novelist John Le Carré, reflecting on the role that foreign language education played in his own life, asserted that "the decision to learn a foreign language is ... an act of friendship ... To have another language is to possess a second soul."[21] We needn't go as far as Le Carré to recognize the potential of a new language to unlock a multitude of unsettling possibilities.

Anti-libraries don't always rest passively, waiting for someone to notice them. They can erupt into public view and demand attention. When Joan Kelly wrote her famous essay, "Did Women Have a Renaissance?" academic feminism was new enough that it formed the anti-library for many areas of inquiry.[22] In 1994, the *American Historical Review* published a short piece with this cantankerous title: "Why Is There so Much Conservatism in the United States

---

[19] Nassim Nicholas Taleb, *The Black Swan: The Impact of the Highly Improbable* (London: Allen Lane, 2007), 1.
[20] François Guillemot, "Death and Suffering at First Hand: Youth Shock Brigades during the Vietnam War (1950–1975)," *Journal of Vietnamese Studies* 4, No. 3 (Fall 2009): 17–60.
[21] John Le Carré, "Why we should learn German," *Guardian*, July 1, 2017.
[22] Joan Kelly, "Did Women Have a Renaissance?" in *Becoming Visible: Women in European History*, ed. Renate Bridenthal et al. (New York: Houghton Mifflin, 1977), 175–201.

and Why Do So Few Historians Know Anything about It?"[23] As these examples suggest, an intervention from the anti-library often comes in the form of an interruption. It is bringing up sources, issues, or perspectives that are so different from the ongoing academic conversation that it can sound abrupt, awkward, maybe a little impolite. Yet publications like these can signal the potential for a paradigm shift of great consequence. It is often the young scholars, not the established academics set in their ways, who notice the opportunities here.

A common suggestion is to seek the equivalent of the anti-library by making sure you read, cite, and discuss the work of scholars from under-represented groups. It makes sense to add the specification that the group you have in mind actually is under-represented, and under-cited, *in the subfield that interests you*. (You can have a look at your cousins' list with this in mind.) A more generic way to find the anti-library is to consider that it is the material that lies in *your* blind spot or outside *your* comfort zone. Exactly what that is will vary considerably from scholar to scholar, and from one project to another.

For example, historians with a commitment to green causes may be drawn to studying activist or conservationist nonprofit groups. Meanwhile, as a recent overview of environmental history remarked, big business has been a very unpopular research area for them: "Private corporations have been understudied despite their importance in capitalist society, above all the giants of chemical industry such as Monsanto, BASF, DuPont, Dow, Union Carbide, and Royal Dutch Shell."[24] Similarly, an oral historian with left-wing sympathies wrote a fascinating, nuanced analysis of how locals in one Italian town told and retold the story of a local worker shot dead by the police in the course of a protest, yet seemingly it did not occur to him to also interview some old cops, who might have had their own competing version—or versions—of the notorious story.[25]

As these examples suggest, anti-libraries *are* anti-libraries for a reason. They make us uncomfortable. They tell us things that disrupt or unsettle what we thought we knew. If you never go looking for the anti-library, though, you risk getting stuck in your own academic "bubble" or echo chamber, and not even knowing it.

The anti-library is not necessarily there to divert you, or demand that you cease and desist from your current project. Potentially, it could open up new areas in which your project is useful and important; you might be holding in your hand the missing puzzle piece for a nearly completed puzzle you didn't know existed. Or the anti-library might show you exciting new ways to do a better job on things that already matter to you.

---

[23] Leo P. Ribuffo, *American Historical Review* 99, no. 2 (April 1994): 438–449; for the complete forum, 409–452.

[24] Simo Laakkonen et al., "The Cold War and Environmental History: Complementary Fields," *Cold War History* 16, no. 4 (2016): 377–394.

[25] Alessandro Portelli, *The Death of Luigi Trastulli and Other Stories: Form and Meaning in Oral History* (Albany: SUNY Press, 1991), 1–26.

A Word About Interdisciplinary Projects

From a certain perspective, the anti-library for historians is what goes on in all the other disciplines. It is probably already clear to you that historians vary in their appetite for theories, theorizers, and generalizations. Yet it would be hard to name a decade in the last hundred years in which historians *did not borrow* from other disciplines. This should stand as a warning to students who bristle when they are assigned books that "aren't history," or indeed to some faculty who look askance at the reading habits of their colleagues. Any new, influential theory of human nature or social structure is bound to find some adopters in our profession. The all-embracing ambition of History as a discipline makes this inevitable.[26]

Some academic journals are avowedly interdisciplinary, such as *History and Anthropology* and the *Journal of Historical Sociology*. Other journals that do not fly their interdisciplinary colors so explicitly, such as the *Journal of Urban History*, have mixed editorial boards. Some entire fields, such as environmental studies, African American history, and women's studies owed much to interdisciplinary collaborations in their early years, and to this day they are often housed in multiple departments, drawing on faculty who have joint appointments.

If interdisciplinary dialogue sometimes results in interesting collaborations, it can also run into difficulties. Harvey Graff reminisces about an initial encounter between social scientists and historians who came together for a dialogue. The historians explained that they were excited to get tips and support, because they planned to re-center their whole discipline around advanced statistical methods. At this point, the conversation became awkward, because the social scientists believed that number crunching had inherent limitations, and *they* had come to the meeting seeking allies for their unpopular views![27]

It should go without saying that a serious foray across disciplinary lines will require engagement with different methods, and more than a few hours in the company of a different textbook than the one you are holding at the moment. It may seem irreverent to approach interdisciplinarity as a time management problem, but—just as with mastering a foreign language—if you are going to encounter a steep learning curve, you owe it to yourself to plan ahead.

That said, exploring a body of theory needn't involve taking secret oaths in the forest, or signing away your future. Perhaps you feel *an affinity for the issues raised* in another discipline. You can express it in exactly that way. If you think network theory has something to offer, you could become—not a practitioner

---

[26] For, one example, see Richard Overy, "'Ordinary Men,' Extraordinary Circumstances: Historians, Social Psychology, and the Holocaust," *Journal of Social Issues* 70, no. 3 (2014): 515–530; see also Ralph Cohen and Michael S. Roth, eds., *History and...: Histories within the Human Sciences* (Charlottesville: University Press of Virginia, 1995), which is even more wide ranging than its title (and tantalizing ellipsis points) suggests.

[27] Harvey Graff, "The Shock of the 'New' Histories," *Social Science History* 25, no. 4 (Winter 2001), 483–533.

of network theory as such—but "someone who's interested in networks." If some historians have already written work inspired by a theory, you have a natural, and user-friendly, starting point.

This is consistent with the "soft" interdisciplinarity that has characterized our discipline for a long time. Many historians feel comfortable with their membership in what John Tosh has called a "hybrid discipline."[28] A soft interdisciplinary approach might begin by asking: "Given my choice of topic, what toolkit suggests itself?"

A good rule of thumb is this: Don't judge an entire discipline by the last famous theorist you've heard of and disliked. The odds are excellent that there are newer thinkers and newer methods; perhaps these developed in reaction against exactly the approach which annoyed you. Theory itself, in all disciplines, is a dynamic entity that grows, renews, and changes. Sometimes historians are well positioned to point out a blind spot or an important exception, performing the function of an anti-library for *them*. Therefore, finding an approach that seems flawed to you can offer a productive friction, a generativity, all its own.

The interplay between gender history and psychoanalysis is an instructive example of this. In the 1970s, Leonore Davidoff made an analysis of Arthur Munby's diary the centerpiece of an article for an academic journal. Munby, a Victorian gentleman, left behind a diary of more than a million words in length—as well as a collection of photographs—cataloguing his erotic fascination with the thick, muscular bodies and calloused hands of "country wenches" and household servants.[29] A bachelor for most of his life, he conducted an intimate relationship over several decades with Hannah Cullwick, a servant who he later secretly married. The two engaged in elaborate role-play involving special nicknames and costumes, mostly organized around enacting different forms of dominance and submission.

In the near absence of any feminist historiography to cite at that time, Davidoff found a generative pushing off point in psychoanalysis. As so often with theory, we could think of psychoanalysis as the tool that was right for the source here, *or* as the catalyst that made it possible to "see" the source as useful to the historian in the first place. She began her classic article with an extended discussion of domestic service, but she also delved into what psychoanalysts had written about the place of nannies and servants in the early sexual fantasies of children under their care.[30] Psychoanalysis also, indirectly, informed her discussion of the recurring themes of dirt and cleanliness in Munby's diary. She balanced this with a careful examination of the ambivalent place of the servant in the spatial and emotional architecture of the Victorian middle-class

---

[28] John Tosh, *The Pursuit of History: Aims, Methods, and New Directions in the Study of History*, 6th ed. (London: Routledge, 2015), 43.

[29] Leonore Davidoff, "Class and Gender in Victorian England: The Diaries of Arthur J. Munby and Hannah Cullwick," *Feminist Studies* 5, no. 1 (Spring 1979), 86–141, see 103.

[30] Davidoff, "Class and Gender," see 89–100.

household. Davidoff's work never strayed far from the norms we would expect a historian to follow, yet it is *informed by* and *in dialogue with* psychoanalytic interpretations. Arguably, both fields were enriched by the encounter.

Does everyone have to go looking for interdisciplinary opportunities? Certainly not. You do owe it to yourself, though, to read the best that's out there on your topic or problem. Other disciplines may be barking up the exact same tree, and it is hard to know this without looking at what they are publishing. It is possible for a parallel or equivalent concept to be hidden in plain sight, in a well-known database of peer-reviewed scholarship, but your search doesn't throw it up. One reason for this is that disciplines do speak their own distinct languages. While some conversations cut across all of the social sciences and humanities more or less simultaneously, in synch with the reception of a theorist such as Foucault, Lacan, or Latour and earmarked with their associated keywords and signature concepts, other subject matter follows idiosyncratic paths in *each* discipline.

For example, historians prefer to discuss a phenomenon by a name that contemporaries would have recognized (antinomian sects, *santería*), whereas our counterparts in some other disciplines are more likely to borrow their vocabulary from theorists, or to coin an abstract concept that might suit any time period or geographical location. If you were hunting among scholarly publications from the mid-twentieth century, an antinomian sect might show up as a case of *deviance* in the language of social science, and santería would be an instance of *syncretism*. (Today, both terms have fallen out of favor, so you would need to investigate what has replaced them; the social sciences, like historiography, present a moving target.) Conversely, an anthropologist with an interest in patriarchy might not know about the rich vein of scholarship developed by historians writing about pronatalism. This is harmless enough, but it results in misleading search results if you are unaware of the correct keyword.

If you have interdisciplinary interests or ambitions, it is important to have a candid discussion with your advisor as early as possible. Find out up front if you are dealing with someone who really has no enthusiasm for interdisciplinary aspects. Historians tend to be skeptical of one-size-fits-all; "the theory needs modification for the circumstance" is a more winning approach.[31] On the other hand, your advisor may surprise you with suggestions about friends they have in other departments who might be an excellent fit for a committee.

Students who feel at home in a borderland region and whose skill set is truly ambidextrous may even want to have a discussion down these lines: Is my project best done in Sociology with input from historians ... or in History, with input from sociologists? For certain projects, this may be the single most important strategic decision that you make. Drifting into a choice without actually considering the possibilities would be a missed opportunity.

If your advisor is already familiar with the interdisciplinary potential of your project, then some terse comments and appropriate footnotes may be quite

---

[31] Tosh, *Pursuit*, 180–204.

sufficient. On the other hand, you may find yourself in the position of educating and orienting your advisor, both to the strengths of the theoretical approach, and its applicability to your project.

In the latter situation, even at the prospectus stage, a thoughtful walk-through is desirable. Aligning yourself with a *theory* or general approach is often wiser than placing the emphasis on the (often prolific) *theorist*. This may exempt you from having to defend other writings by that same theorist with which you may not particularly agree. Restate the theory in your own words, especially as it relates to your project, your sources, and your time period. To avoid ambiguity, cite the specific work that you are drawing from, and reproduce definitions of any important terms. Briefly discussing the theorist's favored examples can be illuminating for a reader encountering new ideas for the first time. Still, it is best to avoid overkill; Bruno Latour may be completely new to you, but perhaps not to your reader.

Conclusion

The next chapter turns to primary sources, but jotting down a miniature lit review right now could be a low-stakes exercise to see where you are with your project. Try crafting a single paragraph in which each new sentence sets out a different comparison, contrast, critique, alliance, or declaration of independence.

The experts said this; where do I fit? is not the most productive way to frame the question. It will leave you feeling self-conscious (or worse). Try some version of these instead:
Here's a scene; what does it lack?
Here's where we are; what if we added so-and-so?

Here's the conversation so far; what comes next?

"I am approaching it like this ... not like that" does not exactly have the ring of academic prose, but it is often this kind of shorthand that academics use when they are speaking to each other, and you may find this is also the way to set it up in a conversation with your advisor.

Here is some slightly more polished language that you might adapt or vary to suit your own needs:
Inspired by ....'s use of ....
In contrast to ...., my project will ....
Akin to ....yet asking instead ....

  Informed by ....

For most student projects, a thoughtful exposition putting some flesh on this skeleton, focusing on just a handful of your cousins (whether books or articles), plus an acknowledgment of some friendly theory, is all the lit review that you will really need to provide.

It's entirely possible that reading the experts will leave you more confused than before. One account of Spanish rule in Mexico might emphasize the fluid, negotiable, and constructed nature of the *castas* system, while another shares evidence that those constructs proved disconcertingly durable—for instance, in the way that women of an Indigenous background were barred from becoming nuns over a period of several centuries.[32] When you spot tension or inconsistencies, be sure to take notes on what you're seeing. Perhaps the historiography isn't fully settled; scholars that should be in dialogue with each other haven't crossed paths yet. It's often at the site of inconsistency, the enticing trouble spot, where excellent new projects are born.

To be sure, it's enough to make your head spin. Sometimes one would hardly guess that these historians are writing about the same century, the same country, the same culture! This may be just the springboard you need, though, to get motivated to take a really deep dive into primary sources. Conveniently, that is the topic of the next chapter.

Further Reading

To appreciate the difference between a thoughtful skeptic and a dismissive (or nihilistic) cynic, the example of how historians approach Holocaust denial is helpful. For this, see: Pierre Vidal-Naquet, *Assassins of Memory: Essays on the Denial of the Holocaust*, trans. Jeffrey Mehlman (New York: Columbia University Press, 1992).

For an instructive debate that hinges on the best way to research and write in a skeptical spirit, see Robert Finlay, "The Refashioning of Martin Guerre," *American Historical Review* 93, no. 3 (June 1988): 553–571 and Natalie Zemon Davis' rebuttal, "On the Lame," 572–603 in the same issue.

Anna Green and Kathleen Troup, eds., *The Houses of History: A Critical Reader in Twentieth-Century History and Theory*, second ed. (New York: New York University Press, 2016) offers an overview of History's numerous interdisciplinary dialogues in the course of the last century.

---

[32] Magali M. Carrera, *Imagining Identity in New Spain: Race, Lineage, and the Colonial Body in Portraiture and Casta Paintings* (Austin: University of Texas Press, 2003); Asunción Lavrin, *Brides of Christ: Conventual Life in Colonial Mexico* (Redwood City, CA: Stanford University Press, 2008).

CHAPTER 4

Questioning Primary Sources

Primary sources can take your breath away: The audio recording of an eyewitness whose voice cracks and trembles; a narrative of a teenage girl who confronted her incredulous father with her intention to shave her head and become a Buddhist nun; the letter from 1632, still stained with the blood of the field marshal who died carrying out the orders it contained; Marie Curie's laboratory notebooks, still so radioactive from her experiments that they are too dangerous to handle today.[1] A brush with something like this is probably what drew you to History in the first place. However, just as a film critic is not the person who is a "buff" or "fan" of cinema, awe of primary sources will only get you so far.

A significant number of History students envision the activity of choosing primary sources as little more than wisely sorting out the correct and incorrect, the reliable and the unreliable, the biased and the unbiased. Having excluded the flawed materials, your work would proceed in an orderly fashion from there. This chapter will seek to complicate that picture.

There is both good news and bad news. The bad news is that the number of problematic primary sources is much higher than most students anticipate. The good news is that these trouble spots are extremely interesting in their own right, and rather than impeding your work, they just might animate and inspire it.

---

[1] The letter from Wallenstein to Field Marshal Pappenheim is displayed in the Museum of Military History in Vienna, Inventory Number NI 1773; Shih Pao-ch'ang, *Lives of the Nuns: Biographies of Chinese Buddhist Nuns from the Fourth to Sixth Centuries,* trans. Kathryn Ann Tsai (Honolulu: University of Hawaii Press, 1994), 20–21; Eoin O'Carroll, "Marie Curie: Why Her Papers Are Still Radioactive," *Christian Science Monitor,* November 7, 2011.

© The Author(s), under exclusive license to Springer Nature Switzerland AG 2024
I. Land, *The Craft of Historical Research,*
https://doi.org/10.1007/978-3-031-68457-9_4

The Past Has No Voice

Pablo Neruda, in his poem *The Heights of Macchu Picchu*, demanded of the mute stones that they divulge the secrets of their long-dead builders, desiring to know every detail about the habits and dreams of the humblest stonecutter—even whether he snored in his sleep. Is Neruda's fantasy of communing with spirits so different from the nineteenth-century historian Jules Michelet's claim to speak for the dead because he had inhaled the archival dust?[2] Most historians today would say that they leave this kind of activity to the poets and visionaries, yet the metaphor persists of "listening to the voices" or "letting the voices speak."

It is a bit odd to speak of serving the past, listening to it, or speaking on its behalf, because—as Keith Jenkins curtly remarked—"the past does not have a self."[3] Even supposing that historians sat down dutifully to take dictation from our sources—presumably, the individuals *did* have selves—consider the paradoxes posed by a slippery narrator. It seems that the poet Shelley "told the story of his expulsion from Oxford at least five different times, never twice in exactly the same way."[4] Decades after the publication of Hannah Arendt's *Eichmann in Jerusalem* popularized the phrase "the banality of evil," a review of the tapes from a secret interview with a Nazi sympathizer revealed Adolf Eichmann to be as flamboyant, boastful, and ideological before his arrest as he was bland and obsequious on the witness stand during his famous trial.[5] These men leave us no choice but to select one version of them to listen to, although this action, perversely, would require dismissing all the others as inauthentic.

Claiming to capture the spirit of a place or the temper of a decade presents similar problems. It might seem, at a glance, that this could not go wrong; after all, a document from Canada in the 1920s could hardly lapse by accident (or cunning artifice) into the mindset of ancient Rome or Tokugawa Japan! Yet here, too, the wisest move is to anticipate inconsistency and build it into your method, or at least to accommodate multiple voices when they appear.

The Canadian student Laura Cameron set out to write her MA thesis on Sumas Lake, a body of water drained in the 1920s.[6] Every day, she drove to her university on a highway that crossed the former lakebed, offering regular reminders of her research topic. Even at the initial stage of her work, addressing the simple question of the lake's size and depth, she discovered that "each

---

[2] Michelet's statement is discussed in Carolyn Steedman, *Dust: The Archive and Cultural History* (New Brunswick, NJ: Rutgers University Press, 2002).

[3] Keith Jenkins, *On 'What Is History': From Carr and Elton to Rorty and White* (London: Routledge, 1995), 22.

[4] Altick and Fenstermaker, *Art*, 35.

[5] Bettina Stangneth, *Eichmann Before Jerusalem: The Unexamined Life of a Mass Murderer*, trans. Ruth Martin (New York: Knopf, 2014).

[6] Later published as Laura Cameron, *Openings: A Meditation on History, Method, and Sumas Lake* (Montreal: McGill-Queens University Press, 1997). Although Cameron now holds a position in a Department of Geography, this Master's thesis was in a History program.

measurement of the lake comes with its own story."⁷ The lake varied in size as the seasons changed, a fact that two-dimensional paper maps could not easily capture. Some writers even characterized the area as not a lake, but a "marsh" or wet prairie scattered with small trees.⁸

Exploring what people felt Sumas Lake *meant* also led Cameron to ambiguous territory. She cites an English naturalist who worked for the International Boundary Commission: It was a "second Eden." She cites a chief of the Sumas Band: It was "one of the greatest spawning grounds there is," frequented by birds of all sorts. She cites a geographer at the University of British Columbia: It was "the great impediment to east-west transportation through the Lower Mainland."⁹ Old photographs showed that the lake was a popular beach and recreation area, as well as a source of valuable fishing for Indigenous people. In the years following World War I, however, most descriptions of the lake focused on its role as a breeding ground for mosquitoes, and as the hidden repository of fertile soil, conveniently located near growing cities, that Canada's returning veterans deserved to farm.

Some students may take it in stride that Adolf Eichmann, for instance, spoke in multiple, inconsistent voices, but would assume on instinct that 1920s Canada did not. If we imagine our role is to capture the spirit of the early 1920s, perhaps the only option is to write a vigorous anti-mosquito, pro-drainage narrative, since that was the most common view. Yet it would be untrue to say, for example, that there were no environmentalists in the early 1920s; Cameron found some.

The fate of Sumas Lake turned on this clash of stories about what Sumas Lake *was*. Ruling out some, or most, of these versions of reality at the outset as unreliable would do an injustice to the evidence, or to any hope of explaining the stakes involved.

Regardless of your time period, location, and topic, telling it like it really was probably means telling a messy story. It's best to embrace this from the outset.

When Is a Source Not a Source?

Most sources are useful in some sense, if only as evidence that a particular point of view existed. Are there situations in which a skeptical scholar actually would reject a source? In *The Historian's Craft*, Marc Bloch offered an example: "When Einhard, while pretending to describe Charlemagne for us, plagiarizes the portrait of Augustus by Suetonius…" Bloch closes his sentence with a provocative conclusion: "…we have really no witness left at all."¹⁰

---

⁷Cameron, *Soundings*, 81. For a similar set of issues, see the discussion of borders and frontier regions in Thongchai Winichakul, *Siam Mapped: A History of the Geo-Body of a Nation* (Honolulu: University of Hawaii Press, 1994), 70, 74–79, 101.
⁸Cameron, *Soundings*, 84.
⁹Cameron, *Soundings*, all from 82.
¹⁰Bloch, *Historian's Craft*, 118.

This is an austere standard. One practical objection, at the outset, might be that we aren't in possession of an abundance of primary sources about Charlemagne, so we should be reluctant to exclude any. But even delving into the substance of Bloch's objection, couldn't Einhard have compared Charlemagne to a different ruler, also admirable, but for a different set of qualities? Presumably, Bloch would have preferred for Einhard to supply an adjective, but maybe the equation of Charlemagne to Augustus—a particular Roman ruler with unique qualities—is not so different from assigning him an adjective such as magnanimous, just, or visionary. We also know that some cultures hold certain types of quotation, elliptical allusion, and imitation in high esteem. Einhard's method of praising Charlemagne was, perhaps, authentic in its own way: It was true to the values of that place and time.

What we need is a method that concedes from the start that any one source is probably partial, quirky, incomplete, or erroneous in some sense. Crosschecking is one of the historian's classic methods because it offers a way forward despite this, and even turns that weakness into an asset. In the absence of written records, Jan Vansina found that it was possible to reconstruct a plausible narrative of African history by comparing different oral traditions; he could test an African court's recitation of its pedigree, wars, and migrations against those of other official versions of history compiled by nearby kingdoms, and against those of smaller units within that same kingdom.[11] Demographic historians of Early Modern Europe worried that their tally of pregnancies and fertility rates was incomplete because baptism records omitted the stillborn babies, but they found that the burial records often made up for this deficiency.[12] Of course, crosschecking has conceptual limits as a research method. Where would I go to "check" what Elvis meant in twentieth-century American culture?

If the key issue is verifying that an event occurred, certain words were uttered, or similar matters, crosschecking is indispensable. It can help us avoid building our arguments and interpretations on weak foundations. For instance, in the course of their expansion into South Asia, Muslim conquerors narrated how they destroyed particular Buddhist monasteries, yet other evidence proves that these exact monasteries survived for a long time afterwards, intact. What lies behind this inconsistency? It appears that the invaders did destroy a modest number of Hindu temples closely associated with the authority of a deposed dynasty, while Hindu temples (and places of worship associated with other faiths) that had no special royal affiliations remained unmolested.[13] Some conquerors—or their chroniclers and court poets—seeking to burnish religious credentials, inserted the language about comprehensive destruction. Each

---

[11] As summarized in Tosh, *Pursuit*, 257.

[12] J. Dennis Willigan and Katherine A. Lynch, *Sources and Methods of Historical Demography* (New York: Academic Press, 1982), 69.

[13] Richard M. Eaton, "Temple Desecration and Indo-Muslim States," in David Gilmartin and Bruce B. Lawrence, eds. *Beyond Turk and Hindu: Rethinking Religious Identities in Islamicate South Asia* (Gainesville: University Press of Florida, 2000), 246–281, see 255.

instance of a false claim, though, had the unintended effect of encouraging later conquerors to dutifully add similar inaccurate litanies of despoiled holy places to their own narratives.[14] Tragically, the exaggerated accounts offer ammunition to those who seek to fuel mistrust and even violence toward Muslims in Myanmar and elsewhere today.

Perhaps the single most famous example of a slippery primary source involves the death of the steel worker Luigi Trastulli in the town of Terni.[15] Alessandro Portelli collected all the evidence that he could concerning this locally famous incident. The young man died in 1949, during a Communist Party-inspired protest against Italy's joining the NATO alliance. In later years, as NATO became less controversial in Italy, it became inconvenient to remember Trastulli's death in that context. Indeed, the idea that once someone had died over this issue seemed far-fetched. A revised memory of the young man's death emerged, with some elements reshaped to conform to visual conventions (to conform to the iconography of martyrdom, Trastulli was pinned against a wall by police bullets) and the assignment of a new motive and context for the demonstration. Surely, Trastulli must have died during the protests several years later against massive layoffs at the factory? This married up "the two most dramatic events of Terni's post-war history into one coherent story."[16] Best of all, in 1953, the workers fought back against the police in an epic street battle, completing the narrative with a satisfying coda.[17] The result was elegant and easy to remember and became the most widespread version of the story, repeated with emphasis, confidence, and the pounding of indignant fists on the table, even by people who were around at the time and should have known better. The only problem was that it was wrong.

Columns of numbers may appear above reproach, particularly to those of us from a liberal arts background who are not accustomed to casting a skeptical eye over them. Yet in this realm as well, there are influential, if unfounded, tales in circulation. In his book *Innumeracy*, the mathematician John Allen Paulos warns about the "semi-attached figure," a statistic that is well known and respected, but circulates without most of its users having any clear notion of what the number means, or how it was derived.[18] Historians have known for centuries that determining the provenance of a textual source is crucial; you should be equally cautious about the provenance of any numbers, graphs, tables, or maps that you may encounter.

It would be convenient if the skeptical reading of a source were always the right reading, but here, too, there are pitfalls. If we find a lone voice contradicted by other sources, is that our cue to discount the lone voice? What if we

---

[14] Johan Elverskog, *Buddhism and Islam on the Silk Road* (Philadelphia: University of Pennsylvania Press, 2010), 131.
[15] Portelli, *Death*, 1–26.
[16] Portelli, *Death*, 14.
[17] Portelli, *Death*, 19–20.
[18] John Allen Paulos, *Innumeracy: Mathematical Illiteracy and its Consequences* (New York: Hill and Wang, 2001), 166.

singled out the one source that was telling the truth, and announced that we had "debunked" it because there was no corroboration? This problem has worried historians for a long time indeed. Edward Gibbon remarked on the difficulty of arriving at an accurate account of the final years of pagan Rome when Christian sources predominate and—directly and indirectly—had eradicated alternative versions of events.[19]

Consider a still thornier situation, the problem of crosschecking a slave owner.[20] The circumstances of slavery, particularly for women, have left us with what Saidiya Hartman has called "an untimely story told by a failed witness," although as she adds, this characterization does not come close to the *kind* of erasure that was inflicted on enslaved women:

> the stories that exist are not about them, but rather about the violence, excess, mendacity, and reason that seized hold of their lives, transformed them into commodities and corpses, and identified them with names tossed-off as insults and crass jokes.[21]

Meanwhile, bystanders—who could serve as witnesses—may not understand what they saw, or notice, or care.

In dictatorships, where telling the truth is a hazardous proposition under any circumstances, it is not immediately evident that lining up several denier sources means that the affirmer is the one who is lying. We might hope for a dictatorship that is two-faced—for instance, its newspapers always lie, but the internal memoranda of the secret police always tell the truth. The reality is often more complicated, not least when the functionaries of the regime seem to have policed their own minds as thoroughly as they sought to police those of others, or they have forgotten how to express themselves in any other register.[22]

Private correspondence should be immune from at least some of the public posturing and posing that we see in so many sources, and historians love to eavesdrop. Yet the authors of texts intended for private consumption still worry and calculate how a message would look to their reader. During World War I, there was a lot of public discussion about the proper letter for a soldier to send home from the front, or receive from loved ones back home. This went so far as the publication of model templates for what uplifting and morale-boosting letters would look like.[23] To be sure, historians can read these with an eye

---

[19] See for example Gibbon, *Decline and Fall*, Chapter XVI, "Conduct towards the Christians, from Nero to Constantine."

[20] Brian Connolly and Marisa Fuentes, "Introduction: From Archives of Slavery to Liberated Futures?" *History of the Present* 6, no. 2 (2016): 105–116.

[21] Saidiya Hartman, "Venus in Two Acts," *Small Axe: A Caribbean Journal of Criticism* 12, no. 2 (2008): 1–14, see 2–3.

[22] Oleg V. Khlevniuk, "Archives of the Terror: Developments in the Historiography of Stalin's Purges," *Kritika* 22, no. 2 (Spring 2021): 367–385.

[23] Miriam Dobson, "Letters," in *Reading Primary Sources: The Interpretation of Texts from Nineteenth- and Twentieth-Century History*, ed. Miriam Dobson and Benjamin Ziemann (London: Routledge, 2009), 57–73, see 63.

peeled for deviations from the script, or change over time, but the first step is an awareness of the approved template and its influence.

If we took a soldier's letter home and marked with a pin every phrase lifted from the newspapers or imitating the wartime speeches of their leaders, and every trite, dutiful sentiment, and every derivative trope and genre-bound practice, we might be left with a primary source studded all over like a pincushion. Yet not many historians would be comfortable setting aside tens of thousands of these painfully self-conscious soldiers' letters as (in Bloch's words) "no source at all."

The private diary might seem like a final refuge. Do we assume that sources confident in their privacy are—in consequence—honest sources? Then it would follow that we must believe human beings are capable of speaking in an authentic voice unconditioned by culture, training, and circumstance, to say nothing of pride or guilt.[24] A sentence beginning "Dear Diary" is not cagey and calculating in quite the sense of Adolf Eichmann on the witness stand. Except in the case of the most unflinchingly candid individual, though, it will be no more honest than people, in general, are honest with themselves.

Despite these challenges, historians have demonstrated many times that a primary source can be a "witness in spite of itself."[25] In his classic work *Night Battles,* Carlo Ginzburg made effective use of the inquisitors' own patterns of questioning to show that they had encountered something they did not expect, and did not understand—a secret group of self-described good witches who combated the forces of evil.[26] Nancy Shoemaker has drawn attention to white settlers who quoted statements from Native Americans referring to systemic deception and oath-breaking *on the part of white settlers;* the most likely explanation is that they were recording what they had heard.[27] The existence of self-interestedness or closed-mindedness doesn't make our primary sources completely impermeable to the truth.

In the records of the ecclesiastical court of Mexico City, Magali Carrera found a case from 1789 concerning Doña Margarita Castañeda.[28] Her baptism, it seemed, got inscribed in the wrong book; her name appeared in the *libro de color quebrado* (the baptismal record of mixed-blood persons, or literally, the book of people of broken color). In colonial Mexican society, this could have serious consequences for any children she might have one day, since admission

---

[24] Chapter Seven of Ann Laura Stoler, *Along the Archival Grain: Epistemic Anxieties and Colonial Common Sense* (Princeton: Princeton University Press, 2008); Nathan Johnstone, "The Protestant Devil": The Experience of Temptation in Early Modern England," *Journal of British Studies* 43, no. 2 (2004): 173–205; Lyndal Roper, *Oedipus and the Devil: Witchcraft, Sexuality, and Religion in Early Modern Europe* (London: Routledge, 1994), 226–248 speak very directly to the difficulties here.

[25] Tosh, *Pursuit,* 112.

[26] Carlo Ginzburg, *The Night Battles: Witchcraft and Agrarian Cults in the Sixteenth and Seventeenth Centuries* (Baltimore: Johns Hopkins University Press, 1992).

[27] Nancy Shoemaker, *A Strange Likeness: Becoming Red and White in Eighteenth-Century North America* (Oxford: Oxford University Press, 2006), 9–10.

[28] Carrera, *Imagining,* 2–6.

to universities, as well as certain professions and guilds, required pure Spanish descent. Therefore, Doña Margarita's husband brought her case to the court's attention, and four different individuals testified that she was held, reputed, and considered to be Spanish, as were her parents. In the end, the court authorized the correction of her baptismal record. The historian's work is made possible, in this situation, by the passionate, anxious investment in pedigree and social status in colonial society. Carrera found a source from *inside* the system that nonetheless illuminated its contradictions.

The Educated Source

What Gail Hershatter has written about oral narratives—they "are as contaminated as any other retrievable fragment of the past. It requires cultivating an interest in and respect for that contamination"—could well be said of all our sources.[29] This language doesn't feel very inviting, though. Words like contamination—or bias—carry such negative associations that it is hard to embrace the task.

Partiality or *interestedness* sound less inherently sinister. These are very human qualities, but such words don't fully capture what's at work in many of our sources. A century ago, the philosopher Alfred North Whitehead wrote:

> Style, in its finest sense, is the last acquirement of the educated mind; it is also the most useful. It pervades the whole being. The administrator with a sense for style hates waste; the engineer with a sense for style economizes his material; the artisan with a sense for style prefers good work. Style is the ultimate morality of mind.[30]

Whitehead wrote to praise, but let's take a moment to examine the richer, more ambiguous territory implied by his statement.

If I am trained in forest management and my job title is "forest manager," I am going to look at trees in a certain way.[31] Yes, it will influence what I notice or omit, but also what pleases me, what dismays me, how I define certain problems, and even what sorts of things I would consider a problem. Taking a page from Whitehead, we might call that an *educated* source.

Of course, not everyone went to forestry school. Hans Asperger was a pediatrician in Vienna who rose to prominence after the Nazi takeover of Austria. Faced with stubborn boys who refused to wear the swastika armband or sing patriotic songs, he developed an innovative diagnosis which foreshadowed later theories of autism. He sent many of his patients to their death as part of a euthanasia program. Edith Sheffer's study of Asperger and his colleagues is based on a deep immersion in their medical doctrines, as well as their detailed

---

[29] Gail Hershatter, *The Gender of Memory: Rural Women and China's Collective Past* (Berkeley: University of California Press, 2011), 24.

[30] As quoted in Williams, *Style*, 199.

[31] A theme developed memorably in James C. Scott, *Seeing Like a State: How Certain Schemes to Improve the Human Condition Have Failed* (New Haven: Yale University Press, 1999).

notes on particular cases; for instance, she explores how they deployed the German word *gemüt* to mark off the qualities that autistic boys supposedly lacked.³² Her careful discussion does not, in any way, minimize or excuse Asperger's behavior under the Nazi regime. Indeed, her own autistic son wrote an afterword to her book. You needn't check your values at the door to acquire a profound knowledge of how a certain kind of training informed the texts—and deeds—of the people you study.

Education isn't necessarily acquired in an accredited training program. You may find yourself working with street smart sources. Ordinary people interrogated by those in power, for example, display a practiced evasiveness.³³ Other sources are steeped in the arts of bureaucratic obfuscation, which is probably not the subject of a formal curriculum anywhere. In 1994, elements within the Clinton Administration fought hard to avoid the use of the word "genocide" to describe the ongoing events in Rwanda. We have an especially clear understanding of this because a memo survives from May 1 warning: "Be Careful. Legal at State was worried about this yesterday—Genocide finding could commit the USG to actually 'do something.'"³⁴

That may sound like an exceptional situation, but what about an entire narrative which, from beginning to end, was contrived to get someone out of trouble? In *Confronting the Classics*, Mary Beard offers this chilling appraisal of testimony about Roman emperors:

> Most senators during most reigns were collaborators... and when regimes changed they made every effort to reposition themselves, usually by excoriating in speech and writing, in ever more gory detail, the dead emperor who had once been their friend. *That writing is the Roman imperial history we have inherited...* [my italics] Tacitus, who devastatingly exposed the corruption of the regime of Domitian (81–96 AD), after the emperor's death, had himself been a beneficiary of Domitian's patronage during his reign and had been rapidly promoted by that 'monster' in the Roman imperial arms race.³⁵

We might guess, or hope, that this strange situation is confined to sources from ancient Rome, but the omissions and obfuscations of officialdom are often woven into the very texture of what we find in the archives. Consider the "Rule of the Bureaucracy," attributed to Dean Acheson (no stranger to the

---

³² Edith Sheffer, *Asperger's Children: The Origins of Autism in Nazi Vienna* (New York: W. W. Norton, 2018).

³³ Ciaran B. Trace, "What Is Recorded Is Never Simply 'What Happened': Record Keeping in Modern Organizational Culture," *Archival Science* 2 (2002): 137–159; Anne Dolan, "Death in the Archives: Witnessing War in Ireland, 1919–1921," *Past & Present* (March 2021): 271–300.

³⁴ Discussion Paper, Office of the Deputy Assistant Secretary of Defense for Middle East/Africa Region, Department of Defense, May 1, 1994. Secret. https://nsarchive2.gwu.edu/NSAEBB/NSAEBB53/rw050194.pdf, accessed May 19, 2024. For context on this document, see Samantha Power, "Bystanders to Genocide," *Atlantic Monthly*, September 1, 2001.

³⁵ Mary Beard, *Confronting the Classics: Traditions, Adventures, and Innovations* (London: Liveright, 2013), 142.

upper echelons of power), which states: "A memorandum is written not to inform the reader but to protect the writer."[36]

Akira Kurosawa's classic film *Ikiru* (1952) is about a mild-mannered bureaucrat who faces an existential crisis as he grapples with a terminal illness. One day, he shocks his colleagues by almost literally cutting through the red tape surrounding a citizen group's request. He tears off a routing slip and crumples it in his hand. Then, to the amazement of his colleagues, he declares that the office which should act on this matter is his own. This action sets a chain of events in motion that is discussed and debated for the rest of the film.

A film like *Ikiru* should remind us that the little self-serving habits and petty rivalries of government offices offer historians an opening. Laura Tabili was looking for primary sources about sailors from Asia, Africa, and the Caribbean who wound up staying in Britain and even marrying local women there. She found it was productive to consult the records of both the Colonial Office and the Home Office on the issue. The Home Office, whose remit was law, order, and immigration, tended to see these men as an irritant and a problem. The Colonial Office, alert in the early decades of the twentieth century to growing anti-imperial sentiment, warned that mistreating colonial subjects had a way of getting into the newspapers in Kingston, Jamaica, and elsewhere, and consistently advocated for a more welcoming, flexible response with an eye to that overseas public opinion. The Colonial Office and the Home Office each analyzed the problem differently, collected different information, and kept different kinds of records—including, in some cases, letters from the wives, and from the sailors themselves. Tabili found a way to turn the partiality and interestedness of each bureau of government to her advantage as a researcher.[37]

Many people are shrewd customers when it comes to text, but forget to apply that same critical lens to visual materials. In Weimar Germany, the photographer August Sander undertook an encyclopedic catalogue of his society, one occupational and social "type" at a time.[38] You might pluck a single portrait from Sander's vast array of photographs and treat it as a simple illustration of your subject matter. Yet a snapshot by Sander could be a posed, contrived, and selective representation, as pointed—in its way—as a satirist's gibe or a propagandist's slogan.

Just as you would for a letter or memo, it's worth inquiring of a photograph: Who produced this? Under what circumstances? If it was reproduced and transmitted, who saw fit to do so? If there was any editing or reframing, what motivations shaped that activity? Most of us don't center our project on such questions, but David Schneer wrote an entire monograph about the Red Army photojournalists who took the first images depicting the reality of the Holocaust

---

[36] Allen L. Otten, "Politics and people: more rules," *Wall Street Journal*, September 8, 1977.

[37] Laura Tabili, "*We Ask for British Justice*": *Workers and Racial Difference in Late Imperial Britain* (Ithaca: Cornell University Press, 1994).

[38] Steve Plumb, *Neue Sachlichkeit, 1918–1933: Unity and Diversity of an Art Movement* (Amsterdam: Brill, 2006), 115–126.

and its immediate aftermath.[39] He explained why most of these men happened to be Jewish, how they navigated the experience of witnessing the destruction wrought upon their own communities, and finally how the photos—such as the images of mass graves or the vistas of liberated concentration camps—got captioned or contextualized in the Soviet media of the day.

Like other primary sources, maps are profoundly embedded in the circumstances of their production. Thongchai Winichakul's *Siam Mapped* is a particularly wide-ranging exploration of the varied agendas of different cartographers.[40] Sacred geography had no concern for accurately depicting relative sizes and distances, and pilgrimage maps represented only the number of days required to actually travel between points.[41] In contrast, some other maps came into existence to favor one side in a colonial land grab—or to justify a claim to mineral rights. Winichakul reminds us that even a historical atlas can reflect an implicit nationalist agenda, amounting to a "codification of the crisis" or even constituting a "lethal instrument" in its own right.[42]

It should be clear by now that the human act of making a record or creating a source is not as random and unintentionally revealing as the fortuitous preservation of a bone in a swamp.[43] Unlike most social scientists, historians work with evidence collected (and preserved) by others. Moreover, the evidence we have is the product of individuals who hoped to accomplish something by picking up a pen, taking a photo, and so forth. If that dilemma provokes you to change your topic from.

what really happened?

to

what can we know about the people who recorded what happened, why and how did they keep the records, and what were the consequences of keeping the records that way?

you would not be the first historian to do so.[44] Kathryn Burns wrote a whole book about the role of the notary public in colonial Peru.[45] Bhavani Raman, taking a close look at just who created and kept the records of British rule in

---

[39] David Shneer, *Through Soviet Jewish Eyes: Photography, War, and the Holocaust* (New Brunswick, NJ: Rutgers University Press, 2012).

[40] Winichakul, *Siam*.

[41] Winichakul, *Siam*, 20–36.

[42] Winichakul, *Siam*, 129, 150–152.

[43] Here, I differ from Gaddis, *Landscape*, 121; see also his remarks in the same vein on 114, 115, and 124.

[44] For a suggestive discussion of the implications of such questions for both archivists and historians, see Thomas Osborne, "The Ordinariness of the Archive," *History of the Human Sciences* 12, no. 2 (1999): 51–64.

[45] Kathryn Burns, *Into the Archive: Writing and Power in Colonial Peru* (Durham: Duke University Press, 2010).

India, found among the "piles of paper and palm leaf" evidence of "informers and delinquent scribes... bribery [and] forced confessions."[46]

In fact, getting a grip on the strengths, weaknesses, and opportunities inherent in a single *source type* might be a task that is just the right size for your small project. In a short piece that could serve as an excellent model for such an inquiry, Joël Glasman offers a careful dissection of how French colonial authorities in Togo did—and didn't—account for polygamy when they filled out paperwork. There was only one space on the personnel form for a police officer's wife, resulting in conflict between the wives about who should be listed. Multiple wives meant that some police officers had more children than the form could handle, although some clerks "glued an additional piece of paper to the bottom of the page" to accommodate the full list.[47] Meanwhile, Glasman notes, patriarchal assumptions led colonial officials to note down the police officer's *father's* occupation and educational background, although in this polygamous society, "it was often the mother who determined whether or not to invest in a child's education."[48] The official paperwork did not include a space to record the mother's education level or how she made a living.

We don't all work on polygamy, but, for example, if you care about immigration, do a study *of* how the census handled people who crossed borders. If you care about patriotism, you could do a study *of* soldiers' letters home. If you are consulting official statistics and learn that "Thatcher's Conservative government notoriously changed the definition of 'unemployed' twenty-three times," then think of it this way—you thought you had one interesting potential topic (British unemployment in the 1980s), and now you have two.[49] In his book on New Orleans, Craig Colten wrote an entire chapter about the myriad ways that the municipal government and public health authorities deployed the term "nuisance" to define problems, shape policy, and justify action.[50]

It's tempting to imagine that you can evade this territory altogether. Surely there are other sources, less contaminated by all this bias, all this interestedness, all this education? Most historians will tell you, from long experience, that the opposite of an interested source is a bored source. Bored sources, however, have a terrible habit of leaving no written record at all.

---

[46] Bhavani Raman, *Document Raj: Writing and Scribes in Early Colonial South India* (Chicago: University of Chicago Press, 2012), 193–4.

[47] Joël Glasman, "Rethinking Colonial Intermediaries: On the Use of Career Records as a Source for African History—A Sample from Togo," in *Sources and Methods for African History and Culture: Essays in Honour of Adam Jones*, ed. Geert Castryck, Silke Strickrodt, and Katja Werthmann (Leipzig: Leipziger Universitätsverlag, 2016), 413–430, see 419 and 420.

[48] Glasman, "Rethinking Colonial Intermediaries," 421.

[49] Michael Blastland and Andrew W. Dilnot, *The Tiger That Isn't: Seeing Through a World of Numbers* (London: Profile Books, 2008), 25.

[50] Craig E. Colten, *An Unnatural Metropolis: Wresting New Orleans from Nature* (Baton Rouge: Louisiana State University Press, 2006), 47–76.

Conclusion

To an aspiring scholar, the works—and words—of other scholars can be the loudest voices in the room. Don't postpone your encounter with the primary sources, though. Looking at material from seventeenth-century England, Kira Newman noticed a sharp divergence between the way that "the government asserted that plague control measures were acts of public health for the benefit of all" and a "popular narrative that portrayed quarantine and isolation as personal punishment rather than prudent policy."[51] Following up on the popular critiques, Newman learned about the numerous ways that the middling sort (small business owners; people who made ends meet by taking in renters) felt the sting of quarantine in ways that wealthier families did not. If she had only encountered the angry testimonials late in her research, it would probably have been too late to do more than drop them in as a colorful quotation. With an awareness of these sources early on, she was able to design her research to explore and expose the inequities of quarantine. If you give them a chance, primary sources can shift your idea of which projects are possible, which are desirable, and even which are urgently necessary.

Be sensitive to what formed your source, but also take care that your source doesn't form *you*, to the extent that it recruits you as its special pleader to the exclusion of all other considerations. Leopold von Ranke once took a scholar to task for populating two chapters with fifty-four footnotes, all to the same source.[52] Reading one hundred boxes of material from the same government office, philanthropic organization, or other entity may fill you with confidence and leave you bristling with quotations and evidence, but on some issue that really matters, you may have just gotten the same version of things, over and over again.

Simple advice such as "immerse yourself in the archives" ignores this fundamental problem. The moment when you break—in a quiet but decisive way—from the senior scholars and the historiographical consensus could be as simple as picking up a different thread than they did, and choosing to let that one be your guide through the archival labyrinth.

Further Reading

Hamish Maxwell-Stewart, "Seven Tales for a Man with Seven Sides," in *Chain Letters: Narrating Convict Lives*, ed. Lucy Frost and Hamish Maxwell-Stewart (Carlton South: Melbourne University Press, 2001), 64–76.

Although the concepts in this chapter are very widely applicable, specialized resources exist for almost every source type, and some journals (ex. *Film and History; Oral History Review*) are dedicated to the opportunities and challenges associated with particular source types.

---

[51] Kira L. S. Newman, "Shutt Up: Bubonic Plague and Quarantine in Early Modern England," *Journal of Social History* 45, no. 3, (Spring 2012): 809–834, see 810.

[52] Grafton, *Footnote*, 44.

There are two particularly good books which deal with kinds of materials I do not dwell on at length in this chapter:

Claire Lemercier and Claire Zalc, *Quantitative Methods in the Humanities: An Introduction*, trans. Arthur Goldhammer (Charlottesville: University of Virginia Press, 2019), see Chapter Two, "Sources and Samples."

Penny Tinkler, *Using Photographs in Social and Historical Research* (London: Sage, 2013).

Keep an eye out for books that deal with the trickier aspects of primary sources, but with a special focus on the country, language, or time period that interests you most. A recent example is Chiara Meccariello and Jennifer Singletary, eds., *Uses and Misuses of Ancient Mediterranean Sources: Erudition, Authority, Manipulation* (Tübingen: Mohr Siebeck, 2022).

CHAPTER 5

Finding a Place to Stand

There is a mystique around originality. It's hard to sort through the swagger and hype, and figure out what the expectations really are in this area. R. G. Collingwood wrote: "…every new generation must rewrite history in its own way; every new historian, not content with giving new answers to old questions, must revise the questions themselves…"[1] This is inspiring language, but we should be cautious about reading too much into it. A *small* contribution is still a contribution to knowledge. Being original can be—and usually is—being original to a *modest* degree. There is, therefore, plenty of room for good scholarship that neither revises the old questions nor compels anyone to look at the whole field differently.

For that reason, I start this chapter with a discussion of what is called incremental scholarship. The truth is that most student projects, like the one you are undertaking now, will fall into this category. Incremental scholarship is both new and different, but in small ways that amount to a refinement or slight extension of existing techniques, explanations, or empirical knowledge. A middle area consists of what might be called "partly original" projects, which break new ground while leaving one foot planted firmly in the approaches and priorities of the existing academic literature. There is also the possibility of a bolder venture that marks a clear departure from what's out there already. For those who yearn to make their mark in this way, I do offer some tips about how to demystify the process that leads to those "eureka" moments of unconventional thinking.

The truth is, though, that there is an originality spectrum. It's wise to settle on a location somewhere along that spectrum where you feel comfortable, that corresponds in some sense to your personality and your goals.

---

[1] R. G. Collingwood, *The Idea of History* (New York: Oxford University Press, 1956), 248.

The World of Incremental Scholarship

One of the great unwritten rules of academic discourse is that if others are interested in a theme, issue, or problem, then this justifies your interest in it. Therefore, situating yourself in a cozy web of affiliations is often the wise stance, and some advisors will deliberately steer you in this direction. It certainly takes the pressure off of you to arrive at a transformative insight or discovery. This is good news for a student project, which by definition is meant to be wrapped up in a limited timeframe.

There is a well-established literature on the standard academic moves to situate and justify incremental projects. Some scholars call it "gap-spotting" and others, a bit more vaguely, refer to finding the area where "more research is needed."[2] In fact, incrementalism is so deeply entrenched in academic life that some methods books treat it as *the* way to determine if a project is viable or desirable, as if no other option existed. Early career researchers are often urged to simply find a humble "niche" where a modicum of originality is possible.[3]

Once you start looking for them, examples of incremental research are easy to find. For instance, Christopher Browning's famous book *Ordinary Men* was a close look at Reserve Police Battalion 101, one group of genocidal killers on the Eastern Front during World War II. Edward Westermann then wrote an article investigating the same themes with respect to a different unit, Reserve Police Battalion 310. This unit had a different demographic profile, skewing younger than 101; it received more propaganda and pep talks; its leaders adopted a different management strategy, seeking volunteers and offering perks to those who took on some of the bloodiest work. Not only was this research publishable, it was welcomed by Browning and others as extending and deepening our knowledge.[4]

The happiest incremental researchers take joy in the recognition that—much as a beehive or wasp nest is an impressive array composed of many smaller, imitative units—their contribution is part of a grand shared endeavor. Adding one narrow chamber to a bustling hive is not an appealing image for many people; one person's *cozy* is another's *claustrophobic*. The incrementalist would say that after conducting a lit review, it is possible to distinguish "what has been done in the field from what needs to be done."[5] The passive, impersonal gram-

---

[2] Mats Alvesson and Jörgen Sandberg, *Constructing Research Questions: Doing Interesting Research* (London: Sage, 2013), 5, 24–37.

[3] As summarized in Thomson and Kamler, *Writing*, 94–95, the "niche" is defined as something smaller than a research "space."

[4] Browning, *Ordinary Men;* Edward B. Westermann, "'Ordinary Men' or 'Ideological Soldiers'? Police Battalion 310 in Russia, 1942," *German Studies Review* 21, no. 1 (February 1998): 41–68.

[5] Boote and Beile, "Scholars," 7.

mar of that statement implies a whole set of presumptions about where the field is, and what is considered valuable. It also implies that the new research can, will, and should follow closely in the footsteps of the old. Not everyone will accept those assumptions.

However, there are advantages to participating in an ongoing shared project. It's easier to make professional small talk, because your project is instantly intelligible to someone working in that field. All jokes about frenemies and evil twins aside, this may offer a glimpse of a less anxious, less adversarial relationship to some of the intellectual cousins that you located in Chapter Three. You are likely to find allies, whether in person or online, and experience all the benefits of joining a supportive community.

For all of these reasons, I expect that many students will find themselves undertaking incremental scholarship in some form. My approach is to strongly encourage you to consider *where* your incremental contribution would be most meaningful and powerful, and Part Two of this book will have a lot of advice about how to go about spotting the best location for it.

Some students become anxious standing in the shadow of prior work and worry that their efforts will appear *too* incremental. Harold Bloom wrote an entire monograph, *The Anxiety of Influence: A Theory of Poetry* around the idea that such sentiments are inherent to creative activity. If, as Bloom suggested, "the only guilt that matters to a poet [is] the guilt of indebtedness," then perhaps you can feel less alone in your unease.[6]

Some linguists and literary theorists, such as Frédéric François, suggest that even actions that are seemingly one hundred percent derivative, such as choosing a passage from an author and quoting it directly, is actually an intellectually complex action more accurately described as "reprise-modification."[7] Common sense tells us this is true in the realms of music (sampling, remixes) and art (collage). In scholarship, as in these other creative endeavors, riffing off of classics and marking out new ground often look like two sides of the same coin.

Deploying a familiar idea in a slightly different context can actually force you to make some tweaks or serious modifications. The sociologist Robert K. Merton coined the term "adumbration," which involves teasing out aspects that were not present in someone else's original idea.[8] Don't underestimate the value of making refinements to an influential approach.

---

[6] Harold Bloom, *The Anxiety of Influence: A Theory of Poetry* (New York: Oxford University Press, 1973), 117.

[7] Christiane Donahue, "When Copying Is Not Copying: Plagiarism and French Composition Scholarship," in *Originality, Imitation, and Plagiarism: Teaching Writing in the Digital Age*, ed. Caroline Eisner and Martha Vicinus (Ann Arbor: University of Michigan Press, 2008), 90–103, see 98.

[8] Robert K. Merton, "Singletons and Multiples in Scientific Discovery: A Chapter in the Sociology of Science," *Proceedings of the American Philosophical Society* 105, no. 5 (1961): 470–486.

Pivot Point: Routes to the Partly Original Project
Most scholarship is, quite visibly, a mixture of old and new. Here are some simple recipes describing the mixture. If you think about it, you'll realize that you are already familiar with examples of some—or all—of these from your prior reading.

Old sample, new question. Just because a source has been visible, accessible, and picked over by generations of scholars doesn't mean that it can't disclose something unexpected if you approach it with a different set of priorities. Themes that come easily to you—perhaps because of the generation you belong to, or the times in which you are living—were perhaps not even on the radar of those who've looked at that same material in the past.

Old question, new sample. It's easy to assume that posing a new question is the most meaningful creative act, but devising a clever new way to address an old question requires creativity as well. Unfamiliar *types* of primary source could be your best friend here. As with the anti-library (discussed in Chapter Three), the quirky unexpected source type will vary, depending on your topic and the source types usually associated with it.

Conduct an "archive audit" of a classic. Historians are—necessarily—very selective about what they quote, and how much context they provide. Access the archive and order some of the materials used in that famous book or article. You will find (one hopes) the small piece of paper that they cited, but also see the hundreds of pieces of paper that they did not. How does that change your view of that event, that era, the operations of that office?

Lost and found. Sometimes excellent scholarship goes unread. If you have the courage to get away from reading just work from the big names in the field, just the prizewinners, and so forth, you can uncover wonderfully quirky new approaches, underused bodies of sources, unexpected theoretical frameworks. Give those unsung scholars credit when it's due, but see how their insights could inform your own project.

Find a good approach, then take it on a trip. "I will do x, but in y context" gives you a confident start. Yet even a straight-up attempt to emulate your role model in a new location, time period, and so forth may force you to innovate. The result may be more fresh (and refreshing) than anyone might have predicted.

THE BOLD AND LONELY PATH

The professional benefits of having your name associated with groundbreaking research are familiar to everyone, but textbooks on academic writing rarely—if ever—speak directly to the student who is looking for ways to maximize their originality. If you are looking to make a big splash with your project, this part of the chapter is for you.

Each year, the MacArthur Foundation gives out twenty or thirty fellowship awards. These have acquired the nickname of "genius grants." In English, we can refer to "a genius," "the genius," or to "a work of genius," but there is no gerund to enable us to discuss "geniusing." Maybe inventing that word would help us all demystify the activity.

Before you hang up a sign outside your study carrel, "Caution: Geniusing Zone," let's consider some ways to go about it. It's helpful to start with the proposition that creativity isn't a thing that you *have*, but a strategy that you might *cultivate*. Creativity is not necessarily a harder activity than normal work. It *is* work—in the sense that it is a deliberate application of effort with a goal in mind—but here, the goal is to crank out fresh approaches. Notice I do use the plural here; for various reasons, many creative ideas don't pan out. So at this early stage in your work, the more ideas the better. It's common to talk about "writing productivity" for academics, but "creative idea output" is another very useful form of productivity. Develop the right habits, and you may find that creativity is your regular companion.

In Chapter Two, I sang the praises of browsing. It's exactly that sort of fluid, open-ended, joyful exploration that can lead you to make the connections that have eluded others.[9] The bibliographies of academic publications heralded as creative or groundbreaking follow a pattern—they tend to cite scholarship that others in their field did not.[10] Those maverick citations turn out to be a very reliable indicator of a scholar who's bringing in a new theory or a fresh analogy. Alberto Manguel, who once worked as Jorge Luis Borges' assistant, speaks in a more poetic vein about listening for the whisperings of a library at night, when "one book calls to another unexpectedly, creating alliances across different cultures and centuries."[11]

The concept of the anti-library, discussed in Chapter Three, gets at a similar phenomenon. People with an outsider's perspective don't spend a lot of energy trying to trick themselves into thinking differently, they just do. Being interdisciplinary is one way to see things as an outsider, but it is far from the only option. Do you know a different language than others have used? Just consulting primary sources in that language could shake things up a lot. In his book *The Messy Middle,* Scott Belsky writes about interlopers in the business world; one argued that his weirdness was his superpower.[12] It can be yours, too. Find a place where you are—in one sense or another—an interloper, and see what happens next.

A more deliberate and self-conscious approach is to position yourself as a contrarian. The term takes its name from the Wall Street investors who spot

---

[9] Alberto Manguel, *The Library at Night* (New Haven: Yale University Press, 2006), 18, 134, 202.

[10] Brian Uzzi et al., "Atypical Combinations and Scientific Impact," *Science* 342, no. 6157 (October 2013): 468–472.

[11] Manugel, *Library*, 14.

[12] Scott Belsky, The *Messy Middle: Finding Your Way Through the Hardest and Most Crucial Part of Any Bold Venture* (New York: Penguin, 2018), 58.

which way the herd is moving, and place bets that things will move in the opposite direction. Make a list of the obvious or popular statements in your field, just to remind yourself that you are not going to say any of them. This doesn't mean that you'll need to adopt a position that might get you banned on your favorite social media platform; a thesis that works even *slightly* against expectations is potentially interesting. For instance, many historians had written about William Morris tapestries and similar exquisite productions, but rather than focusing on "the beautiful and the transcendent," Deborah Cohen decided to write a book about Victorian material culture centered on "the ugly and the ephemeral."[13] The contrarian approach is a bit of a personality test—some people are thrilled to play the iconoclast, but the more contrarian your project is, the more puzzled looks you'll get when you first describe it.

Henry Steele Commager urged his students to "break the spell of the familiar" that has accrued to particular centuries and eras.[14] For instance, writing a whole book about miracles and pilgrimage in twelfth-century Germany would surprise no one. Doing the same for nineteenth-century Germany was startling.[15] Our preconceptions about regions and continents can benefit from the same iconoclastic treatment.

It's possible to break the spell of the familiar without being quite so bold. Figure out what the beaten track is in your little corner of the profession. While researching her book *Captives*, Linda Colley broke her own stubborn habits of relying on archives located in London. Instead, she sought out archives in Gibraltar and Malta, with eye-opening results.[16]

Name your toughest research problem. Now imagine what your project would look like if you put the spotlight directly on that, rather than trying to push it backstage. Jochen Hellbeck's book *Revolution on My Mind: Writing a Diary Under Stalin* drew on a tantalizing, yet infuriatingly suspect, type of source. Was there any way to use diaries kept under a dictatorship well known for its suspicious nature and frequent purges? He could have ducked the issue. Instead, Hellbeck made that question the central theme of the whole book. How *did* Communism shape what went into a private record of this kind? What can we learn about life in Stalin's Russia from the sometimes proud, sometimes uneasy, sometimes guilt-ridden and self-accusatory introspection of these texts?[17] Perhaps your anxieties (about sources, about method, about something else) can themselves suggest a research project, if you re-center it *around the difficulty* in a thoughtful way.

---

[13] Deborah Cohen, *Household Gods: The British and Their Possessions* (New Haven: Yale University Press, 2006), xv.

[14] Henry Steele Commager, *The Nature and Study of History* (Columbus, OH: Charles E. Merrill, 1965), 45.

[15] David Blackbourn, *Marpingen: Apparitions of the Virgin Mary in a Nineteenth-Century German Village* (New York: Alfred A. Knopf, 1995).

[16] Linda Colley, *Captives: Britain, Empire, and the World, 1600–1850* (Princeton: Princeton University Press, 2004).

[17] Cambridge, MA: Harvard University Press, 2006.

The techniques I've suggested here may set up some false expectations that you could jot down some ideas on the back of a napkin, and set off at a brisk pace. This is possible, but unlikely. The poet Amy Fuller likened her creative process to dropping a letter into a mailbox; if she posed it a question, after about six months, she'd get an answer back. The physicist Hermann von Helmholtz felt that his mind worked in stages, starting with saturation, followed by incubation, and finally illumination.[18] If you are attracted to the road less traveled, you should expect a slow uneven unfolding as you research and as you write, even if it is punctuated by moments of clarity. This is not a futile effort; it is a necessary precondition to moving forward, crossing the border into the territory that the poet Kim Stafford calls "what you almost know."[19]

Each of the strategies discussed in this section are ways to *begin* with an innovative trajectory in mind. It's also important to stay alert for openings that will only present themselves as you read further and conduct your research. As early as the 1940s, Merton described the "serendipity pattern" in which new theories are born, or old theories broken, because a chance encounter with an odd, stubborn fact left the researcher puzzled.[20] Among historians, Carlo Ginzburg is most closely associated with this kind of method. As Ginzburg noted, there's nothing small about microhistory; it can be a way to spot icebergs by noticing the little piece that's above water.[21]

It may take a while to figure out the larger significance of what you stumbled on, but surely, the first step is to keep an open mind. Serendipity is beyond your control, but how you react when it happens is an important matter of choice. If you notice something weird, remember that you have the option of not letting it go.

That's Obvious… That's Interesting… That's Absurd

Jack Greene, in an American Historical Association booklet aimed at PhD dissertation writers, seems to imply that boldness is expected and welcomed: "Whether by showing the crucial relevance of a neglected topic or by putting a familiar topic in a new light, your object is to compel scholars in your field to re-evaluate the way they have traditionally understood it."[22] Since I just devoted a whole section to coaching you on ways to achieve this, you can tell that I have some sympathy with Greene's position. Yet, as Thomas Kuhn demonstrated

---

[18] Betty Edwards, *Drawing on the Right Side of the Brain*, fourth edition (New York: Penguin, 2012), 245, 251. See also Efron and Ravid, *Writing*, 205.

[19] Kim Stafford, *The Muses Among Us: Eloquent Listening and Other Pleasures of the Writer's Craft* (Athens: University of Georgia Press, 2003), ix.

[20] Robert K. Merton, *Social Theory and Social Structure* (New York: Free Press, 1968), 157–159.

[21] Jonathan Kandell, "Was the World Made Out of Cheese? Carlo Ginzburg Is Fascinated by Questions That Others Ignore," *New York Times Magazine*, November 17, 1991.

[22] Jack P. Greene, "Defining a History Dissertation and Its Role in One's Future Scholarship," in *From Concept to Completion: A Dissertation-Writing Guide for History Students*, ed. Leora Auslander (Washington, D.C.: American Historical Association, 2009), 3.

some time ago in his influential work on the history of science, challenging people to "re-evaluate" is quite often just a path to dismissive reactions. Kuhn showed how scientists did not abandon theoretical frameworks once someone proved them wrong; instead, it was necessary for a generation to retire or die from natural causes before the new ideas could enjoy universal acceptance. So much for the notion of producing scholarship that would *compel* anyone to accept a new view.[23] So perhaps Jack Greene is setting up a bit of a trap for students who might understand the rewards of taking the more lonely path, but not the risks. In some academic circles, you will find that originality—like toxicity—is best measured in parts per million.

More than fifty years ago, Murray Davis remarked that the reception of new work follows a predictable pattern: A little novelty is received as exciting, but too much prompts a gruff, uncomprehending dismissal.[24] To express Davis' concept, two later scholars developed a delightful (if unscientific) graph to illustrate how the level of interest seems to start low, spike, and then collapse again. If the "number of assumptions challenged" is zero, the reaction is "that's obvious." If it rises to just a few assumptions challenged, the reaction is "that's interesting." Finally, if it completely exceeds their comfort zone, the verdict is "that's absurd."[25] Next time someone recommends a prize-winning book or article to you, have a look and consider where it actually falls on the novelty spectrum. Many prizewinners are only slight innovators, or perhaps there's one particular aspect that was innovative, and everything else is quite familiar and conventional.

In the 1980s and early 1990s, a number of historians expressed discomfort with the newer approaches in the discipline—not on the grounds that they were advancing invalid claims or relying on a scattershot use of evidence—but because they just didn't seem to *connect* with anything else. In particular, to historians accustomed to scholarship about large institutions (a government, a labor union, an army), it seemed that the field was "ramifying in a hundred directions at once [with] no coordination among them."[26] These angry expostulations are less common today, in part because these first tentative gestures toward new themes, new questions, and new types of evidence—such as the history of sexuality—are now enmeshed in a rich web of incremental scholarship inspired by those early publications. Similarly, the first animal-centered histories—such as Harriet Ritvo's work—seemed like another ramification into thin air at the time of their first appearance, although if such a work appeared

---

[23] Thomas S. Kuhn, *The Structure of Scientific Revolutions* (Chicago: University of Chicago Press, 1962).

[24] Murray S. Davis, "That's Interesting!: Towards a Phenomenology of Sociology and a Sociology of Phenomenology," *Philosophy of the Social Sciences* 1, no. 2 (1971): 309–344.

[25] Alvesson and Sandberg, *Constructing*, 68.

[26] Peter Novick, *That Noble Dream: The 'Objectivity Question' and the American Historical Profession* (Cambridge: Cambridge University Press, 1988), 579.

today, it would be in good company, and might even seem unexceptional.[27] Are you comfortable writing about an unfamiliar theme using an unfamiliar approach? That's an option. Just bear in mind that if you go out on a limb, you will have a lot more explaining to do.

I don't mean to create an exaggerated opposition between truly original scholarship and derivative, incremental scholarship. As I've shown, so much of what is published has traits of both. Innovative scholarship will also, as a clever tactical choice, sometimes mask itself as incremental scholarship, to avoid ruffling too many feathers.[28] A deliberate decision to position yourself relatively close to the existing academic literature can be *generative*—it draws credibility, but also strength, by its proximity to where the field is now.[29] A well-designed project may help you avoid the extreme reactions, and just possibly set you up in a sweet spot somewhere in the middle of the spectrum of originality.

One of the most difficult conversations in academia is the one in which you utter a single sentence about your research topic, or maybe you just *begin* to utter the sentence, and you meet with—not a critique—but an abrupt dismissal. It may take the form of a retort: "That's obvious." However, quite often such statements, along with "It's been done," are not meant literally; it says more about the person's lack of appetite for that general sort of thing. A more sincere and precise response would be "Goodness, more of *that*?"

The most difficult conversation for a student is if it is *your advisor* who reacts with a statement such as "It's been done." This is a tricky moment. Your advisor became your advisor because you had some things in common and a reasonably good rapport, so reflect on that before you reply. At the same time, if you conducted a diligent lit review, you arrived at your own sense of the field. Presumably, your intention was not to reprise something already accomplished. So this is the time to be ready with some clarifying questions. It is possible that they know of a piece of scholarship that you do not, in which case you really want to hear about it! But it is equally likely that you aren't communicating clearly. "It's been done, in what sense?" is a good question to ask. What example did they have in mind? If it was a misunderstanding, then you have an opportunity to sharpen your language.

This may even be a chance to articulate something exciting and fundamental about your project. Ashley D. Farmer writes that her book "moves beyond a framework in which men theorized and women organized" and, describing 1970s activists, notes that they "experimented with creating new concepts of black womanhood guided by a Pan-African rather than a American political frame."[30]

You can adopt some version of her structure yourself:

---

[27] Harriet Ritvo, *The Animal Estate: The English and Other Creatures in Victorian England* (Cambridge, MA: Harvard University Press, 1989).
[28] Alvesson and Sandberg, *Constructing*, 92–110.
[29] The concept of generativity first appeared in Boot and Beile, "Scholars."
[30] *Remaking Black Power: How Black Women Transformed an Era* (Chapel Hill: University of North Carolina Press, 2017), 14, 156.

I am interested in looking at it [this way], rather than *[in that way]*.

The topic hasn't been approached through [these kinds of sources]… or *[for this time period]*… or *[in relation to this other thing]*.

It is possible that these adjustments and amplifications will carry the day with your skeptical advisor. They may also suggest a way to reformulate the project that seems sufficiently novel and interesting. Failing that, you may face a more complicated choice about both your project and your advisor.

One of the most common adages about topic choice is that it is crucial to select a topic that is compelling to *you* and that will hold *your* attention. From that perspective, switching advisors may seem to some students like a straightforward solution to any friction. Jonathan Grix offers a valuable note of warning here. A choice of topic that interests you, but seemingly no one else in your program is likely to leave you "isolated in your studies."[31] As he notes, some students shop around a favorite research topic until they find a faculty member who is willing to acquiesce. When their pet project gets the green light, they consider the matter happily settled. Yet this may set you up for disappointments of a different kind. The way that good projects become great projects is by taking on well-informed feedback, advice, and warnings. How will you get this input if you have, effectively, selected an advisor simply for their willingness to leave you to your own devices?

The bottom line is that you do face a decision about just how much you want to stand out from the crowd, and how much you need to shelter under the awning of the common tent. What feels like too much, too little, or just right depends a lot on your personality and style. It should be helpful to check in with your advisor on nagging doubts you may have. On this issue, perhaps more than on any other, it's possible to psych yourself out. You may need a reality check about how novel your project seems to others, and what others with more experience would consider an acceptable (or desirable) level of originality. As with other aspects of your project, this may be an ongoing process of negotiation, feedback, and reappraisal from beginning to end as your project evolves and matures. On important matters like this, keeping the channels of communication open is always the best approach.

Conclusion

Wherever you choose to situate yourself on the spectrum of originality, take special care to differentiate yourself from whatever appears to be your closest counterpart—whether it is a publication by a daunting senior scholar or a piece of student work that you found in a databases of dissertations and theses. Start a running log or notebook about what you owe to it, where you agree and disagree with it, and (as things fall into place) how your project, methods, sources, and conclusions are distinct from it. This will make it easier to explain

---

[31] Grix, *Foundations*, 13.

and signpost those differences as plainly as you can in your final paper. An undergraduate Honors paper that's really just an abridged version of a Master's thesis submitted to a different university will impress no one, and it could easily run afoul of academic integrity standards as well.

Further Reading

Chapter Two, "Envisioning the Thesis as a Whole," in Patrick Dunleavy, *Authoring a PhD* (London: Palgrave Macmillan, 2003) is one of the best short treatments of originality in academic life and thought.

Alan Bennett's play (and later film) *The History Boys,* is—among other things—an extended and witty meditation on what it means to be a contrarian.

Checking in with Your Advisor: Part One Worksheet (The "Vision" Checklist)

(What if...) my topic is _____, considered as _____ rather than as _____

(What if...) my "cousin" books and articles are

_____

_____

_____

Of these, I have the most in common with _____ and a complicated relationship with _____. I may be writing against _____.

(What if...) I am interested in _____ (phenomenon, activity) and a possible interdisciplinary connection would be with _____.

(What if...) a "friendly" theory or conceptual framework would be _____

Typical primary sources for a project of this type are _____, although I might consider alternative sources such as _____.

If I need to acquire a new skill (software, language, paleography…) for this project, it would be _____.

I am most sure about this aspect of the project right now:
_____
_____.

At this point, I am most uncertain about
_____
_____.

When I see my advisor next, what I really want to ask them is
_____
_____.

PART II

Selecting Your Focus

With an overall vision in mind, it is time to consider some practicalities. In Part II, you'll define what you'll probably do, set aside what you probably won't, and make some general reckonings about the best place to settle down, that productive location where you'll get the most bang for your buck. When you can say "to get at *this,* I'll look at *that,*" you have arrived at something more than an interesting idea—you've got a focused plan.

I do not recommend skipping Part I and plunging into this section of the book first instead. As Charles Lipson aptly puts it, "The goal is not just to narrow your topic. The goal is to narrow it in the right way—so your inquiry still matters, so it still offers real insights into larger issues."[1] You need the context that can come only from immersing yourself in the relevant scholarship and appreciating what's been done so that you can envision interesting and productive ways to intervene in that ongoing academic conversation. For example, you will think differently about archives (and digital collections of primary sources) if you know which materials are extensively quoted and discussed already, and which ones have attracted little attention.

Some projects develop in a linear way: A research question prompts a choice of source material that speaks to it. Many projects, though, develop on a spiraling trajectory that looks more like a double helix, an encounter with primary sources inspiring fresh questions, which in turn send you back to the historiography, and so on.[2] Therefore, while the first two chapters of Part II lead you through the process of your first deep encounter with possible sources, a discussion about settling on your true research plan is mostly reserved for Chap. 8, the final chapter of this part of the book. I do offer suggestions along the way about *possible* practical strategies, but it is likely that most readers of this

---

[1] Charles Lipson, *How to Write a BA Thesis: A Practical Guide from Your First Ideas to Your Finished Paper* (Chicago: University of Chicago Press, 2005), 75.

[2] Jerry White, *Rothschild Buildings: Life in an East End Tenement Block, 1887–1920* (London: Routledge and Kegan Paul, 1980), xiii, describes the iterative aspects of his actual research process for the book.

book will entertain multiple versions of their project before committing to a course of action.

Chapter 6 is entitled "Planning for Success in the Archives." Individual circumstances will vary drastically here. You may be writing a local history paper with the most convenient access to most, or all, of the potential materials. This permits a leisurely approach, and frequent return visits. At the other extreme is the "expedition to Mars," involving steep financial burdens and transportation hurdles. In that situation, the archival moment may be long delayed, and when it comes, you'll be conscious of the clock running in the background at every moment.[3] In either scenario, though, archives are a special environment that requires some getting used to. I propose a reconnaissance trip or two, offer some practical suggestions about finding manageable sets of materials, and share some tips about how to turn the archive's quirks to your advantage.

Chapter 7, "Planning for Success in the Digital Realm," explores the options, as well as the difficulties, in this rapidly growing area. We are all digital historians now, whether we use advanced methods or not. It would be overstating things, though, to state that online material is "a thousand times easier to find" than using physical materials in an archive or library.[4] It is quite possible to arrive at what looks like a dead end, even though the database you are using contains millions of pages of material! A zigzag path with many small course corrections is a classic research itinerary, and this remains surprisingly true today even in the era of full text searchable digitized resources. Chapter 7 also offers some perspectives on the choices you may face as you consider whether learning to use "big data" software is a good fit for your kind of project. The chapter concludes with some practical strategies, but also warns about common trouble spots, particularly for the *all*-digital project.

Chapter 8, "Designing Your Project," will help you settle on a chronological scope for your inquiry, consider a latticework of relevant comparisons or contrasts, and look for ways to improve your interplay of primary sources—or perhaps, in the spirit of the social sciences, we could call it your sample. By the end of the chapter, the focus is firmly on stating your research plan, and spelling of out exactly how the materials you intend to use connect to your big questions.

Research isn't about looking at everything, because the truth is that you won't. It's time to figure out what would be *enough*. While, inevitably, you'll have some lingering awareness of paths not taken, your reward for making these tough choices is that you will now have a project that knows when it is finished. This will make an enormous difference in your experience as a researcher and writer going forward.

---

[3] Some libraries and archives will scan material for you and transmit it electronically, with a fee for each page. The costs can add up, but if you know exactly what you want, this opens up a path to do some research using non-digitized materials without physically visiting them. The policies of the particular archive you need may not accommodate this, however.

[4] Helle Strandgaard Jensen, "Digital Archival Literacy for All Historians," *Media History* 27, no. 2 (2021): 251–265, see 253.

The worksheet that appears at the end of Part II will help you compile some notes about where your project stands now. This could be the basis for a conversation with your advisor, or rough notes for a more formal prospectus document. As noted earlier, I encourage you to develop two prospectuses, a Vision prospectus (completed at the end of Part I of this book) and a Focus prospectus completed at the end of Part II.

Books on academic writing and research often assume a constricted orbit, revolving around questions such as "should I discuss this with my advisor?" or "when is it helpful to ask a librarian?" Some projects, however, are best designed in active dialogue with community partners.[5] When he was working on the documentary *The Uprising of '34*, Clifford Kuhn and his team alternated between collecting oral histories and visiting the archives, even using archival material as a prompt to jog the memories of their interview subjects.[6] Such approaches unlock exciting possibilities, but also raise complex questions about the researcher's own role and subject position. A rich literature now exists to guide historians as they consider issues around reflexivity, "shared inquiry," or even "shared authority."[7] Historians working on public history projects—or projects with even a small interviewing component—have been acutely aware of this territory for a couple generations now. The rest of us have a lot to learn from their accumulated insights. These considerations could apply to a wide range of research projects. As a recent publication warned:

> There are far too many instances of researchers using archives without concern for the communities from which the materials came; the stewardship, safety, and vulnerability of the artifacts; or the extractive and sometimes exploitative practices through which the collections they use developed.[8]

A faulty blueprint may be hard to correct later. If this sounds like it might be an issue with your project, consult with the right people, educate yourself about the issues, and take measures now.

---

[5] Erin L. Conlin, "Organizing and Executing Meaningful and Manageable Community-Based Oral History Projects," *The Public Historian* 38, no. 3 (August 2016): 50–77.

[6] Clifford M. Kuhn, "A Historian's Perspective on Archives and the Documentary Process," *The American Archivist* 59, No. 3 (Summer 1996): 312–320, see especially page 317. See also Penny Tinkler, *Using Photographs in Social and Historical Research* (London: Sage, 2013), 173–194.

[7] Katharine T. Corbett and Howard S. (Dick) Miller, "A Shared Inquiry into Shared Inquiry," *The Public Historian* 28, no. 1 (Winter 2006): 15–38; Michael Frisch, *A Shared Authority: Essays on the Craft and Meaning of Oral and Public History* (Albany: State University of New York Press, 1990), 215–224; Jones, "Distressing Histories."

[8] Ashley D. Farmer et al., "Toward an Archival Reckoning," *American Historical Review* 127, no. 2 (June 2022): 799–829; see also Temi Odumosu, "The Crying Child: On Colonial Archives, Digitization, and Ethics of Care in the Cultural Commons," *Current Anthropology* 61, suppl. 22 (2020): S289–S302.

Part II sets you up for an extended period of research that is, normally, the most isolated part of the process. Don't pass up the opportunity to check in with your advisor before taking that big plunge. Whether or not you submit a formal Focus Prospectus, the worksheet at the end of Part II should give you some talking points to make that conversation more productive.

CHAPTER 6

Planning for Success in the Archives

There is a stark difference between working with primary sources in a classroom setting and in the unstructured environment of the archive. A collected volume of primary sources preselects interesting ones, winnows them down to the most striking excerpts, and perhaps juxtaposes contrasting ones against each other. It's usually not hard to figure out why they were included, and if you do need more guidance, they come surrounded by section headings and other interpretive material.

Likewise, any old scrapbooks, photo albums, or keepsakes connected to your family came to you with the associated stories and context, in this case supplied by a relative. Perhaps your first brush with old documents came instead at a museum or historic site; these places, too, make a point of displaying only what is rare, unusual, or significant. As a boy, I visited Washington, D.C., and saw the US Constitution in the Rotunda for the Charters of Freedom. The Constitution resides in a purpose-built treasure room, flanked by murals commissioned in the 1930s. The parchment, under glass, rests under a spotlight like a glittering jewel.

Archives aren't like that. You can expect density, messiness, and a lack of prioritization. To be sure, everything has a number, a box, and a place, but nothing whatsoever is tagged "important" (or, in the unlikely event that it is, it might not be what you were looking for at all). The archive is the place where you really find out that "history is a kitchen midden and not a sacred temple."[1]

Although you are welcome to go to the archive and wait for good things to present themselves—or expect them to be presented *to* you by a helpful,

[1] Edgar Bruce Wesley, "Let's Abolish History Courses," *The Phi Delta Kappan* 49, no. 1 (September 1967): 3–8; see 7.

© The Author(s), under exclusive license to Springer Nature
Switzerland AG 2024
I. Land, *The Craft of Historical Research*,
https://doi.org/10.1007/978-3-031-68457-9_6

encouraging person—the results usually fall short of that. Before the Internet, the first visit to an archive was often a speculative, inefficient endeavor, "the fishing expedition necessary to discover whether a fishing expedition might be desirable."[2] Even today, not every archive has an online catalogue or a web presence, but sometimes you will have an opportunity to assess in advance what's there and whether it might be useful. Your time in the archives is perhaps still weeks or months in the future, but it's never too early to start thinking now about how you will approach the task when you get there and devising possible strategies for using the material.

Thinking Critically About Archives

As the official repository of administrative and legal documents, archives have a long history.[3] Perhaps it is this association with power that fed into the perception that such documents are the most deserving of preservation and the worthiest objects of study. Nineteenth-century historians of such different stripes as Jules Michelet and Leopold von Ranke built up the mystique of the archive.[4] Even Marc Bloch, who worked so hard to broaden our idea of what sources are and what proper ambitions for historians might look like, wistfully remarked: Who would not "prefer to get hold of a few secret chancellery papers or some confidential military reports, to having all the newspapers of 1938 and 1939?"[5] Surely, this depends on what question we wish to ask.

Traditionally, archives keep materials in the filing system adopted by the entity that created or donated the records. In most libraries, we would find this custom quaint, if not downright startling. It is a curiosity, for example, that the *Lindisfarne Gospels* are still catalogued today as Cotton MS. Nero D. IV because, in Sir Robert Cotton's collection (long ago absorbed into the British Library), it was "the fourth book in, on the fourth shelf down, in the bookcase with the bust of Nero at the top."[6] Yet a version of this, expressed as "respect for the *fonds*," remains standard practice in many archives around the world.[7]

Preserving an antiquated filing system from a government office that may no longer exist may seem strange, but it has many practical benefits. It allows

---

[2] Putnam, "Transnational," 381.

[3] Adrian Cunningham, "Archives as a Place," in *Currents of Archival Thinking*, ed. Heather MacNeil and Terry Eastwood, 2nd ed. (Santa Barbara: Libraries Unlimited, 2017), 53–79; Eric Ketelaar, "The Panoptical Archive," *Archives, Documentation, and Institutions of Social Memory: Essays from the Sawyer Seminar*, ed. Francis Xavier Blouin and William G. Rosenberg (Ann Arbor: University of Michigan Press, 2007), 144–50.

[4] Grafton, *Footnote*, 34–61.

[5] Bloch, *Historian's Craft*, 62.

[6] Terry Belanger, *Lunacy and the Arrangement of Books* (New Castle, DE: Oak Knoll Press, 2003), 13.

[7] Any introductory textbook about archival science will discuss "respect for the *fonds*," provenance, and original order.

multiple generations of researchers to understand each other's citations since the material was not rearranged in the intervening years. More subtly, preserving the original sequence and structure of the papers means that many aspects of the mindset and priorities that produced that structure are preserved for study.

At the same time, of course, perpetuating the tacit logic of a regime of power (a slave trading enterprise; a colonial ethnographic museum) can have some troubling resonances.[8] It also means that from your point of view, like material may not be stored with like; perhaps the *fonds* are ordered by administrative provenance and chronological order, but the material is not ordered thematically. Or if it is, it's aligned with themes that someone, long ago, imagined were important. These won't necessarily correspond with the themes and categories that might interest you.

All archival cataloguing systems have a logic and a set of priorities. This means that at every step of the way, you have an invisible partner who is "co-producing" knowledge with you.[9] This is a challenge at so many levels. Can you discover how to *think with* this logic? *Think in spite of* this logic? *Make the most of* what that logic enables? You will have plenty of opportunities to practice your nimble mindset and creative thinking. Sunil Amrith related his struggles when the paper trail concerning migrant workers dropped off in one *fond*, only to reappear elsewhere, when a different government department was charged to address the issue.[10]

Arlette Farge remarks that in a way, what the historian does is build their own—new—archive out of the materials they use, in dialogue with the documents themselves and also with the archive's filing system. She calls it "a joint process of contradiction and construction."[11] George Chauncey's book *Gay New York* is a good example of what Farge has in mind here.[12] In the course of his research, Chauncey became deeply conversant with the logic of police records, medical examinations, and depositions taken by psychiatrists. All of these bodies of documents emerged from a regime of gender identity that was deeply hostile to the lives he was trying to understand better. Despite this, he never lost sight of his own priorities and questions.

Official paperwork has been—and remains—the default source material for many historians. This won't meet the needs of all projects, though. A study of

---

[8] Verne Harris, "The Archival Sliver: Power, Memory, and Archives in South Africa," *Archival Science* 2 (2002): 62–86.
[9] As mentioned in Jensen, "Digital," 253.
[10] Sunil S. Amrith, *Crossing the Bay of Bengal: The Furies of Nature and the Fortunes of Migrants* (Cambridge, MA: Harvard University Press, 2015), 137.
[11] Farge, *Allure*, 63.
[12] George Chauncey, *Gay New York: Gender, Urban Culture, and the Making of a Gay Male World, 1890–1940* (New York: Basic Books, 1994).

family photographs in the Vietnamese diaspora remarks that "this paper turns not to official archives… but rather to collecting projects that have recently been initiated from within the Vietnamese diaspora itself."[13] Specialists in ephemera have questioned whether an elitist bias underpins the very distinction between manuscripts and ephemera, since cheap printed matter (e.g., broadside ballads) was the only reading material that large sectors of the population might ever encounter.[14] Ephemera such as mimeographed newsletters, and flyers from events, form an indispensable source for grassroots activist groups of a certain era. Yet one fledgling collection of LGBT community materials in Canada was, initially, informed that it could not be classified as an archive because it was not acquiring and storing "government records."[15] The long-standing prejudice that privileges traditional archival material over other source types does not take into account a vast, rich range of possible projects, such as studying the "women's handbooks" produced by the Black Panther movement.[16]

In this book, I will adopt an intentionally broad and inclusive definition of *what* an archive might be, *where* it might be housed, and *which* materials it might contain: "Records created or received by a person, family, or organization and preserved because of their continuing value."[17] For example, the Eugene V. Debs papers are held in the Special Collections Department of the Indiana State University Library. This is not an entity that has "archive" in the title, nor are its materials official administrative documents of any kind, but for all intents and purposes, a trip to use this collection is a trip to an archive—albeit a small and specialized one.

For practical reasons, I do—however—maintain a distinction in this book between "the archive" as a physical site where you might request tangible materials, and materials that you will access only online. Adam Crymble wrote in 2021 that "mass digitization was one of the most substantial shifts in the historical profession ever to occur," and it would be hard not to share his

---

[13] Thy Phu, "Diasporic Vietnamese Family Photographs, Orphan Images, and the Art of Recollection," *Trans Asia Photography* 5, no. 1 (2014).

[14] Rebecca Altermatt and Adrien Hilton, "Hidden Collections within Hidden Collections: Providing Access to Printed Ephemera," *The American Archivist* 75, no. 1 (Spring/Summer 2012): 171–194.

[15] Diana K. Wakimoto, Debra L. Hansen and Christine Bruce, "The Case of LLACE: Challenges, Triumphs, and Lessons of a Community Archives," *The American Archivist* 76, no. 2 (Fall/Winter 2013): 438–457, 441.

[16] Farmer, *Remaking Black Power* 111, 115.

[17] This is the first definition that appears in https://dictionary.archivists.org/entry/archives.html, accessed 10/6/2022. The length and complexity of this excellent web resource about definitions of "archive" is a warning sign, of course, that this is contested territory.

excitement, yet it is odd that he puts the statement in the past tense.[18] For instance, in 2020, the US National Archives stated that it had "117 million digital files researchers can use" yet this was "only 1.0 percent of the 13 billion total documents it possesses." Inquiries to two different repositories in Germany, the German Federal Archives and the State Archive of Baden-Württemberg, produced a similar result: Only about 1% was digitized.[19] While the figure will be proportionately higher for some kinds of born-digital archival material you might wish to use, such as emails from the Clinton administration, it is also worth recognizing that some repositories, or collections of interest to you within those repositories, will have obtained no funding for digitization at all.

The introduction of new software may speed up the process of converting manuscript material into a machine-readable version, but the benefits of this have not yet fully materialized. It would be a mistake to assume that even a majority of documents are digitized today, and even what is digitized is quite possibly not transcribed in a way that makes it full-text searchable.[20] If there is digital abundance (measured one way), there is also, considered another way, a surprising degree of digital scarcity.[21]

In one way, however, the revolution has arrived—many new users will "first set foot" in an archive by using its finding aids, in some form, online.[22] While traditional finding aids often took the form of lists of boxes and their contents, an archive's online interface may enmesh you in metadata that could point in any number of directions. The definition of metadata—"data whose purpose is to describe and give information about other data"—sounds bland enough.[23] Consider, however, Michael Kramer's quip that the archivist lays down one layer of metadata, and all he does as a historian is add one more additional overlay of metadata on top of that.[24] When a person attaches metadata to a primary source, it is a profound act of interpretation.

---

[18] Adam Crymble, *Technology and the Historian: Transformations in the Digital Age* (Urbana: University of Illinois Press, 2021), 47.

[19] Simone Lässig, "Digital History: Challenges and Opportunities for the Profession," *Geschichte und Gesellschaft* 47, no. 1 (June 2021), 22.

[20] C. Annemieke Romein et al.'s "State of the Field: Digital History," *History* 105, no. 365 (2020): 291–312, has a great deal to say about the history of machine-readable text and recent developments.

[21] Roy Rosenzweig, "Scarcity or Abundance? Preserving the Past in a Digital Era," *American Historical Review* 108, no. 3 (June 2003): 735–762.

[22] As with the term "archive," I intentionally adopt a loose working definition of "finding aid" in this chapter, also bearing in mind that some vocabulary varies internationally. Thus, the category of "finding aid" might include "card indexes, calendars, guides, inventories, shelf and container lists, and registers," as stated in Gregory Wiedeman, "The Historical Hazards of Finding Aids," *The American Archivist* 82, no. 2 (Fall/Winter 2019): 381–420, footnote 3 on page 410.

[23] *Oxford English Dictionary* s.v. "metadata," accessed 8/21/2022.

[24] Michael Kramer, "Going Meta on Metadata," *Journal of Digital Humanities* 3, no. 2 (Summer 2014), accessed 8 August 2022.

Some of this potential, of course, lurked in seemingly innocuous older vocabulary such as an "inventory" of materials in a collection. Labels, names, and categories come with their own organizational logic, often imposed by some unknown person. The Friends Library, Euston (London), sorted its entire pamphlet collection into two categories, "War Pamphlets" and "Peace Pamphlets." Upon inspection, though—in keeping with Quaker sensibilities—a pacifist approach pervades all, even the "War Pamphlets." Within these two categories, material from different time periods is mixed together, if the cataloguer feels that the subject matter or theme of the pamphlets matches.

An online finding aid could come with an almost limitless number of metadata tags attached to the contents of a single archival box. The potential benefits are vast, of course. One area of interest in recent years has been to use metadata to re-establish links between materials that once were together but now are scattered across multiple repositories.[25] Thus, using one archive's online interface might supply you with research leads to half a dozen other archives that held directly relevant material.

At the same time, it is unrealistic to expect that a librarian or archivist would anticipate all the possible reasons someone might want to consult a source. A series of photos taken in outdoor locations could be scrupulously tagged with metadata such as "women" and "families," but leave an environmental historian frustrated that the presence of trees, mountains, drainage ditches, and fauna went unmentioned. Meanwhile, an architectural historian looking at those same photos might notice the absence of descriptors for railroad stations and rustic resort hotels.

The authors of a 2021 study note that many of the users they surveyed were interested in the possibility of adding their own tags to material.[26] Some wanted to add a tag if the item had been cited in a peer-reviewed article. Presumably, others wanted to add tags about the content of the document, image, or recording that would help researchers who shared their particular interests. There is even the possibility that a person who appears in a photograph would wish to supply information that only they possessed. "Participatory archives" may not have arrived yet at a city near you, but crowdsourced metadata, despite its anarchic possibilities, could enrich the researcher's experience in a host of ways.[27]

---

[25] Ricardo L. Punzalan, "Archival Diasporas: A Framework for Understanding the Complexities and Challenges of Dispersed Photographic Collections," *The American Archivist* 77, no. 2 (Fall/Winter 2014): 326–349.

[26] Emily Lapworth and Su Kim Chung, "The Archives at the Tip of Their Fingers: Exploring User Reactions to Large-Scale Digitization," *Journal of Archival Organization* 18, no. 1–2 (2021): 1–36; see 23.

[27] Timothy Powell, "A Drum Speaks: A Partnership to Create a Digital Archive Based on Traditional Ojibwe Systems of Knowledge," *RBM: A Journal of Rare Books, Manuscripts and Cultural Heritage* (2007): 167–79.

In the midst of this excitement about metadata, old-fashioned paper finding aids are not something to turn up your nose at; in fact, they may offer a possible source of project ideas. Occasionally you will run into a finding aid that has ambitions to be a fairly comprehensive bibliography of an entire subject. The Society of Friends Library holds a volume on *Conscientious Objectors and the Peace Movement in Britain, 1914–1945,* listing unpublished sources (archives; manuscripts) but also printed sources (books and pamphlets published at the time; autobiographies; scholarly monographs; periodicals, including formal reports published by organizations; newsletters and similar ephemera).

Such comprehensive bibliographies are themselves works of scholarship, even if there is no accompanying thesis statement and narrative. They are liable to all the problems of scholarship, including odd choices about periodization, indifference to certain points of view, and simple ignorance of certain sources or methodologies. If the finding aid was created "in" that archive, there is possibly a myopic focus on what is readily available in that archive, but not what exists elsewhere. The authority of a really detailed finding aid is intimidating, yet even here, a skeptical approach is the wisest one. Do not lightly allow a finding aid, even one as helpful as that one, to divert you from the project that *you* thought was important.

Also, if you encounter a tidy handbook of this kind and expect to seize on its contents as a roadmap for your next steps, it is worth considering how many other scholars have already reached that same conclusion and published extensively on this very material. This might even include the scholar who produced the finding aid in the first place!

A "Dry Run" Exercise

For a first-time archive visitor, it is easy to become overwhelmed with the mere mechanics of the experience: registering as a reader, surrendering coats, bags, and pens, obtaining one's seat, ordering and receiving documents, and perhaps handling fragile material.

One way to mentally and emotionally prepare yourself for the archive experience is to break yourself in gently, in a low-stakes environment. Miss no opportunity to improve what we might call your "archive fluency." Your first archive ought to be that of your own university, which almost surely keeps its own records. Perhaps you visit your hometown when school is not in session. Look at the records pertaining to your school district decades or a century ago. Find an archive belonging to the city or the county. You may even know a friendly place of worship, business, or nonprofit, which has its own—perhaps less formal—equivalent of an archive. If the path will be smooth, try them as well.

Don't you need a well-documented, serious purpose to use an archive? You may be surprised how little explanation is requested in most archival situations. Ordinarily, you offer none. Spending time with online finding aids, and perhaps ordering documents beforehand if it is permitted, will sharpen your awareness of what's available and provide you with a ready answer if you get a question about the purpose of your visit.

Ideally, you would encounter as many different archives as you can, just to see what the experience is like: registration, using the finding aids, interacting with staff, seeing how the filing system is set up, getting a feel for the possible range of documents, noticing what's easy and what presents problems.[28] Make the archives as different as you can manage in terms of size, specialization, and so forth.[29] Arrange to spend a day or two in each. Devise a simple project appropriate to each collection, but don't overthink it. It might be something as basic as ordering some maps or something that will be short and a fun browse. After you have spent time in all of the archives, take some time to reflect on the differences between them.

You cannot visit too many archives! Each one is different, and the differences are instructive. In a few archives, documents are still preserved in their original ambiance, perhaps literally in the building where the records themselves were first created. Other archives may have tiny reading rooms that feel like little more than an extension of the archivist's personal office. You can expect a lot of informal conversation with staff in that sort of setting. That said, quite a few archives are modern, vaguely industrial settings, designed for excellence of preservation and speed of document delivery, with the staff hidden almost entirely behind the scenes.

You could do far worse than choose a research topic (or a particular variation of that topic) based on your pleasure in the work conditions in a particular archive or your enjoyment of a particular flavor of archival material. Yet it is hard to see how you could reach such a happy arrangement without being open, in the first place, to trying out a range of document types, working environments, and so forth. As with so many other choices you will face in developing your project, banging your head against the first wall you happen to come across is not a recipe for contentment—or for success.

Even in cases when you run into irritations, be alert to the implications of what you are seeing. Small archives may be slow to answer your initial inquiries. Others—even good-sized ones—may be a little difficult to reach. In some settings, you'll be left wishing that you had access to a car or wondering why the public transport to that location runs so infrequently. The reading room may lack reliable air-conditioning. Perhaps there are few amenities on site, and nowhere within walking distance to buy lunch. I will hazard a guess that the material held in such archives is less visited, and less cited, particularly by researchers who are not locally based. This may offer an opening for the scholar who is willing to tough it out.

---

[28] The list may include basic considerations around accessibility. See, for example, Georgia Geller, "Assistance Dogs and Academia: Supporting the Dynamic Duo," and Erin Pritchard, "A Hierarchy of Impairments: The Absence of Body Size in Disability Accommodation within Universities," in *Disability*, ed. McMaster and Whitburn, 119–128 and 129–136, respectively.

[29] Search tools such as ArchiveGrid: https://researchworks.oclc.org/archivegrid/ offer ways to search both for nearby archives and do some advanced work assessing what they hold that might interest you. At this time, it is stronger for locations in the United States than elsewhere.

Visiting your *nearest* archive just for the experience is also an opportunity to smooth out any snags in your intake process. Don't underestimate how many steps a successful digital workflow will involve. You will learn to photograph the archival tag along with the document. You will keep a running log or annotation so you have a quick way to reconstruct why you took *that* picture. Before embarking on a labor-intensive, high-stakes visit to the main archive you plan to use, try to conduct a small, "dry run" exercise locally. Take photos of documents, capture the citation information you'd need later, check to see that you captured a full and crisp image as intended, and then—in a simple way, since this is just for practice—organize and annotate the images.[30]

A Different Kind of Reading

There is a stunning immediacy to archival documents compared to anything else you may have handled before. What will stand out for you depends on the type of materials, the time period, and the country that you are studying. I remember my delight at first encountering the tiny bundles of related correspondence still held together with the original pins or bits of faded string, and the wax seals still affixed to the documents. I once handled a run of personal letters from the 1840s still bearing the world's first postage stamp, the Penny Black, now a rarity that can fetch high prices at auction.

Arranging the necklaces of lead weights to hold down a recalcitrant piece of parchment for inspection, it is easy to feel that, surely, one is already "doing" history. The novelty wears off faster than you might expect. The average archival document is a memo, an invoice, a list of names, an account book, or a complaint. Our expectations are a bit skewed by renderings in film and television that cut to the chase and show only the moment when something important turns up.[31] Sifting through pages (and boxes) of such petty, quotidian material can be absorbing, but do not be shocked—or ashamed—if you also experience frustration and bewilderment.

You are going antiquing, you are expected to rummage, and one person's junk is another's treasure. The price for this, as with antiquing, is a high degree of randomness and boredom in between the rare "aha!" moments. There is also a risk that you will find nothing worthwhile in any given interval of time and that you will come across things whose very purpose is something of a mystery (what does it *do*? what was that *for*?).

---

[30] New apps are emerging to help with these challenges, such as the one by Capturing the Past at the University of Sussex. Software such as Tropy and CamScanner is widely used. "Personal knowledge management" (PKM) software or "second brain" software is also worth a look.

[31] To be sure, the very *existence* of some archives can be a revelation; Kirsten Weld, *Paper Cadavers: The Archives of Dictatorship in Guatemala* (Durham: Duke University Press, 2014).

There is no guarantee that the run of records that interests you is complete, pristine, or user-friendly. Joël Glassman, trying to reconstruct the lives and careers of the first generation of African policemen employed by the French colonial authorities in Togo, found that only 114 personnel files survived. Yet he knew from other sources that between 400 and 500 African men had served in this police force.[32] He also recounts how the files varied considerably in thickness. One might hope that this would be in proportion to the length of man's career in the police force, but in fact, record-keeping practices were inconsistent. Even the simple task of looking up a named individual, Commissioner Deckon, was complicated by the inconsistency of the records, as this man "began his career under the name Acapossa Félix before becoming Acapossa Cosme, Cosme Félix, and finally Cosme Deckon."[33]

Archival material is often intensely, inescapably intertextual. Documents come with attachments, and the reason certain documents are appended to others often requires a slow process of examination.[34] It is exciting to see a draft rather than a finished, polished, product, but annotated drafts can be something of a puzzle. Perhaps this one was dictated by person A and commented on by persons B, C, and D (whose identity and job description may take some deciphering). Possible marginalia include scribbles, arrows, initials, and scratchings-out in different hands and with varying degrees of confidence and downward pressure. I have also seen archival material that approached the density of a collage, with newspaper clippings pasted in, and annotations added, making pointed remarks about the clippings and indicating who ought to have this brought to their attention. Anticipate something of a learning curve here: "Information that may not seem interesting at first sight can prove to be valuable at a later stage of research: for example, the color of the paper of a document or a handwritten note on a printed form."[35] If you anticipate that really nailing down the flow of information within an organization will be important to you, for instance, it may make sense to take special care to preserve a photographic record of *everything* about such documents, rather than just taking notes on them.

Moir's *General Guide to the India Office Records* includes a lengthy discussion of just how the flow of paperwork and decision-making worked, including a long quotation from House of Commons testimony on the subject.[36] One would hope for something like this for any large organization. A flow chart, plus a cast of characters (not just which jobs existed, but the names of who

---

[32] Glassman, "Rethinking Colonial Intermediates," 416.

[33] Glassman, "Rethinking Colonial Intermediaries," 415.

[34] Sometimes what was *once* a bundle of materials has become—frustratingly—unbundled. My colleague Taylor Easum recounts finding notes such as "map removed by archivist" or "map removed for study by interior ministry."

[35] Claire Lemercier and Claire Zalc, *Quantitative Methods in the Humanities: An Introduction*, trans. Arthur Goldhammer (Charlottesville: University of Virginia Press, 2019), 53.

[36] Martin Moir, *A General Guide to the India Office Records* (London: British Library, 1988), 42–45.

occupied them in your time period) is highly desirable, even if you must compile it for yourself.

Sheets ("f") often appear bound or tied together in a particular order and numbered sequentially in that order. This can result in odd "time travel" moments; replies to a letter can immediately *precede* the letter itself, and other documents resulting from that particular case may appear tens or hundreds of pages away, or in a different run of documents altogether, compiled by a different office or entity.[37] Once you appreciate the main outlines of the problem, it becomes routine to look for a zigzag path through the paper trail.

For example, in the BBC Written Archives, we can find a number of drafts and memos pertaining to the 1942 Empire Day radio broadcast in a folder designated R 34/213/2, "Anniversaries—Empire Day—File 2, 1940–1943." However, if we also consult R 19/305, "Entertainment—Empire Day—1941–1950," we find additional material about that same broadcast, a first draft of the program which is not present in the other folder, and a marked up version of that first draft in which traits of the second begin to appear. The term "entertainment" as pertaining to a vexed, serious, political topic like Empire Day is striking, although the BBC often marked politically sensitive dates (St. Patrick's Day, for instance) with commemorative concerts and dramas. Thus, Empire Day programming did include "entertainment," as well as speeches, interviews, and verbal propaganda. It is in the Entertainment folder where a little surprise turns up, a memo revealing that Eric Blair (George Orwell) was the consultant on the content in this program pertaining to India. Is this important? Only you know the answer. It depends on your project and interests.

Most researchers have to multitask as they seek insight from the sources, *and* gradually get the hang of how their particular run of documents is really organized, *and* start to notice how an organization actually operated. Suppose you are working on the 1970s. The archival trace left by (for example) a bank, a labor union, or a grassroots feminist-and-peace-activist group will all differ. So will the equivalent records from a charity, a church, a military unit, and a government agency. The good news is that you are probably only working with one or two of these source types, so after an initial period of orientation and adjustment, you will become agile at sifting through the material you find. If you come across an archivist or a fellow researcher who is familiar with this material and is happy to orient you, be grateful. You may also find yourself entirely on your own.

---

[37] For the experience of hunting for scattered documents that are actually related to each other, see Evans, *Defense*, 77.

Some sources are, at first glance, simply unintelligible. Administrative shorthand and abbreviations may send you rushing to a paleography manual.[38] In more modern sources, you will encounter an alphabet soup of organizational acronyms and mystifying references to court decisions and numbered regulations. There is also, unfortunately, no law that only people with legible handwriting get to have their documents preserved for posterity! If you spend a good deal of time with a particular style or genre of document, your comprehension and reading speed will improve, but expect a gradual process. Happily, the most common words and expressions that get abbreviated are also the most routine ones. Many of the quirks that disoriented you at first will soon seem easy and familiar.

One of the most helpful, time-saving decisions you may take in the course of your research is to hunt down the training manual pertaining to the material you are using. A pamphlet outlining standard operating procedure in a particular situation could shed light on the behavior you see reported in a source. A textbook that clerks studied on Railway Accounting may amount to a set of instructions for producing the exact type of document that you use in your research. Even documents bursting with personal details and autobiographical anecdotes, such as petitions for redress and appeals for charitable assistance, may follow a prescribed template for exactly such specialized correspondence. Scribes, schoolmasters, and clergymen kept manuals on hand to help the illiterate—or semi-literate—people who asked them to set pen to paper.[39] If the seemingly heartfelt petitions you are reading are chips off that particular block, this is information you want to have. If one petition you are looking at departs in a striking way from the usual template, that is interesting in its own right. Occasionally, you will come across a tertiary source preserved inside a box in the archives (training materials, for instance), but this is more likely a situation in which your detective work in the library and online will have to supplement your activity in the archive itself.

THE HUMAN ELEMENT

You have limits, and in the archive, you will find out about all of them. Even before the era of the digital camera, Arlette Farge posed the question: "Can you read a highway, even if it is made of paper?"[40] The ability to photograph

---

[38] Candida Moss, "The Secretary: Enslaved Workers, Stenography, and The Production of Early Christian Literature," *Journal of Theological Studies*, new series, 74, Pt. 1 (April 2023): 20–56 ranges well beyond the ancient world in its discussion of shorthand and the extremely important author-scribe relationship.

[39] Arun Kumar, "Letters of the Labouring Poor: The Art of Letter Writing in Colonial India," *Past & Present* 246, no. 1 (February 2020): 149–190.

[40] Farge, *Allure*, 4–5.

documents for yourself creates a new kind of labor and seemingly limitless work requirements; "take photos now, think later" can be just as unfulfilling, frustrating, and unhealthy as any other kind of repetitive task. If your body tells you that you are craving fresh air or you just have a need to move around, these, too, are problems with solutions. Working with my crumbling eighteenth-century manuscripts, I found that the dust was getting in my eyes and irritating them. Getting up and washing my face from time to time soothed my eyes and lifted my spirits.

Other challenges are not so easily addressed. In particular, there is now a thoughtful literature about what happens when reading material in the archive becomes an emotionally complex or even traumatic experience for the researcher.[41] Your symptoms of restlessness, or archival burnout, could likewise be a signal of an uneasiness that is more mental than physical. You could be re-thinking an aspect of your project or wondering whether the types of sources you are using now are really the right ones for the job. Perhaps you are simply gestating an insight about the material you are reading, and you have not articulated it consciously quite yet. We don't usually consider taking a brisk walk or changing up your routine to be a formal, productive part of research activity, but that might be exactly what your project needs today.

Observing the other researchers at work is an inevitable part of the archival experience. Imposter syndrome comes in many forms; I, at least, have doubted my calling as a historian more than once when I beheld fellow researchers who could sit immobile for hours at a time, with seemingly no problems with eyestrain or bad backs, only stirring from their desks when the final closing bell dismissed them.[42] It is worth remembering that the archives are not a race, and they are also not a contest. Have compassion for yourself, but also for your peers. Some of the people you see pursuing their work with an almost superhuman intensity are cringing at the prospect of something that is about to run out: a clock, a stipend, childcare, or all of the above.

Going to the archives also, inevitably, means conversations with others about your project. You will get used to summing up your project in a line or two, and hearing others do the same. For many of us, this was the first experience with socializing—across the widest possible range of ages and seniority—with academics outside of a classroom setting and beyond our own university. These encounters can vary a lot. As a student in the archives, you can meet kindred spirits who become lifetime friends and allies; you can pick up random, unexpected, and useful information from strangers (although it usually won't relate to your project itself); you can meet with benign, if polite, indifference.

---

[41] Marisa J. Fuentes, *Dispossessed Lives: Enslaved Women, Violence, and the Archives* (Philadelphia: University of Pennsylvania Press, 2016).
[42] Lau, "Slowness," speaks well to these general themes.

A 2004 study noted that historians, when asked about their favorite information sources, listed "finding aids, footnotes, catalogues, and archival sources" but, strangely enough, archivists weren't often mentioned.[43] That is unfortunate, because getting in touch with the right archivist can be a revelation.[44] Potentially, they will know about material that isn't even catalogued yet. They can help orient you to the subtle differences between a finding aid and a container list. They may be sufficiently specialized that they understand, better than any other living person, the organization of the particular records you wish to use. I have encountered archivists who spontaneously produced documents that I did not order, but that they thought would interest me. You have probably noticed how your advisor often knows others in their field and can immediately think of citations that might be useful to you; similarly, you may discover that an archivist in one location is well versed in what is held *elsewhere* and may be more than happy to put you in touch with other archivists.[45]

While the archive, portrayed in this way, can look like a lot of fun as well as a terrific networking opportunity, I do not wish to romanticize it. For example, every researcher has faced disparaging remarks at some point. Professionals usually exhibit very high levels of confidence—perhaps this is inherent to professional culture as such—but bear in mind that the opinion of everyone you meet is human and fallible. This includes senior scholars. It also includes archivists and other personnel, who may consider themselves gatekeepers, particularly when a researcher arrives from overseas and starts asking about unexpected documents for unclear reasons. In some archives, obtaining a reader's card is only the beginning of a longer process of building trust and credibility.

You may also draw comments about the appropriateness of your research interests. Once, in the process of doing research on small, provincial ports, I encountered a librarian in Greenock, Scotland, who dismissed outright the notion of doing local history research using local repositories; by definition, she explained to me patiently, anything *important* had been moved to London. If there is a fundamental misunderstanding or a gap in their knowledge, the most well-intentioned advice will still be misguided. There's no need to stay and quarrel, but don't let the doubters distract you from what you know is right.

---

[43] Catherine A. Johnson and Wendy M. Duff, "Chatting up the Archivist: Social Capital and the Archival Researcher," *The American Archivist* 68, no. 1 (Spring-Summer, 2005): 113–129; the study is discussed on 115.

[44] Eric Foner, "Black History and the Reconstruction Era," *Souls: A Critical Journal of Black Politics, Culture, and Society* 8, no. 3 (2006): 197–203; see 198.

[45] Johnson and Duff, "Chatting," also note points of friction and dissatisfaction and reflect upon why some researchers have a better experience than others. See also Heather MacNeil, "What Finding Aids *Do*: Archival Description as Rhetorical Genre in Traditional and Web-Based Environments," *Archival Science* 12 (2012): 485–500.

Just as others may—most likely inadvertently—come across as imperious or hurt your feelings, you should be mindful of the impression you make on others in the archives. Many archivists feel—not only underfunded—but unappreciated, for example, in the routine announcements from historians that they have "discovered" a document. Of course, almost invariably the document in question was preserved, tagged, catalogued, and ultimately delivered into the hands to the researcher through the labor of library or archive staff.

We can do better. It is common to send a student undertaking an oral history or public history project to peruse the relevant specialized journals for insights, but despite the centrality of archives to most historians' work, a missing element in our formal education is an introduction to the prominent journals in the archives field itself. If you make yourself aware of the new thinking in these fields, the next time you visit a library or an archive, you may think about the whole experience differently.

Practical Strategies

As an archival researcher, self-care means not expecting that you'll perform miracles every day—or every week. A good rule of thumb might be to plan out three things overall that you hope to accomplish in the course of this project: two major easy tasks and one major hard task. This protects you on both ends: You'll spend many days busy, happy, and visibly productive; you won't lack for sources; yet also, the tougher part of your project can stand as your signature achievement, a source of pride, and perhaps the beginnings of your unique academic brand.

Consider what an easy task might look like. For example, "follow the money" projects are usually feasible because archives are so often nothing but administrative, legal, or business records. Perhaps instead, you're going to pin down what that labor union did, or how this charity operated, and you know you can achieve that by reading their committee minutes or reviewing the materials in their In and Out boxes. You can sleep well at night knowing that even if there are no eureka moments, you will have a substantial and coherent body of material.

Next, consider your one hard task. This is the aspect of your project that will carry some kind of "wow" factor. What will impress? Is it tough paleography? A quantitative achievement? An unusual source type? This might be a time to look back at your historiographical cousins. Within that family of adjacent scholarship that you have located, what is the hard task that others have not undertaken?

Pivot Point: Finding your Stack of Needles
Don't rely on luck. "I will find a needle in a haystack" is a terrible research strategy for a student project. Imagine some ways that you could locate a *stack of needles* all together somewhere. My first stack of needles was an accidental discovery. In an archive in Edinburgh, after a day or two of paging through arid meeting minutes and account books associated with an eighteenth-century charity, I ordered the box marked "Miscellaneous." There, I found a whole collection of petitions by sailors' widows, lengthy, eloquent, and detailed. In the course of the petition, the widow often related—very nearly—her whole life story.

Your particular stack of needles may take a different form, but generally speaking, this is the combination of traits you are looking for:

1. dozens, or hundreds, of pages of rich material
2. all located in the same archive
3. it is all of the same source type
4. it speaks directly to your interests and needs

If you learn the logic and motivations of the archival *fonds*, you may realize that someone long ago took the time to assemble a ready-made primary source kit for you. During World War II, would-be Conscientious Objectors faced a sometimes dismissive local board. Since pacifists faced similar lines of questioning, the Quakers and their allies systematically sent note-takers to all of these hearings to generate a comprehensive record of what happened there. The Friends Library in Euston has a hefty collection of transcripts from these hearings.

With your stack of needles, you can delve deep.[46] You do not have to suffer anxiety that you won't find enough or that your finished product will appear thinly sourced or "anecdotal." Nor will you need to spend extra money and time racing around to multiple archives.

It's helpful to run on two agendas. The first is your promise to work with what you've already found. The second is your "speculative" agenda. This may involve a pet interest: If only we could know how they felt about so-and-so. It could simply be an openness to new opportunities: You want to investigate the set of ten boxes an archivist just told you about, but you had no idea existed.

---

[46] Jon Shelton's "Letters to the Essex County Penitentiary: David Selden and the Fracturing of America," *Journal of Social History* 48 (2014): 135–155, is based on a rich array of material found in a single archival box.

You might decide to give a different archive altogether a try. Or perhaps a recurring, obsessive theme in the sources you are reading right now suggests a different twist to your entire project.

Thus far, I have expressed the two-track method in terms of time management and ease of access; in a project of this size, you simply don't have time to do two or three difficult things. There are ways to make a virtue of necessity, however. Social scientists have observed that even though no source or method is perfect, pursuing Source Type B and C with an eye to compensating for the shortcomings in Source Type A has a beneficial effect known as "triangulation."[47] In that spirit, you might ask yourself: Is there a possibility of using archival material to supplement, cross-reference, or complicate a picture derived from oral histories?[48] What digitized resources exist that can extend the reach of what you are finding in the physical archive?

Whether or not you consider mixing methods, getting into the habit of asking "what *else* can I look at?" is likely to make your project deeper and more interesting. For centuries, historians have found it useful to contrast the secret memoranda of two governments on matters of policy, war, and espionage that concerned them both. In the more modern era, varying regimes of declassification of secret material have sometimes prompted historians to look overseas, even if their research topic concerned the activities of their own government.[49]

We can generalize from this: If you find two distinct sets of archival sources that both speak to the same event or situation, then your project can be, at its essence, "let's set Source X and Source Y in dialogue and see how the picture changes." Indeed, examples of this approach are easy to find, once you start looking for them. Jennifer Foray used the *Wehrmacht*'s own administrative documents for her article about the German occupation of the Netherlands, but with an awareness of the scholarship produced by others on the same subject matter using different kinds of material, such as Bart van der Boom's monograph, which was based on "44 Dutch diarists of various ages, professions, religious and political affiliations, ages, and locales."[50]

---

[47] Kim Peters, *Your Human Geography Dissertation: Designing, Doing, Delivering* (London: Sage, 2017), 148–155.

[48] Noah Riseman, "Contesting White Knowledge: Yolngu Stories from World War II," *Oral History Review* 37, no. 2 (Summer/Fall 2010): 170–190.

[49] Richard Colin Thurlow, "The Historiography and Source Materials in the Study of Internal Security in Modern Britain (1885–1956)," *History Compass* 6, no. 1 (2008): 147–171; see 164, note 6.

[50] Jennifer L. Foray, "The 'Clean Wehrmacht' in the German-occupied Netherlands, 1940–5," *Journal of Contemporary History* 45, no. 4 (October 2010): 768–787; see 773, footnote 14.

One way to reduce an archive to manageable, digestible pieces could be to adopt a sampling technique of some kind.[51] Not every random sample is as random as you might think. You could use the alphabet and read only the files associated with a few particular surnames beginning with a particular letter. This technique, however, may skew your sample to over-represent one group (such as Italian-Americans).[52] There are other considerations here. If you are trying to get a sense of the workings of a particular office, then sampling the forty-eighth letter in a box, or jumping into the forty-eighth box in a series, could deprive you of the more holistic sense of what was going on in that office in a particular period.[53] A slow, comprehensive, sequential reading would grant you some "before" and "after" context, a sense of the personalities and priorities of the staff, and so forth. The value of sequential reading versus some form of sampling, then, depends on the type and style of research you hope to conduct, and the sorts of things you plan to look for.

On the other hand, your project might hinge on measuring the impact of a discriminatory practice. The historiography or related social science literature on it highlights statistical findings, and among your primary sources, you notice that claims made by a municipality, government agency, or corporation themselves drew on statistical concepts and assertions about data. You could find yourself interested in comparing two or more populations or demographic groups for yourself and generating some fresh results.

In that scenario, a reasonable first stop would be an introductory course on statistics, or a textbook such as Claire Lemercier and Claire Zalc's *Quantitative Methods in the Humanities: An Introduction*.[54] The time to familiarize yourself with this conceptual toolkit is probably quite early in your research process. For example, modest percentage differences *that appear in a small sample* are not considered statistically significant.[55] Lemercier and Zalc offer several pages under the heading "The Ten Commandments of Inputting Data."[56] Good luck applying those methods as an afterthought!

We don't require students of History to take the equivalent of the Hippocratic Oath ("first, do no harm"), but maybe we should. John Arbuthnot, compiling London's vital statistics in 1710, entered a value twice—once, correctly, for 1674, but then again for 1704.[57] The result makes it appear as if 1704 was a

---

[51] Lemercier and Zalc, *Quantitative Methods*, 41.
[52] Lemercier and Zalc, *Quantitative Methods*, 43.
[53] This kind of sampling (forty-eighth box, etc.) is discussed in Lemercier and Zalc, *Quantitative Methods*, 41–42.
[54] Charlottesville: University of Virginia Press, 2019.
[55] For sample sizes in relation to chi-squared and ANOVA tests, see Lemercier and Zalc, *Quantitative Methods*, 46–50.
[56] Lemercier and Zalc, *Quantitative Methods*, 57–60.
[57] Howard Wainer, *Graphic Discovery: A Trout in the Milk and Other Visual Adventures* (Princeton: Princeton University Press, 2005), 2–3.

terrible year for disease, drastically different from the years before and after it. Yet there was no outbreak of plague, merely a clerical error that no one caught. This error is more than 300 years old, but you could be the next Arbuthnot, and it might take a good long while before anyone sets the record straight. More recently, a historian failed to transcribe a single word, "not," and quoted an important sentence as saying the opposite of what it really did.[58] It would be nice if the evidence could cry out in pain when we make blunders like this, but unfortunately, it cannot.

There are more subtle opportunities for error. You wouldn't want to quote a defense attorney as arguing that their client was guilty, but this is exactly what might happen if you seized upon a line that came early in their closing statement. It is always important to remain on the lookout for the source that summarizes or caricatures an opponent's position without in any way agreeing with it. This is a common issue with older, longer, and more grammatically complex texts. Perhaps one equivalent of this in the artistic realm is the political cartoon that reproduces offensive tropes or hypocritical stances, for the sole purpose of mocking them.

The example of the misunderstood source is a useful reminder that although we imagine we are simply gathering material in the archive, we are also drawing conclusions about what we read, and this in turn shapes our note-taking practices. For example, as you turn the pages, you will ask yourself questions such as

> Am I likely to need to quote from this later?

Implicitly, the answer to this question relies on other determinations, which you may make almost subconsciously:

> What's going on in this document?

> Is it important?

As a result of these snap judgments, you may make early decisions that are not easy to rectify later. For example, when the FBI furnished Martin Luther King Jr. with evidence that he had made a factually inaccurate statement about the personnel at their Albany office, he failed to respond. You might encounter a file on this in the archive and jot down a summary note to yourself:

> FBI officials were offended that he did not return their phone calls.

or

> They assumed the worst about King as a result.

---

[58] Evans, *Defense*, 103.

There is nothing inaccurate about such notes. For some purposes, they might be quite sufficient. If the full scope and depth of the FBI's reaction at that moment is important for your project, though, you will probably want to be able to reproduce the wording of the internal FBI memos that asserted King "obviously does not desire to be given the truth" or that the man himself was a "vicious liar."[59]

Even if you are photographing more or less everything, taking document-by-document notes on the possible significance of what you are finding in which places will enable you to retrace your steps later. A summary note about this FBI document, for instance, could remark on the strong, emotional wording. Or perhaps you knew that J. Edgar Hoover would later embark on a vendetta against King, but evidence of such severe suspicions about King's character and motives as early as January 1963 was startling to you. Of course, many research projects evolve over time, so it is not always possible to anticipate what you must jot down and which archival documents you truly need to photograph. Do your future self a favor! Give that industrious scribbler the richest set of options that you can.

Conclusion

This has been a chapter about planning. However, anyone who has worked with archival material will tell you to be prepared for surprises. Fiona Paisley came across accounts of A.M. Fernando, an Australian Aborigine who confronted Londoners at Hyde Park's Speaker's Corner in the 1920s and 1930s. Standing in front of a handmade backdrop of toy skeletons, he accused the British Empire of "wholesale slaughter" and, when challenged, urged his listeners to "look [it] up."[60] The British government's surveillance reports on his activities made it possible for Paisley to fill in many details of what a one-man anti-imperial activist campaign on a shoestring budget could look like.[61] Cases like this are so exceptional that it is hard to imagine that anyone would arrive at an archive with a plan to find them. It pays to keep an open mind and rejoice if something falls into your lap.

While historians tend to think of archives as the place where we find things, *not finding things* is a more common experience than you might expect. As Verne Harris has remarked, the reality is that what really got preserved is only "a sliver of a sliver of a sliver" of what once existed.[62] Asking

---

[59] Beverly Gage, *G-Man: J. Edgar Hoover and the Making of the American Century* (New York: Viking, 2022), 543.

[60] Fiona Paisley, "History Lessons in Hyde Park: Embodying the Australian Frontier in Interwar London," in *Critical Perspectives on Colonialism: Writing the Empire from Below*, ed. Fiona Paisley and Kirsty Reid (New York: Routledge, 2014), 85–101; see 97.

[61] Fiona Paisley, *The Lone Protestor: A. M. Fernando in Australia and Europe* (Canberra: Aboriginal Studies Press, 2012).

[62] Harris, "Power," 65.

what can I look at instead?

or

what's the new question?

are frequent moves in the successful research process. This is one reason why I emphasize that nimbleness is one of the researcher's most desirable traits. Indeed, you will notice—if you peruse both this chapter and the one that follows—that this nimble mindset will help you navigate the archives, the digital realm, and mixed archival-and-digital projects equally well.

Further Reading

Ann Laura Stoler, *Along the Archival Grain: Epistemic Anxieties and Colonial Common Sense* (Princeton: Princeton University Press, 2008).

Michelle Caswell, "'The Archive' Is Not an Archives: Acknowledging the Intellectual Contributions of Archival Studies," *Reconstruction* 16, no. 1 (2016), https://escholarship.org/uc/item/7bn4v1fk, accessed May 19, 2024.

Bodie A. Ashton, "The Parallel Lives of Liddy Bacroff: Transgender (Pre)History and the Tyranny of the Archive in Twentieth-Century Germany," *German History* 42, no. 1 (March 2024): 79–100.

Elaine Treharne, "'Terrible Letters': Bad Handwriting and its Implications, 1020–1220," *SELIM: Journal of the Spanish Society for Medieval English Language and Literature* 28 (2023): 79–96.

Jane Traies, "The Perils of the Recording," *Oral History* 48, no. 1 (Spring 2020): 75–85.

Ricardo Santhiago and Miriam Hermeto, eds., *The Unexpected in Oral History: Case Studies of Surprising Interviews* (New York: Palgrave Macmillan, 2023).

CHAPTER 7

Planning for Success in the Digital Realm

Today, announcements of new digital resources appear regularly. For instance, Total Digital Access to the League of Nations Archives Project (LONTAD), completed in 2022, offers researchers access to 14,200,000 pages of material.[1] Yet including this information in your prospectus raises more questions than it answers. It's okay to be excited about the possibilities. However, "I've found a relevant resource, it is vast" or "I've found a relevant set of data to download" should be quickly supplemented with statements such as "here's what I could do with it," "here's what it's especially good for," or "here are some particular avenues I can pursue."

Search results can be exhilarating. Once the glitter of newness wears off, though, you'll be left with many of the classic issues that historians have always struggled with in relation to primary sources. Accumulating, for example, a great deal of quantitative data without a plan is not likely to generate a substantive result. What to count? Why are you counting? Should you be counting? The idea of writer's block doesn't conjure up the image of an anxious scholar staring at a blank spreadsheet, intimidated by the array of empty cells, waiting for inspiration to strike. Yet some of the most important steps in the process do occur before data collection begins.

Indeed, the very word "data" is a bit controversial in digital humanities circles; Johanna Drucker even proposed replacing the word altogether, because while "data" implies a certain rawness (it's just what's out there), a term like "capta" would acknowledge the role of a conscious process of selection at work.[2] Data always arises out of a particular research process; a different process would have thrown up different material. You should expect your advisor

---

[1] It is accessible at http://archives.ungeneva.org, accessed 10/9/2022.
[2] Matthew Lavin, "Why Digital Humanists Should Emphasize Situated Data over Capta," *Digital Humanities Quarterly* 15, no. 2 (2021).

to ask you some hard questions—now, or further down the line—about just how you are proposing to work with your chosen digital materials and what you hope to achieve with them.

This chapter will get you started on the process of having answers ready for those questions.

Thinking Critically About Digitization and Digitized Materials

What are the hallmarks of the historian's craft? For centuries, spotting forgeries and discerning the tricks of slippery and self-serving primary sources featured at the top of that list. A recent overview adds that today, an additional fundamental research skill—in a way, closely equivalent to those—would be acquiring a grasp of "the logic of digital library and archival information systems" and, indeed, the "commercially driven strategies for selection and indexing of companies such as Google and Bing."[3]

This is a bold, and somewhat disconcerting, statement. However, there are many reasons to take it seriously. Getting the most out of a database sometimes requires that you become, in a small way, a student of why that database exists, who brought it into being, how the designers made decisions about what to include. It is even necessary, in many cases, to inquire *how* it was digitized. Writing in 2013, Tim Hitchcock observed that "in terms of the overall quantity of digitized historical material available, only a tiny fraction has been produced in a university environment under academic leadership."[4] This shapes the end product at many different levels. Users of eighteenth-century digitized material in English have learned to run alternative searches (Irish/Irifh) to allow for transcribers, or software, that could not accommodate older orthography or printing conventions.[5]

We can only digitize what survives, and what survives is not always complete, representative, or comprehensive. According to Gale, its publisher, Eighteenth Century Collections Online contains "180,000 titles (200,000 volumes) and more than 32 million pages, making ECCO the premier and irreplaceable resource for eighteenth-century research."[6] However, consider the example of Thomas Dyche's *Guide to the English Tongue*. We know that from 1733 to 1748, this book went through 33 editions, with 275,000 copies in total printed. From that date range, little more than a handful of copies survive.[7] A large database can give the impression of such vastness that it seems

---

[3] Romein, et al. "State of the Field," 308.
[4] Tim Hitchcock, "Confronting the Digital: Or How Academic History Writing Lost the Plot," *Cultural and Social History* 10, no. 1 (March 2013): 9–23; see 10.
[5] Crymble, *Technology*, 33–34; see also Lapworth and Chung, "Archives," 14.
[6] Gale, "Eighteenth-Century Collections Online," https://www.gale.com/primary-sources/eighteenth-century-collections online, accessed June 21, 2024.
[7] Philip Gaskell, *New Introduction to Bibliography* (Oxford: Oxford University Press, 1972), 163, claimed that only five copies survived worldwide from that date range, although a glance at online catalogues (such as Harvard's and the Bodleian) shows that this number is a little low.

like a plausible proxy for what was going on at the time, what had commercial success, and so on. Yet a screen throwing up a modest number of search results hardly conveys the cultural presence—the heft—of a book like *Guide to the English Tongue*. Down these same lines, a recent article—expressing some reservations about the excitement around the potential of the Google Ngram viewer—notes that "even the Google Books corpus, which is said to host 5% of all the books ever printed, does not represent 'language' or 'culture': it, like many corpora, is restricted in its representativity."[8]

Predictably enough, for-profit digitizers emphasize the product's features and not its shortcomings. Information that might make a database appear less important or less impressive is often buried in the digital "fine print" or allowed to rest in silence. When you start working with any new digital resource, a good first step is to see whether it states "clear criteria for inclusion of texts"; some do, while others do not.[9] Helle Strandgaard Jensen remarks: "The Georgian Papers Programme, funded by the Royal Collection Trust and others, have a page called 'What's in the catalogue?'. However, from a methodological standpoint, it would be equally interesting to know what is *not* in the catalogue."[10]

Mislabeled or poorly described digital resources can throw up hidden treasures. I didn't expect *British Newspapers 1600–1900* to contain some newspapers from Barbados and Jamaica or for *Early English Books Online* (*EEBO*) to have some materials at least allegedly published in Louvain, in Amsterdam, and in Paris. *EEBO* also includes many titles that are not in the English language!

Part of what makes a digital resource usable is the set of labels, categories, hierarchies, tags, keywords, and metadata attached to its materials. Yet, as discussed in Chap. 6, assigning these is not a value-neutral activity. It is possible to impose blatantly inaccurate or misleading tags on material, as when Susan Bordo's *Unbearable Weight: Feminism, Western Culture, and the Body* was listed in Google Books under "Health & Fitness."[11] While using a physical archive often involves becoming familiar with the odd logic of *fonds* ossified long ago, using a digital source may require some attention to a brand-new system of cataloguing imposed during the digitization process, to say nothing of poorly chosen or erroneous metadata that someone added.[12]

There is also, of course, the simple yet crucial question of *what* was targeted for digitization in the first place. The Wellcome Trust is interested in the history of healthcare, and funds accordingly. Not every topic has a rich foundation with a soft spot for that material, though. The preoccupations of the wealthiest countries also shape what gets digitized. Qatar, for instance, helped digitize materials in the British archives related to the Persian Gulf region; similar documents that happened to concern Southeast Asia caught Singapore's attention. The global

---

[8] Romein, et al. "State of the Field," 304.
[9] Lemercier and Zalc, *Quantitative Methods*, 146.
[10] Jensen, "Digital," 256.
[11] Janine Solberg, "Googling the Archive: Digital Tools and the Practice of History," *Advances in the History of Rhetoric* 15 (2012): 53–76; see 65.
[12] Tinkler, *Using Photographs*, 106–124.

North, for now, has the most money available for digitization, and its digitization initiatives are sometimes marred by oversights that reflect that geographical bias. The Trans-Atlantic Slave Trade Database—originally based at Harvard and later at Emory University in Georgia—only added Portuguese-language sources as a final touch, many years after the project commenced.[13] The disconcerting result was a million new entries in the database and field-transforming insights about the role of Brazilian ports in the slave trade, begging the question of why Portuguese-language materials weren't among the first in the queue.

In the early years of digitization, a number of historians issued warnings that the history of minority groups—already marginalized—was under-represented in this new arena as well. Likewise, the archives and publications of radical organizations weren't in the queue for scanning. To some extent, nonprofit funding bodies offered grant money to rectify this problem, as in the case of the Bracero Oral History Project and also the Digital Transgender Archive. Brown University Library created a digitized version of *Radical America*, a campus publication affiliated with Students for a Democratic Society. Moreover, while it is indisputable that "commercial enterprises such as ProQuest are digitising collections that they can sell," companies remain alert to new opportunities.[14] We now have ProQuest Black Newspapers, one component of a large and growing Diversity, Equity, and Inclusion catalogue of databases from the same publisher.

It would be unwise to generalize from any of this, however. For the foreseeable future, the already-digitized will remain an uneven, and somewhat unpredictable, patchwork. For example, suppose that you are aware of a digitized version of the minutes and ephemera of a pro-choice group from the 1970s. This does not imply—or even shed light on the probability—that its counterpart, an anti-abortion group from the same era, has attracted the interest of someone with the organization and funding to do the same for it. Did the stars align to produce the ideal set of online resources for your particular project as you initially conceived it? Maybe, maybe not. A major part of your work at this planning stage is to assess where you'll need to supplement digital resources with non-digital resources and vice versa.

The Zigzag Path

In Chap. 6, drawing on the old adage about the difficulty of searching for a needle in a haystack, I proposed that a smart strategy for archival research was to find a run of paperwork that amounted to "a stack of needles." This strategy relied on familiarizing yourself with the logic of provenance. Perhaps someone in the past collected lots of relevant material in one place. Because archives

---

[13] David Eltis and David Richardson, eds., *Extending the Frontiers: Essays on the New Transatlantic Slave Trade Database* (New Haven: Yale University Press, 2008).
[14] Jensen, "Digital," 255.

maintain material in the original *fonds*, it could be all together in one spot, waiting for you to pick it up.

The digital realm offers a tantalizing alternative. What if, to aid your search for needles, you could obtain a powerful magnet? A full-text search function, or really good metadata, might enable you to pull *all* the needles out in an instant. Better yet, you could target not just one haystack with your magnet, but many haystacks, or very nearly *all* the haystacks. Lara Putnam expresses this idea in a provocative statement: "For the first time, historians can *find*, without knowing where to look."[15]

As my choice of section heading suggests, I would like to lower your expectations and prepare you for some difficulties. Even, if in the end, you learn to draw on the digital realm as a powerful resource, before you reach that point, a series of false starts and reappraisals—a zigzag path—is likely. Even assessing *which* digital resource best fits your interests, or contains what you would need for your project, may be a time-consuming process.

Where to start? Some journals now run reviews of websites and digital resources alongside reviews of new books in the field. Other digital resources have elicited so much interest (or consternation) that there are roundtable discussions about them in print somewhere. Really, anything written about the digital resource from a user's perspective will help you. For example, an article about digital collections of oral histories by Red Army soldiers from World War II focuses on one database, *iremember.ru*.[16] The article notes areas of unevenness or weakness in the source material: "Interviewees frequently cut off the conversation when sticky topics—such as executions or rapes—are raised."[17] While Jewish veterans of the Red Army are present in *iremember.ru*, "members of national minorities" within the Soviet Union are not well represented at all.[18] Depending on your exact reasons for seeking out oral history testimony from Red Army veterans, this information might prompt you to reappraise how useful this resource would be for your particular project. No matter how powerful a search function is, it can't locate material that is not present in the database! However, this article's footnotes provide a quick overview of several other similar digital collections, each with their own origins, remit, and quirky characteristics. Thus, you might have started with the expectation that you would rely on *iremember.ru*, but conclude instead that a different Red Army oral history digital resource had more promise for your project.

Once you have settled down to explore a particularly promising resource, you may find that your first attempts at plugging text into a search box leave you feeling a bit bruised and discouraged. On your first try, you might get *no*

---

[15] Putnam, "Transnational," 377.

[16] Iva Glisic and Mark Edele, "The Memory Revolution Meets the Digital Age: Red Army Soldiers Remember World War II," *Geschichte und Gesellschaft* 45 no. 1 (January–March 2019): 95–119.

[17] Glisic and Edele, "Memory Revolution," 114.

[18] Glisic and Edele, "Memory Revolution," 102.

results. The digital realm can feel like it's meant to be a solitary journey, but don't pass up the chance to include a consulting stage. Your local reference librarian may be in a position to help. There could also be a user community online of other researchers who are more experienced with the ins and outs of this resource. While online databases often present an anonymous façade, in fact there are usually people behind the scenes who you could contact as well. Jensen remarks, "Asking an archivist to provide more details about their system's design can prove extremely helpful."[19]

One of the terms for the words used by indexers and cataloguers is "controlled vocabulary." For instance, indexers could reach an agreement that "gender fluid" is a useful tag to attach to certain people who appear in the historical record. When adopted consistently, this could make it easy for any researcher to locate similar information wherever it might occur. *If* everything is scrupulously tagged with metadata, *and* the metadata corresponds to your interests, this could be enormously useful. You can request an index of categories used by that digital archive; perhaps you're just using the wrong search terms.[20]

Don't expect everything to come tagged with metadata, though. In fact, many of the most common digitized resources are newspapers and court proceedings. Here, a strong grasp of the exact words that someone *in the past* would have used becomes indispensable. With new technology, even handwritten manuscripts and previously recorded oral histories may soon become full-text searchable as well.[21] If librarians and archivists speak a great deal about controlled vocabulary, then it's worth pointing out that running a full text search on a database of old material throws you very much into the realm of what we might call *uncontrolled* vocabulary.

For example, suppose that your project is about queer lives in Britain in the 1930s. You are well aware that "gender fluid" was not a term used in newspapers at the time. But what to search for instead? Some browsing may reveal that "sexual indeterminates" *was* a term in circulation then, although what exactly this may have meant could require some investigation. In Oxford University slang, queer people were sometimes referred to as the "arty" set, as opposed to the "hearty" heterosexual students.[22] Whether any of this corresponds to "gender fluid," of course, would involve some thoughtful historical inquiry and a hard look at the context in which terms were deployed. Despite the impressive potential inherent in full text searchable content, we can already see where the analogy to a powerful magnet that will quickly pull the needles out for us breaks down.

---

[19] Jensen, "Digital," 258.
[20] Jensen, "Digital," 257.
[21] For handwritten manuscripts, I am referring to software such as Transkribus.
[22] For my examples of language here, I have drawn on Ross Brooks, "Beyond Brideshead: The Male Homoerotics of 1930s Oxford," *Journal of British Studies* 59, no. 4 (2020): 821–856.

With this in mind, despite the pressure you may feel to get big results and insights right away from a large database, it's wise to plan for a slow early immersion phase. It's not so different from a first, awkward encounter with a physical archive packed with unfamiliar material—you'll want to take the time to orient yourself. For example, you can dutifully look up the occasional obsolete noun in the *Oxford English Dictionary* or a similar authoritative reference work, but really getting a grip on the language of a time period is a more complex process. The historian of emotion Barbara Weinstein warns that a future scholar looking for expressions of anger in mid-twentieth-century America might not know to search for a phrase such as "I blew my stack," but this was really how some people talked.[23] Meanwhile, the sort of person who would say instead, "I became angry" could represent a very particular subpopulation associated with educational level, class background, race, or gender.

It's generic advice that the successful researcher reformulates their search terms again and again.[24] For historians, though, this activity is intertwined with the task of adjusting to the particular (and peculiar) vocabulary used in the time period that we study. Slowly identifying all possible names, alternative names, and nicknames for your topic, even if they are euphemisms, pejorative, or otherwise problematic can feel like a bit of a chore, but it can also be a valuable exercise in reconceptualizing your own project.

In fact, a close inquiry into what people in that place and time called something can also help you refine your own sense of what you are doing, what you are asking, and what you hope to work with as evidence. How a problem was named often speaks to how that problem was defined and imagined. What did municipal planners consider a "nuisance"? Another word that is very versatile in municipal and legal contexts is "vice." Inquiries such as

> how did the word "nuisance" operate in this legal and administrative context?

or

> how did the scope and mission of the city's "vice squad" change over these decades?

are threads you could spin out into an entire section of your final paper. They might even prompt a reconsideration of what you think your project is really about.

A lack of good search terms can stop a research inquiry in its tracks. For this reason, I have devoted extra space here to the circuitous path of finding the right vocabulary. However, this is only one of the many detours and plot twists

---

[23] Barbara Rosenwein, "Problems and Methods in the History of Emotions," *Passions in Context* 1 (2010): 1–32; see 18.
[24] Solberg, "Googling," 64.

that you may encounter. In a candid article reflecting on a research project that started in a physical archive and later ramified outward into the digital realm, Julia Laite remarks that today, "We can now easily chase many people out of the archive or, at least, from one kind of archive into another."[25] She supplies a vivid example: Lydia Harvey appeared in one archival document

> as a destitute and ill young woman soliciting on the streets of Piccadilly; but in another place (the digitized newspaper from her hometown of Oamaru), she smiles on stage after winning a silver purse in a local beauty contest. In my first book, Lydia Harvey was deployed as symbol of one facet of prostitution. The irony of this became acute for me as I learned more about her life and discovered she had spent longer as a photographer's apprentice, a hospital matron, and a wife engaged in "domestic duties," than she had spent selling sex.[26]

Laite wrote this as a reflection on what she'd missed by relying only on visits to a particular, physical archive. Yet the opposite problem is also possible. A researcher who confined themselves to digital resources could unwittingly compromise their project as well.

Hearing about a zigzag itinerary among different search terms and across different databases is, perhaps, not a big surprise to you. However, it's a rude awakening when digital material—which in theory could be accessed from anywhere on the planet—turns out to be only available on-site. A 2019 article in the journal *Archives and Manuscripts* mentions examples in several countries where copyright law mandates that born-digital materials (archived emails, web content, and other items) are usable only when you are physically in the library that holds them.[27] If your local library or institution does not subscribe to a digital resource that is behind a paywall, even older materials may require a travel plan.

For a host of reasons, then, adjusting your expectations will boost your morale and help you muster the requisite patience. Just as research in a physical library often follows a convoluted path, it is perfectly normal to cycle through different database options; to alternate between browsing in a digital source and trying new keyword searches as a result; to read materials sequentially for a while, and then revert back to yet another keyword search.

In a case of "be careful what you wish for," you may also suddenly find yourself so successful in assembling digital materials that you discover you have a different problem—you wonder how you could possibly find the time to read it all. The next section tackles some of your options in that situation.

---

[25] Laite, "Emmet's Inch," 974.
[26] Laite, "Emmet's Inch," 974.
[27] Lise Jaillant, "After the Digital Revolution: Working with Emails and Born-Digital Records in Literary and Publishers' Archives," *Archives and Manuscripts* 47, no. 3 (2019): 285–304.

Is a "Big Data" Approach Right for Me?

In 1999, Margaret Cohen coined the term "the Great Unread."[28] As a literary critic, what she had in mind was the vast number of obscure nineteenth-century novels still unexamined by her peers. Historians can easily conjure up their own examples of runs of text amounting, sometimes, to millions of pages. The term "distant reading" emerged to describe the effort to use technology to, in some sense, read the Great Unread. A textbook offers this definition: "Big data is simply more data than you could conceivably read yourself in a reasonable amount of time or, even more inclusively, information that requires, or can be read with, computational intervention to make new sense of it."[29]

Of course, many kinds of source types are susceptible to a big data approach. "Distant reading" now has an equivalent, "distant viewing," for the use of software to process art or photographs on an equally grand scale. Big data has also transformed the possible maps that historians could create. For example, Geographical Information Systems (GIS) software makes it practical to calculate the "friction surface" of an area, taking a host of variables into account, including the slope and the soil type, as well as variation depending on the season of the year.[30] Drawing on this kind of information, *ORBIS: The Stanford Geospatial Network Model of the Roman World* allows users to simulate different travel choices as "discrete cost outcomes."[31]

Tutorials and handbooks exist to get you started on digital mapping, just as others exist to walk you through the steps of "scraping" text from an online source, cleaning it up, and sifting through it.[32] That literature often does a better job of explaining the steps of such a process, and the tools available for it, than it does to address the question of why you would want to do it in the first place.

Let's consider the answer to that. What large-scale, sophisticated digital intake methods promise is the ability to download material that is already on the web (or possibly, to upload it from your device) and massage it into a format that is susceptible to searching and reordering in myriad ways. This means you needn't confine yourself to using *existing* databases, digital maps, or interactive websites. Instead, you could choose the material that interests you most and then create your *own* digital resource. Plug-and-play templates do exist for the most common needs that would occur to historians.

Of course, writing your own code is clearly more work. What would you get in return? You could escape the limitations of the default search functions

---

[28] Cohen's term is discussed in Shawn Graham et al., *Exploring Big Historical Data: The Historian's Macroscope*, 2nd ed. (Singapore: World Scientific Publishing, 2022), 71.
[29] Graham, *Exploring*, 4.
[30] Trevor M. Harris, "GIS in Archaeology," in *Past Time, Past Place*, ed. Knowles, 131–143; see 136.
[31] Graham, *Exploring*, 15.
[32] Graham, *Exploring*, 57.

embedded in many databases.³³ For instance, instead of merely looking for words and phrases, it could be easier to discover which words are found most often *in company with others*. Searching a large array of text in that way potentially throws up new connections and affinities that have eluded other researchers.

One of the chief attractions of a big data approach is the possibility of detecting subtle patterns. Vincent Brown made use of digital mapping to explore new dimensions of a slave revolt in Jamaica in the 1760s. While the textual sources don't tell us what the rebels were thinking, Brown argued, plotting their movements on a map helps us "discern some of their strategic aims and to observe the tactical dynamics of slave insurrection and counter-revolt."³⁴ A study of 132,747 letters from Tudor England was able to discern a distinctive style of writing adopted by women as well as bring to light some of the patterns of networking and influence that women mobilized to achieve their aims; the authors note that "a piece of code that took a few hours to write can reveal something that previously necessitated years in the archive."³⁵

Perhaps the best case for pursuing a big data project is that *for the subject matter that interests you*, it seems like the most obvious approach. Frédéric Clavert was interested in the popular memory of World War I in Europe. Seizing upon the occasion of the centenary of the war's outbreak, he crunched the data for three million tweets relating to it, representing 500,000 different Twitter accounts and using almost 125,000 different hashtags in various European languages.³⁶

Of course, not all big data approaches rely on textual sources. Geoff Cunfer found a way to recontextualize the Dust Bowl.³⁷ He knew that there had been events quite similar to the Dust Bowl before the 1930s and that the established historiography was not engaging with them. He did not know what the overall picture would look like when he assembled his maps and climate statistics. It was credible, though, that compiling evidence about a longer time period and a wider geographical range across all of the Great Plains would produce a new, useful, potentially transformative picture. At the very least, it would provide the missing context for the anomalous, anecdotal evidence he had observed so far from the 1890s. Therefore, a big data approach suited his interests and needs.

---

³³ *The Programming Historian* has free tutorials on how to code (https://programminghistorian.org/). If you would like to see some of these techniques in action, you can browse relevant journals: *Current Research in Digital History*, *Digital Humanities Now*, *Reviews in Digital Humanities*, and *Computers and the Humanities*.

³⁴ Vincent Brown quoted in Graham, *Exploring*, 16.

³⁵ Ruth Ahnert and Sebastian E. Ahnert, *Tudor Networks of Power* (Oxford: Oxford University Press, 2023), 110.

³⁶ Frédéric Clavert, "Échos du centenaire de la Première Guerre mondiale sur Twitter," *Matériaux pour l'histoire de notre temps* 3–4, no. 121–122 (2016): 18–25; for the hashtag figure, see his article on methods, "#WW1. Les commémorations du centenaire de la Première Guerre mondiale sur Twitter (avril 2014-avril 2016)," *Ricerche Storiche* 46, no. 2 (2016).

³⁷ Geoff Cunfer, "Scaling the Dust Bowl," in *Placing History: How Maps, Spatial Data, and GIS Are Changing Historical Scholarship*, ed. Amy Hillier and Anne Kelly Knowles (Redlands, CA: ESRI Press, 2008).

Pivot Point: Seven Practical Strategies for the Digital Realm

1. *Pick two easy, safe things to do and one harder, riskier thing.* This was my suggestion in Chap. 6, but it is very exportable to the digital context. If handwriting daunts you, perhaps you can include two relevant databases that are heavy on printed sources or typewritten material, setting time aside to puzzle out those messy scribbles later.
2. *Try imagining how your project would work better as a partnership between different repositories and source types.* One digital resource is good; two or three might be better if they complement each other in useful ways. Digitized and non-digitized materials can also combine for a winning recipe.
3. *Realign your project to take advantage of the digital resource that does happen to exist.* There are enough digitized collections now that you have many interesting choices.
4. *With any new software, consider that there's a learning curve.* Applying *one* new technique to *one* set of data is probably a realistic goal.
5. *Search across the database, but also figure out how to read sequentially within the source.* If an immigrant's file is stamped with a warning—"liable to become a public charge at time of entry"—you'd only know if that was a common designation if you'd looked at many such files.[38]
6. *Remain alert to digital shortcomings in the rendering of size, scale, and color.* Be prepared to pivot and seek physical access to a source if that is appropriate.
7. *Always cite your sources.* We incur ethical and professional obligations as *users* of digital compendia. If a digital resource was integral to your project's success, you need to credit it in some visible way

Taking Your Database for a Test Drive

Digital resources make it possible for students to develop a more advanced and sophisticated prospectus than they could have in past generations. Do you have an idea for your research? Try it out now. See whether what you are turning up corresponds to your expectations, complicates the picture, or perhaps suggests that the truly interesting path lies somewhat athwart your original vision.

Suppose you've already looked a bit and found *one* example of what interests you. A single example is probably best considered as a provocation to find more evidence. If the existence of additional examples is just a hope or a twinkle in your eye, then you are embarking on a digital "fishing expedition." For a project with the clock running, that's a gamble.

---

[38] Ngai, *Impossible Subjects*, 77.

Before you drop the name of a database into your research prospectus, devote a few days to browsing it. Get a good general feel for the source. You may spot problems. For example, you may be excited to learn that you can access a long continuous run of digitized material. Is it consistent over that run, though? To make sure that you'll be getting what you actually need, sample that stream at more than one point. If your materials are going to be mainly digital, this assessment of viability is a reality check that you don't want to skip.

Even a quick dive into the digital realm may be an eye-opening process of discovery. Suppose that you are researching a socialist politician, Eugene Debs. You assumed he was a non-religious, or even anti-religious, figure. After all, he read Voltaire as a young man and was sometimes called an atheist.[39] Yet a search in the textual evidence from the period turns up some odd language that occurs in close proximity to the man's name: "vagabond carpenter," "the martyred Christ of the working class," and the name of Jesus.[40] Did sympathetic Christians choose to view the socialist leader through that particular lens? Or did Debs himself encourage these associations? As so often, the results of one search may prompt you to undertake another.

One possible next step would be to hunt for those same terms in Debs' own public utterances and published writings. Or you might decide to search for published scholarship on Debs and Christianity and discover that you are not the first person to notice this connection.[41] Other lines of inquiry open up, however. How prevalent was Christian rhetoric and imagery in the speeches of Debs' socialist peers? How about in a much wider sample of all politicians of his generation, or for that matter in all the mass-circulation newspapers and magazines of his era? Here, distant reading really does open up new vistas, and you have a set of keywords to look out for now. Indeed, if you find that biblical references saturated the texts from this era in general, you might become intrigued by a different American socialist leader who did *not* conform to that pattern. Thus, a short digital inquiry has led you to envision your project somewhat differently or even given you a new research topic.

A traditional, non-digital research method might well turn up similar results, but it would require long immersion in Debs' speeches, his published works, and the other written records of the era. In contrast, software can throw up patterns for your inspection quite quickly. Using digital resources, you could cycle through the phases I have described above in a matter of days or even hours. You might end up writing a very different research prospectus than you expected!

An exploratory visualization also offers a chance to view your project, and your options, in a new light. What would your material look like mapped out,

---

[39] In what follows, I have drawn information and examples from Jacob H. Dorn, "'In Spiritual Communion': Eugene V. Debs and the Socialist Christians," *Journal of the Gilded Age and Progressive Era* 2, no. 3 (July 2003): 303–325; for Voltaire, see 307.

[40] Dorn, "In Spiritual Communion"; see 312 for this language.

[41] For example, you would quickly come upon Dave Burns, "The Soul of Socialism: Christianity, Civilization, and Citizenship in the Thought of Eugene Debs," *Labor* 5, no. 2 (2008): 83–116.

tallied in a table, and arranged as a graph? It's one thing to say that in 2020, the death rate in New York City shot up 50% from the previous year. It's another to see a graph showing *200 years* of death rates in which the advent of COVID still shows up as a sharp spike.[42] From one perspective, you don't know anything new. Yet sometimes seeing your evidence this way changes your impression of what your evidence really means. Perhaps, instead of a pattern or strong trend, it could be an outlier or exception that catches your eye.[43] That might send you back to the drawing board, but with a new idea in mind.

As an introductory statistics textbook will alert you, there are many different ways to count, just as a book such as Mark Monmonier's *How to Lie with Maps* points out that *how* you map things makes a huge difference. Thus, we can refine the question further: What if you mapped, counted, or graphed the material you are finding using a different method or adding a new input? For example, reflect on what we *expect* to see mapped versus what we *could* map instead.

There is a potential for a mapping or graphing project to do more than display or inform; it can transform the way we think about a region or a relationship or a process. Richard White has argued for visualization not primarily as a means of documenting what's already known, but rather as

> *a means of doing research* [emphasis in the original]; it generates questions that might otherwise go unasked, it reveals historical relations that might otherwise go unnoticed, and it undermines, or substantiates, stories upon which we build our own versions of the past.[44]

Particularly if you have some prior experience with the techniques, and the relevant software, an *exploratory* visualization or two could help you develop your sense of what you can really do with the materials you have found so far.[45] This will hardly be a crisp and finished picture, but it might be the equivalent of a concept sketch. Just as with the preliminary findings about Eugene Debs and his unexpected Christian rhetoric, this could form the basis for a conversation with your advisor about next steps.

Conclusion

There is no reason to presume that the best project is one that uses physical archives. If you find that you will rely primarily on digitized materials, though, you should nevertheless ask yourself: When I don't approach this through the

---

[42] "Covid Was Bad in New York City. See How Bad on a 200-Year Timeline," *New York Times*, April 7, 2023.

[43] Graham, *Exploring*, 161.

[44] Richard White, "What Is Spatial History?" Stanford Spatial History Lab, February 1, 2010, https://web.stanford.edu/group/spatialhistory/media/images/publication/what%20is%20spatial%20history%20pub%20020110.pdf, accessed 8/27/2023.

[45] Graham, *Exploring*, 159. Free software options for creating mapping and network diagrams include Palladio; for charts and graphing, you can use Data Wrapper. I am indebted to Sean Fraga for these suggestions.

box or folder, *what is lost?* A frequently voiced regret is that search results pop up on the screen divorced from provenance and context. Lara Putnam has observed:

> Working with tax data or police correspondence in a national archive forced you to read through a lot of evidence of political struggle and state formation even when what you really wanted to get at was grain prices or prostitution—and vice versa. Analog exploration of written sources—the longtime bread and butter of our craft—built in multidimensional awareness.[46]

The software doesn't mind if you bring multidimensional awareness along for the ride. Yet interfaces do shape our habits. Adam Crymble quotes a historian who noted that as a user of physical archives, she would never read a single document from a folder without looking at anything else in the folder, yet using a digital interface, she found herself "forced" to do exactly that.[47] There are often ways around the default user experience, but every inconvenience introduces a point of friction that requires effort and attention to overcome, and not everyone can take the time to slow down and do it.

Quick search results may encourage the single-minded researcher to do the opposite: Gallop forward faster and more heedlessly. In 2014, Ted Underwood warned, in a prescient essay:

> It's true that full-text search can confirm almost any thesis you bring to it, but that may not be its most dangerous feature. The deeper problem is that sorting sources in order of relevance to your query also tends to filter out all the alternative theses you didn't bring.[48]

Five years later, Cokie Roberts—a well-known journalist—made national news when she announced that nineteenth-century American newspapers contained no advertisements for abortion. Historians retorted that plugging appropriate nineteenth-century vocabulary into the search box produced not only *some* results but a plethora of results.[49]

Yet perhaps focusing too much on the egregious cases and the occasional scandal means that we lose track of the ways that the speed and ease of the digital realm can subtly reshape the research process of even the most careful and sophisticated scholars. After they were digitized, two Canadian newspapers were cited *ten times more* in PhD dissertations and in a prominent academic journal. Other Canadian newspapers, undigitized, saw no increase. Among

---

[46] Putnam, "Transnational," 396.

[47] Crymble, *Technology*, 33.

[48] Ted Underwood, "Theorizing Research Practices We Forgot to Theorize Twenty Years Ago," *Representations* 127 (July 2014): 64–72; see 66.

[49] Karin Wulf, "What Naomi Wolf and Cokie Roberts Teach Us about the Need for Historians," *Washington Post*, June 11, 2019; "From the Editor's Desk: Outrages," *The American Historical Review* 124, no. 4 (October 2019): xiv–xvii.

other things, this meant that historians were now more likely to cite media based in Canada's biggest cities, reducing the visibility and influence of newspapers from smaller, more provincial locations.[50]

Cultivate a sharp, critical awareness of what your chosen mode of access makes easy and what it makes hard. How could access to digital resources silently reshape the scholarship that you will produce or even the sort of project that would occur to you in the first place? One of the loudest voices in today's information ecosystem is the readily accessible database of digitized materials. Don't let it dictate terms to you. The *digitized* source may not be the *best* source; it may not even speak very well to what you were trying to learn about in the first place! Indeed, if you are hoping to excite and surprise people with your results, the smart move might be to direct your efforts toward materials that are more obscure and harder to access.

Perhaps a different peril here is the risk of the never-ending project.[51] The digital realm really is large enough to torment a guilty scholar forever. The good news is that a properly delimited project will offer you an escape from this trap. In Chap. 1, I proposed the idea of the Archimedean Point. The next chapter is all about finding that ideal spot, centering yourself there, and building a project that is the right size and also that speaks in a substantive way to important questions.

Further Reading

Lara Putnam, "The Transnational and the Text-Searchable: Digitized Sources and the Shadows They Cast," *American Historical Review* 121, no. 2 (April 2016): 377–402.

Estelle Bunout, et al., eds., *Digitised Newspapers—A New Eldorado for Historians? Reflections on Tools, Methods and Epistemology* (Berlin: Walter de Gruyter, 2023).

Shawn Graham et al., *Exploring Big Historical Data: The Historian's Macroscope*, 2nd ed. (Singapore: World Scientific Publishing, 2022) is a textbook with step-by-step guidance and advice for big data projects, although it is primarily oriented toward projects involving text.

Tim Cole and Alberto Giordano, "Digital Mapping," in *Doing Spatial History*, ed. Riccardo Bavaj, et al. (London: Routledge, 2022), 274–287.

Gillian Rose, *Visual Methodologies,* 5th ed. (London: Sage, 2023) includes a useful discussion of big data approaches to photos, magazine covers, social media posts, websites, hashtags, and more.

Cian T. McMahon, "Tracking the Great Famine's 'Coffin Ships' across the Digital Deep," *Éire-Ireland* 56, no. 1 & 2 (Spring/Summer 2021): 81–109 is a good example of transparency about methods, and candor about what digital resources made a project possible.

---

[50] Ian Milligan, "Illusionary Order: Online Databases, Optical Character Recognition, and Canadian History, 1997–2010," *Canadian Historical Review* 94, no. 4 (December 2013): 540–569.

[51] Solberg, "Googling," 68, for remarks on the risk of "research inflation."

CHAPTER 8

Designing Your Project

Going forward, you need a plan that covers where you need to look, how much is enough, and some sense of when you are finished. This chapter, intentionally, comes right after two chapters about conducting scouting expeditions in the archives and the digital realm. Although you have not yet "done your research" in the fullest sense, you know a great deal more than when you started.

Earlier, you wrote a preliminary prospectus or expressed your plan in an email to your advisor. If you were writing that email today, what information would you include? Is your thinking about your project fully aligned with what you actually *know* now? It's time to take that knowledge fully on board, actively reappraising and revising your plan as needed.

Why is a plan so important? In Chap. 5, I discussed the value of unexpected, even visionary new approaches. Sometimes it feels as if the approach—the vision—is, itself, the project. It's important to distinguish, though, between *problem finding* and *problem solving*.[1] A piece of scholarship that mostly just says "wouldn't it be nice if…" is tantalizing if it appears in a state-of-the-field review essay. Most readers, though, expect a lot more from a standalone piece of scholarship. This chapter will help you complete the circuit and not only identify an interesting problem or a novel angle of approach, but flesh out your plan to do something about it.

I am not here to tell you how many archival boxes you'll need to examine or how many court cases you need to read in the online database. A rough plan for this is best approached in direct consultation with your advisor. Don't be too surprised, though, if you ask your advisor a series of questions about *quantity* (how many boxes) and they respond with a series of questions about *purpose* (why those boxes).

---

[1] Silvia, *How to Write*, 105.

Let's clarify your purpose and develop some goals that match it. This chapter will help you transition from a research topic to a research question, and ultimately to a research plan. At the same time it pushes you to engage with the tough issues that are implicit in making such plans: Why here and not there? Why this and not that? What sources, why this periodization, why this location? Jotting down even tentative, preliminary answers to those questions may, in turn, push you to reconsider and refine what you are really hoping to achieve. It's also a way to assess which iterations of your project are easier to accomplish than others.

A standard reference point for a student project is the scope and ambitions of an academic journal article. This remains true, in a rough sense, whether your target length falls shorter than that—or quite a bit longer. It is helpful to notice that most academic journal articles observe what are known as the classical or Aristotelian unities. They deal with:

- a relatively short period of time
- a particular place
- a single event or situation

The unities of time, place, and action were originally devised for theater. Although there is no need to be dogmatic about it (and I do mention some interesting exceptions to the rules in this chapter), the classical unities are quite well suited to the constraints that you face right now: a ticking clock and a circumscribed length for your final product.

That said, accepting narrow parameters only increases the pressure on you to figure out the position that's just right. There's a proverb about real estate: "It's about three things: Location, location, and location." That's a good mantra for scholarship, as well. The first section of this chapter, "The Art of Changing Your Topic," will help you take what you now think are simple declarative statements about your project:

I will cover the period from 1920 to 1940

and rephrase them as questions:

Will I cover the period from 1920 to 1940?

Doing this with the elements of your project, one by one, will help you see all of the choices that you really have. Much of this chapter is devoted to three areas where every History project could use a good, hard, thoughtful checkup: your comparative or contextual framework, your chronological span, and your methods of sampling.

The next step is to draft a brief research plan that will set your agenda going forward. It will sketch out, perhaps in just a single sentence, how your project is both doable *and* significant. The final subsection offers you some tips as you weave all this together.

The Art of Changing Your Topic

Let's start with a deceptively simple question: What interests you? Until you have examined alternatives and explored variants, you won't have a complete or precise answer. Therefore, I'm encouraging you to investigate this in a self-conscious and deliberate way. I refer to this as "changing your topic" because that is often how students conceptualize it, especially if the suggestion comes from someone else! From my point of view, it is really exploring facets of the topic, rather than abandoning one topic for another. In fact, Natalie Zemon Davis likened her own research process to turning a diamond in the light and suddenly noticing the gleam from a new side of the jewel.[2]

Some research guides warn against reading "around" the topic because it is potentially a never-ending task, and could just become a form of procrastination. For that reason, this isn't a phase you'd want to indulge in indefinitely. Yet for many projects, it turns out to be in the "around" where the action is, or where the sources are. I would modify the conventional wisdom, then. Before you tunnel down, pause and look around first. You might be two steps and a little hop away from a more interesting version of the same project that first caught your eye.

The Oxyrhynchus papyri offer an instructive example here. On January 11, 1897, Bernard Pyne Grenfell and Arthur Surridge Hunt began digging into ancient refuse mounds near this small settlement in Egypt, seeking papyrus preserved in the arid climate. Oxyrhynchus was chosen partly because it was a known center of early Christianity, with a large monastic population.[3] To their delight, one of the first papyri they excavated turned out to be a page from an unknown apocryphal book of the New Testament.[4] Six seasons of excavation ultimately produced 500,000 "pieces and scraps" of papyri, amounting to 700 boxes of material.[5]

The hope of finding copies of lost works by luminaries such as Euripides or Sappho also motivated the archeologists, whose interests were deeply informed by their education in Greek literature. Yet the "literary papyri"—whether biblical or secular—made up only about 10% of the total.[6] It also transpired that "middle-brow taste was very conservative," meaning that copies of Homer—replicas of text that scholars already knew well—accounted for four times as many papyri as any other author.[7]

Meanwhile, the researchers lumped 450,000 documents into a vague "non-literary papyri" category. While Grenfell enjoyed quoting the letter from a

---

[2] Natalie Zemon Davis, *A Passion for History: Conversations with Dennis Crouzet*, trans. Natalie Zemon Davis and Michael Wolfe (Kirksville: Truman State University Press, 2010), 8.

[3] Peter Parsons, *City of the Sharp Nosed Fish: Greek Lives in Roman Egypt* (London: Weidenfeld and Nicolson, 2007), 14.

[4] Parsons, *City*, 15.

[5] Parsons, *City*, 17.

[6] Parsons, *City*, 24.

[7] Parsons, *City*, 152.

petulant boy ("If you don't take me with you to Alexandria, I won't eat I won't drink so there"), it took a while for scholars to fully grasp—and celebrate—the potential of Oxyrhynchus as "a unique dustbin of vanished lives," a whole "waste-paper city" containing "sales and loans, wills and contracts, tax returns and government orders, private letters, shopping lists and household accounts" to say nothing of "the worm's-eye view of Christianity on the march in Egypt, as seen in the lives of its followers and the circulation of its texts."[8] Ironically, then, most of what the archeologists uncovered was only truly usable for academic purposes if they were ready to reevaluate their deeply entrenched values and expectations.

This tension between what we imagine we want to find and what we do find and should be grateful to find is so fundamental that it crops up again and again in historians' actual research practice. You, too, may want to pause at this stage and reflect on what all your hard work has uncovered so far. What seems important *now*? What seems potentially useful *now*? Given the material on hand, what are the pursuable lines of research as you see them *now*?

Imagine your project as you've defined it to yourself, to your advisor, and in conversations with others. Picture yourself as surrounded by alternatives in every direction. Then slowly and systematically look around for them. That means *all* the directions—we can be very close to something, but if we never look up toward the ceiling and down toward the floor, we may never notice it. Or imagine a big city with cross streets. You may think you know what your topic "is," but that could be like knowing the street name without any sense of which intersection. How would your topic look different if you expressed it as "at the corner of x and y"? Would it help to get in an elevator and look out a window so you get a different view of the surrounding neighborhoods? Most people never do anything like this with their project unless they are really pushed to try it.

A student of mine who was researching the history of the Heath candy bar, manufactured in her hometown of Robinson, Illinois, might have explored the intersection of candy bars and public health; candy bars and the history of advertising; candy bars and the history of chocolate as a commodity; candy bars and the presence (or absence) of unionized labor where the manufacturing took place; and small candy companies and the emergence of food conglomerates. Instead, she embarked on an unexpected journey into the world of military logistics.[9] It turns out that the Heath bar survived because it was included in US Army rations during both World Wars. It kept longer, without spoiling, than some other chocolate treats. The Army prized it for that reason, so the company won an exemption from sugar rationing. By preserving factory jobs, that also extended a lifeline to the small town's economy.

In this example, the reappraisal followed the lines of the city streets visualization I proposed: At which cross street or intersection did she feel her project

---

[8] Quotations in this paragraph are from Parsons, *City*, 24, 211, 216, xxvi, 196, respectively.
[9] The student was Heather Coombes.

actually belonged? There are many other possible ways to approach the reappraisal process. For ideas, try re-reading your earlier notes, whether from yesterday or last month. This may induce a little introspection. Take the time to notice what you have been noticing! This is a time-tested technique for capturing fresh insights and coming at things from a new direction.

Here are some provocations to consider as you re-read your notes and reflect on what you've learned about your area of interest so far.

> **Pivot Point: Eight Ways to Change Your Topic**
>
> 1. *Is your project centered on the right source type?* Maybe you are now aware of a different kind of source that would meet your research needs better.
> 2. *Is there an opportunity to move the spotlight to the point of greatest conflict or transition?* This could be a brilliant move for a host of reasons, even if it means reconsidering the starting or ending dates of the project, or reappraising where the project is situated geographically.
> 3. *Is there something (someone; some entity or organization) you didn't appreciate was important when you started your research, but you do now?* It's not too late to consider refocusing the project on just that.
> 4. *Could you reconsider the scale?* Entertain the possibility of a plausible broader version of your project. How about a plausible narrower, tighter version—what would that look like?
> 5. *If your focus is biographical, what other options exist?* Behind (or around) every project focused on an individual, you should imagine a cloud of alternatives. That could mean focusing on a different individual. It also could involve a focus on something *other* than an individual: a club or artistic circle, the groupthink mentality of a particular institutional setting, and the changing demographic composition of an activist movement, among others.
> 6. *What if you flipped to the mirror image of what you thought the project was about?* You can make a little game of this for any research topic: Just reverse it or turn it on its head. Does your project work best as a study of sex workers *or* as a study of the town's vice squad?
> 7. *Would your study of causes be more fresh and interesting as a study of consequences?* Historians ask *why did it happen*, but that's not our only calling; it's also valuable to ask *why did it matter*. Sometimes certain consequences are well known, but no one has really examined the impact in an unexpected location or context.
> 8. *Could you simply relocate your project to where the primary sources are most rich and concentrated?* Once again, it may be worth changing the starting or ending dates or looking at a different location, if it's better documented or the documents are more interesting.

After considering these options, you may also find that more or less by accident, you have taken steps toward refining your *research topic* into a *research question*. A research topic is just an expression of a general curiosity. Charles Lipson offers the example of two hypothetical titles, *Boys and Play* and *Why Boys Play Rough*.[10] This neatly captures the difference between a research topic and something like a worthwhile research question. Notice that a research question is more nuanced and answerable.

"It's interesting how..." is always better than just saying, "It's interesting." The person who begins a statement "it's interesting how..." has begun to narrow down and focus: "How did a body of men with no experience of middle-class forms of civic engagement orchestrate such a large-scale and sophisticated political campaign?"[11]

Indeed, Louis Gottschalk observed that research questions formulated around "the *why*, the *how*, and the *with-what consequences*" tend to be more intellectually interesting than questions formulated exclusively around words such as *who*, *what*, *when*, or *where*.[12] One advantage of *how* and *why* questions is that they challenge us to not take things for granted; framing it this way implies, perhaps, that the outcome was not inevitable. Of course, you can pair this with versions of *who*, *what*, *when*, or *where*, such as "why did that occur in *this particular place*?"

If you are leaning toward a formulation that calls for more description and detail, rather than more analysis and evidence, then you are still too close to just having a topic that captured your interest, rather than a fully developed research question. Also, avoid questions that contain, or appear to contain, their own answers. The most intriguing scholarship is the sort that might elicit continuing thoughtful discussion and disagreement (at least about the nuances). It's not encouraging if it appears you have sorted things out already! For similar reasons, a research question that could readily be answered "yes" or "no" is also not a good idea.

If you think you might have a tentative research question now, this would be a good time to jot it down for later reference. Of course, having a good question is only half of the task. By the end of the chapter, I'll have you sketching out a one-sentence research plan following the formula "to get at *this*, I'll look at *that*."

---

[10] Lipson, *How to Write*, 185.

[11] Emma Griffin, "The Making of the Chartists: Popular Politics and Working-class Autobiography in Early Victorian Britain," *English Historical Review* 129, no. 538 (June 2014): 578–605; see 581.

[12] Louis Gottschalk, "A Professor of History in a Quandary," *American Historical Review* 59, no. 2 (January 1954): 273–286; see 280.

COMPARED TO WHAT?

When Raymond Grew, who later would edit the journal *Comparative Studies in Society and History* for a quarter century, first mentioned his interest in comparative approaches to a colleague at Princeton, that person retorted: "When historians don't know enough to write about one place, they write on two."[13] Yet a historical profession without the wider vision provided by comparisons and contrasts would be much the lesser for it.

To appreciate why, consider a work like Kenneth Pomeranz's *The Great Divergence*, which is an extended exploration of Britain's industrial takeoff in contrast to China in the same period.[14] Pomeranz shows that a remarkably long list of economic ingredients for that recipe were present, but in China, the "take-off" did not occur. Such a magisterial work can take the better part of a professional lifetime to conceive, research, and write. Don't let that leave you feeling that useful comparison is beyond your reach. Donald Bloxham's article in the journal *Holocaust and Genocide Studies* offers an example of what comparison and contrast can look like in a shorter format publication.[15] It mentions multiple examples and countries almost in the same breath, but in a carefully circumscribed context—asking the tough questions about the role, motivation, and conduct of mid-level bureaucrats during episodes of genocide. A statement such as "the Armenian Genocide featured the fewest administrative perpetrators relative to the scale of the crime" is not a set-piece comparison, offering an account of a whole genocide and then following it with a complete narrative of a different one.[16] Rather, Bloxham is engaging in comparative *reasoning*, using an outside reference point to suggest what may be special, interesting, or even surprising about the material at hand.

Comparative reasoning is more common than you might think. It is one of the major ways that historians find meaning in past events, or discern possibilities for interpretation. Bathsheba Demuth made a choice to write not just about the Iñupiaq in Alaska, but also about the Chukchi in Siberia.[17] Both of these Indigenous groups had a long-standing relationship with reindeer, but the Iñupiaq found themselves inside the United States, while the Chukchi, across the Bering Strait, lived in the Soviet Union. The US. Reindeer Service, established in 1908, drew on ideologies and methods dear to the heart of planners in Washington, D.C. The Iñupiaq could become "yeomen farmers" or perhaps holders of shares in a joint stock corporation.[18] Eventually, bureaucrats

---

[13] Raymond Grew, "On the Society and History of *CSSH*," *Comparative Studies on Society and History* 50, no. 1 (2008): 9–20; see 9.

[14] Princeton, NJ: Princeton University Press, 2001.

[15] Donald Bloxham, "Organized Mass Murder: Structure, Participation, and Motivation in Comparative Perspective," *Holocaust and Genocide Studies* 22, no. 2 (Fall 2008): 203–245.

[16] Bloxham, "Organized Mass Murder," 232.

[17] Bathsheba Demuth, *Floating Coast: An Environmental History of the Bering Strait* (New York: W. W. Norton, 2019).

[18] Demuth, *Floating Coast*, 157–158.

debated how to make the operations of the Reindeer Service fit into the goals of the New Deal.[19] Exasperation took the form of Social Darwinist invective or racist put-downs; the Iñupiaq who did not accommodate the latest Reindeer Service initiatives were said to have a "mentality... about that of a fourteen year old."[20] Under Stalin, in contrast, the issue was how to integrate reindeer productivity into the Five Year Plan and collectivization.[21] The terms of invective and disdain were also different: Soviet planners worried about the pernicious influence of "*kulaks* and shamans" who did not support the new order.[22]

There is nothing wrong with doing a project just on the Iñupiaq. Yet it's not far-fetched to propose that a serious interest in the US Reindeer Service demands a serious interest in comparable regimes of management. This is true of a host of other inquiries as well. Try to articulate what amounts to a successful reform of an entrenched bureaucracy, or what counts as revolutionary, or what looks and feels egalitarian, or what causes economic prosperity. It is actually quite difficult without some comparative frame of reference. Of course, sometimes the comparison is left merely implied; we suppose that the reader shares our sense of what examples are pertinent. In those situations, the comparative aspect is present, but there are overlooked opportunities to clarify, revise, and critique it.

It's also possible to undertake comparative reasoning *within* the same location by considering change over time. In his study "Parading in Early Victorian Toronto," Peter Goheen placed great emphasis on a single parade on Wednesday, October 15, 1851.[23] Why? Prior to this, some of the most familiar public demonstrations in Toronto were the riotous Orange Order parades, which involved provocative banners, divisive slogans, and the burning of enemies in effigy. In contrast, Goheen argued, a celebration of the breaking of the sod for Toronto's first railroad was a *Canadian* event (rather than a Protestant tradition imported from Britain). Moreover, it was an inclusive event with no sectarian associations. Without this context, October 15, 1851, would seem unremarkable.

Every working historian has struggled with questions such as "how much information do I need to accumulate before I'll be in any sort of position to begin writing" or, indeed, "how will I know whether what I've got here is a finding worthy of the name?" You may derive some comfort from considering the process of establishing—for example—that *this* parade was meaningfully different from *previous* parades. Already, there is something quite meaningful to say. Nor, as the Toronto example shows, does a thoughtful comparative

---

[19] Demuth, *Floating Coast*, 165.
[20] Demuth, *Floating Coast*, 164.
[21] Demuth, *Floating Coast*, 161–162.
[22] Demuth, *Floating Coast*, 165.
[23] Peter G. Goheen, "Parading: A Lively Tradition in Early Victorian Toronto," in *Ideology and Landscape in Historical Perspective: Essays on the Meanings of Some Places in the Past*, ed. Alan R. H. Baker and Gideon Biger (Cambridge: Cambridge University Press, 1992), 330–351.

approach necessarily require that you violate the unities of time, place, and action.

Let's suppose that your interests are leading you to a multi-site project that really does violate the unities. Now is the time to consider how you will do that without exceeding the reasonable bounds of your time and energy. For example, a full-scale comparison of the Green Party in Germany with the Campaign for Nuclear Disarmament in Britain may be unrealistic for you to undertake at this time. On the other hand, studying the influence of activist A from country B on nonprofit C in country D is well within your reach. There are plenty of possible project ideas—even transnational comparisons—that are adequately focused to make completion possible, but are far from narrow in their vision.[24]

As Demuth's adoption of an Alaska-Siberia comparison shows, the *axis of comparison* is, itself, another choice. What might you gain by comparing things, places, or people that usually aren't mentioned in the same breath? As you come across new scholarship, get in the habit of noticing explicit and implicit comparisons. Which comparisons seem productive? Which seem to be more trouble than they are worth? Seeing how others deploy comparison can be a useful tutorial for how you might do it yourself.

Don't underestimate the value of comparative context. It is often what establishes the stakes of the academic inquiry. I'll concede that a few topics—like cavalry charges, million-dollar lawsuits, and humanitarian measures to save refugees—carry a natural drama of their own. Most really don't. Clearly, something has captured your attention. But not all readers are susceptible to your quirky sense of what is fun and important. You just might convince them, though, that what's going on is *interesting*. If you want to establish why the design of playground equipment or the custom of keeping pet squirrels is a compelling thing to learn more about, then context is key. It could make the difference between a project that's meaningful to you, and one that's meaningful to others too.

FROM WHEN TO WHEN?

Historians have a nearly inexhaustible appetite for discussing periodization. This isn't just fussiness for its own sake; we've learned—both as readers and as writers—that broadening or narrowing the chronological scope of an inquiry can decisively change it for the better or for the worse. So while you are keeping that sharp eye out for comparative reasoning, you can also notice the choices that each work of historical scholarship makes about timeframe. And

---

[24] See, however, the thoughtful critique of older forms of comparative history presented in Michael Werner and Bénédicte Zimmermann, "Beyond Comparison: Histoire Croisée and the Challenge of Reflexivity," *History and Theory* 45 (February 2006): 30–50. They inaugurated an "entangled histories" approach, which is particularly relevant for transnational comparative projects.

there *are* choices here. Just because you have material going up to 1966 doesn't mean that your paper ought to use that as its ending date.

It is common to zero in on a short period of time. Peter Stansky found inspiration for a book in a provocative quotation from Virginia Woolf, "On or about December 1910, human nature changed." Each chapter of Stansky's *On or About December 1910* explores a different facet of London's intellectual and cultural life in that historical moment.[25] It's possible to narrow the analytical aperture still further, to a week or even a twenty-four-hour period. Perhaps the prize for the tightest chronological focus goes to John Keegan. Here is an excerpt from his account of the Battle of Midway:

> At 1025 Nagumo stood poised on the brink of perhaps the greatest naval victory ever promised an admiral, certain to be spectacular in itself and destined to alter the balance of power between the Western and the Asian world for decades to come. At 1030 he confronted not victory but disaster.[26]

Keegan singles out the crucial events of a period of just *five minutes*. In contrast, some processes are so gradual that the appropriate chronological scope is very long indeed. Particularly in fields such as agricultural and environmental history, it is possible to find academic journal articles that span centuries.[27]

While there is no generic advice to tell you *when* to place your focus, it often helps to center your project on a place or time when some kind of transition occurred. Change is the historian's friend, not only because it gives you something to explain, but also because contemporaries' experience of change tends to generate a written record that's packed with potential insights (from would-be reformers, from conservatives, from bystanders, from people affected in one way or another by the change). Perhaps change makes them more self-conscious, whereas people living in what they perceive as a static period are less observant, less critically minded, and less reflective. A tough choice involving competing priorities—merely the *possibility* of change—can call forth articulate advocates to express a dizzying array of proposals.[28]

It's no accident that Laurel Thatcher Ulrich's remark—"Well-behaved women seldom make history"—first appeared in an academic journal article reflecting on the difficulties of *research*.[29] If historians love change and transition, we absolutely adore misbehavior and conflict. It generates copious records. Bankruptcies or industrial accidents can lead to detailed testimony

---

[25] Peter Stansky, *On or About December 1910: Early Bloomsbury and Its Intimate World* (Cambridge, MA: Harvard University Press, 1997).

[26] John Keegan, *The Price of Admiralty: The Evolution of Naval Warfare* (New York: Viking, 1988), 204.

[27] Daviken Studnicki-Gizbert and David Schecter, "Environmental Dynamics of a Colonial Fuel-Rush: New Spain, 1522 to 1810," *Environmental History* 15, no. 1 (January 2010): 94–119.

[28] Zachary M. Schrag, *Princeton Guide to Historical Research* (Princeton: Princeton University Press, 2021), 59.

[29] Laurel Thatcher Ulrich, "Vertuous Women Found: New England Ministerial Literature, 1668–1735," *American Quarterly* 28 (1976): 20–40; see 20.

under oath. A project centered right on top of a scandal will never run short of primary source material. Even relatively humble misunderstandings may generate a copious, and revealing, paper trail.

A crisis, then, *could* be a year of international drama such as 1939. On their own modest scale, though, small nonprofits, large labor unions, and political parties can also face emergencies. Even households and individuals experience shocking incidents that break unwritten norms. Perhaps only some of your primary sources identify the event as noteworthy, and others disagree. That disagreement, too, makes for interesting reading.

Despite the opportunities here, students are sometimes quite reluctant to consider switching up their starting or ending date. There is nothing wrong with having a special affection for a certain time period; most historians would cheerfully confess to that. Perhaps two statements describe you right now, "I am interested in colonial prisons," and "I study the eighteenth century." Suppose, though, that you came across a rich set of primary sources, or a fascinating historiographical debate, that pertains to colonial prisons in the *nineteenth* century. How would you react then? It is well worth your time to read just a little more broadly and run a thought experiment or two. *What if* you started earlier or ended later? How would your project take on a new shape, or ask different questions, as a result?

As historians, another point of resistance is a vague feeling that some eras are too modern for us. I am old enough to remember the wave of projects in the 1950s that emerged once that decade felt solidly historical. Periodically, runs of material are declassified by governments—either as the result of the passage of years or perhaps because of a sudden regime change. Sometimes a policy decision by a nonprofit, such as the Rockefeller Foundation, throws a huge body of source material open.[30] There is a thrill to working with primary source material that hasn't been assiduously picked over by other historians. Consider that some people, organizations, and events have yet to find their historians at all.

If you are going to change up your timescales, the units of measurement needn't be decades. Craig Koslofsky wondered about shifting the focus to a different *time of day* and wound up writing an acclaimed book about the history of the night.[31] How about switching your focus to the most interesting point *in the life cycle*? When women's history was a new field of study, scholars discovered that it was exceptionally productive to zero in on young unmarried women and also widows.[32] Each of these phases of life was a controversial transition that generated opportunities for women, but it also prompted wagging tongues, disagreements, opinionated reactions, and sometimes even lawsuits. Similarly, a study of sailors broke new ground by shifting the focus away from

---

[30] Putnam, "Transnational," 383.

[31] Craig Koslofsky, *Evening's Empire: A History of the Night in Early Modern Europe* (Cambridge: Cambridge University Press, 2011).

[32] See for example Linda E. Mitchell, "The Lady is a Lord: Noble Widows and Land in Thirteenth-Century Britain," *Historical Reflections / Réflexions Historiques* 18, no. 1 (Winter 1992): 71–97.

time spent at sea. Seafaring was traditionally a vigorous and risky job for young men. This suggested a new research question: What did the surviving sailors do with the rest of their lives?[33]

Look back over the books and articles you have collected, or try skimming the table of contents for one of your favorite journals, just looking for the timespan each piece appears to cover. Acquiring an eye for how others approach this task may help as you go through your own process of pondering the question "from when to when?" You might also ask your advisor how they approached their own choices in selecting a starting and ending date for one of their projects. That could be a good conversation starter. Even if they didn't have to agonize over it, they undoubtedly can think of examples of historians who did.

What's Your Sample?

Where a historian chooses to find their sources often speaks to the essence of their project, its unique personality, its priorities, and its strengths. What are you going to use, and why? This is one of the inescapable questions in historical research, and you may find yourself revisiting it multiple times over the course of your work on this project. If your advisor seems to harp on this issue, bear in mind that when you tell someone what your sources were, you are indirectly speaking to some of the most fundamental questions about historical knowledge: What can we know? Where could we look? Who (or what) is important enough to include? How much is enough?

Perhaps your project faces some challenges in this area. It's okay to acknowledge that—in conversations with your advisor, in your prospectus, and even in your final written product. In fact, if you are aware of some challenges, it's a sign that your project, and your mastery of the issues involved with it, is maturing. You may start noticing that quite a few books and articles you read contain mini-essays or small digressions to discuss what sources exist for this particular research topic, how the historian handled obviously mendacious or self-serving sources, or why a particular source type deserves respect despite some well-known shortcomings.[34]

Sometimes finding some evidence, any evidence at all, becomes the great adventure that occupies your full attention and ingenuity. In a book on statistics, I came across an astute discussion of the problems with measuring the size of a wildlife population using a proxy: the animals that are found as roadkill.[35] As historians, we can relate very well to the challenge of how to count invisible animals that may or may not exist. Notoriously, any activity that was stigmatized,

---

[33] Daniel Vickers, *Young Men and the Sea: Yankee Seafarers in the Age of Sail* (New Haven: Yale University Press, 2007).

[34] For example, Browning, *Ordinary Men*, 147–158.

[35] Blastland and Dilnot, *Tiger That Isn't*, 101–102.

or outright illegal, is hard to assess. Yet it would be reckless to take the paucity of evidence as proof that it was rare.

Lucien Febvre wrote a famous book entitled *The Problem of Unbelief in the Sixteenth Century*.[36] Historians have struggled even more, though, with the challenge of assessing the extent and depth of *belief* in this same period of European history. Church attendance is a poor proxy for piety. A failure to attend church is not necessarily a reliable indicator of heresy or skepticism. Reports from spies about secret assemblies and unsanctioned religious observances could be true, or just the fabrication of an informer who expected payment for a juicy tidbit.

Despite these daunting obstacles, Eamon Duffy found ways to measure the strength and resilience of Catholic piety during the disruptions of the English Reformation. First, he demonstrated that prior to the Reformation, Catholic religious teaching communicated more widely, and more effectively, than many scholars had thought. He accomplished this through a close examination of the ubiquitous church decorations, as well as the popular forms of "extra-liturgical piety" such as devotion to the Wounds of Jesus.[37] Second, through a meticulous examination of churchwarden's account books and parish inventories during the reign of Queen Mary, he uncovered a pattern of Catholic religious objects which were "purchased" during a wave of Protestant iconoclasm, kept safe, and then lent back to the churches promptly when a Catholic returned to the throne. Others were sold back for a token amount.[38] In cases where the originals were smashed or burned, Duffy remarks on how expensive it must have been to repopulate every church with devotional objects, from rood lofts to copes, vestments, bells, and towels. This "demanded resources of manpower, cash, and availability of craftsmen which parishes could not readily command. Yet command them they mostly did...."[39] These devotional practices snapped back, with vigor, under Mary. It seems that allegiance to the old ways was far from anemic.

Perhaps we expect a crisp answer to the research questions "who believed?" and "how ardently did they believe?" In that case, Duffy's findings fall short. Yet his methods commanded instant attention and respect from Reformation scholars. Queen Elizabeth I, facing down advisors who were anxious about religious nonconformity, once retorted that she could not see into people's hearts. Historians can't either, but that doesn't stop us from trying to find a different approach that gets us closer to the answers we seek.

When people take in your final product, one of their first questions will be "what were the sources?" You want the answer to that question to be an impressive one. Bear in mind, though, that the most impressive project isn't

---

[36] Lucien Febvre, *The Problem of Unbelief in the Sixteenth Century: The Religion of Rabelais*, trans. Beatrice Gottlieb (Cambridge, MA: Harvard University Press, 1982).

[37] Eamon Duffy, *The Stripping of the Altars: Traditional Religion in England, 1400–1580* (New Haven: Yale University Press, 1992), 233.

[38] Duffy, *Stripping*, 549–550.

[39] Duffy, *Stripping*, 547.

always the project that consulted the largest number of sources or which somehow had the biggest sample. As Gillian Rose once suggested, the deepest level of research design is aligning the method with the sort of question you are really asking.[40] One of my students undertook a project about feminists on our campus in the 1970s, but failing to find a record of any self-identified feminist organizations, she wrote a strong paper about the Women's Health Center, which turned out to be a place where a range of feminist concerns found practical expression.[41] Your approach to sampling may be simply a statement roughly in this spirit:

> I can't answer that very well, but with this evidence, I *can* get at a related question in a productive way, so listen up.

The trick here is to remain open to a particular source type that wasn't on your radar when you first thought of the project.

From Research Question to Research Prospectus

New to writing a formal prospectus? I have good news for you. It really comes down to just two things. You'll need to spell out why your project is worthwhile (establishing *significance*) and sketch out a practical roadmap (showing that it is also *doable*). Your advisor knows that there are many possible projects, but quite a few of them are weak in one of these areas. For example, you could plow through some sources that happen to be handy and plentiful. That doesn't guarantee that you'll produce any findings that will seem consequential. Likewise, a project that begins with no notion of which archive would meet its needs is likely to over-promise, and under-deliver, no matter how visionary its aims may sound. There's also a need to demonstrate a nice, tight fit between what you are trying to get at and the sources you propose to use. Ample documentation may survive from the 1790s (or the 1190s), but what makes you confident that it's the right kind of documentation for your needs? Discussing your research prospectus with your advisor is also the best time to agree on parameters that will keep your project at a nice, manageable size. The right-sized project is your path to good time management and mental health.

In our discipline, we are unlikely to start with a hypothesis. We certainly don't use that word. It is both acceptable and desirable, though, to start with an *aim*.[42] Stating what motivates your interest ("I am working on A because I want to find out B" or "I am working on A in order to help us understand C better...") is, indirectly, a way to signal what you think the significance of your

---

[40] Gillian Rose, *Visual Methodologies: An Introduction to the Interpretation of Visual Materials* (London: Sage 2001), 29.

[41] The student was Brooke Truax.

[42] D. G. Evans et al., *How to Write a Better Thesis*, 3rd ed. (Carlton, Victoria: Melbourne University Press, 2011), 98.

inquiry is.⁴³ Suppose you jot down your version of these lines and notice that the components are misaligned. A is a body of sources that you really can access, but it's *not* shedding a lot of light on B. Or you're excited about working with A, which does speak well to C, as you just wrote, but it speaks even *better* to D. That's maybe your cue to switch things up a bit. In other words, drafting the research prospectus can be a kind of thought experiment that may help you foresee difficulties and devise a different path, if necessary.

A widely respected guide to academic writing offers this advice: "If you are free to work on any problem, look for a small one that is part of a bigger one."⁴⁴ Small sounds good, but how are you supposed to identify the big problem? What's the guarantee that your notion of a big (important, complex, relevant) problem aligns with what others might think? This is another occasion when your cousins—the most nearly adjacent scholarship that you were able to find—will come in handy.

Re-read your cousins' work with the "big problem" question in mind. In their view, what are the important themes, unresolved puzzles, or more generally the needs of the field going forward? You can jot down one of their statements and integrate it into one of your own sentences: "Following Peter Borsay's call for a greater focus on green space by urban historians…."⁴⁵ They say the field needs to go somewhere. You can volunteer to do exactly that. Of course, you may not feel a cozy affinity or allegiance to the historians who have worked on your topic so far. If your stance is more oppositional, it's fine to start out with "Despite…" or "Although…." Your contribution might be to undermine a lazy assumption that deserves to be questioned. Or perhaps the picture is incomplete, and there's a need to supplement it with evidence from a new kind of source. Regardless, by naming a historian, a stance, a familiar conclusion, or some other piece of received academic wisdom, you've found a launching pad.

Now, articulate a plan to really do something about it. This statement is what will lie at the heart of your research prospectus. Elaborate language isn't necessarily your friend here. You want to strip away hints and ambiguities and come right out and say some version of: "To get at *this*, I will look at *that*." This establishes that you don't just have an interesting question in mind. You've located evidence that will speak to that question. Perhaps it will speak to it in a clever, unexpected way. As I remarked in the Introduction, vision tempered by focus often looks like genius.

Can I guarantee that your advisor will be thrilled? I can't. As I discussed in Chap. 5, there are many possible variables at play here, including your advisor's temperament, their attitude toward novelty, and their enthusiasm for your

---

⁴³Wayne C. Booth, et al., *The Craft of Research*, 4th ed. (Chicago: University of Chicago Press, 2016), 44–45.

⁴⁴Booth et al., *Craft*, 60.

⁴⁵Jon Winder, "Revisiting the Playground: Charles Wicksteed, Play Equipment and Public Spaces for Children in Early Twentieth-Century Britain," *Urban History* 50, no. 1 (February 2023): 134–151; see 134.

particular interests. Still, "to get at *this*, I will look at *that*" protects you on two sides: By situating your work in relation to published scholarship, you show that you meet the *significance* criterion, yet your specific idea about well-chosen primary sources demonstrates that the project is *doable* and not just a question that would be nice to answer.

An example may help here. Suppose you are responding to some history of science scholarship that emphasizes how climate and habitat were only gradually recognized as key concepts for how plants and animals fit into their environment. Your particular research question is

> How did French *savants* think about habitat, climate, and ecosystems in the 1700s?

This seems like an interesting theme to pursue, but it's not immediately clear how to proceed with it. For one thing, such terms weren't commonly used in this period or lacked their modern meaning.[46]

You're aware of one celebrated case when these themes erupted into the historical record. The French naturalist François Perón spent years in Australia, organizing all his specimens by latitude. Upon the expedition's return to France, he grew agitated and wrote letters to museum staff begging them to respect his system when they unpacked the vessel. They did not, and much of his information was lost.[47] Despite his years of meticulous record keeping, his specimens from tropical reefs were tossed in with those from temperate and even chilly subarctic waters.

The fate of Perón's specimens *could* imply that his ideas were unconventional. In that case, the disposition of his boxes shows us something noteworthy about the intellectual history of the era. On the other hand, perhaps his wishes were ignored because he lacked the right social prestige and professional cachet. Or maybe he just had an annoying personality!

It would be a shame, then, to rely on just this one case. We need a better sense of the whole spectrum of attitudes toward habitat and environment in this period. Marie-Noëlle Bourguet decided to look at the people who used thermometers and recorded temperatures—whether they were natural history collectors, gardeners, or botanists—because it was likely that they were also going to be the people who were thinking about relevant issues.[48]

---

[46] Etienne S. Benson, *Surroundings: A History of Environments and Environmentalisms* (Chicago: University of Chicago Press, 2020), 11, 18.

[47] Richard W. Burkhardt, Jr., "Unpacking Baudin: Models of Scientific Practice in the Age of Lamarck," in *Jean-Baptiste Lamarck, 1744–1829*, ed. Goulven Laurent, (Paris: Éditions du Comité des travaux historiques et scientifiques, 1997), 497–514.

[48] Marie-Noëlle Bourguet, "Measurable Difference: Botany, Climate, and the Gardener's Thermometer in Eighteenth-Century France," in *Colonial Botany. Science, Commerce, and Politics in the Early Modern World*, ed. Londa Schiebinger and Claudia Swan (Philadelphia: University of Pennsylvania Press. 2005), 270–286.

This is a great example of "to get at *this*, I will look at *that*." It's also a reminder that the best method for your project might involve zeroing in on something that wouldn't have especially interested you just a little while ago. Bourguet, perhaps, had no special fascination for thermometers as such. However, the thermometer users were a proxy for the content that interested her. Assembling evidence about thermometer use offered her a way to compile a tidy set of relevant primary sources. After all, even documenting a *lack* of interest in measuring temperatures would shed some light on the problem.

If it was narrative on a grand scale that first drew you to History, then articulating a research plan that's delimited and localized this way may look puny by comparison. Don't feel like your achievement here is insignificant. In fact, a standard warning in methods books is that asking the "unmanageable or over-scaled question" is a recipe for trouble.[49] In the long run, a sharpened focus will reduce your stress and increase your project's interpretive depth and power.

In Chap. 1, I spoke of the Archimedean Point where you could accomplish big things even while standing on a small spot. How to know when you've arrived at your Archimedean Point? When you are able to state concisely and with confidence: To get at *this*, I will look at *that*. Or perhaps, here's the problem or puzzle that has engaged others; here's how I will address the problem.

It is possible to reprise some examples from this chapter in just that way:

> To get at the scope and depth of Catholic piety in England, I will look at the inventories of religious objects that appear on the pages of the churchwarden's account books.

> Some have suggested that climate and habitat were undertheorized concepts in the life sciences of the eighteenth century. A comprehensive survey of how French botanical garden keepers and natural history collectors used thermometers in their work should help us evaluate and contextualize that claim.

Sentences like these demonstrate what vision tempered by focus looks like in practice. If you are looking for more inspiration as you formulate a provisional research plan of your own, you will find that laudatory book reviews—and the statements released by prize committees about the winners—are an excellent place to find this kind of thing expressed concisely.

A one-sentence research plan may sound like it is much too short. There's sometimes a temptation to list lots of source types, as if more is necessarily better, and proof that you've been diligent and busy. It's also possible to just gesture toward the interplay of multiple source types, for example, saying that you will "weave together" evidence from two or more kinds of material. If this is the best you can do at this stage of your project, it's not the end of the world, but a more interesting and effective approach would be to construct a couple

---

[49] Patrick Dunleavy, *Authoring a PhD: How to Plan, Draft, Write, and Finish a Doctoral Thesis or Dissertation* (New York: Palgrave Macmillan, 2003), 20.

of *to get at this, I will look at that* statements that each pair off one source type with one expected benefit. Help your reader take in at a glance how using source type B compensates for a weakness in source type A.

For instance, you might be engaged in a project like Matthew Frye Jacobson's in his book *Whiteness of a Different Color*.[50] Frye acknowledged the difficulties both in writing about his subject matter and in researching it: "How... to render something at once so thick and so vaporous as *ideology* in a thin black line of linear prose?"[51] His book drew extensively from vivid, if often vague, pronouncements in popular magazines, yet he balanced this type of evidence with court cases in which the exact race of the defendant was at issue. For instance, in one miscegenation trial from 1922, a Sicilian immigrant's status as a white person was disputed.[52] The litigation showed just how seriously some people took racial categories, and also—because court cases must have outcomes—it illustrated how judges and juries handled the ambiguities that arose at the point where the rubber met the road.

While it's possible to express a research plan in just a sentence or two, a prospectus of a few pages could give all the ideas room to breathe and nail down some additional specifics. There's room for a very short lit review, for example, and a quick guided tour of the primary sources and how you will access them.

A final word about motivation. As the geographer Kim Peters aptly put it, research design is a way of answering the question "Can I actually do this study?"[53] Yet the process of formulating your research plan is also a good time to reflect on where your heart is. There are a number of projects that will pass her test: They are doable. Many might be interesting. Some would be fun. Others would be a bit of a headache, but worth the trouble. From among these, though, which plan do you really want to execute? Which facets or iterations of your project make you genuinely excited to do more? That is probably where you belong.

Conclusion

Won't new sources, methods, and questions occur to you as you go? Absolutely. Yet by the time that happens, you will already have accumulated a large amount of material on the basis of your original plan. It's worth remembering the old saying, "As the twig is bent, so grows the tree." Do your best to develop a viable plan now.

---

[50] Matthew Frye Jacobson, *Whiteness of a Different Color: European Immigrants and the Alchemy of Race* (Cambridge, MA: Harvard University Press, 1998).
[51] Jacobson, *Whiteness*, 11.
[52] Jacobson, *Whiteness*, 4.
[53] Peters, *Your Human Geography Dissertation*, 71.

With this in mind, before you invest additional days, weeks, and months with a particular set (or combination) of source materials, ask yourself:

- Reflecting on the historiography, what am I doing that others haven't? If my contribution will be in the form of incremental scholarship, how is this extension of our knowledge valuable?
- Am I investigating the small, specific, or particular in a way that does not lose sight of the large and the general (or of a comparative context)?
- Am I asking a big question about a delimited source base, locality, time period, spatial category?
- Where am I looking? What do I hope to find there? What is my evidence or reasoning that it *will* be there? Given what I am looking for, where else could I look?
- Are my primary sources appropriate to, and aligned with, my research question *as it is formulated now*?
- Is my lit review appropriate to, and aligned with, my research question *as it is formulated now*?

Then block out some serious time to think through your overall research design as best you can, collect another round of advice from librarians and archivists, and make sure you are aware of all your options.

After that period of reflection, it will be time to fill out the "Focus" checklist at the end of this chapter. Consider your tradeoffs as you design your project. I guarantee that there *will* be tradeoffs. Narrowing your focus means missing some things. Remember that making your project smaller is not an admission of defeat, though. In almost every case, the smaller iteration of your project will be more focused, deeper, and potentially more insightful.

Likewise, choosing a method means you are eschewing the strengths that would have come from other methods. In making these tradeoffs, you are facing a problem that every scholar you have ever read faced as well, so you are in good company.

You may squirm a bit at stating your project quite this bluntly; it's laying the structure bare and opening yourself to critique. But this is exactly the value in expressing it clearly and honestly right now. A good conversation with your advisor about a research plan framed in this way should put you on very solid ground going forward.

Whether or not you are expected to submit a formal prospectus, it's time to get your advisor caught up on your latest thinking and see if they have feedback. Assuming they don't send you back to the drawing board, it will be time to dive in. I'll leave you in peace for a while as you carry out your research. Part III of this book will check in with you again, as you begin to articulate major claims, and even the beginnings of a thesis statement.

Further Reading

Wayne C. Booth et al., *The Craft of Research*, 4th ed. (University of Chicago Press, 2016), although it is not aimed at students of History, is a classic on these matters.

Todd Donovan et al., *The Elements of Social Scientific Thinking*, 11th ed. (Boston: Cengage, 2013) and similar guides to research design speak well to many of the themes of this chapter (for example, the concept of taking a sample), as viewed through the lens of other disciplines.

Checking in with Your Advisor: Part Two Worksheet (The "Focus" Checklist)

The most accessible large body of primary source material for my project is _____.

What is your "sure thing"? One or two straightforward research tasks that I can accomplish with that source material are:

_____

What is your "signature" or more challenging component? I would also like to attempt a more difficult activity with primary source materials such as an archival expedition, or a more speculative use of digitized materials:

_____

A useful framework (of comparison, contrast, context) for my subject matter is _____.

If I picked an earlier starting date, a later ending date, or adopted a wider or narrower time scale, it would be _____.

Would the topic that interests me look different if I looked at it in a different location, such as _____? How about a different spatial scale (zooming in, zooming out), such as _____?

I can anticipate this issue _____ with sampling, or using my primary sources as evidence. I could address this by

_____

As a result of my forays into the source material, do I now have new keywords to search for? What about a new skill that I now feel I need to learn? _____

My research question *could be*
_____
_____
_____?

My one-sentence research plan *could be*
_____
_____
_____.

The working title of my project *could be*
_____.

When I see my advisor next, what I really want to ask them is
_____
_____.

PART III

Developing and Supporting Your Thesis

In 1910, Albert Bushnell Hart, the President of the American Historical Association, conjured up an arresting image of evidence sliding into place with no other guidance than the force of gravity. Hart believed that this was the model offered by scientific inquiry, but was quick to add:

> History, too, has its inductive method, its relentless concentration of the grain in its narrow spout, till by its own weight it seeks the only outlet. In history, too, scattered and apparently unrelated data fall together in harmonious wholes...[1]

This passage is laden with old-fashioned assumptions, but it does capture something about the *internal* process—the almost physical sensation—as ideas take form. In a wordless, subtle way, we reach a moment where we've persuaded ourselves, without quite knowing how it happened.

Persuading others is another matter. On its own, that imposing pile of evidence that wound up at the end of your chute—in Hart's analogy—may not look like much of anything to your readers. With that in mind, Chap. 9 is entitled "Imagining Claims and Counterclaims." Here, and indeed throughout Part III, you will encounter many references to how others might balk, quibble, or snipe at your proposals.

You may shrink away from such language. Isn't the word "claim" what we use for an opinion that takes some liberties with the truth? If an irritating person persists with their claims, you might mutter softly (or loudly), "You have issues—what's your problem—don't argue with me." Yet the most ordinary books on academic writing come bristling with references to problems, issues, claims, and arguments.

A call for a thesis statement is, in a sense, nothing more than a call for honesty: What does your project really intend, attempt, and accomplish? The reader needs to see your examples and evidence, but they also will want an

---

[1] Albert Bushnell Hart, "Imagination in History," *American Historical Review* 15, no. 2 (January 1910): 227–251, see 233.

explicit statement of the reasoning that holds it together, and what you think it all means.

If you are not making those things explicit, you are falling short somewhere—whether it is a failure to be forthcoming to your readers, or a lack of clarity within your own mind. If you don't ever make your reasoning explicit, you're not giving the reader a chance to evaluate whether or not it is sound. You are also cheating yourself of the opportunity to catch careless errors in your own thinking.

What is the opposite of honesty in academic writing? There's a temptation sometimes to emit a nebulous cloud of words, much like an escaping squid uses ink to confuse a predator. Your subject matter, and even your argument, may be complex. But the reader deserves to see your priorities and follow your reasoning.

Don't underestimate how much the thesis statement will help you as well. As Donald Murray urges, you yourself deserve an answer to the question "What is the one thing I must say?"[2] It will guide you in managing your time, priorities, and energy. Eventually, once all the supporting material is in place, it will leave you with a sense of completion, and of a job well done.

Chapter 9 walks you through the process of drafting a possible thesis statement. It usually requires a few false starts before you get a sense that it is coming together. I offer some warnings about common logical fallacies and other ways that a would-be thesis statement can misfire. There is a separate section dealing with claims about causation and contingency, which are particularly tricky territory. I also provide some advice about the process of reappraising and re-evaluating. Until you have really explored the likely counterclaims and critiques, you don't know your own thesis very well at all.[3]

Settling on a good thesis statement is, of course, only part of the challenge. However interesting your claim might sound, you won't seal the deal with your reader until you develop, support, extend, or refine it. You can't do that unless you marry it up, in some sense, with a body of evidence. Yet the moment you move to *support* your claim, the task becomes different.

Which type of evidence speaks most effectively to the claim? Perhaps you've decided to deploy a graph and a map, but you have little experience creating content in either of these formats. Or you're going to drop in some photos, but you need to decide which ones, and how to caption and contextualize them. For each type of evidence, the conventional rules and methods vary, as do the classic pitfalls that lie in wait for beginners.

An influential book by the philosopher Stephen Toulmin, *The Uses of Argument,* focuses on exactly this issue. Toulmin put the spotlight on warrants, which implicitly authorize the move from a *certain type* of evidence to a *certain*

---

[2] Donald M. Murray, *The Craft of Revision,* 5th ed. (Boston: Thomson and Heinle, 2004), 46.
[3] The famous formulation of this is John Stuart Mill, *On Liberty* (1859), Chapter 2.

kind of conclusion.⁴ For our purposes here, this is a reminder that the considerations involved in evaluating a graph as fair, accurate, and persuasive are not identical, or interchangeable, with the standards for evaluating whether a quotation is handled in a fair, accurate, and persuasive way. Likewise, what we'd consider a reasonable interpretation of a photograph doesn't line up neatly with the process required to assess the merits of a map. For this reason, Chap. 10, "Supporting Claims with Evidence," has separate sections devoted to verbal, numerical, visual, and spatial warrants, respectively.

Maybe you're tempted to skip directly to a section in Chap. 10 that you know will have an obvious application. However, nearly every project has opportunities to use more than one type of evidence. I hope that reading about all four types will make you more astute and enterprising about pulling in less familiar materials. Perhaps you weren't expecting to use one evidence type (political cartoons? census records?), but it could turn out to be a lifesaver.

From beginning to end, Part III encourages you to play devil's advocate and investigate whether the overall design of your argument will stand up to scrutiny. To achieve that, you needn't anticipate a skeptical reader who's disposed to question everything you have set down on paper. As Toulmin noted, if we kept questioning every warrant, nothing would get done; it would be as if our discipline did not admit any warrants at all.⁵ However, the odds are excellent that *some* readers will raise *a few* serious questions. Your reading in the historiography—and, in particular, among your cousins, as defined in Chap. 3—should help you anticipate the challenges here. What is the likely objection to your particular claim? What is the common reservation that scholars bring up about the type of evidence that you rely on the most?

Working out the trouble spots on these issues sets you up to succeed at all the subsequent stages of the writing process. The implications here go well beyond reaching a sense that you are on solid ground with your overall position. It can shed light on the perennial question "how much evidence is enough?" With a clear idea of how your thesis relates to your evidence, it will be much easier to think about organization and your use of space in the paper, right down to the level of the individual paragraphs in which that evidence will appear.

In contrast, the student who's merely told to "write up their findings" may include all sorts of material, leaving it to the reader to sort through the relevant, the semi-relevant, and the irrelevant that wound up at the end of the chute. My aim in Part III is to invite you to undertake a more deliberate and artful process, crafting a thesis and considering how to back it up in a coherent, persuasive way. The worksheet at the end of Part III offers you a chance to reconnect with your advisor and talk through some of these issues out loud.

---

⁴ Stephen Toulmin, *The Uses of Argument*, rev. ed. (Cambridge: Cambridge University Press, 2003), 91–92.
⁵ Toulmin, *Uses*, 98–99.

CHAPTER 9

Imagining Claims and Counterclaims

As an illustrative example for his textbook on rhetoric, Erasmus wrote and rewrote one sentence of greeting—"Your letter pleased me mightily"—150 different ways.[1] This performance still makes for entertaining reading five hundred years later, but many writers will balk at the idea of devoting this much attention to a single sentence.

The good news is that there are only a few places in your paper that require anywhere near this level of attention. One of them is your title; another is your thesis statement. What your readers see there will shape how they read and understand everything else. The title and the thesis statement should be the most eloquent parts of your final product. If you are going to think clearly, state memorably, and argue persuasively, these are the places to do it.

Since we're not in a contest with Erasmus, let's imagine stating the same thing *fifteen* different ways. If you try, you'll find that what you wind up with is *not* the same thing after all. It's fifteen different patterns of emphasis, fifteen different messages, fifteen slightly—but maybe significantly—different answers to the same question. For this reason, an afternoon spent tinkering with your thesis statement might start out as just a polishing session, but wind up somewhere much more substantial.

In general, a successful thesis statement is

- Simple enough to state concisely
- Specific and plainly stated (no softening or euphemism)
- Evidence-based (you may even mention the type of evidence in your thesis statement itself)
- Consequential (e.g., the contribution is not just at the level of bringing us more detail on the topic)

[1] Erasmus, "Copia," in *The Rhetorical Tradition: Readings from Classical Times to the Present*, ed. Patricia Bizzell and Bruce Herzberg, 2nd ed. (Boston: Bedford St. Martins, 2001), 605–609.

- Different from what someone would get out of a textbook-style narrative
- In dialogue with the best and most closely related scholarship
- Somewhat novel, in the sense that it moves the scholarly conversation forward
- Intellectually honest (fair to opposing positions and interpretations)
- Intellectually modest (makes claims or draws conclusions that don't exceed the scale of your project or the nature of your actual findings).

If your first impulse is to write a thesis statement down the lines of "it's a crime and scandal that more hasn't been written on this astounding subject matter," then you're suffering from what might be called "lily pad myopia." If most of us are blatantly overlooking your frog and your lily pad, it's because most of us aren't lying on our stomach in that section of swamp. The infinite regress of historical detail means that a sense of significance is fractal: You can zoom in limitlessly, each time experiencing a rush of portentousness as hitherto unseen objects loom large.

It's time to come up for air. It's understandable that you've been immersed for a while in your own chosen sources and your own thoughts. What you need to do now is to look back to your notes from Chap. 3 on your cousins, and more generally, your lit review. This is the conventional wisdom from which, perhaps, your work departs. Reviewing your notes on where the field stands now will help you assess whether you are addressing some of the bullet points above—notably the ones about whether your thesis statement is "consequential" and "novel." Setting your conclusions in direct dialogue with others' work is also one of the most efficient and straightforward ways to help other people share your enthusiasm for the material that fascinates you.

It may be tempting to avoid taking a stand on anything. However, a thesis-free paper—however long, however detailed—is likely to come across, in the words of the proverb, as "The mountain labored, and brought forth a mouse." Moreover, a weak thesis is an improvable thesis. Stating your claim plainly, without weasel words, is more than just a way to jump through a hoop and meet academic expectations. Really hearing yourself say the thesis "out loud" is the best way to give yourself a chance to step back and critique it.

You already knew that you'd be expected to generate a thesis statement, but I want you to take it a step further and articulate *the best claim that you can, given the evidence you have assembled*. With this in mind, I will walk you through some exercises to help you get a draft thesis statement down on paper, but more importantly, I will also challenge you to carefully consider the most likely counterclaims. This isn't always pleasant, but it is an indispensable step. Whatever position you take, consider: From what direction would a challenge come? If you can "foresee the objections and reservations real readers will have regarding your arguments," that will give you a chance to modify your thesis statement to make it more clear, more nuanced, more complex, more reasonable, more resistant to the toughest charge anyone could throw at it.[2]

Will you have only one claim? Is it possible to have more than one thesis statement? In a long, complex work of History, it is not unusual to have more than one sentence (or paragraph) that clearly possesses some degree of thesis statement energy. For instance, in Beverly Gage's biography of J. Edgar Hoover, she writes:

> "McCarthyism," the word that came to capture the sordid side of anticommunist politics, would turn out to be mostly a surface phenomenon, a wild media drama of accusation and counteraccusation, of truth and lies. "Hooverism," the less popular term, came first, lasted longer, and mattered more.[3]

Yet anticommunism is not the only theme in Gage's book. She remarks on the FBI director's uneasy encounter with two former protégés who

> represented two sides of Hoover's legacy: Moore the professional lawman, ostensibly devoted to expertise, local-federal cooperation, and scientific methods; Hanes the passionate conservative and standard-bearer for segregation, willing to stretch and evade the law in order to promote his cause.[4]

Those themes and tensions, perhaps even more than anticommunism, resonate in nearly every chapter and subsection of the biography. In a book that exceeds 800 pages, I do not doubt that another reader might locate additional passages that would deserve consideration here, or that Gage herself, if invited to join the conversation, might offer a subtly different reading of her own work.

In books about academic success or the writing of research papers, there is no shortage of generic advice about thesis statements. Beyond the basics, which I have just shared with you, their suggestions are often not especially useful for students of History. Policy-oriented disciplines expect you to identify a key issue and then offer some sort of solution to the problem, which usually isn't in the cards when we are dealing with past events. Advice emanating from the social sciences may nudge you toward statistical concepts such as sample size and correlation. Unless you and your advisor are on the same page with the decision, you should steer clear of any reference to things being correlated. This has a specific association in statistics; very few historians use formal social science methods to that extent. Another suggestion you may encounter in many templates for academic writing is that a thesis statement would include the word "because"; historians have a sufficiently fraught relationship with that word that I devote a whole section of this chapter to the pitfalls there.

---

[2] Andrea A. Lunsford, *Everything's an Argument*, 2nd ed. (New York: Bedford St. Martin's, 2000), 103.
[3] Gage, *G-Man*, 386.
[4] Gage, *G-Man*, 545.

Warning you off certain language, though, doesn't go far in helping you understand how historians *do* articulate claims. The wordy, narrative-oriented writing style favored in our discipline means that it is sometimes difficult to spot thesis statements in our favorite books and articles. Moreover, trends in philosophy and theory have distanced many of the humanities disciplines from older notions about claims and proof. So this chapter, necessarily, begins with some reflections on where historians fit into these conversations.

What Do Historians Think About Truth?

Perhaps it sounds old-fashioned to suggest that you'll assemble evidence to support your conclusions. It's helpful to consider an example. F.A. Hayek's book *The Road to Serfdom* was published in 1944. It argued that encroachments on economic freedom—such as those favored by socialist political parties—would inevitably compromise other forms of freedom, including individual rights and democratic political norms. Winston Churchill gave a speech in 1945 that sounded like it drew inspiration from its pages; it implied that if the Labour Party won the next election, it could mean the end of democracy in Britain. When Hayek himself heard about the speech, he believed that Churchill had read his book.[5] We might venture a thesis statement:

> Under Hayek's influence, Churchill wrote his infamous "Gestapo speech" or "Crazy Broadcast" that some speculate cost him the 1945 election.

Yet just because Hayek's book had seen the light of day doesn't mean that all conservatives immediately read it, liked it, and started to draw inspiration from it. Churchill's own formative years as a politician and speechwriter already lay far in the past. In particular, what should we do with the information that 1929 Conservative Party campaign posters had sported slogans such as "Socialism would mean inspectors all round" and "If you want to call your soul your own, vote Conservative"?[6] If your thesis statement put the spotlight firmly on Hayek's 1944 publication, this would be a big problem. It would be reckless to leave yourself open to accusations of either distorting the overall picture or suppressing evidence.[7] A single piece of evidence can make all the difference. At the very least, it can *disprove* something.

To the question "Can we agree on any facts?," most historians would answer yes. While what we expect to develop is one interpretation among many, not one fact to rule them all, sometimes we must insist that a statement is factually incorrect. As in the case of Churchill's "Gestapo" speech, new information in the form of a fact can make an interpretation less convincing.

---

[5] Richard Toye, "Winston Churchill's 'Crazy Broadcast': Party, Nation, and the 1945 Gestapo Speech," *Journal of British Studies* 49, no. 3 (July 2010): 655–680, see 665.

[6] Toye, "Churchill," 665.

[7] On this point, see also Evans, *Defense*, 126.

However, if you wander into an academic debate at random, you're more likely to catch historians debating which facts are relevant, than which facts are factual. Any conversation about relevance, though, leads us quickly into more ambiguous territory about what sort of history we value, what sorts of questions matter most, and why. For this reason, sometimes the most important things that historians say are not statements about facts.

The reception of E. P. Thompson's work illustrates this well. Perhaps the most-quoted line from *The Making of the English Working Class* is his stated aspiration to rescue certain groups from "the enormous condescension of posterity."[8] We might debate whether, in the terms of Aristotelian rhetoric, this is an example of *pathos* (tugging at our heartstrings) or *ethos* (inviting us to agree in the spirit of shared values). It is, in any case, more like a mission statement than a thesis statement.

Thompson's thesis also appears in his Preface, when he says:

> The working class did not rise like the sun at an appointed time. It was present at its own making.[9]

This is a good example of how a thesis statement doesn't always encapsulate *all* the elements (there's a claim here, but no reasoning or evidence), or, indeed, tease out all the contexts and implications. Yet Thompson's statement has proven to be a very helpful provocation. It was, in the best sense of the word, suggestive. The rich conversation that flowed out of, around, and in opposition to Thompson's statement shows how productive it was, even if our first rejoinder is only "it was present, in what sense?"

The responses to—and refinements of—Thompson over the years amount to almost a subfield all by itself.[10] To mention only one example, Carolyn Steedman, Alison Light, and Selina Todd have asked what happens if we "rewrite the history of the working class to place servants at the centre, rather than at the margins, of this narrative."[11] While Thompson looked for early examples of labor unions, protest, and public articulations of defiance, class conflict looks different when it is enacted in an intimate domestic space, with the workers rarely coming into contact with each other. A clash of mistress versus maid, intriguingly, features women on both sides of the conflict. A servant might also experience their work as a temporary life stage or a short-term expedient, rather than perceiving it as a meaningful occupational or class category. Each of these insights subtly—or not so subtly—revises what we imagine Thompson's terms "working class," "present," and "making" might even mean.

The complex reception of Thompson's classic is also a reminder that academic debate does not always follow what specialists in rhetoric call an

---

[8] E.P. Thompson, *The Making of the English Working Class* (New York: Vintage, 1966), 12.
[9] Thompson, *Making*, 9.
[10] Burton and Fortado, eds., *Histories of a Radical Book*.
[11] Selina Todd, "Domestic Service and Class Relations in Britain 1900–1950," *Past & Present* 203, no. 1 (May 2009): 181–204, see 182.

agonistic process, in which one side expects victory of the sort that is only demonstrable through an opponent's defeat. Some arguments are better characterized as exploratory or invitational.[12] Urging "look here instead" is not quite a thesis statement on its own, but paired with a thoughtful suggestion about what we can find in that other place, it comes close. *Rogerian* argument, named after the psychotherapist Carl Rogers, actively seeks out a middle ground and considers a "win-win" outcome as not wishy-washy or intellectually dishonest, but as a positive accomplishment.[13]

When students seek to complicate the terrain already explored by their former teachers and mentors, or when scholars with similar interests and values congregate to discuss the legacy of a classic work such as Thompson's *Making*, the behaviors we would associate with invitational or Rogerian argument are often present. This is more than mere etiquette—these alternative modes of argument express a genuinely different vision of what the shared search for truth should look and feel like. Incremental scholarship, discussed in Chap. 5, understandably takes this tone quite often. A thesis statement, then, *could be* a pointed, pugnacious contention. But historians do not always take that path.

Is it possible to convey a thesis through narration alone? Consider how often historians put the spotlight on hypocrisy, unintended consequences, valiant failures, and good intentions gone horribly wrong. Few of us would explicitly self-identify as the authors of tragedies, but portraying a situation as tragic is an interpretive lens of a sort. Claudia Koonz's *Mothers in the Fatherland: Women, the Family, and Nazi Politics* is a helpful example to consider here.[14] It forces us to confront the reality that women—newly empowered with the right to vote—cast many votes for the Nazi Party, no friend to feminism. Moreover, Koonz shows that after Hitler came to power, some women eagerly seized on the bits of power available to them as petty officials or functionaries of the regime.

If poignant storytelling were the only standard, perhaps *Mothers in the Fatherland* could have been a short book. For instance, Leni Riefenstahl was a respected film director at a time when there were almost no women in that role anywhere in the world, yet she became irrevocably associated with her work filming Nazi political rallies. It would not take many words to evoke the irony, or the tragedy, of Riefenstahl putting her exceptional talents at the disposal of the Nazi state. In fact, I just did.

Mothers in the Fatherland, in contrast, is more than five hundred pages long, because historians care about breadth of scope, as well as the quantity and quality of evidence. Koonz delves into the workings of the Women's Bureau, the experience of officials in the Teacher's Union, the impressions of intellectuals who hoped to somehow compromise with the new regime, the somewhat

---

[12] Lunsford, *Everything's an Argument*, 5.

[13] Lunsford, *Everything's an Argument*, 6–7.

[14] Claudia Koonz, *Mothers in the Fatherland: Women, the Family, and Nazi Politics* (New York: St. Martin's Press, 1987).

distinct trajectories of Protestant and Catholic women, and more. She also complicates the picture when the evidence demands it. Female concentration camp guards exceeded their male colleagues in gratuitous cruelty, yet even the most ideologically loyal women expressed shock at the *Lebensborn* program when they became aware of it.[15]

It is also worth noticing that Koonz's book also contains thesis statement language of the conventional kind. Here, she is helping us understand *how* things worked and where Nazi women fit into the larger system:

> Looking back at Nazi Germany, it seems that decency vanished; but when we listen to feminine voices from the period, we realize instead that it was cordoned off. Loyal Nazis fashioned an image for themselves, a fake domestic realm where they felt virtuous.[16]

When you share your first draft, I doubt that your advisor's critique will be that you didn't tell the story well. They are much more likely to say "are you sure that quotation supports the point you are trying to make here?" or "I don't follow your reasoning in this part." The focus of this chapter will be on preparing you for that kind of dialogue, and those kinds of objections. It's this analytical exposition that you really need to get right.

Even castles in the air have load-bearing walls. With that in mind, before I encourage you to get creative and brainstorm possible thesis statements, I need to cover a few things that I hope you *won't* write down.

Avoiding Common Errors

It's easy to find books that round up famous logical fallacies. Those lists can be a bit tedious, but they are a necessary reminder that having *a* logical structure for your claim doesn't mean that it'll be accepted as a *valid* logical structure. For instance:

> From the moment that President Reagan said "Mr. Gorbachev, tear down this Wall," it was clear that the Soviets, weakened by economic failure and foreign misadventures, could not refuse him.

Thoughtful people will be quick to offer other possible explanations for the exact timing of the collapse of Communism in East Germany, from the acquiescence of the East German border guards to the actions of the exuberant crowds and Gorbachev's order for the Soviet troops to stay in their barracks. This error in argument was recognized as such, and named by the Romans: *Post hoc, ergo propter hoc* (this came after that, therefore the one thing caused the other). I suppose, if you fall into this error, that puts you in a long and

---

[15] Koonz, *Mothers*, 399–400; 404.
[16] Koonz, *Mothers*, 17.

time-honored tradition! Still, it's not company that you'd want to keep. This is the sort of thesis statement that will get sent right back to you for revision.

Yet many of the common mishaps aren't failures of logic, as such. Some statements aren't even specific enough to be wrong.

> Juries remained all male in Athens, as women were seen as incapable of public duties.

Using passive voice often sets you up for trouble. Seen as incapable, by whom? Historians will always resist language that implies a general consensus that may not have existed. Occasionally, you might deploy passive voice just to register a prevailing norm, but your thesis statement ought to name the suspects. What's especially frustrating about a formulation like "women were seen as incapable" is that it throws off this offhand, vague remark at exactly the point where you ought to be the most specific (who, when, where, how) and precise about the relationships involved.

Placeholder explanations leave a relationship, activity, or dynamic dangerously vague. Consider a statement like this:

> The dictatorship failed because of economics.

When it comes to the dictatorship's economic record, what claim is that sentence even making? Was it rising inflation that ate into the standard of living? Was it the relationship between interest rates, unemployment, and the stock market? Was it an experiment with central planning and import substitution that went horribly wrong? We have no idea. When I see statements like that, I want to retort:

> She broke up with me because of psychology.

Like the first statement, this tells us nothing about what went wrong, yet what went wrong is at the heart of the matter. The good news here is that expressing yourself more clearly can also mean developing a real explanation or interpretation, rather than gesturing toward a direction from which you hope an explanation might appear.

Writers are not in the habit of spelling out what they consider common sense; yet my common sense might be—in your eyes—a startling or unreasonable assumption. To help clarify the situation, we use the term *warrant*, which in the realm of rhetoric is defined as a general principle that connects a reason to a claim.[17] A very old use of the word appears in an antislavery poem from 1781: "Canst thou ... Trade in the blood of innocence, and plead Expedience

---

[17] Booth et al., *Craft*, 155.

as a warrant for the deed?"[18] This example should serve as a reminder that accepting or rejecting a warrant is a very important choice for the reader, and they *do* have a choice.

Every field of study and subject matter area has its set of shared assumptions, habits, and conventions. In conversations between experts, these are left implied, or are stated in an extremely compressed form.[19] For instance, an article in the social sciences that deploys statistical methods normally won't define common statistical terms. It would be even rarer for it to defend the value of quantification in the first place!

Practitioners operating within a theoretical or ideological framework also display this behavior. Perhaps one school of serious film criticism is premised on the notion that a great film must be enigmatic and unsettling. A roundup of the contenders at this year's Cannes Film Festival will jump in, without prologue, and start demonstrating whether the new work meets that standard. As this example suggests, the warrant is often simultaneously the least articulated part of an argument, *and* the connective tissue that enables the other parts of the argument to interact successfully.[20]

To appreciate why warrants are so important, it is helpful to recall your own experience of reading a text with an implicit warrant *that you didn't like*. This can be positively distressing. For instance, a libertarian writing for other libertarians might, understandably, take certain presumptive shared values as a given, and perhaps even a body of context and past experience. Yet for someone outside that circle, reading such a text can be rather like swallowing a telescope when you thought it looked like a small lozenge. Does this mean that libertarians can never write successfully for anyone else? They can. But they have some explaining to do.

For similar reasons, take special care to explain any interdisciplinary warrants that you use. Not everyone knows, or agrees with, particular strands of postcolonial theory or intersectional feminist analysis. The list goes on. Here is a thesis statement that will perplex some readers:

> The eighteenth-century coffeehouse offers a perfect illustration of how social capital is the glue that holds societies together.

Perhaps a few of your readers have never heard of social capital. Others, better informed, will quickly think of *alternative* conceptual frameworks that appeal to them more. For example, tight-knit circles can be unfriendly to outsiders. Perhaps the coffeehouses in question were notable for excluding women. To readers thinking down those lines, the reference to social capital will

---

[18] *Oxford English Dictionary*, s.v. "Warrant" (N1), William Cowper poem cited as an example under 8a, accessed 1/22/2023.
[19] Booth et al., *Craft*, 158.
[20] Lunsford, *Everything's an Argument*, 107.

look—not like a foundation stone for a towering edifice—but like an assumption that needs defending.

There is no perfect remedy here, but moving from an unstated warrant to a stated warrant will help. You can show some humility by using language such as "inspired by …" or "in the tradition of …" which signals to readers that you are grounded in a particular framework of analysis, although you know that this is not the only possible framework. Thus, rather than slipping in the warrant as if it were a principle that commands universal assent, you can present it as a lens that you will deploy. Owning your warrants and devising language that makes them clear to your readers also offers you a chance to reflect critically on your own assumptions. Are you comfortable relying on this warrant as much as you do?

Many rhetoric textbooks discuss warrants almost solely in terms of values (a cherished principle, a favored concept, an attachment to a particular goal or pet issue). The examples supplied here are consistent with this. However, warrants are also important in the context of using special types of primary sources as backing for your claims. This is not really about subscription to an ideology or adherence to a theoretical lens, but rather we are dealing with "specific principles of reasoning that belong to particular communities of researchers."[21] Some of us support our reasoning with numbers. Others rely on visual evidence. We will return to those considerations in Chap. 10.

Take some time to reflect on every important term or concept that shows up in your claim. You would not write a thesis statement—even in draft form—that included an obviously derogatory term like "loose women." After spending weeks immersed in social work bulletins from the 1950s, though, you might articulate a thesis about "juvenile delinquents," a term that characterizes human beings purely as a problem and perhaps prejudges desirable policy outcomes. Seemingly unexceptional language can carry worrying baggage:

> At the height of the crisis, a moderate faction made their voices heard and saved the republic.

Moderate is, of course, a term that only has meaning relative to some standard of comparison. This thesis statement might trouble readers who are aware that these so-called moderates took very immoderate positions on an important issue. Perhaps this faction only appears moderate if it is compared to some really militant extremists, in which case the label is a little disingenuous.

Abstract terms are ripe for quibbles and misunderstandings about definition. When you say "capitalism" or "patriarchy," what do you have in mind? What counts as "rural"? Even designations such as "liberal" or "reactionary" may raise eyebrows. A heated debate once raged about whether or not the eccentric Protestant sect known as the Ranters even existed. Of course, expecting the Ranters to keep minutes at their meetings, and maintain a list of dues paying

---

[21] Booth et al., *Craft*, 157.

members, is probably asking a bit much for such an irreverent sect. Yet doubts persisted—if the whole notion of Ranters was the overblown bogeyman of fearmongering pamphleteers, then responsible historians should steer clear of applying that label to any real person.

A closer look at that particular controversy shows that the various scholars weren't actually adopting the same working definition of Ranter. Some treated it as "persons who are known to have called *themselves* Ranters," while others thought in terms of "persons called Ranters, or reputed to be such, by others," "people moving in a demonstrably Ranter-like milieu," or perhaps "people known to have believed several of the religious tenets associated with Ranters."[22] In such a climate, you owe it to your readers to make it clear which definition you have adopted. Kathryn Gucer found a way to stake out her own distinct perspective and build something like a thesis statement around it:

> In this debate about the Ranters we can see the process by which pamphleteers invented a linguistic means of talking about religious diversity before it was an accepted feature of English society.[23]

As the Ranters example suggests, sometimes one or more participants in a conversation need to spell out either their claims, their warrants, or their definitions. Until this occurs, it may not be apparent what the root of the disagreement actually is. Sorting this out may generate assent when it would not otherwise be forthcoming, or it may just help the conversation move forward to the next logical stage. You can't control what others do, but if you are honest, explicit, and clear about your own argument, you are doing your part to clarify the whole situation.

Darrell Huff, in his book *How to Lie with Statistics*, offered some advice in a sarcastic spirit: "If you can't prove what you want to prove, demonstrate something else and pretend that they are the same thing."[24] This goes on too often, and not just in the realm of statistics. One of the most common subterfuges is to offer the reader a false choice, to force them to pick the alternative you are offering. A whole subgenre of "special topics" readers for History students once adopted binary opposites as its stock in trade, reducing *every* possible controversy to two choices. Titles included *Huey P. Long—Southern Demagogue or American Democrat?* and *The Medieval Mind—Faith or Reason?*[25] Pedagogically, there is probably a place for this, particularly if the target readership is the student who is encountering—for the first time—the idea that credentialed, respected historians might disagree about something important.

---

[22] Ariel Hessayon, "The Ranters and Their Sources: The Question of Jacob Boehme's Supposed Influence," *Sciences et Techniques en Perspective* second series, 16, no. 2 (2014): 77–102.

[23] Kathryn Gucer, "'Not Heretofore Extant in Print': Where the Mad Ranters Are," *Journal of the History of Ideas* 61, no. 1 (January 2000): 75–95, see 75.

[24] Darrell Huff, *How to Lie with Statistics* (New York: W.W. Norton, 1993), 76.

[25] David Hackett Fischer, *Historians' Fallacies: Toward a Logic of Historical Thought* (New York: Harper & Row, 1970), 10–11.

You are not writing for that readership now. Offering a false choice or an exaggerated contrast like this is known as putting up a "straw man"—you aren't engaging with a real opponent that might put up a fight, you're trotting out a lifeless doll that's guaranteed to lose.

Another notorious fallacy is false comparison. For instance, someone might say "being President is a lot like being a restaurant owner"—presumably followed by "and I've been a restaurant owner, so let me tell you ...."[26] In the History classroom, we occasionally encounter this kind of thinking:

> They did it this way when I served in the U.S. Army in 2004, therefore they must have done it that way in 1962.

Not so. Indeed, that policy or rule may have existed in 2004 precisely because it was absent in 1962, and the Army learned from its mistakes.

Despite our training to avoid anachronism, professional historians are not immune to the temptations here. G.A. Williamson, writing his translator's introduction to Eusebius' *History of the Church* in 1966, remarked:

> No one can read Eusebius's account of how the cathedral of Tyre, with all its elaborate symbolism, rose from the ashes, without thinking of Coventry. Truly that generation and this are one.[27]

Williamson referred to an event familiar to many of his readers:, the obliteration of the historic Coventry Cathedral by the Luftwaffe during World War II, and the subsequent inauguration of a rebuilt Cathedral—with much fanfare—on the site of the ruin.

It may seem harmless enough for Williamson, no doubt genuinely moved, to bring up Coventry. Yet are the situations even similar? Eusebius described the dedication of the new church in Book X, but just pages earlier, in Book IX, we learn about the gruesome fate of the pagan adversaries who destroyed the old church. They were purged and tortured. Artworks honoring them were "flung from a height to the ground and smashed."[28] With these legacies of mistrust and surviving tensions between neighbors, Tyre has more in common with a deeply divided post-conflict society such as today's Bosnia than it does with post-1945 Britain. The Coventry analogy actually works to obscure this.

To be fair to Williamson—and to the many others who have drawn on their subject position while researching and writing—if we felt no kinship at all with people in the past, if we detected no ways in which their moment might speak to our own, we might not be motivated to write history at all. When we elevate

---

[26] Harry Phillips and Patricia Bostian, *The Purposeful Argument: A Practical Guide*, brief 2nd ed., (Stamford, CT: Cengage Learning, 2015), 133.

[27] Eusebius, *The History of the Church from Christ to Constantine*, trans. G.A. Williamson (New York: New York University Press, 1966), 10.

[28] Eusebius, *History of the Church*, 378.

this to a point-for-point equivalence, however, it becomes anachronism and false comparison.

Like many fallacies, this is easier to detect in others than in yourself. Perhaps this particular fallacy is so tempting because lived personal experience is so immersive and profound. Your life may not have included Williamson's experience of living through a war and then watching a city reborn from rubble. But you have other lived experiences that may evoke this profound sense of affinity. For example, a historian who has experienced post-traumatic stress disorder could write about shell-shocked soldiers in World War I. A historian who once earned income from sex work could write about sex workers in that same town one hundred years earlier. The list of possibilities is rich and varied. These are all powerful experiences and they are a legitimate wellspring of creative, interesting research *topics* and research *questions*. Like Williamson, you may choose to acknowledge your experience and your sense of affinity at some point in your paper.

However, the place to incorporate this is in not your thesis statement. There is no amount of evidence derived from your experience in today's world that will establish something about what appears to be the "same" subject position in a different time and place. This is not about diminishing or invalidating your experience; it is about showing a fundamental respect for how people in the past may have thought, felt, or experienced something differently. Consider, too, that—as in the case of Coventry and Tyre—it is exactly in the *differences* where the most surprising and interesting dimensions of the material may emerge.

Finally, an overly ambitious or dismissive thesis is one of the easiest ways to trigger the reader's skepticism.

Based on my examination of these sources, we can dispose of Historian A.

Many admired historians have had a few flaws exposed. If your aim is to take issue with one aspect of a well-known book, be clear what you are rejecting, but also what you don't dispute in the book. "I've discredited this person" or even "I've discredited this approach" is in most cases an unnecessarily tough proposition for you to defend. A strong paper *does* have to be historiographically grounded, but it *doesn't* have to be either a crisp affirmation or a conclusive rebuttal. For example, if the existing scholarship on an era discusses change a great deal, then simply by making the choice to explore what did *not* change, you can gently redirect the conversation.[29]

There's no reason that a moderate position must be evenhanded to the point of incoherence. Even when we articulate a conclusion, it is okay (and even desirable) to express both what we know and what we don't know, in a clear and forthright manner. Why, then, are moderate positions so uncommon?

[29] Judith Pollmann and Henk te Velde, eds., *Civic Continuities in an Age of Revolutionary Change, c.1750–1850* (New York: Palgrave Macmillan, 2023).

Perhaps it is because people who have invested a great deal of time and effort in a project intuitively feel that big work should justify big claims. If you're feeling that temptation, remember that adopting a vigorous "change" thesis will predictably draw a quibble or pushback about continuity, and vice versa. Advisors will have more respect for the student who qualifies their position than for the strong advocate who won't listen to the voices of moderation. You can start by listening to the voice of moderation in your own head. It may have a soft voice, but it's there if you listen for it.

Drafting a Provisional Thesis Statement

It's time to get something down on paper. If "articulating my thesis" sounds too daunting, think of this task as drafting a quick guided tour or progress report of where your research stands now. The trick, though, is stating it in a compact, clear way. In the first decade of the twentieth century, Max Weber's formulation of his thesis in *The Protestant Ethic and the Spirit of Capitalism* ran to 138 words.[30] Writing guides today counsel brevity: "The argument only needs to be a paragraph or perhaps even a sentence, capturing your main idea."[31]

How could you possibly express something that big in a single sentence? If you're feeling anxious on this point, it's helpful to look at some examples of scholars who managed to pack something very close to an entire thesis statement into their title itself. These are some terrific role models for concise writing. We've already seen some examples by historians, including *Mothers in the Fatherland*. In an earlier chapter, I discussed Christopher Browning's *Ordinary Men*, about Holocaust perpetrators from unexceptional backgrounds who received little indoctrination. Historians like titles that put the spotlight firmly on a turning point or transition, like Beth L. Bailey's *From Front Porch to Back Seat: Courtship in Twentieth-Century America*.[32]

Once you start looking for book and article titles that get the reader more than halfway there, you'll find they are quite common: "Frederick Law Olmstead: Landscape Architecture as Conservative Reform."[33] You may have heard that a thesis statement should be something intellectually robust enough that a person could disagree with it. Some titles, on their own, are so assertive that you may feel you disagree with a book that you haven't even opened yet. Some titles rebut earlier titles; James Scott's book *Seeing like a State* prompted an article by Fernando Coronil, "Smelling like a Market."[34]

I hope these examples have boosted your confidence that you, too, could express something complex and important in a compact format. Try to be this

---

[30] As quoted in English translation in Lipson, *How to Write*, 114–115.
[31] Lipson, *How to Write*, 113.
[32] Baltimore: Johns Hopkins University Press, 1988.
[33] Geoffrey Blodgett, *Journal of American History* 62, no. 4 (March 1976): 869–889.
[34] Fernando Coronil, "Smelling Like a Market," *American Historical Review* 106, no. 1 (February 2001): 119–129.

brief and you may feel that a whole sentence or paragraph really gives your thesis statement room to stretch out!

Don't panic if you are jotting down claims that are something less than earth shaking. Originality in a thesis statement can take modest forms:

> The declassified material confirms the importance of the North/South divide in Pope John Paul II's thought about global issues.

Notice that this language also nods to what primary sources informed the research. This thesis statement does so as well:

> A review of the secret correspondence undermines the impression that the Vatican and the Reagan Administration thought, and acted, with unanimity on international affairs.[35]

Many historians frame their thesis along such lines, basically saying, "[I]f we approach it through these sources, we see things differently in the following ways."

Even in your fully developed thesis statement, you won't be saying *everything*, but you will be connecting the important dots for the reader. Be sure to move the academic conversation forward from where it is *now*.

> These days, it won't impress too many people if you assert "Gender was important."

Maybe there's a need to refine *how* gender was important, or correct a particular misunderstanding in this area. Thavolia Glymph's formulation in *Out of the House of Bondage* is a good example:

> Mollie's desire to put her money on her "back" and Wilborn's to own pillows might superficially seem to smack of a lack of political awareness, [however] ... The dresses, pillows, and other material purchases black women made testify to the meagerness of black people's lives in slavery and to the promise of fullness in freedom.[36]

Refining the picture needn't come across as a stark negation of what others have written. I suppose you could take "Reagan was a transformational figure who inspired many and recast American politics for a generation" and posit the opposite: "Reagan accomplished nothing in office." Here we have an unexpected thesis, but it is overdone. "Reagan was a partly transformational figure"

---

[35] These two examples are my summary of Marie Gayte, "The Vatican and the Reagan Administration: A Cold War Alliance?" *Catholic Historical Review* 97, no. 4 (October 2011): 713–736.

[36] Thavolia Glymph, *Out of the House of Bondage: The Transformation of the Plantation Household* (Cambridge: Cambridge University Press, 2008), 205.

is nuanced, but not in a precise or particularly useful way. What do you have in mind here? Perhaps it is the fact that the Department of Education survived two terms of Reagan as President, even though he ran on a platform promising to abolish it.[37] How about this:

> Although Reagan has the reputation of being an ideologically-driven and transformational figure, at the end of his eight years in office, several of the pledges in the 1980 Republican platform remained unimplemented, because ...

We needn't agree with this statement to appreciate that it gets at a different, less predictable conclusion. "Although ... because" thesis statements are explicitly recommended in many books on writing, since—in a small number of words—they pack in complexity, a sense of significance, a crisp takeaway conclusion, and even a nod to the alternative possible viewpoints that will occur to some readers.[38] However, dropping in that little word "because" sets you up, potentially, for so many problems that the whole next section will take a closer look at that tricky area.

Writing About Causation, Contingency, and Change over Time

In his rhetoric textbook *The Office of Assertion*, Scott Crider explores different styles of formulating a claim, remarking that "vital verbs" lend excitement to your writing. He offers this example from a student paper on *The Iliad*: "Agamemnon's imprudence releases Hektor's rampage."[39]

Such sentences are probably more appropriate and plausible on this person-to-person scale, although just because it's a tidy turn of phrase doesn't—in itself—make it the most accurate characterization of what happened. Consider the work that same verb, "to release," performs in a different sentence, such as this one about the U.S. Presidential campaign of 1988:

> Lee Atwater's unscrupulous political advertisements released the deluge of racist "dog whistle" messaging that followed in the coming decades.

That's proposition to consider. It might even be true. But perhaps it is only one way to write about the trends in American political discourse after 1988, and not the best way. Vivid imagery—Atwater released the deluge—sometimes veils a claim about causation. Worse, it might be a claim that you would recognize as such, and possibly shy away from, if you saw it typed out in colder, less

---

[37] B. B. Kymlicka, "Introduction," in *The Reagan Revolution?* ed. B.B. Kymlicka and Jean V. Matthews (Chicago: Dorsey Press, 1988), 3–21, see 18; Lou Cannon, *President Reagan: The Role of a Lifetime* (New York: Simon & Schuster, 1991), 86, 176, 813.

[38] Booth et al., *Craft*, 125.

[39] Scott F. Crider, *The Office of Assertion: An Art of Rhetoric for the Academic Essay* (Wilmington, DE: ISI Books, 2005), 87.

artful prose. This is by no means an injunction to avoid forceful modes of expression. Particularly in a thesis statement, though, make sure you are not getting carried away by the sound of your own voice.

More than fifty years ago, Arthur Schlesinger, Jr. warned: "The besetting sin of the historian is to tidy up the past—to impute pattern to accident and purpose to fortuity."[40] Yet in the 1990s, Richard Evans wrote that historians "generally see it as their duty to establish a *hierarchy* of causes and to explain, if relevant, the relationship of one cause to another."[41] This is a bit of a quandary, to say the least. Should we show humility by steering clear of any talk about causation? Or do we have such confidence in our mastery of cause and effect that any competent historian could tell Lee Atwater to please take a number and get in line, since he's only the third most important cause of the decline of American political discourse?

The first question to ask yourself is whether your project calls for *any* statement about causation. It is certainly not mandatory. Maybe all you want to do is to describe a process. Many excellent thesis statements are centered more on the *how* than on the *why* of things. David Garrioch's *Making of Revolutionary Paris* doesn't establish the suppression of the Jansenists as *the* cause of the French Revolution, but he makes a strong case that it exposed, and worsened, serious rifts in that society.[42] For her part, Rebecca Spang, in *Stuff and Money in the Time of the French Revolution*, implicitly shifts the focus from the debate on causes to asking whether we've reckoned sufficiently with all of the revolution's *consequences*.[43] Thus, "X caused Y" is one way that some historians express their ideas, but it is far from the only one; nor is it the one generally acknowledged as the best.[44]

If you do feel a claim about causation coming on, the next step is to consider whether it will stand up to scrutiny. Some statements about causation have a nice ring to them, but they have more value as a literary device than as an analytical formulation:

The revolution arose out of a time of turmoil.

---

[40] Arthur Schlesinger, Jr., "On the Writing of Contemporary History," *Atlantic Monthly* 216, no. 3 (March 1967): 69–74.

[41] Evans, *Defense*, 135. For a counter-argument, see Robin Briggs, "'Many Reasons Why': Witchcraft and The Problem of Multiple Explanation," in Jonathan Barry, Marianne Hester, and Gareth Roberts, *Witchcraft in Early Modern Europe* (Cambridge: Cambridge University Press, 1996): 49–63, in particular 53.

[42] Berkeley: University of California Press, 2004.

[43] Cambridge MA: Harvard University Press, 2017.

[44] I will not consider counterfactuals, another area where there has been plenty of ambivalence in the profession. It's not difficult to posit a counterfactual, but trickier to envision how to research one in any depth. See, however, Martin Bunzl, "Counterfactual History: A User's Guide," *American Historical Review* 109, no. 3 (June 2004): 845–858; Gary J. Kornblith, "Rethinking the Coming of the Civil War: A Counterfactual Exercise," *Journal of American History* 90, no. 1 (June 2003): 76–105. If this approach interests you, be sure to check with your advisor first.

There might be a valid and interesting claim implied here somewhere, but it is left much too vague. As it stands, this thesis statement feels circular or repetitive. There is a special name for such formulations: "tautology." You don't want to remind anyone of the joke:

> Studies show that the people who celebrate the most birthdays tend to live longest.

Some claims about causation are more substantial. At least we could agree or disagree with this one, or consider what evidence to assemble for or against it:

> Nancy Pelosi was a successful politician because she was so good at networking.

Just accumulating evidence that Pelosi both networked adeptly and was a successful politician is not sufficient to support that thesis statement. How would you answer if someone presented evidence about other politicians who networked just as well, but failed?

You may not be in the habit of watching out for the word "because"; after all, in many sentences, it does little more than clarify the context of the claim.

> Reagan's transformational reputation is overstated because, although it was a goal articulated in the 1980 Republican platform, he did not abolish the Department of Education.

The word "because" in that thesis statement has little more force than an interjection such as "consider this!" On the other hand, this statement asserts a claim about how politics really worked:

> Reagan could not muster the political support to abolish the Department of Education because…

This is an important and maybe interesting claim, but depending on how you finish that sentence, it is contestable from a dozen different directions. A different formulation might imply some familiarity with Reagan's motives and the workings of his mind:

> Reagan did not really *want* to abolish the Department of Education because …

This is perhaps a supportable claim, though it will require strong primary source evidence to back it up.

Avoiding overblown claims about causation isn't as simple as just avoiding the words *caused* or *because*. English is rich in oblique language about how one thing led to another. Constructions like *gave rise to, led to, stemmed from, resulted in*, and *as a result* are ascribing a cause, although the claim doesn't seem quite as vigorous. Nouns such as *factor* are softer, but they too imply some form of causation; even if we demote Lee Atwater to a factor rather than a cause, he's one of the hands stirring the pot.

Softer—and perhaps more accurate—language includes *shaped, affected, expedited* (or *delayed*), *contributed* (or *inhibited*), *encouraged* (or *discouraged*), *influenced*, or even *played a vital role*. A social scientist would be quick to point out that here, too, potentially powerful claims are afoot, but at least you are on firmer ground within our discipline—many historians actually do write in this way.[45]

We are also open to an acknowledgment that many things are going on at once. Natalie Zemon Davis' famous article, "The Reasons of Misrule," conceded that the ritual appointment of "boy bishops" and similar festive transgressions reinforced existing structures. Yet also, these not-quite-serious jokes served as a means of conveying social critique and even veiled threats. This wasn't just waffling on her part. As her witty concluding paragraph suggested, when reckoning with such liminal and anarchic activities, wouldn't an overly tidy thesis statement miss the point?[46]

Don't send a metaphor to do the work of a thesis statement. To be sure, some linguists have proposed that all human language is metaphorical.[47] You may have noticed one or two metaphors in my book! Yet beware—elaborate metaphors have a way of warping everything that comes into contact with them. If you venture on an analogy to a chess game, you'll quickly find yourself fretting over just how to explain which people were pawns, kings, knights, and bishops, taking on unnecessary claims and implications along the way. Not every metaphor is as blatant as the chess analogy. Consider expressions such as "they reaped what they sowed" and "the chickens came home to roost." If such claims tempt us to frame rebuttals in the language of agriculture (or poultry farming), then as a thesis statement, they are a misdirection. Jot down the metaphor if you must, but come back to it later and try the Erasmus technique—how else could you state it?

Appeals to "decline" (or, for that matter, "progress") are also veiled causal claims that don't stand up to close scrutiny; an empire may decline, but any notion of a slope that makes it easy to slide lower is just a metaphor. Plenty of people who'd never indulge in those sorts of physical analogies fall into a different trap, relying on an appeal to a zeitgeist or spirit of an age. Although the Renaissance, the Age of Reason, and the Victorian era are all names that we assign to time periods, they exerted no magical force field that governed thought and behavior and possibility. Perhaps what you meant is that this century was different because of such-and-such phenomenon that was new. Write your thesis statement about that phenomenon, instead of implying that it's the time period itself that made things happen.

---

[45] Werner and Zimmermann, "Beyond Comparison," offer some cautionary words on these matters. See also Julia Leikin, "From Comparative to Entangled Histories," *Kritika: Explorations in Russian and Eurasian History* 22, no. 1 (Winter 2021): 173–82.

[46] Natalie Zemon Davis, "The Reasons of Misrule: Youth Groups and Charivaris in Sixteenth-Century France," *Past & Present* 50 (1971): 41–75.

[47] George Lakoff, *Women, Fire, and Dangerous Things: What Categories Reveal about the Mind* (Chicago: University of Chicago Press, 1987).

My examples in this section have followed a long-standing habit in our discipline: I've singled out people (individuals or groups) as causes. However, a human-centered historiography is no longer the only game in town. Some historians have explored the possibility that a non-human system—infrastructure, a piece of technology—could itself be an agent, shaping or nudging outcomes.[48] An increasing environmental awareness has also spurred inquiry into more-than-human agents. Depending on your project, these are important avenues that you might pursue, and there is some intriguing scholarship already published down these lines.[49] Nevertheless, you'll want to tread carefully, and make deliberate choices. If Lee Atwater's significance is debatable, then so is the agency of an insect, or a river.

The Art of Changing Your Mind

A recent book on academic writing remarks, "Only when each new source confirms what you think, rather than troubling it, will it be time to settle on a thesis."[50] Well, maybe. Write the thesis down, but stay in touch with your inner skeptic. It is true that sometimes the academic debate only moves forward when a series of scholars announce bold, but untenable, propositions and—in a chaotic process—eventually correct and moderate each other. I hope this chapter is beginning to show you, though, that it is actually possible to have a dialogue with yourself that results in some refinement of your thesis, some unburdening of unnecessary baggage, perhaps before anyone else even sees it for the first time.

Playing devil's advocate with your own propositions is easier said than done, of course. I can urge you to think like a debater or a courtroom lawyer, anticipating the other side's best retort, but this isn't the easiest advice to follow unless you have had lots of practice at it. You can listen really carefully to others when they do it for you, but this feedback usually arrives so late in the game that you don't have much of a chance to act on it. One way to simulate another interlocutor is to get in the habit of asking what scholars of a slightly different persuasion might say about your claims. If you lean to explanation A (or primary source type A), immerse yourself in scholarship by proponents of B, C, and D, and you will eventually hear their little voices in your head, picking apart your claims, and suggesting their favored alternatives.

Suppose that you are writing about masculinity. Those with long experience in reading about this topic have observed, wryly, that historians of nearly every time period and location have solemnly announced their discovery: Masculinity

---

[48] David A. Mindell, *War, Technology, and Experience Aboard the USS Monitor* (Baltimore: Johns Hopkins University Press, 2000); Donald Mackenzie, *Mechanizing Proof: Computing, Risk, and Trust* (Cambridge, MA: MIT Press, 2001).

[49] Debjani Bhattacharyya, *Empire and Ecology in the Bengal Delta: The Making of Calcutta* (Cambridge: Cambridge University Press, 2018); Lisa Onaga and Dominik Huenniger, eds., "Magnifying Insect Histories," special issue of *Isis* 115, no. 1 (2024).

[50] Schrag, *Princeton Guide*, 64.

was—just there and then—in crisis.⁵¹ None of this means that such propositions are not interesting, or that all of them are exaggerated, but if your thesis places a lot of emphasis on a decisive moment or a startling contrast, it is a good exercise to entertain the possibility that other historians might demarcate things differently. After that process, you may find that your thesis is not "isn't it remarkable that there was a crisis of masculinity," but "here's how this crisis of masculinity was different." As ever, a sharp awareness of the historiography is the way to save yourself from embarrassment and really figure out what your insight brings to the table.

What if you uncover evidence, or a line of reasoning, that altogether refutes your own initial position? If that happens to you, don't be shocked—it's the wisdom behind Peter Elbow's statement: "Writing is, in fact, a transaction with words whereby you *free* yourself from what you presently think, feel, and perceive."⁵² If this sounds a bit too New Age-y, you might prefer Elbow's brisker line: "When you start out trying to write X and it comes out Y," a recurring situation in his book *Writing Without Teachers*, and one that he welcomes.⁵³ Elbow celebrates the messiness as evidence of growth, and remarks: "[R]egressing and falling apart are a crucial and usually necessary part of any complex learning."⁵⁴

Falling apart sounds worrying, particularly since you are a student with a deadline. Having second thoughts—or getting critical feedback—when you thought you were nearing the finish line can be a nerve-wracking experience. That said, there are usually ways to refine your position without abandoning it. A slightly revised research focus might actually make your project more interesting. Suppose your project on Churchill's 1945 speech was focused on Hayek as the fountainhead of that kind of anti-socialist rhetoric. You encountered a setback when you learned that such language was plentiful before Hayek set pen to paper. Now you have a new task, documenting these other possible influences on Churchill and evaluating their impact on his speech. Is this a delay? Definitely. Will your project (and eventual, revised, thesis statement) be better as a result? Undoubtedly.

Sometimes, as we have seen, the challenge is not to your mastery of the facts, but to the assumptions that underlay your approach as a whole. Perhaps you are the enthusiast for eighteenth-century coffeehouses. You might feel a little stung to hear that some of them were remarkably exclusionary spaces. Once you get over the initial vexation, though, you might expand your inquiry and explore where everyone else was hanging out. Juan Pedro Viqueira Albán's book about Mexico City features a whole chapter about a different sort of eighteenth-century gathering place, the ball courts where people gathered to

---

⁵¹ David Morgan, "The Crisis in Masculinity," in *Handbook of Gender and Women's Studies*, ed. Kathy Davis et al. (London: Sage, 2006), 109–123.
⁵² Peter Elbow, *Writing Without Teachers* (Oxford: Oxford University Press, 1973), 15.
⁵³ Elbow, *Writing without Teachers,* 70–71.
⁵⁴ Elbow, *Writing without Teachers,* 136.

watch *pelota* matches. This spectator sport was so popular that the merchant elites started imposing high ticket prices to keep out the "riff-raff" whose "drunkenness, insolence, and provocations were a continual embarrassment."[55] Even demanding money for a ticket did not obtain the desired results; in a pointed gesture directed at those who did not adopt European-style clothing, they imposed a dress code at the entry gate to ban "those who walk around in skins or wrapped in counterpanes, sheets, or blankets."[56] Albán weaves this example, among others, into a larger thesis statement about urban modernity in Mexico more generally:

> [A]lthough modern society proclaims the integration of all groups into social life as its goal, financial inequalities ensure a sufficient discrimination within public spaces.[57]

We do not always know what sort of interpretive framework or thesis statement a historian may have entertained at one point or another in their process of research, drafting, and revision. Perhaps Albán did not have this thesis statement in mind from the beginning. He might even have started out as an adherent of an optimistic spin on coffeehouses. However, he was sufficiently open to different ways to think about the material that it was possible to eventually arrive at this more unexpected interpretation of how merchants, in dialogue with Enlightenment ideals, refashioned the public sphere in Mexico City.

One reason that these kinds of halfway-through-the-project reappraisals are so valuable is that they take what was, perhaps, already an interesting thesis statement and then complicate the picture further. A zest for complexity is as basic to the genre of academic writing as suspense is to the spy thriller, or sentimentality to the greeting card. It's possible to inject complexity by what's known as *qualifying the claim*. I don't recommend just adding adjectives or adverbs from a formulaic template:

> Hitler was a tyrant, probably.

This is a qualified claim, but won't satisfy anyone. For historians, qualifying a claim ("this was true sometimes") is less helpful than supplying nuance through logic and counter-example:

> The Nazi regime certainly had totalitarian ambitions, but the outcome of their campaign against cigarettes—which lasted for years and enlisted every trick in their propaganda arsenal—was an overall *increase* in smoking.[58]

---

[55] Juan Pedro Viqueira Albán, *Propriety and Permissiveness in Bourbon Mexico*, trans. Sonya Lipsett-Rivera and Sergio Rivera Ayala (Wilmington, DE: SR Books, 1999), 187 and 192.
[56] Albán, *Propriety*, 200.
[57] Albán, *Propriety*, 217.
[58] This sentence is my summary of Robert N. Proctor, The *Nazi War on Cancer* (Princeton, NJ: Princeton University Press, 2000), Chapter Six.

Some of the best thesis statements stand out—not for their unexpected boldness—but for their unexpected subtlety. Vicente Palermo wrote: "Argentinian nationalism is unique; but it is not exceptional."[59]

Your observation of *what doesn't fit* may be worth reformulating as an interesting claim in its own right. In her study of the representation of women in Ottoman political cartoons in the early twentieth century, Fatma Müge Göçek assembled examples of "three contradictory images of women [either] as asexual heroines, as immoral vixens, or as stolid mothers."[60] Rather than despairing at the failure of her evidence to fall into alignment, Göçek argued that it was exactly this ambiguity and ambivalence about women that mirrored the "checkered trajectory of their gains" in this period, and may even have worked to impose a limit on how far emancipation could really go.[61]

When do you know that it's time to stop revising your thesis statement? Do you declare victory when you've arrived at a thesis statement so crystal clear, so logical, so compelling that all will bow down before its wisdom? I'm here to tell you that is not going to happen. In History, as in other walks of life, it is quite common for an idea to meet with a mixed reception. The same idea that delights one person may prompt rejection by a second, and a "so what?" response from a third.

Is that just a matter of varying tastes? Looking more closely, we can probably spot different cognitive styles in these strong and disparate reactions. The historian J. H. Hexter reflected on how some of his colleagues habitually looked for useful generalizations (the "lumpers") or cheerfully picked generalizations apart (the "splitters").[62] In a famous essay, Isaiah Berlin explored similar territory: "The fox knows many things, but the hedgehog knows one big thing."[63] For example, some scholars have a single favorite method (such as quantification) or a single theoretical lens that they apply. These people—Berlin's hedgehogs—are confident and accomplished, but they aren't on the lookout for alternatives. Others cultivate an eclectic toolbox of methods and stay on the lookout for multiple sources of causation for historical events; Berlin's animal analogy, appropriately, was to the sly fox. That style has also been likened to *bricolage*, after the French word for a person who tinkers, or assembles contraptions out of spare parts. Each of these deep-set mental habits has a profound, if usually unstated, effect on how we hear or receive new information and ideas.

---

[59] Vicente Palermo, *Sal en las heridas: Las Malvinas en la cultura argentina contemporánea* (Buenos Aires: Editorial Sudamericana, 2007), 437 (my translation).

[60] Fatma Müge Göçek, "From Empire to Nation: Images of Women and War in Ottoman Political Cartoons, 1908-23," in *Borderlines: Gender and Identities in War and Peace, 1870-1930*, ed. Billie Melman (New York: Routledge, 1998), 47-72, see 48.

[61] Göçek, "From Empire to Nation," 48.

[62] For a discussion and critique of those terms, see William G. Palmer, "The Burden of Proof: J.H. Hexter and Christopher Hill," *Journal of British Studies* 19, no. 1 (1979): 122-129.

[63] Isaiah Berlin, *The Hedgehog and the Fox: An Essay on Tolstoy's View of History* (New York: Clarion, 1970), 1.

Not everyone is self-aware enough to see the reason for their own reactions. You may just be told an approach is obviously wrong, or completely unconvincing. One of the best things you can do for yourself is learn where you fall (e.g., on the fox-hedgehog spectrum) and understand the strengths that go with that. Also, get in the habit of anticipating how the "opposite" intellectual personality would react, because you will see this pattern unfold again and again as you share your ideas with others, starting with your advisor. Most of us can benefit from a dose of that alternative worldview. It's one way to spot rookie mistakes, and overlooked opportunities for nuance, in our own thinking.

At the same time, don't let that sort of critic make you forget your project's actual strengths. Differences in cognitive styles predictably result in asymmetrical excellence. The splitter will never quite understand lumping, will never undertake it except under duress, will never excel at it. Every academic discipline, nonetheless, needs at least a few lumpers. And speaking as an unrepentant fox, I don't want to live in a world where all the thesis statements are written by hedgehogs.

Conclusion

Arriving at the right thesis statement is a gradual process for most people. As anyone who has written a lot will tell you, you may have to write pages to arrive at that one sentence which eventually becomes your thesis statement. It's not unusual for the elegant, brief expression of your complex idea to only really come together near the end of your writing process. It may slip in as you compose a paragraph that wasn't anywhere near the beginning, and had no pretensions to be grand or profound. I hope that reading this chapter, at the very least, will help you spot a good thing when it comes.

Uncertainty about your thesis statement, or a lack of ideas in that area, could reflect a growing sense that your project is in need of a reappraisal somewhere. You may have had a clear plan when you completed Part Two of this book, but having examined the evidence, now you have doubts. Perhaps your findings are not as conclusive as you had hoped. Perhaps you have encountered problems with your sources. Perhaps you are feeling, after conducting your research, that your own question, or the one you borrowed from the historiography, is the wrong question. Any or all of these could make it hard to focus on a thesis statement, or make it hard to formulate a draft of one, even when you diligently sit down to attempt it.

These problems could actually be a blessing in disguise. Addressing the unresolved issue will clear the path ahead. Remember, as you draft possible thesis statements, you are making your thought processes explicit to the reader, but also to yourself. It is perfectly understandable that jotting down possible wordings for a thesis statement could make you realize that "all along" you've been trying to do Y, instead of X. If you feel genuinely confused and torn because you have ideas for *multiple* thesis statements, there are a couple of possibilities. Perhaps you can envision some claims as supporting of, or subsidiary to, another. It is also possible that—while focusing on one thesis—you have been incubating another, bigger idea that needs attention and room to grow.

If you are feeling a little discouraged just now, a textbook on rhetoric offers this memorable advice: "Arguments can't be stamped out like sheet metal panels; they have to be treated like living things—cultivated, encouraged, and refined."[64] If you are struggling with how to reformulate your claims, you are likely to find that your advisor will welcome that conversation. Bring along some of your jottings about alternative ways to express your thesis. Erasmus would be proud.

Further Reading

Booth et al., *Craft of Research*, 4th ed. (Chicago: University of Chicago Press, 2016): Chapter Eight, "Making Claims" and Chapter Ten, "Acknowledgements and Responses" offer many helpful templates and suggestions.

Albert Sonnenfeld, "Napoleon as Sun Myth," *Yale French Studies* 26 (1960): 32–36 demonstrates that a position can be coherent, erudite, and adduce supporting evidence, yet still be nonsense on stilts.

Joseph M. Williams, *Style: Ten Lessons in Clarity and Grace*, 8th ed. (New York: Pearson Longman, 2005) has wise remarks about clarity at the sentence level which also may help you decide upon the wording for your thesis statement.

---

[64] Lunsford, *Everything's an Argument*, 91.

CHAPTER 10

Supporting Claims with Evidence

Poor Wile E. Coyote pedals in the air. He's working so hard at it. What could possibly go wrong? Yet it is hard to argue with gravity. As your fingers traverse the keys and your paper starts to take shape, the good news is that there aren't any actual cliffs to worry about. However, if you drop a graph, a picture, a map, or a direct quotation into your paper—under the impression that it will pretty much speak for itself—you may discover that you're doing bicycle motions in thin air, like Mr. Coyote just after he exits the cliff edge.

As discussed in Chap. 9, warrants are the connective tissue that makes arguments work. In particular, they are what allows your evidence to support your claims. One might even say that they are what allows your evidence to count *as* evidence. A careless approach in this area may set you up for a situation in which you believe you've backed up your claims, but a reader concludes that your backing isn't fit for purpose. In History papers, we don't—and can't—present an ironclad proof according to set rules, as one might in Euclidean geometry. Nevertheless, you want to present your evidence in a convincingly productive way. Your goal is to reduce, or eliminate, the credibility gap between you and your skeptical reader.

In his book *Authoring a PhD*, Patrick Dunleavy included a chapter entitled "Handling Attention Points."[1] As a social scientist, he imagined that the most common "attention point" would be a graph or another type of data visualization. Of course, for historians, it could just as easily be a photograph or a long block quotation. By its size, length, or format, some material is so conspicuous, or so deeply implicated in your exposition and argument, that you just know that for a few moments, at least, it will have your reader's undivided attention. It would be nice if they would come away nodding with understanding and agreement.

---

[1] Dunleavy, *Authoring*, 157.

In this chapter, I differentiate between four different types of attention point: verbal, numerical, visual, and spatial. To be sure, these are not the only possible types of evidence. For example, a growing number of historians are interested in the material, the tactile, and the embodied. Penny Tinkler's excellent book on how to use historical photographs remarks that the materiality of photographs might deserve our analytical attention.[2] An example of this would be the creases that show someone folded them to carry in their pocket or wallet. Yet I predict that very few readers of this book are undertaking an analysis of creases. Words, numbers, pictures, and maps—in some form—are still the most common forms of backing that feature in student work, and in academic History publications as well.

Of course, it is possible to tackle a research topic that would naturally draw on more than one evidentiary realm. W.J.T. Mitchell has introduced provocative terms such as *imagetext*; while that sounds grandly theoretical, it captures the everyday complexities inherent in such common source types as a comic strip, a piece of photojournalism, or an advertisement.[3] Michaela Schäuble's fieldwork on Croatian landscapes of commemoration and martyrdom is a good example of a project that took multiple evidence types seriously.[4] She considered the design of Communist-era monuments and smaller improvised post-Communist shrines. She also analyzed the words spoken at sermons to the assembled pilgrims on important occasions. In addition, to get a deeper sense of place, she hiked the pilgrimage routes herself. Adopting the terms used in this chapter, her project sat at the intersection of the visual, the verbal, and the spatial. For simplicity's sake, however, I focus on one type of backing at a time. This makes it easier to highlight the best practices associated with each, and also the rookie mistakes that you will want to avoid.

Reading this chapter may also help you sort out what sort of warrant you actually need. That might seem obvious, but I also make sure to bring up examples where the key issue turns out to be different from the first thing that catches the eye. With this in mind, I encourage you to read *all* the sections of this chapter. It may help you if a sudden pivot becomes necessary. It could even pique your curiosity enough to get out of your comfort zone and draw on a new source type, just because you can.

Verbal Warrants

It would be a rare History paper that did not draw at least a little on words as a form of evidence. Never assume that a quotation makes your point for you, though. The act of spelling out what *you* think the quotation means may also

---

[2] Tinkler, *Using Photographs*, 99–104.

[3] W.J.T. Mitchell, *Picture Theory: Essays on Verbal and Visual Representation* (Chicago: University of Chicago Press, 1994), 83. An entire academic journal, *Word & Image*, explores the possibilities here.

[4] Michaela Schäuble, "How History Takes Place: Sacralized Landscapes on the Croatian-Bosnian Border," *History and Memory* 23, no. 1 (Spring/Summer 2011): 23–61.

help you clarify your own reasoning, or even help you refine your own conclusions. Without guidance, readers have a way of rebelling or drifting off in unpredictable directions. They may simply overlook the portion of the quotation that speaks to you with such urgency. If it's important to your argument, always slow down and explain.

Some snippets of text seem to cry out for quotation. They're passed along and excerpted until a dog-eared version arrives at the reader, bearing marks from who knows where. Along the way, there are many opportunities for the introduction of errors, some quite substantial. It's an old adage that "whether or not history repeats itself, historians repeat each other."[5] Don't become part of the problem! Your credibility begins with you going directly to the source and reporting back. If it's important to your argument, that may well mean consulting it in the original, examining its original context, seeing it in its original format.

I admit it's rare that a historian will possess equal mastery of every language that might be relevant. Yet there are many situations in which—without a high degree of language proficiency—you'll be unable to understand what a text actually says. Sometimes even your primary sources *themselves* will make fastidious distinctions about word choice or grammar. Diego de Mesa, questioned by the Spanish Inquisition about his statement that one who observed the laws of Moses could go to Heaven, asserted that "he could not remember whether he had used the preterit (*fue*) or the imperfect (*era*) when he described the old law as valid, the former implying a completed action in the past, the latter, a continuing action."[6] This corresponded to the difference between saying that *before Christ*, following Jewish law sufficed, and saying that a non-Christian dispensation *remained* a valid path to salvation in Diego de Mesa's own era. Making the second statement would have put him in considerable peril.

If you are not quite ready to wade into such distinctions, you might rely on someone's translation efforts. However, translators have many opportunities to make choices, some of which reach to the heart of a passage's meaning; any translated text, as Kate Briggs puts it, is something that we receive "twice-written."[7] Even seemingly reputable translations, such as those put out by Penguin Classics, can present hidden perils.[8]

Paragraph 141 of Hammurabi's Code contains a remark about severe legal action against a wife who has dared to "belittle her husband."[9] Yet a different

---

[5] Hackett Fischer, *Historians' Fallacies*, 25.

[6] Stuart B. Schwartz, *All Can Be Saved: Religious Tolerance and Salvation in the Iberian Atlantic World* (New Haven: Yale University Press, 2009), 141. In some situations, a confident grasp of the nuances of *two* languages may be necessary: M. Kittiya Lee, "Cannibal Theologies in Colonial Portuguese America (1549–1759): Translating the Christian Eucharist as the Tupinambá Pledge of Vengeance," *Journal of Early Modern History* 21, no.1–2 (2017): 64–90.

[7] Briggs, *This Little Art*, 31.

[8] Venuti, *Translator's Invisibility*, 27–28.

[9] Hammurabi, *The Code of Hammurabi, King of Babylon*, trans. Robert Francis Harper (Chicago: University of Chicago Press, 1906), 49.

translation simply says that the woman has "neglected her husband."[10] To discuss in any serious way how patriarchy worked in that society, every word in this law requires close attention. If you had the skills in Akkadian, you could walk your reader through the issues here. If you are relying on translation, you have an obligation to track down multiple translations of this law, showcase them, and discuss the implications of each. Clearly, without having a deep grounding in the possible shades of meaning and alternative translation possibilities, it would be reckless to spin out a whole line of interpretation that relied on Hammurabi's use of the word "belittle."

If your argument relies at all on your sources' exact choice of words, then consulting dictionaries is a must. For a reality check about how many meanings a word can possess, have a look at the entries in the *Oxford English Dictionary*. It preserves a variety of alternative and now-obsolete meanings, and may shed light on euphemisms that had a definite association for contemporaries. The entry for a single word in the *OED* can go on for pages. There is not, however, the equivalent of a reference work like the *OED* for every language you might want to read. Sometimes there is no substitute for consulting dictionaries and other reference works that actually date from the time period you are studying. In other situations, especially if the usage is quirky or the context is unusual, you must puzzle out a word's weight and implications, one source at a time.[11]

Historians sometimes argue that the invention of a new word was, in itself, proof that something changed. In his article "Unbelief in Early Modern Europe," David Wootton remarked on some earlier scholarship which had established that "words such as atheist, deist and libertine first appeared, initially in Latin and then in the vernacular languages of Europe, in the 1530s."[12] We might speculate that such beliefs weren't imaginable in earlier periods if no one had even taken the trouble to devise a word for them. Yet tales of the Three Imposters—Christ, Moses, and Mohammed—circulated in medieval Europe, even if they were always carefully attributed to someone other than the author.[13] This would seem to be atheism, even if it lacked a name.

When historians seek to reconstruct a working definition of a word as it was really used, they sometimes go well beyond what any dictionary can offer.[14] Wootton himself encountered this problem. He found that in seventeenth-century usage, "The defining characteristic of an atheist was not that he or she denied the existence of God, but that he or she did not believe in a divine

---

[10] Hammurabi, *The Oldest Laws in the World*, trans. Chilperic Edwards (London: Watts & Co, 1906), 21.

[11] Denise Kimber Buell does this with Greek words such as *genos* and *ethnos* in *Why This New Race: Ethnic Reasoning in Early Christianity* (New York: Columbia University Press, 2005).

[12] David Wootton, "Unbelief in Early Modern Europe," *History Workshop* 20 (Autumn 1985): 82–100, see 88.

[13] Wootton, "Unbelief," 89.

[14] Miller, *The Street Is Ours*, 5–7 offers a long, nuanced discussion of the Portuguese word *logradouro*, but only mentions dictionary definitions at the very end.

economy of rewards and punishments, in heaven and hell."[15] The *OED* entry for "atheist" hints at this possibility (living *as if* there were no God), but offers no examples that speak unequivocally to that sense of the term.[16] Yet in Wootton's sources, it was the most common meaning of the word.

As the atheist example suggests, while it's possible to point to a word's presence, it would be better to develop a robust claim based on the word's context. Where does the word occur? Who's using it? How often? In what sorts of situations? To what end? This gives you a chance to describe the work that a word performed or the role that it played in a larger discourse.[17]

This isn't just important for intellectual history projects like Wootton's. For example, professional jargon and bureaucratic expressions were often *actionable* vocabulary. Designating someone as a "tramp" in the 1870s could empower the authorities to treat them as part of the undeserving poor because it served as a synonym for an unemployed person who was "apparently healthy."[18] Depending on your source material, the exact nuances of slang or dialect could be important. The Introduction to George Chauncey's *Gay New York* explores the many shades of meaning evoked by words such as "queer," "trade," and "fairy."[19] Within the same time and place, outsiders used those words in a vague way, perhaps as a term of disparagement, but if a person applied them to himself, they carried a different weight.

Sometimes the historian's point is merely to establish *what was said*. More often, though, we are bringing in words to speak to something rather different: *Here's what people did*. The term "smoking gun" entered the language from the Watergate hearings; if you caught someone admitting something in very explicit terms, that might be crucial for your overall argument. On December 23, 1963, we know that FBI officials met for nine hours about what counterintelligence methods they might adopt against Martin Luther King, Jr. Perhaps the list of tactics discussed at the meeting establishes what you need the reader to see: "they discussed how to use wiretaps, bugs, press leaks, photographs, gossip-spreading, physical surveillance, tax inquiries, anonymous letters."[20] However, if you dropped in a summary statement such as

> FBI agents proposed trying to bait or frame Dr. King,

readers might wonder what such a plan would have involved, or doubt whether you had the hard evidence to back up such a bold claim. Here, it is important

---

[15] Wootton, "Unbelief," 86.

[16] *Oxford English Dictionary*, s.v. "atheist," accessed March 10, 2024.

[17] Stefan Collini, "The Idea of 'Character' in Victorian Political Thought," *Transactions of the Royal Historical Society*, 5th ser., 35 (1985): 29–50.

[18] Michael B. Katz, *In the Shadow of the Poorhouse: A Social History of Welfare in America*, rev. and updated edition (New York: Basic Books, 1996), 95.

[19] Chauncey, *Gay New York*, 1–29.

[20] Gage, *G-Man*, 584.

to quote from the planning memo that bluntly inquired: "What are the possibilities of placing a good looking female plant in King's office?"[21]

Of course, establishing that someone set that idea down on paper doesn't prove that it was embraced, or even taken seriously. Quoting that proposal, but not, for example, a dismissive reaction that is recorded from someone else in the meeting, would be a dereliction of your duty as a historian. Most of us would flinch away from the suggestion that we had "cherry-picked" quotations, but if we are eager to find support for a particular line of interpretation, it can exercise a subtle influence on what we notice and what we don't.

Consider four possible ways to describe the reception of *Star Wars* in 1977.

a. The early reviews were not enthusiastic, but one reviewer acknowledged "a touch of genius" and "real inspiration" in the decision to "set its sci-fi galaxy in the pop-culture past, and to turn old-movie ineptness into conscious Pop Art."
b. Film critics found the first Star Wars film poorly made, immature, tedious, and full of bad acting. One remarked that "the excitement of those who call it the film of the year goes way past nostalgia to the feeling that now is the time to return to childhood."
c. Remarkably, early critics of Star Wars missed the spiritual depth that has captured the hearts of generations of fans and, in recent years, even led some people to list their religion as Jedi. Writing in the *New Yorker*, Pauline Kael commented that Star Wars was "an epic without a dream" and added that it lacked "a sense of wonder."
d. Pauline Kael is often cited as an example of a critic who didn't get Star Wars. Yet her so-called bad review from 1977 shows a curmudgeonly respect for its popularity with kids. "An hour into it, children say that they're ready to see it all over again," Kael observed. She also put her finger on the special appeal of the Princess Leia's character, who became a feminist icon for generations of women. Kael herself was unimpressed, writing that "the high-school-cheerleader princess-in-distress talks tomboy-tough." Yet it is Leia—not Luke Skywalker, not Obi-Wan Kenobi, not Darth Vader—who made enough of an impression that *her* name appears in the short review.

What I did here was to invent four very different short assessments that all quote from just one source, the review by Pauline Kael.[22] Each one quotes her actual words, but to end the conversation there misses the point—Kael's review was genuinely complex and contradictory, so extracting just a line or two without acknowledging the whole text allows you to position Kael on almost any

---

[21] Gage, *G-Man*, 584.
[22] Pauline Kael, "Contrasts," *New Yorker*, September 18, 1977.

side of the question. Perhaps the review is best characterized as a film critic thinking out loud and processing something new, whose undeniable appeal is a bit of a mystery to her. A more balanced summary might use the words "despite," "yet," and "nevertheless" quite often. For instance:

> Kael denied that *Star Wars* possessed a sense of wonder, yet scrupulously observed that it seemed to elicit one in children.

We don't always have sources that are engaged in such a rich (and confusing) dialogue with themselves. Every historian should come prepared for conflicting testimony, though. A single page in Thavolia Glymph's *Out of the House of Bondage* often contains quotations both from the slave owners *and* from enslaved people. Although our instinct is to cherish the words of a primary source, it is sometimes necessary to note that a source is probably lying, exaggerating, or characterizing a situation in self-serving way; if the motivations behind this are not going to be immediately clear, you will need to set them out and walk the reader through what is going on in the source.

Indeed, behavior that we would condemn in a historian is often utterly routine in the historian's sources. This sets up an interesting paradox. Loyalty to the sources in all their pristine integrity could mean that we diligently reproduce language that is saturated with the prejudices and agenda of a very partial observer. This is another situation where judicious paraphrase or summary is useful. Glymph offers an overall summary of the language *around* the 1861 slave conspiracy at Second Creek, Mississippi, without supplying numerous direct quotations:

> While the court seemed most interested in allegations that the conspirators planned to 'take' white women as one of the spoils of the rebellion, the slaves themselves returned repeatedly to the subject of white women's violence.[23]

Her turn of phrase here is interesting for several reasons. Glymph establishes the background context (the court's preoccupation with white women's bodies) without dwelling on that theme or reproducing any of the associated language—other than the verb "take." She also puts the emphasis firmly on the defendants' tendency to consistently revert to subject matter *that they were not asked about*. Documenting a recurring preoccupation in your sources, especially one that is articulated "against the grain" of a situation, is always a strong method of demonstrating that you are doing something more than cherry-picking the evidence.

No one imagines that a written record is ever a perfect mirror of someone's motivation or inner mental state. Nonetheless, historians often do move beyond documenting *what was done* and inquire *why it was done*. Julie Cruikshank noticed a short remark—just twenty words—in the report of the

---

[23] Glymph, *Out of the House of Bondage*, 41.

Comte de La Pérouse, who led a French scientific expedition to the Pacific in the 1780s. He wrote: "[A] religious respect for the asylums of the dead is universal, and I was willing that this should remain inviolate."[24] She reproduced his exact words. Just as importantly, she supplied a whole page of context. La Pérouse was writing about his decision regarding the wrecked remains of a local boat belonging to the Tlingit people and the fate of some corpses that it contained. Like other government-funded expeditions of this period—James Cook's Pacific voyages may come to mind—his expedition was under orders to "collect and classify material objects," but he did not confiscate the wrecked boat and deliver it to the *savants* in Paris. He chose to interpret the wreck as a cemetery, and honored it as such. Cruikshank situates this decision as part of a pattern; despite orders to collect skeletal remains, particularly "the bones of the head," La Pérouse also declined to allow his crew to continue robbing a grave that they had opened. Indeed, he listened to Tlingit informants who explained their funeral customs and made sure that whatever his men had disturbed, they "replaced everything with scrupulous exactness."

Cruikshank guides us through each quotation and indicates how, together, they amount to a striking pattern. She also provides an overall summary that differentiates her reading of the evidence from some other historiography and theory: "A template of a coherent, crushing colonialism leaves no room for unexpected surprises." While we cannot claim to have a complete accounting of what went on in La Pérouse's head, he was clearly capable of thinking beyond the commonplaces of Enlightenment discourse around "exploring" and "collecting."

In some situations, the sticking point with your readers probably won't be over your interpretation of the text on the page, but in establishing that *these are the words that made a difference*. We have a record of the text of sermons delivered in such-and-such colony, but why should we believe that the words were heard, understood, or had any particular effect?[25] What makes us imagine that a particular feminist newsletter really raised consciousness? In recent years, the debate over the influence of imperial propaganda evolved into a discussion about how many people in the metropole knew about their overseas empire, or cared that it existed. Perhaps you found a particularly arresting passage about schools under construction in Rhodesia, or railroad bridges spanning rivers in India. The crucial question could be: In how many media outlets did it appear, with what circulation, and reaching what target demographics? An inquiry that began with a focus on verbal evidence could well evolve to refocus on an issue with numbers, counting, and sampling.

---

[24] Julie Cruikshank, *Do Glaciers Listen? Local Knowledge, Colonial Encounters, and Social Imagination* (Vancouver: University of British Columbia Press, 2005): this and all other quotations in this paragraph are from 147.

[25] Vicente L. Rafael, *Contracting Colonialism: Translation and Christian Conversion in Tagalog Society Under Early Spanish Rule* (Durham: Duke University Press, 1993), 1–3.

Numerical Warrants

The historian who's tempted to rephrase Julius Caesar and declare, "I came, I saw, I counted," is in for a rude awakening. William Aydelotte's warning from almost sixty years ago is still pertinent today: While your numbers themselves may meet with assent, your conclusions drawn from the numbers may not.[26] Books like *A Mathematician Reads the Newspaper* and *The Tiger That Isn't: Seeing Through a World of Numbers* offer a quick, witty, and user-friendly introduction to the many pitfalls here.

One of the most common numbers that historians will encounter—and this is a crucial difference between what we do and what most other disciplines do—is the result of a quantification *undertaken or assembled by someone else* in the past. It's important to go back to basics here: Don't forget to ask why the primary source exists in the first place. Counts, quantifications, and estimates may look dry, but like words, they can be selective, argumentative, or just plain disingenuous. If you can't go back and generate your own count—and often this is impossible—then summarize or cite others' summaries with care.

Jennifer Foray encountered a claim that during World War II, more than 50,000 illegitimate children were born to Dutch women as the result of contact with German soldiers. She supplies a footnote that discusses the rival figures for this, adding some commonsense considerations (the occupation force was "no more 125,000 men at its peak," so 50,000 conceptions might imply a high degree of sexual activity, not to say fertility), and a comparative study of the issue using evidence from Denmark.[27] She strongly implies that a figure between 10,000 and 15,000 illegitimate children is more likely, but not without supplying her readers with more than 200 words of context about where all these figures come from, as well as what reasoning and evidence (if any) was supplied to back them up. Conversely, an uncritical approach could lead you to produce a graph that's based on someone else's flawed numbers. That will just reproduce their misrepresentations, lending them an air of credibility they never deserved in the first place.

Sometimes the bad numbers that come to us are the result of carelessness; in other situations, there's a deliberate effort to deceive. Darrell Huff related an anecdote about the Chinese province that reported strikingly low, and then remarkably high, population totals within the same short period. "The first census," he remarked dryly, "was for tax and military purposes, the second for famine relief."[28] What you want to avoid at all costs is becoming the mouthpiece for someone else's self-serving press release, or the white lies of a mid-level manager trying to cover their tracks.

With this in mind, you'll want to avoid formulations such as "It is estimated that ...." If the figure is important, then don't bury the source for it in a

---

[26] William O. Aydelotte, "Quantification in History," *American Historical Review* 71, no. 3 (April 1966): 803–825, see 818–819.

[27] Foray, "'Clean Wehrmacht'," 779, footnote 29.

[28] Huff, *How to Lie*, 136.

footnote. Let the reader know who did the estimating, and under what circumstances. Jane Doe, in 1837? Historian John Smith, in 1937? You, in the twenty-first century? How was the estimate reached? Some descriptive adjectives give the reader hints, but not enough information. For instance, it's not unusual to refer to a *conservative estimate*, but you might explain what was conservative about it, compare it with other estimates, and situate it in relation to any non-quantitative evidence we may have.

The discipline of statistics itself has a history. Therefore, the numbers you encounter in primary sources are themselves, potentially, the product of fads, feuds, and paradigm shifts in that discipline. Get in the habit of considering who created the numbers, why, where and how the supporting information was collected, and what techniques were applied to the data before it was shared in a digested form to a wider readership. The historian of mathematics Stephen Stigler has remarked that it would be unfortunate if we ignored "the interplay between statistical concepts and the scientific and practical problems that spawned them."[29] Yet it is equally important to bear in mind that the so-called problems were sometimes spawned in the first instance by the discourse of statistics itself. For example, a nineteenth-century panic about rising crime rates was incited—not by a crime wave—but by improvements in data collection.

Perhaps you yourself are going to do the counting. Historical records bear their own "native" categories (terms specific to that time and place), and this presents challenges to any would-be quantifier. For instance, records of "nationality" in France between the two World Wars turned up some entries apparently imposed by a petty official in a hurry (a person's nationality was "indeterminate"), and other self-identifications which are so eclectic that they pose a puzzle for any would-be tabulator ("Armenian Brazilian") and a few ("Russian refugee") which seem to reflect "the status they hoped to be granted."[30] Any statistical summary that you produced using these inputs would represent a complex compromise between these varied "native categories" plus any others that you chose to impose on top of them.

A different kind of "native category" that's pertinent for anyone using archives is the administrative unit. West Virginia separated from Virginia in 1863. If you needed to calculate the size and productivity of a typical Virginia farm from 1860 to 1870, some odd things would happen to your data series in the later years of that decade. Only *some* of them would involve the end of slavery, postwar malaise, and the policies of Reconstruction!

Books on statistical methods tend to spend little time on patchy data, but for many subfields of History, that's all we have. Within our profession, quantifiers are usually drawn to exhaustive data sets like modern tax and criminal records, or the height measurements of entering cadets from military academies, so it is easy to forget that other kinds of material exist. Perhaps you are studying a

---

[29] Stephen M. Stigler, *Statistics on the Table: The History of Statistical Concepts and Methods* (Cambridge, MA: Harvard University Press, 1999), 87.

[30] Lemercier and Zalc, *Quantitative Methods*, 64.

once-in-a-generation crackdown on queer people; stray trade figures from unusual caravans; evidence from pirate shipwrecks. If there are few data points, it could be misleading to graph them at all. At the very least, rather than connecting them with continuous lines that imply a steadier flow of evidence, it is best to represent rare and scattered samples as individual data points.[31] Likewise, if you have a sample of four, it would be pretty silly to remark on what the top quartile of the distribution looked like.

Oscar Handlin remarked in the 1970s: "No matter how ingeniously the numbers are tortured, in the end the adjective chosen depends upon the ability to set the evidence in context, as historians should do with any other material."[32] This is still true in the profession today. Even in the case of numbers, the warrant is expressed in words. Therefore, your responsibility goes well beyond just sharing the numbers. You must decide what's the most honest and accurate way to convey their meaning to the reader. For instance, a familiarity with the standard language used to discuss probability could be just what you need to discuss your sources' claims about cancer risk, industrial accidents, or once-in-a-century floods.

Using the *wrong* language to characterize numerical evidence can mislead you, your reader, or both. Reporting an average is a classic example here. One big outlier, or a cluster of outliers, can skew a whole distribution. You may know what's wrong with the notorious, yet still common, claim that in some early society (a Paleolithic village; Shakespeare's England) people had a gloomy outlook since the average life expectancy was only twenty-five. High infant mortality, when averaged in, creates a very misleading impression!

Here's another example of how averages can deceive. In 1999, a British newspaper ran a story about how average family wealth was growing in Britain, but the mean (at £7136) was far ahead of the median figure of a mere £750. What was going on? Thirty percent of the population, almost one out of three families, "had no savings outside of their home and pension, and around 10 per cent (mostly single parents and out-of-work couples) had no savings at all."[33] As with the life expectancy problem, visualizing (or creating) a scatterplot or some other graphic representation is the place to start your thinking, even if you plan to express the salient points in words alone. For instance, instead of mentioning the average, you could state that 40% of the population had no cash or liquid investments to sell in an emergency.

Sometimes, when the average hides a more complex picture, a simple visualization is what your reader needs. For example, in 1995, the average age of a foreign correspondent for a U.S. media outlet was 44 for men and 38 for women. This disparity doesn't seem large. Yet Stephen Hess noted that women,

---

[31] Stephen Few, *Now You See It: Simple Visualization Techniques for Quantitative Analysis* (Oakland, CA: Analytics Press, 2013), 152–153.

[32] Handlin, *Truth in History*, 222.

[33] Pat Hudson, *History by Numbers: An Introduction to Quantitative Approaches* (London: Bloomsbury Academic, 2000), 92–93.

as newcomers to the profession, skewed a lot younger, and they were particularly underrepresented among the most senior foreign correspondents, who often got the most visible and influential assignments.[34] For illustrative purposes, I invented a set of numbers that would produce the pattern that Hess describes. Then I used a box-and-whiskers graph to display it (Fig. 10.1).

In my invented set of numbers, I made the age of the youngest journalist the same for both men and women (27), and also the age of the oldest journalist was almost the same (67 for the men, 66 for the women). Yet that 66-year-old journalist, who broke barriers in an earlier generation, stands out quite a bit among the women; her next youngest colleague is only 51. The men's ages are more or less evenly distributed, while the women are mostly made up of a strong generational cohort falling between the ages of 31 and 44.

In my box-and-whiskers graph, the overall contours of this are visible at a glance. The top and bottom of each box represents the upper and lower quartile of the distribution. The lines at the end of each "whisker" indicate the extremes, and a true outlier, the 66 year old among the women, appears as a dot. The line running through the box corresponds to the median, while the X indicates the mean (or average).

This particular graph does not convey how many men or how many women are in the sample; I invented ages for exactly 20 of each. So what you see in the graph—the apparent "size" of the box—is purely about how extended or compressed the *distribution* of ages was. If that is what you need to convey, then the graph suits its purpose. Matching up the form of visualization with the point you need to make is a classic challenge, but fortunately it is the subject of

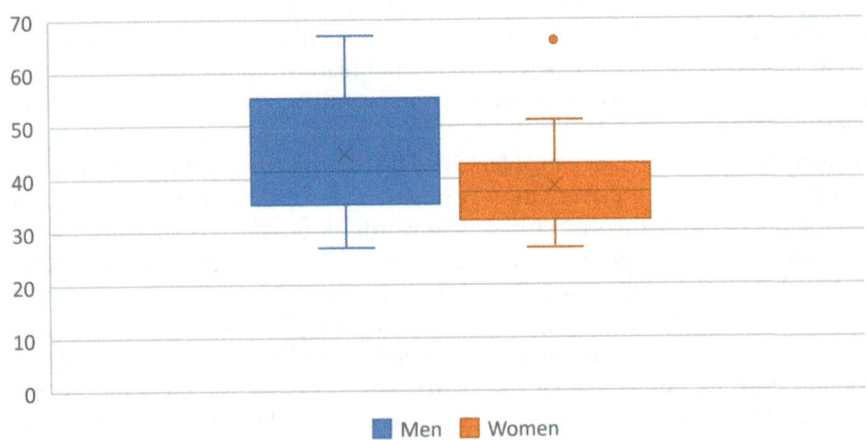

Fig. 10.1 Ages of foreign correspondents, 1995. (Graph by Isaac Land)

[34] Stephen Hess, *International News & Foreign Correspondents* (Washington, D.C.: Brookings Institution Press, 1996), 23–24.

a number of respected handbooks, some of which I list in the Further Reading section of Chap. 12.

The idea of a *per capita* rate is probably familiar to you. For instance, the Soviet Union lost the most people in World War II, but adjusted for population size (deaths *per capita*), Poland tops the list, and less familiar contenders such as French Indochina become prominent.[35] In some situations, you will need to supply a different reference point or benchmark to make a figure intelligible. Paulos gives the example of the headline "500 dead in carnage over 4-day holiday weekend"; given the daily toll of dead on the highways, he remarks, 500 dead in 4 days was not exceptional.[36] Perhaps if the weekend really was bad, the most honest characterization—rather than the raw number of deaths—would be to indicate it was 10% above average.

Precision, by itself, will impress no one if it appears that you are precisely measuring the wrong things. You don't want to elicit something down the lines of D.C. Coleman's sarcastic comment:

> The heights of soldiers or marines are brought in to inform us about the standard of living. Lacking output data, we use trade figures which are themselves often based on customs returns or other tax statistics; parish registers and hearth taxes stand in for vital statistics; excise figures for industrial output. The figures, once gathered in, invite processing ... and out come the results to two places of decimals.[37]

If Coleman had to worry about a quick, misleading result in 1995, in today's world widely available statistical software offers an even faster route to even more trouble. Working through software tutorials may not convey the concepts *behind* the options on the drop-down menu: "Although it is possible to leave the mathematics to a computer, it is dangerous to use statistical techniques without being fully aware of the conceptual foundation for mathematical processes."[38] If you think you need statistical software, taking an elementary statistics course first is probably a good precaution.

Even the most math-averse historians still regularly find themselves working with one kind of number: An amount expressed in a currency. If, for instance, an ancient law code stipulates a penalty of one talent of silver, was that a large fine or a slap on the wrist? Even if you come across a reference to a currency that still exists—such as the British pound—the first point to recognize is that there is no straightforward way to express what that tax, fine, or income would buy in today's money. Find a benchmark from that same time and place, such as how much a manual worker would earn in a day. Then build up a framework

---

[35] Ken MacLean, "History Reformatted: Vietnam's Great Famine (1944–45) in Archival Form," *Southeast Asian Studies* 5, no. 2, (August 2016): 187–218.
[36] Paulos, *Innumeracy,* 168.
[37] D.C. Coleman, "History, Economic History, and the Numbers Game," *Historical Journal* 38, no. 3 (September 1995): 635–646, see 641.
[38] Hoover and Donovan, *Elements,* 119.

of reference points around your benchmark. Bear in mind that one particular item—a chicken, for instance—has been plentiful in some locations, but elsewhere was a rare commodity. So look for the examples that naturally spring up in the time and place that you are studying.

Edward Tufte once remarked that all quantitative reasoning comes down to "compared to what?"[39] If there's an important question in your project that takes the form of asking "to what extent ..." then you may already be in quantification territory. An exploratory statistical analysis can help you transition from a hunch to something much more substantive. It could also correct for misleading conclusions derived from a suspicion, or a single vivid instance. If any aspect of your argument relies on an implied quantification, it is better to evaluate any vulnerabilities in this area now, rather than experiencing a deer-in-the-headlights moment when someone questions you about it later.

Visual Warrants

It's never been easier to drop an image into your work in progress. Always be clear, though—both to your reader and to yourself—about why you included it. Perhaps you see the picture as merely illustrative. It's there to indicate *that* there was poverty, *that* there was brutality on the battlefield, *that* a policy drew ridicule. This is one possible approach to visual evidence, and not all of us have the appetite to delve deeply into photography or art. Yet even here, you have some basic obligations to know where the picture came from, and share that information.

Alert readers won't be surprised to learn that "what kinds of photos are made and why, and how they are presented, circulated and used" is very revealing of a society's character—or, indeed, of the photographer's outlook.[40] Yet this awareness, in the abstract, doesn't mean that they know the details in this particular circumstance. Darren Newbury, who studied South African photographs, remarked that they were not just "images of" apartheid; they were "literally images within apartheid."[41] In such situations, offering the merest descriptive caption and no backstory is a form of negligence, if not outright historical malpractice.

Symbolism is another area that requires explanation, but also caution, on your part. It may disappoint some *Da Vinci Code* fans, but there aren't any professors of "Symbology," and you'd be hard put to find an art historian or film studies scholar publishing today who'd think we could pull out a visual grammar or visual dictionary and get solid answers to what's going on in an

---

[39] Edward Tufte, *Visual Display of Quantitative Information*, 2nd ed. (Cheshire, CT: Graphics Press, 2001), 74.
[40] Tinkler, *Using Photographs*, 87.
[41] As quoted in Tinkler, *Using Photographs*, 108.

image.⁴² A more influential approach is to study *visual culture*.⁴³ This approach acknowledges that the what, how, and why—the very purpose of art—will vary from one culture to another; in addition, some characters, objects, gestures, scenes, and even colors will appear according to widely used, consistent, and enduring conventions that are nevertheless particular to that time and place. The term *iconography* was originally coined as a way to sort out the standard practices of early Christian art, but many visual cultures have iconographic systems of some sort, whether we are speaking of Buddhist religious sculpture or Victorian political caricature.⁴⁴ These codified practices and shared understandings observably reach well beyond the whims or habits of any individual artist—although as I discuss below, there is still room for creativity, eccentricity, and resistance.

For historians, there is no substitute for patiently learning the particular rules of the visual culture that interests you. Often the best way to get started is by reading an excellent piece of scholarship analyzing *an* example of that visual culture, ideally within the same medium or genre, even if it was not produced by the artist whose work you need to interpret. Another shortcut is to learn the standard names of important recurring elements. In representations of the Buddha, each hand gesture (*mudra*) is assigned a conventional meaning. In Fig. 10.2, the Buddha touches the ground with his right hand. This might seem like a minor detail to someone unfamiliar with *mudras*. Yet it evokes a dramatic moment in the story of the Buddha's Enlightenment, when he calls on the earth to support him in his struggle with the demon Mara. This specific gesture has a name, *bhumisparshamudra*.

We might infer from this a deeper underlying iconographic convention: No hand gesture in Buddhist art will be accidental. At the very least, a claim assigning significance to a hand gesture in Buddhist art is likely to come across as a warranted, permissible reading of visual materials. This does not generalize to all art forms in all cultures; if you think the position of the hand is crucial in a twentieth-century Canadian photograph or a Paleolithic cave painting from Spain, readers are persuadable, but you'll have to work harder to convince them.

Meaning is multifarious and contestable. Thus, even the most iconic symbols can have more than one meaning. For instance, what did the Phrygian cap denote in 1792? We might expect this would be completely straightforward. Isn't that the cap of liberty, after all? In Thomas Rowlandson's cartoon (Fig. 10.3), it is present, but despite its association with the Jacobins, it is appropriated to represent the superior version of liberty associated—for Rowlandson—with British orderliness, conventional morality, and respect for

---

⁴² W. J. T. Mitchell, *Picture Theory: Essays on Verbal and Visual Representation* (Chicago: University of Chicago Press, 1994), see, for example, 111–112.

⁴³ This term originated in Svetlana Alpers, *The Art of Describing: Dutch Art in the Seventeenth Century* (Chicago: University of Chicago Press, 1983), xxv. For more recent conceptual work around this and related terms, see Gillian Rose, *Visual Methodologies*, 5th ed. (London: Sage, 2023).

⁴⁴ For example, Mary Cowling, *The Artist as Anthropologist: The Representation of Type and Character in Victorian Art* (Cambridge: Cambridge University Press, 1989).

Fig. 10.2 "Plaque with Scenes from the Life of the Buddha," twelfth century (India: Bihar or West Bengal). (Metropolitan Museum of Art, New York. Open Access image, Accession Number: 1982.233)

private property. Neil Hertz observes that we find it "calmly taking its place among the benign attributes of British Liberty, propped on a rod beside her throne."[45] Just as the word "liberty" was up for grabs in 1792, so was the meaning of the Phrygian cap.

If you are going to propose a symbolic reading, you are on much sturdier ground if you have ample evidence that the interpretation had currency at the time. For instance, does a Phrygian cap propped up on a rod automatically count as a phallic symbol? Hertz does offer a Freudian interpretation of the Phrygian cap, but he takes the trouble to offer numerous examples of people in the 1790s who were obsessed over its erect or flaccid shape.[46]

Another general rule: Interpretations that embrace many things about a picture, rather than just one or two things, are more compelling.[47] If you leave "a disproportionate acreage of the canvas ... unaccounted for," it probably won't satisfy.[48] Of course, sometimes the composition or color scheme of an image conveys emphasis, or guides the eye to a particular location. We can perhaps smile at the extensive discussion in academic journals over whether the egg in Piero della Francesca's *Brera Altarpiece* of 1472 is really an ostrich egg,

---

[45] Neil Hertz, *The End of the Line: Essays on Psycho-Analysis and the Sublime*, 2nd ed. (Aurora, CO: Davies Group, 2009), 222.

[46] Hertz, *End of the Line*, 216–224.

[47] David Carrier, *Principles of Art History Writing* (University Park, PA: Pennsylvania State University Press, 1991), 40.

[48] Carrier, *Principles*, 172, quoting Leo Steinberg.

Fig. 10.3 Thomas Rowlandson, "The Contrast" (1792). (Metropolitan Museum of Art, New York. Open Access image)

and if so, what that means; yet a glance at the painting itself, which makes the egg a focal point, tells us that an interpretation of *this* painting that does not address the egg will seem inadequate.[49]

Sometimes it is important to discuss not only *what* was shown, but also *how* it was shown. Honoré Daumier's "Last Council of the Ex-Ministers" (Fig. 10.4) appeared in *Le Charivari*. The scene is simple enough: "[T]he final session of Louis-Philippe's cabinet being upset by the appearance of the figure of the Republic in the doorway."[50] Undoubtedly, many political cartoons of 1848 sought to capture the revolutionary moment.

Yet it was *this* cartoon that made such a great impression. Jules Michelet, recalling it several years later, reminisced to Daumier about the way that "she comes *home*; she finds *thieves* at the table. ... She has the *strength* and the *confidence* of the *mistress of the house*. She, and she alone, is *at home* in France."[51] The historian Laura O'Brien remarks that the figure of the Republic here is "almost supernatural."[52] It's not just her otherworldly body, rendered in lighter lines, that accomplishes this, but also the way that most of the ministers seek to

---

[49] Isa Ragusa, "The Egg Reopened," *Art Bulletin* 53, no. 4 (1971): 435–444; Millard Meiss, "Not an Ostrich Egg?" *Art Bulletin* 57, no. 1 (1975): 116.

[50] Laura O'Brien, *The Republican Line: Caricature and French Republican Identity, 1830–52* (Manchester: Manchester University Press, 2015), 74.

[51] O'Brien, *Republican Line*, 74.

[52] O'Brien, *Republican Line*, 74.

Fig. 10.4 Honoré Daumier, "Dernier conseil des ex-ministres," March 9, 1848. (National Gallery of Art (U.S.A.), Corcoran Collection, gift of Dr. Armand Hammer. Open Access image)

avert their eyes, as if they might turn to stone, or dissolve. Consider the overall composition of the cartoon as well. It doesn't just depict scampering politicians. Their weird anatomies seem to combine into a composite beast that is far too large to fit through the window where one of them—part of it—tries to escape.

Daumier also depicted the massacre at the Rue Transnonain, a brutal military reprisal against a civilian uprising (Fig. 10.5). The title is simply the location and the date: April 15, 1834.

Laura O'Brien sums up the image in this way:

> The central figure in the image is a man in a bloodied nightshirt, lying prone over the body of a dead child whose skull has clearly been split open. In the shadows to the left of the print lies the body of a woman and to the right that of an elderly man, underlining the fact that several generations of one family had been murdered.[53]

[53] O'Brien, *Republican Line*, 40.

Fig. 10.5 Honoré Daumier, "Rue Transnonain, le 15 avril 1834." (Metropolitan Museum of Art, New York. Open Access image)

Yet as O'Brien also notes, the style is part of the message as well. "Rue Transnonain" nearly has the realism of a photograph. For contemporaries familiar with Daumier's usual cartoonish broad brush, this signaled his serious documentary intent very loudly indeed.[54] Whether you are working with material like this, or with advertisements, or propaganda, you may find that readers need short explanations like these to help them see each image through your eyes.

There is a difference, of course, between offering a guided tour of an artfully designed image and convincing the reader that an image *had* an effect. There is something of a stereotype that visual material, because it does not place much reliance on reading skills, must be more in touch with the pulse of the masses than textual material. This is not always borne out by the evidence. A police raid on the offices of the satirical publication *Le Charivari* in 1835 resulted in the preservation of a list of 1406 subscribers, along with their residential addresses. As O'Brien remarks, despite the anti-regime flavor of the cartoons published by *Le Charivari*, "It is telling that very few of the paper's Parisian subscribers at this time resided in the traditionally working-class neighborhoods in the east of the city."[55] She adds that "in economic terms little differentiated the editors and publishers from the middle-class characters they

---

[54] O'Brien, *Republican Line*, 40–41.
[55] O'Brien, *Republican Line*, 11.

mocked in their publications."⁵⁶ We don't always have such precise information, but it should not surprise you if your advisor asks what we know about the means of dissemination, who could afford access, or what sort of public your images actually reached in practice.

On August 28, 1968, in what many at the time described as a police riot, Chicago cops attacked protesters and journalists alike in front of the Democratic National Convention. In the simpler media landscape of that era, it is not difficult to quantify viewership; we know that 90 million Americans—half of the U.S. population at the time—saw the live coverage of the events in Chicago.⁵⁷ The protesters, conscious of the television cameras, started to chant, "The whole world is watching," as if those who watched could only reach one conclusion.⁵⁸ However, a subsequent Gallup poll found that 56% of Americans felt that the police had behaved correctly.⁵⁹

The mixed reception of the images that came out of Chicago offers a helpful example of what Penny Tinkler is getting at when she makes the seemingly enigmatic statement, "You do not learn much from looking very closely at photos."⁶⁰ So much of a photo's life occurs outside its edges. A person harboring a mistrust of long-haired hippies might view the Chicago footage through that lens. Another viewer, noticing only that the situation was out of hand, might welcome a stern response from law enforcement. Don't jump to conclusions about the work that an image performed in the world. There is nothing automatic or inevitable here. Historians will be happiest with you if you keep the focus on how an image *was* received.

Visual materials can be beautiful, arresting, disturbing. Still, it's important to keep an open mind about what kind of evidence is really the most pertinent and telling. For instance, a traveling slideshow, "The Last Great Wilderness," is credited with heading off the Reagan Administration's plan to open the Arctic National Wildlife Refuge for drilling. It's possible to document the 250 slides that audiences saw. Yet Finis Dunaway has offered an interpretation that puts the emphasis at least as much on the presenters as on the presentation itself. Previous critics of the proposal had expressed it in terms of conservation of a wild, untouched place. The slideshow, however, emphasized the human urgency of the Indigenous perspective. Since the proposed drilling zone was in the middle of a caribou calving area, it expressed the stakes in terms of food security and "Indigenous cultural survival."⁶¹ This message was underscored

---

⁵⁶ O'Brien, *Republican Line*, 96.
⁵⁷ David Culbert, "Television's Visual Impact on Decision-Making in the USA, 1968: The Tet Offensive and Chicago's Democratic National Convention," *Journal of Contemporary History* 33, no. 3 (July 1998): 419–449, see 446.
⁵⁸ Culbert, "Television's Visual Impact," 444.
⁵⁹ Culbert, "Television's Visual Impact," 447.
⁶⁰ Tinkler, *Using Photographs*, 64. Tinkler is paraphrasing Annette Kuhn here, who is well known for her analysis of a different genre, the family photograph.
⁶¹ Finis Dunaway, *Defending the Arctic Refuge: A Photographer, an Indigenous Nation, and a Fight for Environmental Justice* (Chapel Hill: University of North Carolina Press, 2021), 21.

through the presence of a representative from the Gwich'in Nation at each showing. It seems likely that images played a role in the presentation's success. Yet we also know that this slideshow succeeded where—for example—nature documentaries and *National Geographic* photojournalism failed. An inquiry that began, perhaps, with an examination of visual evidence could turn to a careful consideration of the words and actions of the Gwich'in activists themselves.

Spatial Warrants

In 1976, Paul Boyer and Stephen Nissenbaum published *Salem Possessed*. They included a simple map, sketching out the boundaries of the village in the barest outline and denoting residents through three different letters.[62] *A* stood for an accuser, *W* for an accused witch, and *D* for a person who spoke out as a defender of the accused. A startling pattern is visible at a glance: Accused witches and their defenders generally lived close to each other, while those who made an accusation lived on the opposite side of the village. The Salem map serves as a reminder, in our era of elaborate visualizations, that something you could scribble on the back of an envelope can also be very effective.

Yet statements about spatial relationships won't always be this stark or crisp. Your point may even be the opposite, that the boundaries are blurry and the indicators equivocal. Furthermore, the Salem map's strengths and weaknesses were two sides of the same coin—its clarity was what made it so powerful, but its intense focus on a single dimension meant that other dimensions weren't visible at all. It was easy to see whether an accuser did, or didn't, live near an accused witch. The gender of the villagers—on whatever side of the matter—was left out.

If you provide a map, you should remain deliberate about your purpose in doing so, conscious of what that method of mapping emphasizes, and candid with your reader about what it shows, as well as what it omits. Perhaps, if different maps would suggest different conclusions, the solution is to provide several maps to orient your reader. You can explain how each illuminates a distinct perspective.

Beginners should be aware that plugging values into mapping software can easily result in a product that looks crisp and professional, but is quite misleading. In his book *How to Lie with Maps*, Mark Monmonier offered an example of four maps, *each* depicting "occupied housing units lacking a telephone, 1960."[63] The only difference between the maps was the "class breaks" that determined the differences in color—for instance, do we change from gray shading to black shading when a threshold is crossed between 14% and 15%?

---

[62] Paul Boyer and Stephen Nissenbaum, *Salem Possessed: The Social Origins of Witchcraft* (Cambridge MA: Harvard University Press, 1974), 34.
[63] Mark Monmonier, *How to Lie with Maps*, 2nd ed. (Chicago: University of Chicago Press, 1996), 41.

Between 29% and 30%? The underlying data was exactly the same in all four maps, but each presented a drastically different picture.

Not only is this slippery territory, but it is slippery in several different ways. I created a set of numbers that correspond to the information implied by Monmonier's sample maps. Most states cluster in the mid- to high teens. Maine, New Hampshire, and Vermont differ from each other by only a point or two. In Fig. 10.6, I present those numbers in the form of a bar graph, arranged from high to low.

The quip that "a map is just a bad graph" isn't universally true, but examples like this one give you some idea what inspired it.[64] If the differences from one state to another aren't very large, then perhaps the whole mapping project is suggesting contrasts that aren't really there.

A more subtle point is that on all of these maps, large states (in this example, Maine) make a disproportionate visual impact and small states (Rhode Island) will seem less important. With this effect in mind, Dona Wong offers a general principle: "No mapping unless geography is relevant."[65] A map will make the reader think in terms of spatial warrants, even if you are advancing none, so use maps sparingly.

Finally, in the telephone ownership example, we started with an unexamined premise: Mapping at the level of entire states was the way to go. A moment's reflection will suggest that urban-rural differences would show up much more

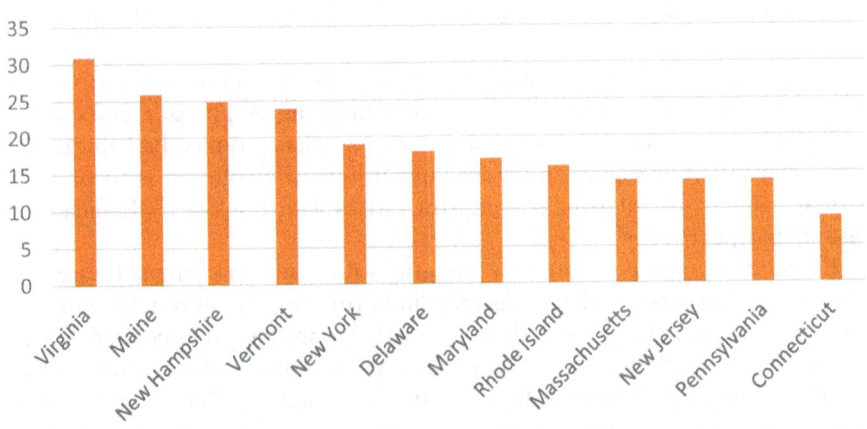

Fig. 10.6 Telephone ownership. (Graph by Isaac Land)

[64] Ian N. Gregory, "'A Map Is Just a Bad Graph': Why Spatial Statistics Are Important in Historical GIS," in *Placing History*, ed. Knowles, 123–150.

[65] Dona M. Wong, *Wall Street Journal Guide to Information Graphics: The Dos and Don'ts of Presenting Data, Facts, and Figures* (New York: W. W. Norton, 2013), 90.

clearly if we paid attention to variation on a smaller scale. Is the solution to demarcate and shade individual counties, not entire states? Even within a single county, however, a lot of complexity and variation might still exist. For instance, Washtenaw County, Michigan, includes liberal, affluent Ann Arbor, yet there are also many rural areas within its boundaries.

If your map reports on anything quantifiable—anything that might be susceptible to statistical reasoning—then deciding on a scale for your map sets you up for what geographers call the "areal aggregation problem."[66] How does the presence of Ann Arbor in Washtenaw County skew the numbers for the county as a whole? Changing the scale down to municipalities, townships, or precincts—or up to the level of Detroit, plus its suburbs, exurbs, and communities within driving distance—would throw some patterns sharply into focus, yet others would disappear. Worse, if you fail to investigate *how* these different methods of aggregating and disaggregating could reshape your results, you might rush to unwarranted conclusions.

With the software available today, you might wonder if the solution here is to provide an interactive map with appropriate affordances so that your readers could explore the data—and possible visualizations of that data—for themselves. In your paper, though, you will still want one (or more) static maps that capture what *you* think is important. Your responsibility is to offer a concise and pointed summary—whether in words, maps, graphs, or a combination of these—of what stands out to you, and what you believe the reader needs to see.

Maps reducing the world to x, y, and z coordinates (latitude, longitude, and elevation) are not the only way to think about space. For example, a study of perceptions of the U.S.-Mexican border asked schoolchildren in Tijuana and San Diego to draw pictures of the border, what it was like on the other side of the border, and so forth. The researchers found a striking contrast: "All the children in Tijuana identified and associated the border with the metal fence that divides the two countries," while the San Diego children rarely acknowledged the fence; "the great majority of the group had not seen it, and some did not even know of its existence."[67] Across a conventional city map, the eye roves unimpeded, with godlike perspective and godlike freedom. It's worth asking yourself whether you are you creating—or using—a map that leaves an impression that is fundamentally different from the way that some residents would have understood and experienced that space.

As a good-sized urban center, Tijuana at least enjoys the benefit of falling into a category that cartographers conventionally honor with *a* place on the map. Depending on who is doing the mapping and who got consulted, the U.S.-Mexico border might also include numerous "empty" spots that are actually areas of significance and memory to Native American groups, such as the

---

[66] Monmonier, *How to Lie*, 140–150.

[67] Norma Iglesias-Prieto, "El otro lado de la línea/The other side of the line," in *GeoHumanities: Art, History, Text at the Edge of Place*, ed. Michael Dear, et al. (New York: Routledge, 2011), 143–153, see 146, 149.

pilgrimage site of Quitobaquito Springs and the graveyard at Monument Hill.[68] A different kind of omission is evident in some maps of the United States, including the ones I saw growing up. They truncate at the border, leaving the immediately adjacent nation vague, or actually blank and unlabeled, as if it did not exist at all.

Geographers have learned to think in terms of a *functional region*, in this case the Rio Grande borderland that joins the United States and Mexico in a complex set of linkages and interdependence.[69] Of course, it is likely that people living in that border region thought about linkages and interdependence long before the geographers got around to theorizing it! If you set out to make a map of that functional region, you might well center it *on* the Rio Grande, instead of treating the international border as the edge of a picture frame.

Maybe what you are really trying to communicate about a space is best expressed in words. For example, it would be hard to express in a diagram or blueprint what was lacking in a new public housing project, or what amenities the new residents missed from their old neighborhood. *Space* and *place* are not opposites, but as you examine your own argument more closely, you may find that your claim is less about distances, configurations, and adjacencies, and more to do with the investment of meaning in that unique location or the particular texture of emotion associated with it.[70]

An attentiveness to emotional resonances reminds us that privacy, secrecy, and safety have their own intimate geographies. Servants might live in fear of their master grabbing them on the dark stairwell. Illicit lovers might pay special attention to the line of sight from a particular balcony. On an even smaller scale, one middle-class memoirist described a childhood memory of how the maid gave her access to the romance novels that she kept hidden in her room. "Beneath Karoline's underclothes in the bottom drawer" is not a spot we'll find marked on many maps, but in the right context, this could be a very important location.[71]

A sense of place can also adhere to public spaces and public experiences. It's not difficult to find a map and share it with your readers. If, however, it was the variety of languages spoken there and the cosmopolitan spectacle of diverse religions that counted the most, then you need to assemble and present your evidence accordingly. Is your claim primarily about *space*? Is it about a sense of *place*? Or do your readers need to understand how space and place were both a factor? It is perfectly reasonable to provide some contextual details and a map for orientation purposes, but most of the evidence and orientation that you provide should speak directly to the needs of your actual argument.

---

[68] "Blasting in Construction of Border Wall Is Affecting Tribal Areas," *New York Times*, February 11, 2020.

[69] Susan Hanson, ed., *Ten Geographic Ideas That Changed the World* (New Brunswick, NJ: Rutgers University Press, 1997), 145–162.

[70] Yi Fu Tuan, *Space and Place: The Perspective of Experience* (Minneapolis: University of Minnesota Press, 1977).

[71] Davidoff, "Class and Gender," 96.

One type of spatial warrant that I have not yet mentioned is geographical determinism. Claims about the inherent character of entire civilizations (such as the "Asiatic mode of production"; "the Islamic city") were once common, and as warrants, they stood largely unchallenged for a very long time.[72] Some determinist explanations have manipulative origins intended to give the stamp of approval to someone's imperial ambitions. As David Arnold has written, some Europeans envisioned India as "an extension of the more familiar Orient of the Middle East and Persia (or even the Holy Land of the Bible)" while others positioned it as "a transitional zone between the deserts of Arabia and the exuberant landscapes of Southeast Asia," but "it was India as tropical that had most widely come to prevail by the mid-nineteenth century."[73] Arnold noted:

> India's tropicalization ... countered the appreciative evaluation of India's ancient achievements by Orientalist scholars with an insistence upon the subordination of the country (and, implicitly, its civilization) to the dominant power of nature.[74]

Confusing India with the Holy Land is not a pitfall that will ensnare many scholars today. Yet many types of primary sources are contaminated by problematic language freighted with geographical determinism. It can take subtle forms. For example, after reading enough memos and reports submitted to the World Bank in a particular decade, what concepts might creep into your own reasoning? Some assumptions about the necessity of "development" as a surefire fix for poverty, perhaps, or a preoccupation with a homogenous entity known as "the Third World."

Most recently, the theoretical position that borderlands are wondrously blurry and hybrid in character eventually had to reckon with the uncomfortable realities of some actual border towns and port cities. The existence of cosmopolitan communities that enshrined routine discrimination, punctuated by pogrom-like riots, prompted a rupture between the "celebratory" school of interpretation and more critical, or "post-celebratory," appraisal.[75] While it is easy to brush aside the most outdated concepts, it seems that ascribing agency to space is a hard habit to break.

Conclusion

At the beginning of Part III, I mentioned one historian's metaphor involving evidence accumulating like the percolation of grain down a spout. There are many problems with this analogy, but perhaps the greatest is its implication

---

[72] Malte Fuhrmann, *Port Cities of the Eastern Mediterranean: Urban Culture in the Late Ottoman Empire* (Cambridge: Cambridge University Press, 2020), 11, 12, 23, 29, 30.

[73] David John Arnold, *The Tropics and the Traveling Gaze: India, Landscape, and Science, 1800–1856* (Seattle: University of Washington Press, 2014), 36.

[74] Arnold, *Tropics*, 36.

[75] Fuhrmann, *Port Cities*, 17; see also Will Hanley, "Grieving Cosmopolitanism in Middle East Studies," *History Compass* 6, no. 5 (2008), 1346–1367.

that evidence is best understood as an accumulation of volume or weight. Just as a longer paper—or article, or book—is not necessarily a more convincing piece of scholarship, there is no reason to assume that abundance, by itself, will compel your reader to assent if they don't feel that all this detail really amounts to evidence. In this chapter, we've looked at a number of possible situations where there was a mismatch between the backing and the claim. In that situation, supplying more of the same won't help at all.

A different way to think about your task here is to reflect on what you have gathered so far and decide what your *single most valuable piece of evidence* is. Is it a quotation? A number? A picture? A map? Something else? By all means, bolster that piece of evidence with other material, but it's often helpful to consider the simplest possible situation. Where does your favorite example fit into your argument? Why should the reader accept it as important and persuasive? What makes it count as evidence? Clear answers here will offer you a firm foundation to build on.

In the sciences, a standard venue for sharing research results is the poster session.[76] As the name suggests, projects are summarized within the confines of a poster. It is possible to take in the research question, the methods, and the results, all at a glance. We don't have any strong tradition of this in the humanities. However, there is a lesson to learn from this compact format. Your readers should be able to see, without difficulty, *why* you put the spotlight where you do, *how* you have assembled evidence, and *on what grounds* you think that this evidence amounts to something.

Of course, since you're not in the sciences, you'll be producing something much more extensive than a poster. Part IV will be your companion as you undertake the writing process, but having an overall sense of your thesis, warrants, and backing will supply you with the preliminary scaffolding for that great construction. Having a clear mission is the best cure for writer's block. It will provide guidance, and maybe even inspiration, down to the level of writing individual paragraphs and sentences. Footnotes may look different to you now as well. It's possible to fret over "why do I cite," "when do I cite," and "how much do I cite," but if you have an awareness of which of your main points will require extra support—and discussion at length—in the research paper, you may be surprised by how straightforward the answers are here.

---

[76] For a quick overview of what a scientific poster would contain, see Adelheid A.M. Nicol and Penny M. Pexman, *Displaying Your Findings: A Practical Guide for Creating Figures, Posters, and Presentations*, 6th ed. (Washington, D.C.: American Psychological Association, 2010), 163–176.

Further Reading

Miriam Dobson and Benjamin Ziemann, eds., *Reading Primary Sources: The Interpretation of Texts from Nineteenth- and Twentieth-Century History* (London: Routledge, 2009). Despite its title, this volume touches on a number of issues that are pertinent when working with words from any century.

Claire Lemercier and Claire Zalc, *Quantitative Methods in the Humanities: An Introduction* (Charlottesville: University of Virginia Press, 2019).

Gillian Rose, *Visual Methodologies*, 5th ed. (London: Sage, 2023) is wide-ranging, but probably chapters 10 and 11 will be of the most interest.

Penny Tinkler, *Using Photographs in Social and Historical Research* (London: Sage, 2013).

Konrad Lawson, et al., *A Guide to Spatial History: Areas, Aspects, and Avenues of Research (2022)* https://spatialhistory.net/guide/ , accessed 8/5/2023, highlights exemplary theoretical approaches and classic works that deploy them.

Riccardo Bavaj, et al., eds. *Doing Spatial History* (London: Routledge, 2022), delves into a greater variety of specific examples, situations, and primary source types than the Lawson volume.

If your source material doesn't neatly fit any of the categories discussed in depth here, it's still important to seek out appropriate reference points for how historians use that kind of evidence. Examples include Susan Broomhall, "Imagined Domesticities in Early Modern Dutch Dollhouses," *Parergon* 24, no. 2 (2007): 47–67; Katrina Navickas, "'That Sash Will Hang You': Political Clothing and Adornment in England, 1780–1840," *Journal of British Studies* 49, no. 3 (July 2010): 540–565; Deidre Lynch, "Bugs in Books," in *Manuscript Albums and Their Cultural Contexts: Collectors, Objects, and Practices*, ed. Janine Droese and Janina Karolewski (Berlin: DeGruyter, 2024), 167–188; Troels Myrup Kristensen, "Iconoclasm," in *The Oxford Handbook of Roman Sculpture*, ed. Elise A. Friedland et al. (Oxford: Oxford University Press, 2015), 667–680.

Checking in with Your Advisor: Part III Worksheet

A good way to warm up here is to re-visit your research plan from the end of Part II. Re-word it as a progress report about

- What you (mostly, really) looked at,
- What your approach was,
- What you concluded.

You can draft that as an email to your advisor. You don't have to send it, but they would probably like to hear from you just about now.

Recall that in Chap. 9, I proposed generating 15 different versions of your thesis statement. Try setting down a few different versions to look at now. The prompts below may help you get started.

You'll find that "throughout history …" thesis statements are vanishingly rare in academic writing by historians. In contrast, associating a time period with a noteworthy change (e.g., "the 1920s were the turning point") is common, whether the timescale is in days, weeks, years, or decades. Give that a try using your own subject matter:

_____
_____
_____.

Now, look at your claim itself. Is it

- Bold enough to be interesting?
- Measured enough to be credible?
- Sufficiently aligned with the surviving evidence to seem warranted?

Did you position your thesis statement right on top of the trickiest, most fraught, most complicated aspect of the subject matter? If not, how would it look if it were re-centered on that?

Do you signal some of that complexity within your thesis statement (perhaps using an "Although ..." clause)?

Which of your claims will be the most surprising, unfamiliar, or unsettling to readers?

What is the most likely objection to the position that you are taking? Is there a plausible alternative explanation that you need to address?

Describe in a couple of sentences your *favorite* piece of evidence and how it supports your thesis statement:

_____
_____
_____.

Does most of your evidence come from the verbal, numerical, visual, or spatial realm? What steps are you taking to guard against the common pitfalls associated with that kind of evidence?

Do you still think that this evidence type is the most effective way to explore the themes or aspects of the primary sources that interest you most?

Has the process of considering a thesis statement, warrants, and backing led you to realize that it's time for a return visit to your primary sources? Or do you realize you need to consult *different* primary sources than those you used before?

At this stage, what are you most certain about?

_____
_____.

What are you most unsure about?

_____
_____.

Earlier, you jotted down a working title for your project. Do you have an idea for a different title now?

_____
_____

When you see your advisor next, what you really want to ask them is:

_____
_____
_____.

PART IV

Writing Up

In his memorable piece, "Eight Hitchhiker Inscriptions from a Highway Railing at Barstow, California," the American composer Harry Partch set graffiti to music.[1] Partch approached this unlikely material with respect, curiosity, and even affection. His first contribution, then, is to make us slow down and really pay attention. Then, of course, we need to consider his selection of these particular scribblings out of who knows how many others. Why eight inscriptions? Why *these* eight? Beyond this, though, his musical arrangement allows us to hear the words on his terms.

On the page of an academic text, the framing and contextualization of quotations, images, or statistics can achieve something similar. You have spent a lot of time accumulating backing for your claims, but it is the selection and arrangement that gives your evidence a chance to sing.

I assume by this point that you are fairly clear in your own mind about *what* your overall claims are, and *which* evidence is best suited to support them. This was covered in Part III of this book; hesitation at the "writing up" stage is quite possibly a symptom of someone who has unfinished business with those issues.

Your journey to this point was a bit convoluted, as you sifted through different kinds of primary source material, different possible versions of your project, different conclusions. While it's okay to come to your insights in a roundabout way, readers have a limited tolerance for roundabout *structure*. You don't want a situation where it's hard for the reader to spot where your best evidence lines up to support your most important claims. Yet, in our discipline, there is no handy standardized template of sections and section headings. You're the ringmaster of this particular circus, so you have some decisions to make about which acts you'll trot out, and in which order. Chapter 11, "Structuring Your Paper," is there to demystify this for you.

---

[1] The composition itself is only about ten minutes long. It is not difficult to find recordings of it online, or to access a transcript of the text.

Your detailed, guided tour of the evidence is probably the most important part of your paper. In developing this material, you will face a new set of choices: weighing how much or how little evidence is needed to make a particular point, assessing whether and when you must contextualize, excerpting and highlighting without sacrificing elementary fairness and intellectual honesty. Chapter 12, "Crafting Your Exposition," considers the opportunities and challenges that occur down at this level, as you formulate individual paragraphs, sentences, captions, and footnotes.

Chapter 13, "Working with Feedback," deals with the emotional rollercoaster of the project's late stages. At times like this, it's helpful to remind yourself that often the difference between good work and great work is the willingness to act on outside input. "Writing is rewriting" has nearly achieved the status of a proverb; Donald Murray even came up with a list of "twenty ways to unfinal a draft."[2] One writer likens the revision process to "cleaning house, getting rid of all the junk, getting things in the right order, tightening things up," while another draws the analogy to a stick-like, frostbitten tree "leafing out" to take its joyous warm weather form.[3] It is possible, then, to approach revision in a spirit of gratitude, as the moment when your paper becomes most fully and successfully itself.

If this is true of your paper as a whole, it is also true of your title. Although most rough drafts do have a title of some sort, your best and most informed thinking about a title will come at the end of the process. Often, you realize that your focus has shifted, or you understand your own conclusions better, suggesting the need for a new title. Therefore, the section on giving your work a title (and writing an abstract) is in Chap. 13.

Not all readers of this book will experience a *viva voce* defense at the conclusion of their project. I do include a discussion of the defense at the end of Chap. 13 because this, too, is an opportunity to receive input. You may experience a more informal version of a defense, in which someone—perhaps just your advisor—urges you to make corrections and further revisions prior to submitting the true final version of your paper.

Our critics—and even our own false starts and half-baked ideas—are ultimately helping everyone clarify what's going on. This conviction is captured neatly in the title of a book that is steeped in the rhetorical tradition: *Thank You for Arguing*.[4] Listen well, take notes and gather ideas, bearing in mind that a close reading is a compliment; you motivated someone enough to really engage with the material, and they saw enough potential in it to prompt suggestions to make it even better.

---

[2] Murray, *Craft*, 218–220.

[3] Ellen Goodman and Elizabeth Cooke, quoted in Murray, *Craft*, 3 and 19–20 respectively.

[4] Jay Heinrichs, *Thank You for Arguing: What Aristotle, Lincoln, and Homer Simpson Can Teach Us about the Art of Persuasion* (New York: Three Rivers Press, 2013).

CHAPTER 11

Structuring Your Paper

John Lewis Gaddis has remarked that "Historians don't like to display ductwork."[1] Yet as Gaddis' own statement tacitly concedes, the ductwork is there, and we'd be in trouble without it. To continue with his metaphor, perhaps many of us would consider a building ugly if the walls were transparent, but we also are rather attached to heating, cooling, electricity, and the conveniences of plumbing.

In academic writing, there are some unavoidable, important tasks. At some point in your paper, you'll need to set up your problem; supply the relevance and context; acknowledge the historiography; possibly supply some necessary orientation and define key terms; acknowledge any difficulties or ambiguities about your primary sources; walk your reader through the available evidence; discuss reasonable conclusions that we can draw from it.

Our peers in the social sciences face similar tasks. However, many disciplines have standard section headings, a predictable order, and even a numbered structure (one subsection might be designated 1.3.2). In contrast, I've never seen a publication by a historian with a section marked "literature review." It's uncommon to have a separate section that explains what method was adopted. Even a "conclusions" section—bearing that name—is not invariably present. Social scientists sometimes call our approach a "literary" style.[2] While experienced readers know what to look for, the structural elements are left extremely understated. This sets up some problems for anyone undertaking the "writing up" phase in our discipline for the first time. It's natural to turn to your own favorite pieces of scholarship in a search for role models, but in the absence of section headings and signposting, the text does not give up its secrets easily.

Nor is pure storytelling a viable path forward. The hazard of a narrative that only *implies* a thesis is that the reader will miss it. A mere recounting of events,

---

[1] Gaddis, *Landscape*, 92.
[2] Dunleavy, *Authoring*, 82.

however competent and accurate, probably doesn't rise to the level of academic History writing. At the same time, narrative has been a *part*—even a signature part—of our disciplinary toolkit for millennia. Before considering alternatives to storytelling, the first section of this chapter addresses this sometimes fraught issue head on.

Are We Storytellers First?

In the early years of the eighteenth century, Felipe Tendeur, a soldier serving in what is today Colombia, was arrested by the Spanish authorities for possessing "a book in Dutch called Prayers and devotional songs for seamen." Tendeur's insouciant remark that he "read the good parts and left out the bad ones, and that he could read the books that he liked" did not impress the Inquisition.[3] Open Stuart Schwartz' book *All Can Be Saved* to a random page, and you are likely to encounter other lively anecdotes featuring sassy characters like Tendeur.

These tiny, delightful narratives (an accusation, a trial, the defendant's remarks, the court's verdict) may keep us turning the pages, but Schwartz presents them only as examples, comparing and contrasting to make a point. Indeed, he sets up the section that includes Tendeur with these lines:

> I want to examine three American cases of the eighteenth century in which religious tolerance was expressed and in which a desire for freedom of thought played a central role. All these cases involved relatively unlettered, simple men, one a soldier, the others mariners, but all were literate, all set a high priority on freedom of conscience and on what they could read, and all expressed an admiration for lands where such freedom seemed to be a reality.[4]

Many individual paragraphs of *All Can Be Saved* follow a style that would not be out of place in a work of fiction. Yet Schwartz' goal is to map out the patterns of blasphemy and various forms of irreverent freethought in the Spanish-speaking world and help us understand their reception. Because Schwartz's overall structure is analytical, Tendeur pops up on page 231 and lingers for a few paragraphs, but doesn't reappear later in the book, or interact with the other people under discussion. A reader expecting an overall story would be disappointed.

Sometimes, though, narrative performs some heavier and more serious work for us. Historians are united, as a discipline, by our particularly strong belief that context matters. As Marc Bloch once put it, we would not simply write about an eight-year conquest, or a fifteen-year process of religious conversion; it matters to us that this is Caesar conquering Gaul, or Martin Luther

---

[3] All quotations in this paragraph are from Schwartz, *All Can Be Saved*, 231.
[4] Schwartz, *All Can Be Saved*, 227.

undergoing a crisis of faith.⁵ Faced with a gradual development, we are wary of offering a quick description. Jonathon Glassman's book *War of Words, War of Stones: Racial Thought and Violence in Colonial Zanzibar* offers a harrowing analysis of how the rhetoric of ethnically polarized political parties can erode the norms of civil society.⁶ Although, at first, newspapers in Zanzibar published editorials expressing concern, and the authorities convened an investigative commission to inquire into the origins of the violence, a cycle of escalating fear and hatred wore down the old habits of everyday coexistence. Every inflammatory rumor seemed plausible, and a pretext for instant retaliation. The culmination of this process was the deadly riots of 1964. A quick rundown is possible, but Glassman's book-length exposition, deliberately, matches the pace of the slow erosion of norms that he describes.

In Chap. 9, discussing thesis statements, I entertained some possibilities for the *one* sentence that might sum up Beverly Gage's biography of J. Edgar Hoover. However, we shouldn't lose sight of the message that Gage sent simply through the physical extent of her book itself. It runs to 864 pages. She is far from unique in feeling that there would be something incongruous about offering a short treatment of complex subject matter; PhD candidates in History produce, on average, the lengthiest doctoral theses of any discipline. We are committed to discussing change over time without losing sight of the stubborn uniqueness of a particular moment and place and situation. As a tool to approach that task, narrative is hard to beat.

Indeed, narrative is such a familiar technique that we sometimes speak, a little too loosely, about ourselves *as* storytellers. It's not unheard of to circulate tips from screenwriters or novelists.⁷ If you browse this kind of material, you also owe it to yourself to read some words of caution. For instance, the documentary film makers Alexandra Juhasz and Alisa Lebow have warned: *"Not everything should be molded into a story*, not everyone fits its constricting contours nor finds their most meaningful incantation in its familiar folds."⁸ As an anthropologist, Dominic Bryan brought a profound awareness of the power of ritualized storytelling. It was exactly this that prompted his misgivings. If our culture would like to assign historians the role of the "high priest of commemoration," he remarked, maybe we should refuse it.⁹ It's worth taking a moment to unpack what is at stake here for historians.

---

⁵ Bloch, *Historian's Craft*, 35.
⁶ Bloomington, IN: Indiana University Press, 2011.
⁷ Ann Curthoys and Ann McGrath, *How to Write History That People Want to Read* (Sydney: University of New South Wales Press, 2009), 145.
⁸ "Beyond Story: An Online, Community-Based Manifesto," *World Records Journal* 2, no. 3 (2018), https://worldrecordsjournal.org/beyond-story-an-online-community-based-manifesto/, accessed 3/7/2024.
⁹ Dominic Bryan, "Ritual, Identity, and Nation: When the Historian Becomes the High Priest of Commemoration," in *Remembering 1916: The Easter Rising, the Somme and the Politics of Memory in Ireland*, ed. Richard S. Grayson and Fearghal McGarry (Cambridge: Cambridge University Press, 2016), 24-42; also very pertinent here is the discussion of Ronald Reagan's speech at Bitburg in Robert Braun, "The Holocaust and Problems of Historical Representation," *History and Theory* 33, no. 2 (May 1994): 172-197.

First, there's a risk that the search for an attractive, relatable, compelling, or suspenseful *story* may start to dictate what sort of topics we explore—and which we avoid. "People like stories about other people" is well-intentioned advice.[10] Still, environmental historians have shown the value of animal-centered or more-than-human approaches. Fernand Braudel suggested that events—in the traditional sense of the word, anyway—were little more than "surface disturbances, crests of foam that the tides of history carry on their strong backs."[11] We needn't agree with this statement as a universal generalization to concede that some thesis statements are more about process than event, or more about stasis than change. The bottom line is that some subject matter really does come brimming with characters, motivations, scenes, turning points, and snappy dialogue—and some subject matter doesn't. If your research didn't turn up a single thing that would turn a screenwriter's head, that's okay.

In fact, it could be a good thing. The storytelling imperative has a bad habit of eating up your time and attention. It may suggest a need for protagonists and antagonists in ways that warp your interpretation of the material. If a storyline seems especially tidy, it can even crowd out alternatives, or make them hard to imagine. As Jean M. O'Brien has pointed out, in New England a host of expressions couched in narrative-friendly language—*the first birth, the last Indian*—made settler colonialism seem like "the most natural framework" for anyone writing the history of a town.[12] Some might speculate that we could always find a different storyteller to tell a better story. Ultimately, the problem runs deeper than that. By relying on the all-too-human yearning for "sentiment and closure," a story tends to prepare the reader to feel the right way, rather than wonder about the right things.[13]

There's a coziness associated with the recitation of the old beloved campfire story, its instantly recognizable cast of characters, its rehearsal of familiar tropes, its predictable conclusions. This impulse toward coziness is not the instinct you want to be listening to right now. While successful academic writing doesn't need to be harsh, dissonant, or strange, we do expect novelty. Telling a familiar story with no substantial change is *the* approach most likely to elicit the dreaded "so what?" from an academic reader.

A good story well told isn't the same thing as a good argument well made. Modern academic writing requires us to lay out our logic, make fine distinctions, clarify our stance in relation to rival interpretations, and justify our use of evidence. This is valuable because it allows others to critique our choices and advance the conversation, but even before that happens, it also permits us to

---

[10] Schrag, *Princeton Guide*, 312.

[11] Joyce Appleby, et al., *Telling the Truth*, 83.

[12] Jean M. O'Brien, *Firsting and Lasting: Writing Indians Out of Existence in New England* (Minneapolis: University of Minnesota Press, 2010), 6, 7, 107.

[13] Jill Godmilow and Ann-Louise Shapiro, "How Real is the Reality in Documentary Film?" *History and Theory* 36, No. 4 (December 1997): 80–101, see 84.

examine our own work with an unflinching honesty. Sentence by sentence, paragraph by paragraph, a storytelling style works to obscure exactly these aspects of your writing—if you even remembered to include them.

You may have an advisor who explicitly discourages storytelling. If so, that's because—like me—they have seen too many students get in trouble with it. Clearly, if participants (or historians) have cast some doubt on the order of events, it might be desirable to offer your readers a rundown of what happened. It's even possible that at some point, your meticulous reckoning—who was where, when, doing what—will speak directly to something at the heart of your thesis statement itself. If narrative is used sparingly in your paper, slowing down and offering a blow-by-blow account just there could lend an intensity to a special passage that readers absolutely must notice.

Suggesting that you could *make judicious use of narration*, but *avoid telling a story,* may sound like an ambiguous—or even untenable—distinction. However, writers practice these prudent balancing acts all the time. For example, it might be helpful to describe a scene in 25 words, as a quick, evocative orientation. At that same point in your paper, though, 250 words of description would probably come across as overdone. There's even an expression, "purple prose," for self-indulgent passages like this.

Academic writing can be fun, engaging, and thought-provoking without imitating other genres. What academic readers crave is a historian with something interesting to *say*. A thoughtful interpretation is spellbinding. A clever use of evidence will leave them at the edge of their seat. Don't feel that you must stifle your creativity, either. As you consider which method of exposition might best fit your argument and your source material, you'll also have plenty of chances to invent solutions and explore your own potential as a writer.

From Writer's Block to Building Blocks

The process of filling blank pages with words is a bit mysterious, and everyone comes at it in their own idiosyncratic way. I will have a lot to say in this chapter about the deliberate listing, outlining, or sequencing of parts. The truth is, though, that it's possible to jot down a clever outline in a matter of minutes and then freeze up when it comes to producing actual text.

A different method, unapologetically, starts in the middle. Advocates of the "reverse outline" technique point out that you can write a draft and later pull structure out of it, studying your own writing as if it were someone else's, observing what each paragraph actually does. With the reverse outline in hand, you have the ability to consider what works, what doesn't, and what remains to do.[14]

This approach results, eventually, in a "discovery draft" that eventually *decides* what it concludes, without necessarily having a clear vision in mind at

---

[14] Rachael Cayley, *Thriving as a Graduate Writer: Principles, Strategies, and Habits for Effective Academic Writing* (Ann Arbor: University of Michigan Press, 2023), 133–139.

the outset.¹⁵ That can work. Once you see your claims and backing all together on the page for the first time, take stock. Ask yourself what's missing, what argument feels misaligned with the evidence, and what would work better in a different location. Even incorrigible outliners-in-advance like me often find that once we have written a fair amount, we discover that we aren't arguing quite what we expected! I also regularly find that my sections grow, shrink, disappear, or split in two as the writing process continues.

There are some risks to a write-first-and-ask-questions-later approach, though. You may wind up with a draft that contains only an *implied* thesis statement. The same goes for warrants. As I noted in Part Three of this book, that is a recipe for trouble!

One way to reduce the risk of an undisciplined rough draft is to start by writing about your best evidence. Exxon CEO Rex Tillerson was considered a climate change moderate who sought to redirect his company's stance, but when information came to light that his behind-the-scenes strategy and private remarks were quite different, it was referred to as "obituary-changing."¹⁶ You may not have eye-opening, show-stopping evidence quite on this scale, but in the course of your research, it's a near certainty that you've found a run of primary sources that you feel requires us to rethink something. Donald Murray reminds us of the importance of the *revealing detail*, the *significant phrase*, and the *haunting image*.¹⁷ We could probably add some terms to his list; maybe your findings are best expressed through a *killer statistic*.

Whatever has captured your eye, spend a page or more walking a reader through just this and really teasing out the implications, as you understand them. See if you can discuss those examples or anecdotes or pieces of information *as evidence*, in other words as backing for your thesis statement. Supplement this kernel of writing with other material, counterbalancing it, comparing and contrasting. Before you know it, the middle portion of your paper is well underway.

After the dust has settled on those first few pages, though, it might be time to think about the overall design. Before you proceed with this chapter, I'd like you to make some preliminary notes. Whether or not you choose to call this an outline is up to you. Maybe it's a to-do list. But I'm going to go out on a limb and say that *every* paper needs the following five items tucked away somewhere.

One introductory paragraph In plain language, sketch out what's at stake and why we should care. It's often a good idea to imagine a historian reading this who does not work on your continent, time period, or subspecialty. Explain to *that* person why the puzzle or problem that interests you fits into a larger puzzle, problem, context, or controversy.

---

¹⁵ Murray, *Craft*, 50.
¹⁶ Christopher M. Matthew and Colin Eaton, "Inside Exxon's Strategy to Downplay Climate Change," *Wall Street Journal*, September 14, 2023.
¹⁷ Murray, *Craft*, 175.

One paragraph of lit review Acknowledge your debts. Nod toward what was missing in the historiography. Suppose I asked you to list five pieces of scholarship that, together, define where the field's been. Tell me about those, and where your project fits in.

One paragraph of "background" and historical context Suppose there are five things every reader of this paper needs to know up front. What are they?

One paragraph about what makes your study different from what's gone before To get at *this,* you looked at *that.* Discuss the special strengths and weaknesses of the surviving primary sources for your particular topic. Explain your choice of primary sources. This is a great place to sum up not just what you looked at, but how much you examined—25 archival boxes? 175 court cases? Six pieces of memoir or autobiography from an often overlooked minority group? The complete meeting minutes of a grassroots organization over a ten-year period?

One paragraph of findings As much as possible, match up each finding with your use of sources. I looked *here,* which showed *that...* As we can see *from...*

One thing you might notice about these five paragraphs is that they are many of the things that a book review would cover; indeed, some excellent book reviews do little more than this. Therefore, if you are feeling skeptical that such things are possible in 250 or 500 words, have a look at some recent book reviews in your favorite area of historical study. It's a little challenging to look at your own work with the dispassionate eye of a book reviewer, but that's a skill worth cultivating.

With these five paragraphs in hand, you probably have placeholders for everything that matters most. For sure, think about what might be missing from my generic skeleton; every project has its own quirky attributes that make it special. You can also anticipate possible objections to your choice of sources or your boldest conclusions, and write about those, perhaps even in a dedicated sixth paragraph of its own.

From these notes, you can gradually build out supplements and subsections that make each of your placeholder paragraphs stronger, fuller, and more comprehensive. What you've got right here *could* form the basic structure of your entire paper. If you think it's inelegant to have the dry academic signposting on display from beginning to end, keep it quarantined in just one or two places. Just don't leave it out.

If you've completed this exercise, you have a sense of an *overall* to-do list for what the paper must contain. Paragraphs are stones in a larger edifice. If you know what you are arguing, you'll have a sense of purpose as you slide them into place. Likewise, if you understand what kind of warrants you are using, you'll know, broadly speaking, what sort of evidence your reader will expect to see. If you are clear on which of your claims are most likely to draw skeptical reactions, you'll have a general idea about which parts of your paper need to be longer, and where the ties between claims and backing should be tightest and most explicit.

This leaves a number of matters still unsettled, though. In what order should all these things appear? How do you manage the relative weight, proportion, and emphasis among the parts? What is the role of introductions and conclusions? The rest of this chapter will explore these questions and help you design a custom-built structure that works well for the needs of your particular project.

How Much Background Should I Give?

It's a fair guess that historians don't need history lessons. What they may need is carefully selected information that relates to the point you are trying to make, the assertion that you want to prove, and the distinctions that you need to draw. I have supplied a diagram (Fig. 11.1) to remind you of this.

A glance at the typical ratio of background to main content in the articles that academic History journals publish will help orient you. Pick one at random, and I will hazard a guess that 5–25% of the article's total space (including footnotes, maps, and illustrations) was devoted to setup tasks. Aim for the low end of this.

That said, you may have noticed that there really are common misconceptions about your subject matter. Perhaps you've already had to explain certain things to friends, family, or your advisor. In that case, a background section that speaks directly to the problem could be very helpful. For similar reasons, define the most difficult words or concepts early on, particularly the ones that

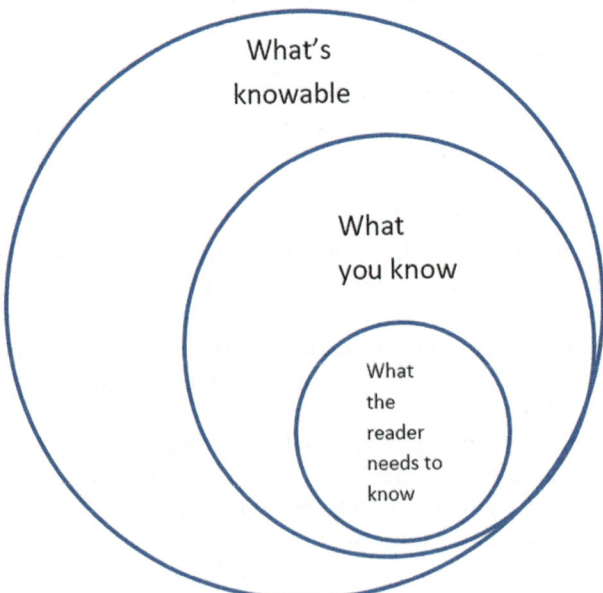

Fig. 11.1 What's knowable; what you know; what the reader needs to know. (Diagram by Isaac Land)

appear throughout your paper. If your primary sources are derived from legal or legislative proceedings, you might need to supply a short tutorial on how courts, or legislatures, operated.

There's no such thing as a generic reader, which complicates your choices here. It's not unusual to have multiple assessors; I'm accustomed to committees of three. Some of those readers will need a true introduction; others may just require a reminder of some key points. A historian with a specialization in gender and sexuality isn't necessarily familiar with the legal and cultural constraints that operated in the location, and the century, that you are writing about. An expert on German history during the Kaiserreich is probably *not* well versed in German-Argentine trade relations, even during that exact time period. So the need for background is uneven, and extremely project-specific.

The best way to handle some things is *not* a background section. As one book on academic writing remarks, "Historical individuals need to be introduced properly—just as in a social situation."[18] Those conversational introductions are often indispensable, but also remember how quick they usually are, almost like little asides tucked into another sentence. When a person's name first pops up in your text, you could just supply a couple key details about them there, and move on.

Similarly, there are many bits of context that you can explain just in passing. In his book about Roman Egypt, Peter Parsons notes that "a folded slip of papyrus was intended to provide all-purpose protection," and he supplies the text, "A EE HHH IIII OOOOO ΥΥΥΥΥ ΩΩΩΩΩΩΩ" with one line of explanation: "Here the seven Greek vowels represent the building-blocks of the universe, and the supplicant invokes them in arithmetic crescendo."[19] Since magic isn't his main focus, this is quite sufficient. A whole background section on this topic would feel like overkill, or showing off. In this spirit, experiment with how much background you can convey in a single sentence. A footnote works well if you're really just glossing a term or providing a simple definition. If it's more a matter of "how much?" or "when?", a single statistic or brief example might suffice.

On the other hand, suppose that your primary sources, your secondary sources, and you yourself are all discussing fine nuances of exactly the same thing, such as the meaning of the term "utopian socialism." Here, a whole page or two of clarification might be valuable, because a reader really might jump to the conclusion that you agree with the other historians, or worse, that the utopian socialists agreed with each other!

If theoretical terms are important to your project, they deserve some attention early on. A vague reference to Latour or Foucault is not as useful, or as intellectually acute, as mentioning which concept you have in mind, and how you yourself understand that concept. Some theoretical terms (governmentality, assemblage, patriarchy) have passed into such wide use that quoting a

---

[18] Curthoys and McGrath, *How to Write*, 143.
[19] Parsons, *City*, 208.

theorist's original definition may *not* capture the way in which you are really deploying it. In some cases, the best place to address theory is in your lit review section. If your debt is really to such-and-such historian who drew inspiration from the theorist, then maybe describing what they did with the concept is all your reader really needs to see.

On the historiography front, you have a responsibility to show you are up to date. Provide a roundup of what's gone on in the last decade. Prior to that, be selective. If you delve into the nearly infinite regress of "begats" of the historiography, be sure you have a good reason for it. "In the tradition of E.P. Thompson..." might kick off a paragraph, but depending on your exact research topic and approach, it's also possible to relegate even a titan like that to your footnotes. You may have a better sense now than when you started about what's truly noteworthy, what needs explanation, and what is so familiar that a nod of acknowledgment is perfectly adequate. For your first draft, a light touch here is sufficient; if your advisor urges that you need more in this section, that's not difficult to address at the revision stage.

Trying to express your relationship to the historiography may send you back, intellectually and emotionally, to themes discussed in Chaps. 3 and 5. You're not alone in this struggle—it's extremely common to find others' work both inviting *and* intimidating, or feel that their contributions are both helpful *and* an obstacle to moving the conversation forward. Finessing your language around that is good manners, but it is also helpful guidance for your readers, who will need to understand both ends of the classic paradox: Every project is, in some sense, derivative; every project is, in some sense, a departure from what went before. It's okay to be honest about that when you situate your work in relation to your closest counterparts.

Perhaps you are using a primary source that is controversial, difficult, or just very unfamiliar. This also could be the place to discuss the sources you didn't use, or the materials you couldn't access. In his account of the responses to the genocide in Bangladesh, Gary Bass took time to explain to his readers that—sometimes at Henry Kissinger's behest—White House officials "routinely sanitized their records of conversations," while in India, materials from a certain date are *said* to be declassified, but the archive "often leaves out the most significant and controversial papers."[20] Generally, if you are working with a source that has a reputation for being problematic, the more you can do up front to explain your approach to that material, the better.

Make a short list of the types of background that you expect your readers will need. Understanding *why* you are providing background will give you a rough guide to how much you need to say, and about what.

Consider these 54 words of background:

---

[20] Gary J. Bass, *The Blood Telegram: Nixon, Kissinger, and a Forgotten Genocide* (New York: Vintage Books, 2014), xvi, 348.

The Weimar police ran the spectrum from the heavily armed *Landespolizei* (stationed in barracks), modeled along military lines and designed for employment in the event of large-scale civil disturbances to a *Gemeindepolizei* (community police) located in rural villages and responsible for finding lost cattle or children and enforcing work and noise restrictions on Sundays.[21]

This passage appeared in an article about police who were repurposed (and to some extent, retrained) to carry out mass murder on a genocidal scale on the Eastern Front. In that context, it serves as a helpful, quick reminder that the individuals came from a wide variety of prewar backgrounds, even if they were all considered law enforcement. The killing fields of Poland could be a jarring—or even devastating—transition for men accustomed to "finding lost cattle or children."

Consider, though, how you would react if you encountered these same 54 words of background in an article about how law enforcement responded to reports of domestic violence during the Weimar period. They would barely scratch the surface of the various kinds of context that you might expect, and need. Just for starters, women are not mentioned. What was family law like in this period? What were the rules of evidence that pertained to cases of assault and battery? What do we know about everyday misogyny among the police force? Were there ingrained assumptions about wife beating that prevailed in popular culture which also shaped how law enforcement reacted to testimony of domestic violence? Would responding to domestic violence resemble a police errand such as "finding lost cattle or children," or were there circumstances where it would be undertaken as a serious criminal investigation? All of this background would belong either in a dedicated section early in the paper, or perhaps as a series of digressions to contextualize particular examples and quotations later in the paper, but the reader would need it somewhere.

What you *won't* find in any article about German policing in this era is a discussion of the Treaty of Versailles, or the causes of World War Two! Supplying too much background, or the wrong kind of background, is a common rookie mistake in History papers. Develop the unfamiliar. Gesture briefly to the familiar. Explain ambiguous terms. Please move things along briskly, though. The background section is the opening act, but it's never the main attraction.

Academic writing is all about the transition from the paved road of consensus to the rugged and thorny terrain of real complexity. If you're offering a god's eye panorama, it's only to disrupt it. If you present a generalization, it's only because you're about to introduce a puzzle that has so far defied solutions.

In that spirit, if you are writing about a concept—such as agency—don't linger too long on a background discussion that does little more than rehearse a familiar dictionary or textbook definition of the word. Present readers with the actual situation when the whole challenge of interpretation hinges on *which* definition of agency we use.

---

[21] Westermann, "Ordinary Men," 43.

Ordering the Parts

What goes where? It's instructive to study the organization of an academic journal article that you admire. It is even possible to mimic that organization, almost down to the paragraph level—an anecdote just here, a thesis statement there. Choose your model wisely, though. The article may be excellent, but perhaps it met expository challenges that aren't yours.

Jane E. Miller discusses a simple but powerful method of exposition that she calls "GEE," standing for Generalization, Example, and Exceptions.[22] This works well for many academic writing tasks, because it accommodates both a clear thesis statement and a nuanced awareness that the world is complicated and changing. It also anticipates that skeptical readers will question the adequacy of any insight that you offer.

To implement GEE, after describing the pattern you see, you'd offer the best evidence you have to support it, and then move on to contrasting these with some exceptional cases. This could be a noteworthy body of contrary evidence, or in a "change over time" paper, it could be a new trend that broke the pattern. It's probably helpful to announce your overall plan to the reader up front, and signpost it with appropriate section headings. Then, when you transition from one part to the next, they won't see it as a sign that you're confused, or inconsistent.

I wouldn't propose GEE—or anything else—as a one-size-fits-all outline. Rather, successful outlines emerge logically from the needs of a particular thesis statement, a particular use of sources, an intervention in a particular controversy. It's sometimes easier to express this about someone else's research topic than about your own. For instance, what sort of outline would develop and support a thesis statement like this?

> Lincoln's Gettysburg Address is a famous speech today, but it had little impact at the time.

Questions naturally follow from this interesting, debatable proposition. How do you know this? How would we measure impact, anyhow? Impact on which sorts of people? If it had little impact, why was that? This paper would focus on a relatively short period of time—the weeks and months following the speech. The body of the paper might consist of a discussion of different media outlets that covered (or didn't cover) the speech, evaluating the response from different possible target audiences, or comparing and contrasting some of the most common reactions to the Gettysburg Address.

Now imagine an outline for a paper with this rather different kind of thesis statement:

---

[22] Jane E. Miller, *The Chicago Guide to Writing About Numbers: The Effective Presentation of Quantitative Information* (Chicago: University of Chicago Press, 2004), 265.

There was a sharp generational shift between the first and second generations of Black Panther activists.

This paper would naturally follow a different structure. Unlike the Gettysburg Address paper, it would examine a timescale best measured in decades. The body of the paper would probably focus on a very small number of individual life stories that are sufficiently well documented to support the inquiry at hand. It would proceed chronologically, explaining what the demarcation was between the two generations and what events and inspirations led to their differing outlook.

Notice that the first two examples each revolved around a yes/no proposition: The Gettysburg Address *didn't* have much impact, the Black Panther activists *did* show a marked generational shift. Consider a third example, a thesis statement that doesn't take the form of a simple affirmation or negation:

> In England, the Reformation subtly reworked the devil's role and meaning, relocating the conflict with Satan to the individual conscience of the believer.[23]

Supporting and developing a position like this would probably involve weaving together a very large number of examples gathered from across a long period of time. Unlike the first and second examples, it is also a statement whose full implications will only gradually become apparent to the reader. For instance, one section might explain that the battle unfolded most often on the pages of personal diaries, where small daily doubts, temptations, and distractions were characterized as the devil's work. Later sections of the paper might help the reader understand where less typical examples, perhaps involving accusations of witchcraft or demonic possession, fit into the bigger picture.

I doubt that any of these ideas for outlines would appeal much to a Hollywood screenwriter. But each are well suited to the needs of the academic project that they serve. Your project, too, deserves a form of scaffolding that is suited to its needs, allows you to showcase your evidence, and gives your main claims room to breathe.

I have mentioned claims, in the plural. When, exactly, is the best place to state your thesis? Should you introduce your thesis in stages, or all at once? Some textbooks imply that single-minded writing is the best kind of writing. To mention an extreme example, one writing guide suggests that

> Each comma, verb, statistic, reference, descriptive detail, transition, summary sentence should relate in a direct way to the central tension of what is being written.[24]

---

[23] I am drawing on themes and concepts from Johnstone, "Protestant Devil" here.
[24] Murray, *Craft*, 67.

This is understandable advice, yet it does not speak very well to a research paper that must present multiple points of view and consider different contributing factors. You deserve an outline that will do justice to the nuance of your thesis statement, and the expectations of an academic readership. The challenge, then, is to offer a structure that keeps the overall argument within sight, but accommodates the complexity of the subject matter. In contrast, an unwavering focus on a single "central tension" might result in an outline resembling the hammering, monotonous verse-chorus-verse structure of a popular song.

When considering the relationship of your outline to your overall thesis, think about how the elements of an architectural form work together.

In Fig. 11.2, each of the supporting arches and gradually ascending domes form a structure that mounts, by stages, to a satisfying silhouette. In this analogy, while the minaret may—in some sense—be the arresting, signature

Fig. 11.2 William Henry Goodyear, "Mosque of Suleiman I," Istanbul, Turkey, 1903. (Brooklyn Museum Archives, Goodyear Archival Collection (S03_06_01_003 image 1711) via Wikimedia Commons)

element, higher than anything else, it is surrounded by material that visually *complements* it and fills out the picture. It's not hard to pick out at a glance what the minarets are, or which dome stands higher than the others. Yet the mosque is not the minaret.

Perhaps the mosque analogy is useful for another reason: It is possible, and indeed common, for a mosque to have more than one minaret, and domes of a lesser elevation than the largest one. In this book, I have emphasized the overall thesis—because its presence offers a guiding star to orient you throughout. Yet the work of topic sentences and section headings has much in common with the work of thesis statements, on that appropriately smaller scale. A highflying thesis statement may actually require a series of supporting subclaims, the rhetorical equivalent of arches or buttresses.

One shortcoming of the architecture analogy, however, is that while the façade of a building is taken in at a glance, readers will experience your written work sequentially, like someone listening to a musical composition, or hearing a poem. Poems often have rhyme schemes; for instance, a Spenserian sonnet follows ABAB BCBC CDCD EE. In music, too, it's not uncommon to introduce themes that may recur at intervals or interweave in a new way.

Psychologists might speculate about how much pattern is just right, but it is safe to say that many people enjoy it when they encounter a series of somewhat predictable, somewhat surprising combinations. As long as it is not too complex, even a casual listener can notice it. They don't need to consult a diagram, or a musical score, to experience a satisfying sense of resonance.

Finding something like an ABCD for your project could give you just enough structure, without abandoning the complexity and nuance that most historians feel is one of the great strengths of our disciplinary style. While there is nothing magical about having four elements, what we are going for here is enough familiarity that the reader will have a pleasant sensation: "Ah, that again" or "oh look, a new combination." If you devised a pattern using the whole alphabet—an A to Z—only the most dogged and obsessive reader would even spot it.

What would your ABCD look like? Perhaps your thesis statement revolves around ideals, motivations, or ideological frameworks which interacted in varying, sometimes surprising, ways. One subsection of your paper might put the spotlight on a situation when B and D worked to reinforce each other. Another subsection might reveal that in another situation, A, B, and C appeared mutually exclusive, provoking tension and prompting a difficult, controversial choice.

Or, you could zero in on a few well-documented individuals whose lives and experiences are illustrative of something discussed in your thesis statement. If certain figures make repeat appearances in the beginning, middle, and end of your paper, there are many potential benefits. It provides continuity, jogs the reader's memory, provides opportunities for empathy, and generally supplies a relatable human face to what might otherwise be an abstract phenomenon.[25]

---

[25] Schrag, *Princeton Guide*, 311–340 offers a vigorous advocacy of such a technique.

Don't bend your exposition out of shape to affirm someone's character arc, though. If "the best art *almost* becomes sentimental but doesn't," then let me suggest that History writing, too, is at its best when it maintains some critical distance.[26] Still, characters that recur—perhaps in interesting, unexpected combinations and differing contexts—could offer the historian's equivalent of an elegant rhyme scheme or musical arrangement.

Paul A. Cohen's book on the Boxer Rebellion suggests still another way that an ABCD framework could generate an effective outline.[27] He has a chapter on ideological, anti-Western motivations as a root of the uprising. There is also a chapter about how the wrath of God appeared to have sent a drought to the plains of north China. Other chapters delve into spirit possession and supernatural forces at work on the battlefield. Cohen's overall structure conveys something about the radical plurality of the Boxer Rebellion—What caused it? What was it? What was at stake? Clearly it depends on who we ask.

A different way to think about what structure really accomplishes for your paper is that it will help direct the reader's attention to what matters most. It's tempting to apportion time, space, and effort evenly among the different parts of your paper, sort of on the principle that you should love all your children equally. The best way to give that one special portion of your paper the additional weight it needs, though, is to allow it to take up more room. Even before you begin to write, you might ask yourself: What will my longest section be?

Perhaps you have more evidence about one thing than others, and you'd like to showcase that and quote from those primary sources at length. Or a more narrative-oriented paper might select a moment of crisis or a moment of decision to feature in its longest section. If you are working with something tricky like oral history, a long discussion of method could be the section that needs the extra pages.

You could also try to anticipate the reader's greatest sticking point or area of reluctance. Intellectual honesty calls for finding a way to write about the toughest, most intractable aspect of your material. Making this your longest section gives you that chance to acknowledge what was at issue here, but also to explain how you addressed it. You may squirm at the suggestion of offering the reader quite this much opportunity to watch you struggle. Yet much of the historian's craft consists in fully inhabiting the question "what can we know?"—in all its contradictions and limitations—without giving up. I promise you that any historian will respect you more for staying with the trouble, rather than pretending it wasn't there.

Once you have some notion of *which* section ought to be the longest, you should consider *where* it belongs. Is it so fundamental that it belongs quite early, since it makes it possible to comprehend the rest of the paper? In some cases, the answer will be yes. Or you could organize your paper to start with

---

[26] Goldberg, *Writing Down the Bones*, 61.
[27] Paul A. Cohen, *History in Three Keys: The Boxers as Event, Experience, and Myth* (New York: Columbia University Press, 1997).

the more familiar and proceed to the less familiar, or from the less disputable to the more controversial or intricate.[28] This approach might place your longest section halfway or two-thirds of the way through your paper. By that point, the reader may be invested enough in your project that they will have the patience to work through some more challenging material.

It's also possible to start from your longest section and build out from there. Suppose you have decided that your longest section falls relatively late in the paper. What ought to come *after* it? A section relating to an aftermath of some sort, a consequence of earlier actions? For example, if your paper delved into an abuse, your last section might deal with the reforms that changed how that industry operated. Similar reasoning might suggest what should come right *before* your longest section. You may find, through a process of elimination, that making just one decision about where an important piece goes determines many things about your overall outline.

The artist Kim Gordon reminisces:

> I used to get self-conscious about drawing when I was a teenager in an art class with a model, and the teacher said, "Don't think of it as drawing. Think of it as designing the page." That really loosened things up for me.[29]

Have fun with it. Play around with your design. You're free to try things on for size, knowing that you'll have a chance to reconsider. In the end, it will settle into an order that feels right.

Beginnings and Endings

This section, deliberately, comes last. Introductions and conclusions are difficult to write. Trying to force it too soon is a recipe for writer's block and self-loathing. Do the lion's share of the work on the first and last pages *as late in the writing process as you can get away with*. That way, you'll come to the task with all the tools that you need.

Whether you choose to go with an anecdote, a remark about past scholarship, or even a thesis statement, your opening should have enough of a spark that it is likely to stimulate intellectual suspense. In other words, the reader should be mildly surprised or even a bit skeptical about *some* aspect, yet the logic and evidence hinted at in your opening pages will make them intrigued enough to want to read further.

Avoid the temptation to be grandiose on your first page. Clichés such as

the mists of time...
throughout history...

---

[28] Booth et al, *Craft*, 181.
[29] Kate Guadagnino, "Advice on Beginning," *New York Times*, April 18, 2024.

aren't just irritating, they suggest that your motives are out of synch with the precise, critical frame of mind that academic writing cherishes. You're writing for someone who'll get excited about the puzzle, the debate, or the conflict. As one book on academic writing puts it, "What seizes their attention is a problem they think needs a solution, and what holds it is a promise that you've found it."[30]

Admittedly, many historians feel it's a little inelegant to name the problem as such. We tend to start with an example, a direct quotation, or some combination of these that *implies* the underlying issue. To adopt some terms from journalism, these serve as the hook or lede.[31] You still want to signal what's afoot, though: Something tricky and complex enough to merit an academic inquiry.

Here's an opening sentence from Michael Camille:

> I could begin, like St. Bernard, by asking what do they all mean, those lascivious apes, autophagic dragons, pot-bellied heads, harp-playing asses, arse-kissing priests and somersaulting jongleurs that protrude at the edges of medieval buildings, sculptures, and illuminated manuscripts?[32]

This is utterly charming. Yet we're not seeing anything right here to explain why we should share his enthusiasm, or what we would gain from a deep inquiry. Vivid language is delightful, but try to segue quickly to an intellectual payoff. Indeed, in the following paragraphs, Camille does just that. His very next lines discuss the theoretical framework for the book. The subsequent paragraphs provide a quick guided tour of what's to come, noting the focus of each chapter. His preface concludes with a short thesis statement.

If you are seeking to engage the reader's heart, but also their brain, you could try opening with a moment of crisis or a setback. The strike of 1905 failed; let's reflect on why. This ingenious solution really was proposed by the Department of Such-and-Such, but the suggestion wasn't taken up; let's examine that. You're not explaining everything at the start, but you are offering something like "a flashlight that shines down into the story."[33] Starting your paper this way could lead you to narrate events in an out-of-order sequence such as 3, 1, 2, 4. By leading with the event, situation, or choice that you see as important, you are making an analytical move at the same time. Perhaps your thesis statement itself reinterprets Event 3, or simply contends that Event 3 or Development 3 was a big deal. Leading with what you think is most important makes your priorities unmistakable for the reader.

---

[30] Booth et al., *Craft*, 232.

[31] Schrag, *Princeton Guide*, 282-284.

[32] Michael Camille, *Image on the Edge: The Margins of Medieval Art* (Cambridge, MA: Harvard University Press, 1992), 9.

[33] John McPhee, *Draft No. 4: On the Writing Process* (New York: Farrar, Straus, and Giroux, 2017), 50.

An even more cerebral opening, of course, would be to jump right into the historiography. Here's where the field was, is, or seems to be going. Here's the unresolved puzzle. Here's the gauntlet thrown down by another scholar but not taken up (until now, of course). While the openly theoretical or historiographical opening may seem like the driest choice, it is a straightforward method of showing where your project fits into the ongoing conversation. At a deeper level, it can be a powerful way to establish a bond with the reader's intellectual and skeptical side. Historians reading other historians will instantly recognize a kindred spirit in someone who's alert to the state of the field, eager to define and differentiate key terms, sensitive to the strengths and weaknesses of different primary source types.

Reciting the way *you* came to know something is usually not the most efficient way to convey material to someone else. You have a sentimental attachment to the story of how you got here, but bear in mind that this may leave others unmoved. There are sometimes ways to deploy a personal anecdote in the service of a higher objective, however.

Carlos S. Dimas begins his book about nineteenth century cholera epidemics in a small Argentinian province with a narrative of his arrival in Tucumán in the winter of 2012 to conduct his research. After some initial investigations, he followed a lead and paid a visit to the community's Italian Society, in the hopes of uncovering some additional archival materials. Although the building appeared cold and deserted, a glint of light from under a door led him to a tentative knock, followed by an encounter with "about twenty elderly women gathered for what seemed a potluck and quilt-making session."[34]

There was no archive, but Dimas found himself in conversation with these descendants of Italian immigrants for an hour. He learned that the topic of his research—a series of epidemics more than a century earlier—was immediately familiar to all of those present. They explained that it was remembered as a transformative event in their community's immigrant experience in Argentina. Dimas remarks that "More than any document, this interaction left an impression on me," ultimately shaping his thesis statement and conclusions.[35] An epidemic, he realized, could be the moment when outsiders became—in some meaningful sense—insiders.

In some situations, it matters a lot *who* the historian is. Your personal experience, or your identity, may intersect with the material in an ambiguous way, a problematic way, an intellectually or emotionally complex way. An anecdote down the lines of what Dimas shared, adopting "an openly autobiographical style in which the subjective position of the author, especially on political matters, is presented in a clear and straightforward fashion" could at least signal

---

[34] Carlos S. Dimas, *Poisoned Eden: Cholera Epidemics, State-Building, and the Problem of Public Health in Tucumán, Argentina, 1865–1908* (Lincoln: University of Nebraska Press, 2022), xiv.

[35] Dimas, *Poisoned Eden*, xv.

your awareness of the relevant issues.³⁶ Even here, a light touch is best. Introductions—whichever flavor you prefer—should be short and simple.

Good openings and good conclusions are not carbon copies of each other. Readers always remember where you left them at the end. This is your last chance to impress, so take it up a notch! Two classic ways to do this are to *revisit* something from earlier in your paper—perhaps from the introduction itself—or to *recontextualize* your project as a whole.³⁷ A good conclusion isn't a repetition of what you said earlier, but—harking back to the discussion of sonnets and musical compositions earlier in this chapter—see if you can make it rhyme.

One way to make content "rhyme" is to revisit an earlier theme, but with a twist. This can leave the reader with a satisfying sense of arrival or accomplishment. Help the reader see something fresh in what was already familiar. Let them reread a quotation or example from earlier in light of what they now know, or in the context of your overall thesis. This then becomes the final insight which shows that the whole journey was worthwhile.

Recontextualizing, or zooming out, is another way to strike a satisfying note in your conclusion. You've dug down into something very granular—the circumstances of a lawsuit, the struggles of a family business, the one-step-forward-two-steps back of an effort to build a political coalition. You did this for a reason. As discussed earlier in this book, that particular conflict or scandal was your Archimedean Point. Yet the conclusion offers you a chance to turn the Archimedean Point into an Archimedean Vista.

It may be helpful to return to Chap. 8 and recall how you looked around in all the possible directions before settling on a spot for your project. In your conclusion, you can use that awareness to describe how your project (and your findings) appear a different and broader context. This isn't the time for another lit review, but you could mention how your findings sit in relation to the work of some of the most prominent historians who have considered related material. Or if you've engaged with interdisciplinary reference points, now would be the time to bring those back and reflect on them. Hopefully, the reader already has a sense of what your project contributed, but this is a chance to show off its value and importance in a new light.³⁸

Many first drafts feature weak conclusions, or even no separate ending section at all. That's understandable if someone wrote the last part when they were weighed down by fatigue, confusion, and even ambivalence. We all encounter moments when we feel a little sick of our own project, or exasperated with ourselves. Not surprisingly, attempting to write a conclusion when

---

³⁶ Jenkins, *On "What Is History,"* 14.

³⁷ I am indebted to Ellen Muehlberger's (@emuehlbe) Twitter thread of April 21, 2021, which supplied a series of ten suggestions to students about conclusions. My short formulation here captures what many of them had in common.

³⁸ Sarah Fox, "Archival Intimacies: Empathy and Historical Practice in 2023," *Transactions of the Royal Historical Society* (2023): 1–25 may suggest some additional possibilities for a "zoomed out" reflection at the end of a paper.

you're physically and mentally worn down doesn't deliver very inspiring results! Even if you're working to a deadline, to the extent that it is possible, set the manuscript aside and come at this particular task with fresh eyes. Leaving your paper alone for a couple hours, or even a couple days, may enable you to get the perspective you need.

If a draft is due now and you don't have a chance to rest up, you can generate a satisfactory conclusion paragraph or two quickly by jotting down a series of sentences that remind the reader of what you chose to do *and what the benefits or payoffs were in each case*. For example, previous scholars focused on the 1930s but you worked on the 1920s, and we can see different things as a result. Others read the case notes of psychoanalysts, but you took a patient-focused perspective, and your primary sources offered a glimpse of something new. As I noted earlier, you already have part of the scaffolding to write this—go back to your prospectus, your research question, or your research plan. It may be necessary to revise some of that language given what sources you really used the most, or what your most interesting findings turned out to be. Still, rewording sentences that exist now is a lot faster, and less intimidating, than facing a blank screen. For now, take a quick victory lap, share your favorite takeaways and research findings, and promise yourself you'll look at the conclusion again during the revision process.

Conclusion

Tinkering with your structure may feel laborious, but ultimately it will make things easier. I am often impressed to discover how moving a paragraph to a different location even allows me to shorten the text, because just setting things in close proximity makes the logical relationships more obvious.

As you write your first draft, you may find that common sense suggests a structure to you, whether or not you anticipated it in your outline. For instance, if you are going to differentiate yourself from the previous scholarship, the place to do that is right after you summarize that scholarship. Anything else will require the reader to either receive a reminder, or supply one from their own memory. John McPhee writes: "Readers are not supposed to notice the structure. It is meant to be about as visible as someone's bones."[39] This sounds like a tall order, but you can make a start at it. Re-arrange the elements so that the number of times you need to say, "as I discussed earlier" approaches zero.

Further Reading

Peter Gay, *Style in History* (New York: Basic Books, 1974) feels dated in some ways, but his reflections on the place of narrative and other literary devices in our writing are still worth a look.

---

[39] McPhee, *Draft No. 4*, 34.

Scott F. Crider, *The Office of Assertion: An Art of Rhetoric for the Academic Essay* (Wilmington, DE: ISI Books, 2005): Chapter Three is pertinent here.

Charles Lipson, *How to Write a BA Thesis: A Practical Guide from Your First Ideas to Your Finished Paper* (Chicago: University of Chicago Press, 2005): Chapter Ten has a strong discussion not only of introductions and conclusions, but also on how to incorporate a similar thought process when you consider the transitions between the sections of your paper.

CHAPTER 12

Crafting Your Exposition

Academic writing reaches for that elusive quality of *having convinced your reader*. It's interesting to consider just when this happens. Is it when the reader encounters your thesis statement? Is it when you wave your hand at the quantity of supporting material that you have assembled? Let me suggest that the moment when things really come together in the reader's mind—the moment when your position becomes not just interesting, but believable—is when the reader spends time with your explanation and contextualization of the evidence.

You may feel quite well prepared for the task. Who better to walk them through this material than you, the person who's spent so much time immersed in it? Yet that very strength can become something of a weakness at this stage of your work. What seems obvious to you now may be far from obvious to many of your likely readers. In a recent history of the Everglades, a direct quotation appears: "A swamp is a swamp."[1] This could mean anything—or nothing. The historian, Chris Wilhelm, knew to surround that quotation with context and commentary:

> Progressive conservationists in the 1920s and 1930s perpetuated these negative views. Zoologist William T. Hornaday insisted that "a swamp is a swamp," and thought the Glades nothing but a wasteland filled with "water moccasins and rattle-snakes." Robert Sterling Yard, a founding member of both the National Parks Association and the Wilderness Society, repeatedly attacked the Everglades as unworthy of national park status.[2]

---

[1] Chris Wilhelm, *From Swamp to Wetland: The Creation of Everglades National Park* (Athens, GA: University of Georgia Press, 2022), 17.
[2] Wilhelm, *From Swamp to Wetland*, 17.

© The Author(s), under exclusive license to Springer Nature
Switzerland AG 2024
I. Land, *The Craft of Historical Research*,
https://doi.org/10.1007/978-3-031-68457-9_12

Wilhelm's achievement wasn't just in locating that quotation, although no doubt it took a considerable amount of reading, sifting, and evaluating to arrive at it; its value only becomes clear when he spells out the explicit ties and connections around it and shows that it was part of an important pattern in the way that influential people viewed the Everglades. With that in mind, walk us through why you share the quotations that you do. Give some thought to the wording of a photo's caption. Explain that graph. Readers will thank you for it.

When in doubt, remember that your overriding mission is not to demonstrate how much work you did, but to convey to the reader how all your parts fit together: To get at *this*, I looked at *that*—and now here's the result. Even down at the level of individual paragraphs—*especially* down at that level—make sure the thread of interpretation remains visible, always elucidating the place of the evidence in your argument.

Much of this chapter is about clarity and candor in various contexts. The concluding section, though, is all about tone. Readers will remember what you said, but they'll also remember *how* you said it. The research and writing process can be a bit of an emotional rollercoaster, and it's not unusual for your first draft to bear the marks of that journey. Even if you resolve to keep sarcastic asides and eye rolling to a minimum, figuring out what note you *should* strike can be something of a puzzle, and there is very little guidance on this topic. I will offer some guidelines as you seek a path forward.

THINKING CRITICALLY ABOUT QUOTATION

As you read this chapter, you are transitioning from a stage in which you took a lot of notes *about* documents or photos *of* documents to a stage in which you are reassembling selected elements of those materials into coherent paragraphs. You'll need to cement them into place using other words—the words that enclose, surround, and connect those quotations. In academic writing, these words are at least as important as the ones that appear between quotation marks.

For this reason, what to say *about* your quotations will form the main focus of this section. Before considering this, however, there are some fundamental challenges to address involving the quotations themselves. We are often in the position that our reader has never seen—and will never see—the primary source that we are quoting from and needs guidance about any quirks, such as gaps in a manuscript, illegible passages, or unconventional spelling. Most historians do their own transcribing, their own translating, and (when they quote) their own excerpting and editing. In cases where authorship or the date of composition is unclear or potentially disputed, they may make determinations—or articulate best guesses—about that as well.

The ethical code surrounding the scholar's special obligation here dates back centuries, to a time when sharing photographs of archival documents, or dropping in a web link to a primary source database, was unimaginable.[3] Even

---

[3] Grafton, *Footnote*, 179–180.

today, however, paywalls and physical distance mean that it is quite possible that your readers either cannot, or cannot conveniently, crosscheck and validate your work. Therefore, you have a special responsibility to preserve the integrity of the text, because you are perhaps the only conduit of that information for your reader.

Consider the quotation, then, as something you could enter as an exhibit in a court of law. The quotation marks are the envelope that keeps the evidence pristine. Tamper with that evidence only for the best reasons, and leave unmistakable marks showing the extent of your intervention. For example:

[emphasis mine] clarifies that a portion in italics was not formatted in that way in the original.

[sic] denotes odd, offensive, or puzzling usage in the original which you have left unchanged. It might just be a word that's not spelled correctly, or a factual error.

... indicates that you have omitted some text. Ellipsis points are an important tool, since it is also desirable to keep direct quotations short and focused.

Scholars who work with ancient texts face additional challenges. Clay tablets, for example, are often damaged and incomplete. This incompleteness is laid bare for the reader in scholarly editions such as *The Harps That Once...: Sumerian Poetry in Translation*.[4] As the title itself reminds us with its ellipsis points, some of these texts have as many holes as a piece of Swiss cheese, or simply trail off!

Presenting text in translation also presents deeper intellectual challenges. How we can represent these texts in a user-friendly way, while respecting their integrity? Most well-informed English translations of Buddhist texts bristle with terms and concepts in the original Pali. This might seem like an abdication of the translator's responsibility, but used sparingly, it is a tribute to the uniqueness and untranslatability of certain things. Not coincidentally, it is often the most fraught, culturally specific, and nuanced words that receive this treatment. In the Buddhist case, for example, many academic works will retain the original Pali (or Japanese, or Tibetan) for words relating to enlightenment or to suffering, two profoundly important concepts in that religious tradition.

Consult with your advisor about the appropriateness of supplying direct quotations completely in the original language. Particularly if your university makes use of committees or outside readers, it may be practical (and humane!) to provide English translations for everything, whether in a footnote, or side by side in the text.

Perhaps the most common approach to these kinds of issues is to provide most of the material in English translation, but to reserve the original language for more complex, debatable, or unusual examples. In his book about German

---

[4] Thorkild Jacobsen. New Haven: Yale University Press, 1997.

Holocaust perpetrators, Christopher Browning discusses one individual who participated in the mass murder of civilians, but shot only children. He explained that it was "soothing to my conscience to release children unable to live without their mothers." Browning clarifies, however, that "the German word for 'release' (*erlösen*) also means to 'redeem' or 'save' when used in a religious sense. The one who 'releases' is the *Erlöser*—the Savior or Redeemer!"[5] This is a rare digression into a translation issue on Browning's part, but these two sentences help us get at a profound insight about this particular primary source.

Of course, shades of meaning and hinted implications can be an issue even when there's no translation involved. You may need to call out your source for a slippery omission or silence. Todd Gitlin discusses a 1965 *New York Times* story which replicated a police chief's reference to "last year's student riots" without questioning the choice of the word "riot" to describe protests. Conscious that his readers, too, might pass lightly over a distinction that he believes is an important one, Gitlin intervenes. "The word *riots* in the reporter's account was not neutralized by quotation marks," he notes, "it was presented as objective description."[6]

I can't anticipate all the special considerations that might apply to your source material, but I can remind you of a longstanding convention in academic writing: *Every* direct quotation will be integrated into one of your own sentences. Why? Because context always matters. Knowing why you are quoting should help you decide what the reader needs to hear right at this moment. Tell them that.

> **Pivot Point: The Care and Feeding of Quotations**
> Don't leave your direct quotations neglected or malnourished! Always indicate to the reader who's being quoted, why they are being quoted, and how this relates to what has gone before and what comes after. Occasionally, a diligent reader could reconstruct some of this information from your footnotes (the date of a letter, the known political affiliation of an author), but your responsibility is to provide this orientation in the main body of your text.

(continued)

---

[5] Browning, *Ordinary Men*, 2nd ed., all quotations from 73.
[6] Todd Gitlin, *The Whole World Is Watching: Mass Media in the Making and Unmaking of the New Left* (Berkeley: University of California Press, 1980), 80.

(continued)

It matters when they said it—
> On February 13, Lincoln wrote...
> After receiving the bad news, Lincoln wrote...
> As early as the 1840s, we can see Lincoln was...
> Recalling events from his boyhood, Lincoln especially singled out...

It matters who said it—
> The Pentagon press release indicated that all troops would receive Geneva Conventions training lasting one hour, covering the following topics...
> Veterans typically remember one important detail about the training they received...
> Junior officers recalled the training differently, remarking that...
> The survivor of the My Lai massacre observed that in his village...

The source's motivation, stance, or background matters—
> The factory owner disagreed with the safety proposals...
> Socialists questioned the legitimacy of the whole project, observing how...

How typical the sentiment was is important—
> Unlike most civil engineers in this era, he felt...
> As most of the petitions remarked...
> Among the letters to the editor, Smith's was unusually concise and candid, but he expressed widely-held sentiments, particularly when he states...

The immediate circumstances of the statement matter—
> Interviewed by the Bracero Oral History project in 2010...
> Deflecting the question, Ramirez said...
> When interviewed by an African-American researcher, the replies to Question 3 became notably different...

The genre, format, or provenance matters—
> In his novel, the survivor of the concentration camp makes up some characters, but also draws on his actual experiences, such as when he...
> Unusually for a letter to the editor...
> This notorious, often-quoted statement appeared only in a footnote to the published version of the sermon:

The tone is important—
> In a sarcastic aside, the student activists requested that the campus police should also...
> The judge paraphrased the legal theory, but only to deride its failure to consider...

Your pages should be dense with these little interjections. If you have a habit of dropping in hefty block quotations, experiment with breaking those up and interweaving them with your running commentary.

(continued)

> **(continued)**
>
> When you quote from other scholars, similar principles apply. Academic phrasebooks, such as those mentioned in the Further Reading section, offer ample guidance in this area, offering model phrases such as how to quote from an opponent: "While some have argued..."[7] Other standard phrases give credit or acknowledge influence. As with quotations from primary sources, the value of such language is that it indicates where the quotation fits into a larger structure. Does it continue your train of thought and support it? Does it form a departure or a direct contrast to what went before?

It's not a great oversimplification to state that all quotations are *either* there to speed the reader up, *or* to slow the reader down. Each time that you quote, know which one you have in mind. Are you suggesting that the issue is more straightforward than it looks, or less? Are you making a point memorably, and in the most user-friendly way possible? Or are you inviting the reader to study something, consider it from multiple perspectives, even refer back to it later on?

Understanding your purpose for quoting—in each instance—should help you answer one of the most common questions, which is *how long* the quotation needs to be. Depending on your objective, just quoting part of a sentence, or even a single word, may be enough. On rare occasions, there are reasons to break this rule and make the quotation or excerpt exceptionally long. In 1984, an American magazine published a dead woman's hospital bill in full, with annotations explaining the medical procedures, which parts her insurance company covered, and where this one example fit into the bigger picture.[8] Quoting a couple line items from the bill would not have conveyed this. Offering a paraphrase or summary would also have fallen short. As a commentary on the American health care system, the relentless length (with new charges accumulating for each new item of care that she received) and the excruciating detail was, itself, the point.

You may hesitate to chop up a passage. It is true that when we make decisions about excerpting, something is inevitably lost. One of the best times to quote directly is when the original wording makes a much deeper impression on the reader and conveys insights that no other method could. For instance, in 1865, the Rev. John Jones wrote:

---

[7] Robert A. Harris, *Using Sources Effectively: Strengthening Your Writing and Avoiding Plagiarism*, 2nd ed. (Glendale, CA: Pyrczak Publishing, 2005), 41–42, 76, 91, 92.

[8] David Hellerstein, "The Slow, Costly Death of Mrs. K----," *Harper's* 268 (March 1984): 84–89.

> The dark, dissolving, disquieting wave of emancipation has broke over this sequestered region. I have been watching its approach for months and marking its influence on our own people. It has been like the iceberg, withering and deadening the best sensibilities of master and servant, and fast sundering the domestic ties of years.[9]

A summary could remark simply that slave owners expressed confusion and dismay at the unprecedented developments. A paraphrase might single out Jones and nod to his sense that emancipation was experienced not exactly as an event, but as a process. None of that would capture the way that Jones fitfully adopts and then discards one metaphor after another. His awkward wording lays out his deep uneasiness right there on the page.

Since you are not offering the reader an anthology of primary sources, though, you have a practical requirement to keep most direct quotations short and purposeful. What you're assembling is a lot like a curated playlist or collection. Notice that the skill in assembling such things—and the value that they possess—is inherently about selectiveness. When you quote, your reader should feel that you are singling out what's best, what's most important, what's most representative, or what's most tellingly dissonant. Parsimony is also a wise practice because it means that when quotation marks do appear, they'll capture the reader's attention. You may find yourself in a balancing act, quoting the source directly at times, but supplying clarification and correctives by paraphrasing and summarizing other portions of that same source.

If an opinion was rare, against the grain, or possibly—some might have imagined—unthinkable in that place and time, then sharing the exact words will set the record straight. What if your point is the opposite one, though: It is interesting because it was part of a pattern, because it was representative, maybe even typical? In contrast to the more quantitative social sciences, which rely on the conventions of statistics, historians have no conventional method of denoting how common a statement was.

Occasionally, you will see a historian crunch the numbers:

> Of the sixty-six witchcraft pamphlets published [in England] between 1563 and 1735 only three fail to mention a witch's reliance on the Devil to help inflict maleficium, that is, harmful magic.[10]

As a general rule, though, you'll notice that historians don't try to settle arguments by weighing up quotations as if they were cabbages on a grocery scale. The standard approach is to write a thematically unified paragraph that provides a succession of closely related examples.

---

[9] Glymph, *House of Bondage*, 144.
[10] Charlotte-Rose Millar, "Diabolical Men: Reintegrating Male Witches into English Witchcraft," *The Seventeenth Century* (2020) 36, no. 5: 693–713, see 698.

Perhaps you are seeking to show how the written record can help us discern what sorts of things fell in the realm of the usual or the everyday. Thavolia Glymph's *Out of the House of Bondage: The Transformation of the Plantation Household* contains sentences such as "Peace accords were as fragile as the last dish broken or the most recent failure of a household slave to move fast enough" and "The cowhide whip is ubiquitous in the slave narratives."[11] General statements like this appear regularly in her book, punctuated with the occasional direct quotation, which focuses the reader's attention on the especially vivid examples, the ambiguous cases, and the exceptions. This also enables her to budget the reader's time and attention effectively. Where it is important to draw their attention to the phrasing, emphasis, and word choice—or perhaps the circumstances in which something was written down—then the spotlight comes on and the pace slows down.

Glymph also assembles a collection of testimonials from indignant white women whose slaves had self-emancipated or effectively gone on strike, leaving them with the housework. The examples all come from a period of a few months spanning the Spring and early Summer of 1865. Gertrude Thomas reported that the ironing had "piled up with flies swarming all over it"; another former mistress recounted her ordeal "doing the washing for six weeks, came near ruining myself for life as I was too delicately raised for such hard work." Tryphena Fox managed to incorporate her incredulity into the rhythm of her sentence, expressing her morning as one unthinkable step after another: She had "the pleasure of going over to the kitchen (across the yard) & cooking my own breakfast & bringing it out to the house myself."[12]

How many quotations does Glymph need to make her point? I have supplied three that she used; her paragraph contains more. Would it be more convincing if there were, say, fifteen or thirty quotations down these lines? Perhaps, instead of looking for a magic number, we should consider what the tone of these three slave owners conveys not just about the authors themselves, but the anticipated views of their intended readership. They believed that their peers and their extended family would share their slack-jawed incredulity. In a single paragraph, Glymph gives us a sense of the collective spasm of disorientation when a whole system came crashing down.

Many of the general principles discussed in this section also apply to numbers, pictures, and maps. For example, it's perfectly acceptable to pull one statistic from a larger compilation, though this is a kind of quotation, so explain what the reader needs to know about who did the compiling, and with what motivations. Information out of context is potentially misleading:

---

[11] Glymph, *House of Bondage*, 37 and 35 respectively.
[12] All quotations in this paragraph are from Glymph, *House of Bondage*, 143.

You can, for instance, express exactly the same fact by calling it a one percent return on sales, a fifteen percent return on investment, a ten-million-dollar profit, an increase in profits of forty percent (compared with 1935–39 average), or a decrease of sixty percent from last year. The method is to choose that one that sounds best for the purpose at hand and trust that few who read it will recognize how imperfectly it reflects the situation.[13]

This gleeful passage from *How to Lie with Statistics* refers to intentional manipulation, but sharing a number without understanding its original context is also a violation of the covenant between the historian and the reader.[14]

You often need to acknowledge in some way what's going on in the *whole* source. For example, sometimes it's fine to reproduce the lower left-hand corner of a painting with a simple caption including the cautionary word "Detail." If there's something pertinent going on elsewhere in the picture, though, you have just as much of an obligation to indicate this as if you were excerpting a few words from a longer text.

A historian's analysis of Buffalo State Hospital presented "before" and "after" photos and offered the contrast as evidence of overcrowding. However, the first photo, from 1901, was from promotional material released when the hospital first opened; as Penny Tinkler has remarked, this professionally produced photograph of a nearly empty facility is unlikely to document actual conditions there on any given day in the hospital's early years.[15] Astute readers will know a decontextualized excerpt when they see one. If you build on weak foundations, the entire edifice may be easy to knock down.

The Artful Footnote

Jacques Barzun once offered the lovely, and still pertinent, suggestion that you should "write a note whenever you think an alert person might feel curiosity about the source of your remarks."[16] This is the modern approach to footnotes in academic writing. You may encounter writers from past generations who used footnotes for digressions, endearing asides, and witty jibes at their rivals.[17] Since you are writing in the twenty-first century, if you have anything really clever to say, don't bury it in a footnote. From time to time, you may define a

---

[13] Huff, *How to Lie*, 84.

[14] New technologies raise new, worrying opportunities for tampering: Tara Tran, "Colorizing Photos from the Past: The Ethics of Making History," *Perspectives on History* 59, no. 5 (May 2021).

[15] Tinkler, *Using Photographs*, 36.

[16] Jacques Barzun and Henry F. Graff, *The Modern Researcher*, 5th ed. (Boston: Houghton Mifflin, 1992), 307. For this reason, even epigraphs at the start of a paper or the beginning of a section really ought to have footnotes attached, although too often, they are omitted.

[17] This tradition is celebrated in Chuck Zerby, *The Devil's Details: A History of Footnotes* (New York: Simon and Schuster, 2002).

term or clarify a subtle point in a footnote, but don't overdo it. Readers will expect that a footnote "records the origin of, or the authority for, a statement in the text."[18]

In that spirit, if you are quoting a passage directly, or even offering a paraphrase or summary, you must supply a footnote with a page number—or something equally precise—every time. Of course, supplying a precise citation for an archival document will look a little different from what you'd furnish for a line of religious scripture; the equivalent information about a graph, a map, or a photo would be different in turn.[19] There's no way to predict which piece of evidence or which assertion will stimulate the skeptical reader to look for that trail of breadcrumbs, so you are obligated to provide it in every case.

Other disciplines follow different practices, but historians permit only one footnote per sentence. It always appears at the very end, after any terminal punctuation. Faced with a situation where a mid-sentence footnote seems desirable, look for a way to split that sentence into two sentences, permitting two footnotes.

In an effort to direct the reader as precisely as possible, some historians supply little disambiguating catch-phrases to help the reader reconstruct *which* direct quotation came from *which* source, as I do in the footnote associated with the end of the next sentence, which contains three direct quotations from different places. Are footnotes "the scholar's saving alibis and afterthoughts," a source of "amusement, charm, [and] a chance to rest," or, in Anthony Grafton's words, little more than a source of "hints" about what the historian used?[20] Read too much commentary in this vein, and you might despair, both as reader of footnotes and as a prospective writer of them.

Such quibbles notwithstanding, if we say that the footnote supplies the *authority* behind a statement in the text, then we are treating it as a form of backing. Even Grafton concedes that "historians' arguments must still stride forward or totter backwards on their footnotes."[21] For example, if I state that there's a lot of recent scholarship on something, and I then supply a substantial footnote showing citations—each displaying a recent year of publication—this is *the* backing that I provide to support the claim. Likewise, if I tell you that a particular problem provoked a great deal of bureaucratic correspondence, you'd naturally look to my footnote for examples—and you'd be a little surprised if I offered only one. It's indicative that footnotes occupy the bottom of the page; they are the foundation on which everything rests. A weak, absent, or misaligned foundation is a recipe for trouble.

---

[18] Barzun and Graff, *Modern Researcher*, 298.

[19] *The Chicago Manual of Style* is regularly updated and offers advice on an even wider range of source types than I mention here. In the case of archival materials, ask the archivist for guidance if the citation format is unclear to you.

[20] "saving alibis," Leo Deuel, *Testaments of Time: The Search for Lost Manuscripts and Records* (New York: Alfred A. Knopf, 1965), xiii; "amusement," Zerby, *Devil's Details*, 5; "hints," Grafton, *Footnote*, 22.

[21] Grafton, *Footnote*, 4.

Yet in practice, historians don't always populate their footnotes with exactly the information that readers expect. For instance, Carl Bridenbaugh, writing about seventeenth-century towns, made this statement: "Casting rubbish and refuse of all kinds into the streets without let or hindrance was a confirmed habit of both English and American town-dwellers."[22] In his book *Historian's Fallacies*, David Hackett Fischer took him to task for the footnote, which supplied three pieces of information:

> a law was passed against littering in New Amsterdam in 1657... the law was enforced upon an early American litterbug named John Sharp in 1671, and... provision was made in 1670 for weekly trash removal by the car men of the city.[23]

In what sense, he objected, does this support the extent, prevalence, or depth of the alleged bad habit?[24]

A look at the page in Bridenbaugh's actual book, though, turns up a different issue. The footnote in question is *not* placed at the end of the sentence containing the words "without let or hindrance." Instead, it appears later in the same paragraph, after a summary of the laws and prosecutions directed at the bad behavior.[25] Perhaps Hackett Fischer shouldn't have griped about the footnote that Bridenbaugh supplied, but about the claim that appeared without a footnote.

What did Bridenbaugh have in mind when he composed this paragraph and supplied this (one) set of citations? It's not uncommon for historians to offer a footnote that says, in effect, "here's what I looked at relating to this." There's a subtle, but important, difference between such a footnote, and the one that says, "Let me adduce examples of what I just mentioned." Perhaps Bridenbaugh needed to populate his footnote differently. Of course, it's easier to find example of laws and prosecutions than to locate an archival example *of* carefree littering. What sort of written record would that behavior leave behind?

Instead, Bridenbaugh could have spelled out his thinking for the reader in the main text:

> New anti-litter legislation appeared at frequent intervals, but even the threat of prosecution failed to deter these stubborn habits.

---

[22] Carl Bridenbaugh, *Cities in the Wilderness: The First Century of Urban Life in America, 1625–1742* (New York: Ronald Press, 1938), 18.

[23] Hackett Fischer, *Historians' Fallacies*, 44.

[24] Both Gibbon and Ranke were called out by contemporaries who, like Hackett Fischer, wanted to register a complaint about text and footnotes that didn't align. Their indignant replies to the critics speak to a fundamental ambiguity about the true purpose of footnotes that is still unresolved today: Grafton, *Footnote*, 66–67, 100–101.

[25] Zerby, *Devil's Details*, 92–93, refers to this practice as the "consolidation of notes," offering just one footnote to vaguely cover a large body of text, although—as Hackett Fischer's reaction illustrates—authors take this step at their peril.

Someone might disagree with the interpretation, but this—at least—is a sentence that both makes his claim, *and* corresponds to the footnote that he supplied.

This example should help you understand why academic writing by historians comes studded with footnotes at frequent intervals, like rivets or nails. We anticipate some kicks and buffets from skeptical readers! Perhaps this section has also shown you why you don't want to be the scholar who writes their text and tries to tack on footnotes late in the process, perhaps in haste, trying to reconstruct just what you had in mind earlier.

Writing captions and labels for photos, graphs, or tables requires the same spirit that we bring to footnotes. For example, "statistics on workplace safety" doesn't convey the same thing as "statistics assembled by the corporation in 1960 when it faced a lawsuit over workplace safety." The reader has a legitimate need for exactly this kind of information; if it did not appear this way, it would need to appear in the main text somehow. As with quoting words, notice that the consideration is not simply "how does one cite this source?" but fundamentally, "what information will the reader need here?"

Visual Explanations

Even the most hasty reader will notice your pictures, graphs, maps, and so forth. Devote extra care to ensure they are in good working order. They should direct the reader's focus to your top priorities and the heart of your argument. If they can't pass that elementary test, you might be better off without them.

For example, always explain why pictures are there and offer the reader some instruction as to *how* to look at them.

Sara Stevenson has characterized Fig. 12.1, "Willie Liston redding the line" as "a study in concentration, as he cleans and baits, with mussels, the hundreds of hooks on the line—a meticulous and lengthy task."[26] This is clear, brief, and helpful. In my own discussion of that image, though, I needed to help readers notice something else: the composition of the picture as a whole. Liston, I argued,

> comes across as a man of action, in part because Hill uses the lighting and camera angle to reduce the head and neck in proportion to the rest of the fisherman's body, suggesting broad shoulders and a rugged physique. The low hat brim shades his eyes, presenting him as a "type" rather than as an individual. Emphasizing his nose and jawline achieves in a photographic format the same physiognomic effect that [Thomas] Rowlandson deployed to such effect in his caricatures of sailors.[27]

---

[26] Sara Stevenson, *Facing the Light: The Photography of Hill and Adamson* (Edinburgh: Scottish National Portrait Gallery, 2002), 111.

[27] Isaac Land, *War, Nationalism, and the British Sailor, 1750–1850* (New York: Palgrave Macmillan, 2009), 247.

Fig. 12.1 David Octavius Hill and Robert Adamson, "Willie Liston redding the line," 1843–1847. (Metropolitan Museum of Art, New York. Open Access image under the title "Newhaven Fisherman")

It was also important, for my purposes, to emphasize *how* the image was made:

> the contours and texture of the fisherman's clothing stand out with exceptional clarity, right down to details like Liston's rows of buttons or the individual stitches in the inseam of his trousers. Hill's calotype technique enhances this effect; the photograph was printed on ordinary writing paper, whose gritty texture helps convey the "feel" of Liston's weatherbeaten outfit.[28]

Surround an image with commentary and explanation, and at the very least, readers will understand what you *meant* for them to see. Will they follow where you lead? Inescapably, just as with the interpretation of words or numbers, someone could always decide you've gotten it wrong. All you can do is put your best foot forward, express your priorities, and help them follow your reasoning.

Visual aids may be the only way to communicate something too unfamiliar, too intricate, or too large for our everyday thinking. Bear in mind, though, that a visual aid can also be opaque, confusing, or misleading. We "read" graphs

---

[28] Land, *War*, 246.

and maps, just as we read text. People will respond better to legible material! Stephen Few discusses the "preattentive"—what we process without engaging the verbal, calculating, or analytical parts of our brain.[29] The good news is that there are a number of very accessible guidebooks covering this area, informed by research and practical experience. Consult some of the books in the Further Reading section to learn about the ways that layout, color schemes, fonts, and even the angle of your captions can make graphs and tables user-friendly—or the opposite.

Many of those insights apply equally well to maps. For example, a history of religious sectarianism in Canada contained a map depicting streets on which there were both Orange Lodges (a Protestant meeting place) and Catholic Churches.[30] Yet it chose to denote them with crosses (+) and small circles (o), resulting in a dense, alphabet soup texture on the page.

oo+o+++ooo

This leaves the reader squinting! Would it help to use O for Orange Lodge and C for Catholic Church?

OOCOCCCOOO

That's also a bit of a visual blur. While adding color does mean that you should consult an online resource about color blindness issues, when used wisely, it can clarify things a lot. Here are the Orange Lodges and Catholic Churches one more time:

●●●●●●●●●●

A judicious use of color or hue can convey the same information without an increase in ink, or pattern complexity.

For similar reasons, a graph charting ten things is not necessarily superior to a graph charting just one or two—and it's probably worse. Here is a design principle to live by: "A graph should always display as directly as possible the information that people need."[31] A simple bar graph from France in 1967 showed the birth deficit associated with both World Wars.[32] At that time, there was an otherwise inexplicable shortage of people in their twenties (the result of men who did not become fathers in the 1940s), and an even greater gap

---

[29] Stephen Few, *Show Me the Numbers: Designing Tables and Graphs to Enlighten*, second edition (Burlingame, CA: Analytics Press, 2012), 68–71.

[30] Cecil J. Houston and William J. Smyth, *The Sash Canada Wore: A Historical Geography of the Orange Order in Canada* (Toronto: University of Toronto Press, 1980), 46.

[31] Few, *Show Me*, 116.

[32] Tufte, *Visual Display*, 2nd ed., 113.

corresponding to people in their fifties (caused by men who did not become fathers in the second half of the 1910s). Edward Tufte used this graph, which resembles a comb with some missing teeth, to illustrate one of his favorite points about visual explanation: Once you know what you are looking at, just noticing or comparing *shapes* often tells you all you need to know. Readers can take that in at a glance, absorb your point, and move on.

Earlier, I suggested that all quotations are meant to speed the reader up, or slow the reader down. Stephen Few offers a parallel distinction between two kinds of visualizations. The first visualization is the kind intended to quickly highlight something important. The bar graph showing France's missing people is an example of this. Few's second type of visual aid, though, is aimed at organizing and guiding, "in a manner that promotes optimal understanding and use."[33] In short, these are intended for study.

Historians do not make extensive use of this second category, but in some situations they really should. An ambitious map or graph is only one possibility. Perhaps your readers would really benefit from an infographic representing the fifty states' restrictions on gun ownership, in all their variety, in one particular year. They might need a full chronology of the Cuban Missile Crisis day by day, collating events and actions on all sides, or an organizational chart to illustrate the paths of decision making or the flow of paperwork among different departments.

Something like this will probably take up more than one page and require some thinking about layout. Take special care to design the graphic so that the reader can dwell on it a long time, without eyestrain. Don't underestimate the importance of the *size* of the graphic element, as well as the text in the caption and legend. Your goal here is to encourage repeat visits, and drilling down into the detail.

Expecting too much from *one* chart, table, or image is often a recipe for clutter and confusion. Help your readers out! No one is charging you a fee every time you add an image or another graph, so experiment with the benefits of deploying two or three to do the work you'd hoped to accomplish with one.

Match your data visualization to the needs of your argument. For a long time, historians relied upon tables. Dona Wong warns, though, "Rows of numbers do not have any visual impact."[34] If you must use tables, Stephen Few offers advice on format and design choices.[35] You have more options, though. Line graphs are best for showing change over time; bar graphs, especially if arranged in exact rank sequence, communicate fine distinctions of quantity

---

[33] Few, *Show Me*, 140.
[34] Wong, *Wall Street Journal Guide*, 82.
[35] Few, *Show Me*, 155–190.

more clearly than pie charts; scatterplots were invented for the purpose of showing correlation between two variables.[36]

When you select a style of mapping, you face similar considerations. Certain map types will deliver some messages better than others. In fact, some are so well suited to a particular message that they may deliver it by accident! Johanna Drucker has warned, wisely, that when historians adopt software, we should also pause and reflect on the unintended baggage that may come along for the ride. She describes

> a striking visualization created for the digital project *Mapping the Republic of Letters*... [in which] letters between eighteenth-century correspondents move from one geographic location to another as if by airmail. The perfect lines of sight, looking for all the world like a contemporary graphic of air traffic, make the connection between the point of origin and place of delivery a smooth, seamless, unitary motion.[37]

Drucker's reminding us, of course, that *nothing* in the eighteenth century was as smooth as the movement of goods and ideas in our intensely globalized world. Deploy software if it's useful, but don't allow your powerful visualization to tacitly advance its own thesis statement. Drucker has invented terms such as "graphic argument" and "enunciative interface" to express the ways in which such images perform the work of exposition, whether we intend them to do so or not.[38]

To be sure, it is becoming possible to share information in radically new ways. Your research paper could include an annotated video, a three-dimensional fly through, or an interactive data visualization. The new technologies would have looked like magic to a twentieth-century philosopher like Stephen Toulmin, to say nothing of Quintilian, the ancient instructor of rhetoric. Yet the moment we pose a question to this glittering digital oracle, we are back to square one. Do we feel that it speaks plainly? Does it communicate with honesty and fairness? Do we find its reasoning persuasive and its evidence sufficient? On what grounds should we receive it, in the broadest sense of the term, as credible? The old-fashioned conventions of academic eloquence aren't obsolete in the twenty-first century. In some ways, they are more needed than ever.

In a discussion about clarity and transparency, one more issue deserves our attention. If your visualization is derived in whole or in part from others' work,

---

[36] Stephen Few, *Now You See It: Simple Visualization Techniques for Quantitative Analysis* (Oakland, CA: Analytics Press, 2013), 245–279.

[37] Johanna Drucker, "Humanistic Theory and Digital Scholarship," in *Debates in the Digital Humanities*, ed. Matthew K. Gold (Minneapolis: University of Minnesota Press, 2012), 85–95, see 91.

[38] Drucker, *Visualization*, 142 and 163. Also of interest here is Catherine D'Ignazio and Lauren Klein, *Data Feminism* (Cambridge, MA: MIT Press, 2020).

at minimum you need to credit them.[39] One common method is to enlist the humble preposition "after." For example, Erik Seeman supplied this caption to a map: "Drawn by Bill Nelson, after maps in Trigger, *Children of Aataentsic*, and Warren, *Population History of the Huron-Petun*."[40]

This use of "after" with maps and graphs is, unfortunately, vaguer than the language we are able to use when we quote others' words. Perhaps there is a need to carefully explain and attribute which parts were borrowed. In that case, a short, candid discussion in the main body of your text may be in order. When the main point is how your visualization *differs* (perhaps there is a profound error you're exposing, or a disagreement that should be laid out unmistakably), supplying side-by-side maps or graphs—yours, and theirs—could be the path of least resistance.

Here's the bottom line. Whatever technologies you use, and whatever your chosen format of exposition is, your duty is to set out "the entire process of knowledge production, presented with transparency and in precise detail," so that anyone could drill down and perform a skeptical evaluation of the underlying sources and evidence and what you did with them.[41] If you find yourself in a gray area here somehow, a consultation with your advisor should clarify how you can fulfill that obligation in your particular circumstances.

Adopting the Right Tone

We routinely encourage students to proofread, but a quick proofread for *tone*—not just for typos—at the very end of your writing process is probably a good idea. Tone is rarely discussed in classrooms—or in books like this—but it is one of the hardest aspects of academic writing to get right.

Why is it so hard? Sometimes the isolation of the research process itself leaves us without an outlet. When we begin to compose paragraphs, sometimes what comes out is a sharp snap of emotional release, like a taut spring that's finally gotten to unwind. Just as friendships and romantic entanglements can follow a bleak trajectory of "idealization, revision and rejection," it's not unheard of for historians to find—after long immersion in the sources—that they now must write about someone they've come to despise.[42]

As if navigating our own ambivalence or animosity weren't enough, we routinely work with primary sources that were themselves shaped by self-interest, envy, or some form of resentment. Add to this our love-hate relationship with

---

[39] If you are preparing work for publication, conventions of "fair use" or "fair dealing" *may* permit you to excerpt or adapt, but exercise caution—like a photograph, a map or graph could count as a large percentage of a work, or as *an entire work*, for copyright purposes. A librarian with an expertise in intellectual property law would have advice on whether you need to seek permissions here.

[40] Erik R. Seeman, *The Huron-Wendat Feast of the Dead: Indian-European Encounters in Early North America* (Baltimore: Johns Hopkins University Press, 2011), 46.

[41] Lässig, "Digital History," 31.

[42] Jill Lepore, "Historians Who Love Too Much: Reflections on Microhistory and Biography," *Journal of American History* 88, no. 1 (2001): 129–144, see 134.

the scholarship that's preceded us, and we are left with a recipe for a hilarious group therapy session (with some of the participants, of course, long dead).

Our best voice, our most mature voice, resists boiling down conflicts into heroes and villains, geniuses and fools. This is true whether the fault lines are in between nations, factions, various groups within a place of employment, or even within a family. Taking a step back from the language of saints and sinners doesn't mean that you must let anyone off the hook. It just involves shifting the emphasis to explanation: What options did people in the past believe were available to them? What choices did they make as a result?

None of this should involve waffling; the sentence from a Wikipedia article on William Clarke Quantrill—"Some historians remember him as an opportunistic, bloodthirsty outlaw, while others continue to view him as a daring soldier and local folk hero"—is singled out for mockery, and rightly so.[43] It is possible to make all these people three-dimensional for your readers without melting your prose into an enervated puddle of neutrality and "both-sides-ism."[44]

What if the problem is with the tone that your sources themselves take? Presumably, no historian today would write about "slatternly wenches," or refer to human beings as "vermin," just because their source does. When we quote from such sources, it may be unbearable to let certain words pass without comment. Once again, it is helpful to remember that the language surrounding a direct quotation is as important as what takes place in between the quotation marks. Richard Evans offers some excellent advice here:

> historians have far more powerful rhetorical and stylistic weapons at their disposal than mere denunciation: sarcasm, irony, the juxtaposition of rhetoric and reality, the factual exposure of hypocrisy, self-interest, and greed.[45]

Another option, though, is silence. For example, earlier scholars who disseminated colonialist propaganda or outright lies may not deserve another hearing, even in the context of a rebuttal. It's possible to cite someone, but not accord them the privilege of a direct quotation.

If the prejudice *is* the subject matter, there's a tricky balancing act. When the prejudiced language becomes a form of evidence, then it needs to show up on the page.[46] You might show some restraint, though; if references to human beings as "vermin" were common, you can establish that without assailing the reader with five pages of examples.

---

[43] Roy Rosenzweig, "Can History Be Open Source? Wikipedia and the Future of the Past," *Journal of American History* 93, no. 1 (June 2006): 117–146, see 130.

[44] For a chapter that contains many examples of unflinching three-dimensional treatments of complex individuals and groups, see Deák and Naimark, *Europe on Trial*, 112–137.

[45] Evans, *Defense*, 45.

[46] Mikko Toivanen, "The Speech of the Subaltern Transcribed: Quoting Practices and Language 'Errors' in Colonial Travel Writing," *International Journal for History, Culture and Modernity* 10, no. 1–4 (2023): 62–73.

When she was translating the life stories of Chinese Buddhist nuns for publication, Kathryn Ann Tsai encountered a challenging passage. Nun Feng (d. 504 CE) was so pious that, according to the narrative, "As an offering to the Buddha she burned six fingers down to the palms of her hands."[47] Since this was a critical edition of an ancient text, Tsai and her publisher responded to this unusual statement in the conventional way, by supplying an endnote. Readers with the patience (or curiosity) to turn to the back of the book are rewarded with a note that runs for half a page in small print, contextualizing this religious practice and supplying other evidence that there were some people who really did this. In the note, she uses the word "mutilation," to dispel any remaining doubts about the meaning of the line in the original text.[48]

If you quoted this sentence in your paper, though, you would have to balance a number of different considerations. Would readers wonder whether they had read the sentence correctly? Would they speculate about *candles* that burned down to the quick, leaving the pious nun with some injury during her meditation, and suspect that you made an error in transcribing your source, or that the translation was faulty? You could use [sic], discussed earlier in this chapter, to signal that you knew it was a disconcerting sentence. You might introduce the quotation with some prefatory language:

> Inspired by a passage in the *Flower of the Law Scripture*, Nun Feng took the extreme measure...

Yet readers might react with so much shock, or curiosity, that even this would seem insufficient.

Should you, then, stop mid-argument (or mid-narrative) and supply something like Tsai's lengthy endnote, but in your text itself? There are benefits here, but also—perhaps—liabilities. The primary source disposes of the burnt fingers in a single sentence; its main focus is a tale of how Nun Feng sent a perplexed male colleague on a long, difficult journey, at the end of which he achieved enlightenment. She was a sage, revered by her contemporaries. If the historian's goal is to foster deeper understanding and (to the extent possible) respect and empathy, then the challenge is to supply clarification without consigning this whole text—or this woman's life choices—to the realm of the sensational or the exotic.

Tone enters the picture as well when we consider how traditional rivals or adversaries might receive each other's efforts at historical scholarship. In 1604, the German humanist Markus Welser expressed despair that people of different nationalities could ever reach agreement about contentious historical matters:

---

[47] Tsai, *Lives of the Nuns*, 95.
[48] Tsai, *Lives of the Nuns*, 146.

Take the history of Charles V and Francis I—a Frenchman and a German will always tell it differently. And the one will never persuade the other of what he himself thinks is true and would guarantee at any price.[49]

Perhaps. Such statements throw us back, at the very least, to the question of what sort of historical scholarship would make that result *less* likely. Where does fairness and credibility reside? Does it show up in the way that events are narrated? In which elements the historian slows down to explain? In the way that the motivations and decisions taken by historical actors are characterized? Down at the level of individual footnotes, what would we expect to see that would leave an impression of evenhandedness?

Charles V isn't the topic of much vituperation today, but consider the admirable—if difficult—experiment undertaken by South Korean, Chinese, and Japanese historians to write a high school history textbook together that dealt with sensitive, controversial material relating to World War Two. The hope was that schools in all three countries could assign it.[50] The need to write in a way that commands some degree of respect and trust from readers of different subject positions, or different nationalities, is still with us. We could abandon the hope that such a version of history is possible, yet such a conclusion carries civic and political consequences, including some that we might like to avoid.

When you write about other historians, too, moderation is usually the best path. When in doubt, I would suggest that you shift the focus from *How should I speak here?* to the more down-to-earth *What needs to be said here?* Seeking to demolish other scholars is not mandatory and may even weaken your own attempts at persuasion. It is true that in some subfields, the dialogue is quite contentious. Arguments are assessed as strong or weak; debates are won or lost. In many others—I would suggest, the majority—the normal tone is more collaborative.

You may be justifiably irritated with something you read, but a good first step is to see if you can engage a little with that piece of scholarship on its own terms. It's best to offer an evenhanded accounting of what a publication *did* achieve before you note where it fell short. Catching a rival in one factual or logical error is not going to discredit anyone, though it may take their credibility down a notch. While it is possible to accomplish the equivalent of disbarring a lawyer, that is such a rare and extreme circumstance that it is hardly worth our attention here.

A common bad habit is to fixate on a minor point in another scholar's work and take them to task for it as if that were the main focus of their analysis, or part of their thesis statement.[51] What counts as a minor point? Consider how

---

[49] Grafton, *Footnote*, 139.
[50] Zheng Wang, "Old Wounds, New Narratives: Joint History Textbook Writing and Peacebuilding in East Asia," *History and Memory* 21, no. 1 (Spring/Summer 2009): 101–126.
[51] Harris, *Using Sources*, 62.

many pages or paragraphs they actually devote to it. Anyone who has published can be held accountable for what they said, in the context that they said it, but exaggerations do not advance the conversation. Putting words in someone's mouth isn't fair, and it is likely to backfire. Perhaps the concept of civility in academic debate boils down to this: We proceed on the basis of skepticism, staying focused on finding more evidence and better answers, without dwelling any longer than absolutely necessary on the shortcomings of others.

A different challenge arises when you discuss scholarship that has deep affinities or even overlap with your own research and writing. Thinking back to Chap. 3, you'll recall that I had you identify a short shelf's worth of books and articles as your cousins, frenemies, or rivals. That shelf has probably grown a bit since then. Perhaps in the rush to get your own research done and your paper written up, you've not had time to look at this material for a while. Re-reading your cousins at this stage will be a very different experience from reading them the first time. Quotations and examples and concepts will leap out at you now that you barely noticed before.

Having struggled yourself with the primary sources, fretted over how to construct your own claims, and worried over whether you had sufficient backing, you'll read other scholars' work with a lot more empathy. Yet this re-reading will also turn up vivid contrasts. The same material and themes you know so well now looked different to others. Those contrasts may throw aspects of your own findings and conclusions into sharp relief, as if—viewed through the lens of your cousins—you are seeing your own work for the first time. You may surprise yourself by feeling simultaneously more frustrated with the prior scholarship, more conscious of your debts to it, *and* more uneasy about how to differentiate your contributions from what has appeared in print.

Even the most original scholar has many debts to others. I expect that you have a clear idea about what would count as plagiarism in the realm of quotation, but tutorials on academic integrity don't always consider whether an idea or approach can be plagiarized. This is partly because every one of us stand at the end of a vast chain of obligation stretching back so far that its beginnings are not even discernible. A new publication in sociology won't begin by crediting Max Weber or some similar figure for inventing the whole discipline, yet so much that followed was—in some sense—derivative from the fact that he lived, thought, and wrote. This does not even touch upon the sociologist's obligation, for example, to René Descartes for inventing the practice of making graphs with an x, y, and z axis, or to a multitude of feminist activists for inventing feminism. In addition, so much of academic publishing *presupposes* that others will draw on our concepts, methods, or findings. That is why academic publishing exists. We write to be used, and to be useful. I certainly do.[52]

---

[52] You may write your paper differently because you read this book, but it would be very unusual to cite it, unless you quoted from it or otherwise engaged with it directly.

That said, you are also entering a conversation, and it is both ethical (on your part) and helpful (to your readers) to indicate this. The American Historical Association's statement is well expressed: "The best professional practice for avoiding a charge of plagiarism is always to be explicit, thorough, and generous in acknowledging one's intellectual debts."[53] Signposting attribution and derivation in the main body of your text is at least as important as complete and correct citations in the footnotes.[54] It also permits a level of subtlety that no footnote, by itself, could achieve. After all, you have an appropriate desire to acknowledge what you owe to others, but sometimes you need to register only partial agreement, or disagreement.[55] Clarify what's new, what's old, what's in dialogue, what's in conflict. It's part of your job.

Always make it easy for the reader to see when you are borrowing tools from others:

> What we see in the port of Alexandria under British rule is an example of what the sociologist Elijah Anderson has called "the cosmopolitan canopy."

It's tricky to acknowledge your debts without sounding sycophantic, or bereft of insight yourself. "If… then" statements are a way to align yourself with a scholar or a scholarly tradition, while beginning to complicate the picture or move into new territory:

> If, as Elijah Anderson has shown [a], then we might reasonably ask [b].
> If, as Sonya Rose has shown [c], then further research is desirable about [d].

Making it clear where others' ideas end and yours begin also permits you to do justice to your own originality. Here, for example, is E.P. Thompson articulating his famous term "moral economy" for the first time:

> It is of course true that riots were triggered off by soaring prices, by malpractices among dealers, or by hunger. But these grievances operated within a popular consensus… This in its turn was grounded upon a consistent traditional view of social norms and obligations, of the proper economic functions of several parties within the community, which, taken together, can be said to constitute the moral economy of the poor.[56]

---

[53] American Historical Association, "Statement on Standards of Professional Conduct" (updated 2023), https://www.historians.org/jobs-and-professional-development/statements-standards-and-guidelines-of-the-discipline/statement-on-standards-of-professional-conduct#SharedValues, accessed July 28, 2023.

[54] Carol Peterson Haviland and Joan A. Mullin, "Introduction: Connecting Plagiarism, Intellectual Property, and Disciplinary Habits," in *Who Owns This Text? Plagiarism, Authorship, and Disciplinary Cultures*, ed. Carol Peterson Haviland and Joan A. Mullin (Logan, UT: Utah State University Press, 2009), 1–19, see 3.

[55] Harris, *Using Sources*, 89–90, offers examples of possible language here.

[56] E.P. Thompson, "The Moral Economy of the English Crowd in the Eighteenth Century," *Past & Present* 50 (February 1971): 76–136, see 78–9.

Good academic writers know when to acknowledge the received wisdom as well as how to poke holes in it. Actually achieving this balance on the page requires some fine modulations, anticipating where readers might quibble or balk, when it's fitting to signal tentativeness, and when to forge ahead with confidence.

Assessing whether the moment calls for a bold, firm, statement or for striking a moderate and conciliatory stance is one of *the* most important skills in academic writing. Identifying the correct tone—particularly in relation to your academic cousins—may feel like sorting out an etiquette problem, but it could well be the final stage in finding your own voice. This could be the moment when you reach a new appreciation of what you've learned, what you really have to say, and what matters most of all.

Conclusion

You might imagine that you've already devised an outline, composed a paragraph, or articulated a sentence. Yet experienced writers know that you'll revisit many of those decisions. And just as research is an iterative process, you may be surprised at what cascades of small modifications you set off by tinkering with just one location in your draft.[57] As the word itself (*re-vision*) implies, true revision means seeing your work with fresh eyes.[58]

Before turning in your complete first draft, then, let your manuscript rest for a day or two and then re-read it. The need for many small changes will come to light, but this isn't just a proofreading exercise. It is quite possible that you will find you've come full circle and are ready to refer back to the considerations of structure and ordering discussed in Chap. 11. The outline that made sense to you *before* writing the paper—and which served you well enough to generate a readable first draft—may have outlived its usefulness. Moving around a few elements may, in fact, resolve some nagging problems and make your paper clearer and shorter.

Don't tinker with it on your own for too long, though. It's time to get feedback from others. This is where we will turn in Chap. 13.

Further Reading

Joseph M. Williams, *Style: Ten Lessons in Clarity and Grace*, 8th ed. (New York: Pearson Longman, 2005) speaks well to managing the flow of your individual sentences and paragraphs.

John Morley, *Academic Phrasebank: An Academic Writing Resource for Students and Researchers*, 3rd ed. (Manchester: Manchester University Press, 2020).

---

[57] Murray, *Craft*, 21.
[58] Clark, *Writing*, 92.

John M. Swales and Christine B. Feak, *Academic Writing for Graduate Students: Essential Tasks and Skills,* 3rd ed. (Ann Arbor: University of Michigan, 2012).

Stephen Few, *Show Me the Numbers: Designing Tables and Graphs to Enlighten,* 2nd ed. (Burlingame, CA: Analytics Press, 2012).

Dona M. Wong, *The Wall Street Journal Guide to Information Graphics: The Dos and Don'ts of Presenting Data, Facts, and Figures* (New York: W.W. Norton, 2010).

Shawn Graham et al., *Exploring Big Historical Data: The Historian's Macroscope,* 2nd ed. (Singapore: World Scientific Publishing, 2022), see in particular Chapter 5.

Johanna Drucker, *Visualization and Interpretation: Humanistic Approaches to Display* (Cambridge, MA: MIT Press, 2020).

CHAPTER 13

Working with Feedback

Just now, it's tempting to guard your manuscript with the vigilance of a dragon over its hoard. Didn't you just finish it? Patrick Dunleavy remarks on the "magic moment when you can for the first time spread out all your chapters on the floor and physically hold and review all the elements of the thesis as a whole."[1] Whether your paper is long enough to have chapters or not, we can all appreciate the feeling he's describing here. Yet before you know it, a more emotionally ambiguous moment arrives: You will have to read your advisor's feedback.

Whether you are sharing in installments—a bit at a time—or all at once, receiving feedback can be startling. You're about to get reacquainted with your manuscript. Expect some surprises. It may seem odd to suggest that you don't know what your own paper says. In the act of composition, though, we are distracted by the buzz of our own spinning gears. What was clear—or felt clear—in your head as you typed doesn't always make it to the page in an intelligible form, at least not at first.[2] As one book on revision warns, "Syntax often breaks down at the point of discovery."[3] If that's true, then the *weakest* part of your draft right now could well be the lines where you reached (or reached toward) your most important conclusions. You thought you were pretty much finished barring some tweaks and tidying, but perhaps your best writing—your most important writing—still lies ahead.

This chapter begins with some advice about what to look out for as you re-read your paper on your own, reflect on the feedback you've received, and start to make changes. I then turn to the task of finalizing your paper's title, and, if required, writing an abstract for it. You may find these decisions, too, are

---

[1] Dunleavy, *Authoring*, 199.
[2] Erika Lindemann, *A Rhetoric for Writing Teachers* (New York: Oxford University Press, 1995), 3rd ed., 187.
[3] Murray, *Craft*, 220.

informed by the revision process you just undertook. The chapter concludes with some advice on how to think about the defense. Customs vary internationally, but a defense or oral (*viva voce*) exam is a common event at the end of Master's and PhD programs and may occur at the undergraduate level as well. A treatment of the defense might seem out of place in a chapter about feedback. Yet the defense, too, is a chance to listen and find opportunities for improvement.

The Art of Revision

Feedback can take many forms, some easier to digest than others. Let's consider some possibilities. Feedback isn't always synonymous with fault-finding; sometimes the most memorable contribution from a reader is an insight about what works *well* in your existing draft. They may spot a successful section and encourage you to do more of the same. Noncommittal or vague responses are also possible. The Oxford professor of philosophy who returned a 12,000-word chapter with only three words of feedback ("I suppose so") is the stuff of legend, but you, too, may encounter some readers who have surprisingly little to say.[4] If you encounter extensive feedback, you may yearn for that laconic reader. However, profuse page-by-page annotation is a sign that someone invested in your draft enough to stick with it and cared enough to complain about what didn't work for them.

A book on revision offers a list of hypothetical reader reactions. Each of these (in some variant phrasing) is quite common, but notice how different they are from each other:

> How do you know that?
> I don't get it.
> Tell me more.
> Whoa. Back up, I don't understand.
> Get to the point.[5]

Perhaps you'd be delighted to respond to "Tell me more," and you know exactly where to look for the information you'd need. But how long would it take to address—or even resolve in your own mind—the proper response to "Get to the point," or, worst of all, "I don't get it"?

First, let me single out one form of feedback that students sometimes tune out—but shouldn't. When an academic doesn't agree with you or really wants you to change something, they will often express it as: "Oh, you should read so-and-so." This is considered more polite and oblique than explicitly finding fault, but if you don't follow up on it, that's a recipe for trouble. I recommend that you pull out any statements down these lines:

---

[4] Dunleavy, *Authoring*, 140.
[5] Murray, *Craft*, 123.

read this historian
consider this theorist
look at this other primary source

and *do that first*. It's quite possibly the best and most carefully considered feedback that you will receive. Get your hands on that material. Read it carefully. Reflect on *why* someone would send you to it. Implement some kind of discernible change as a result. Thank the person who made that suggestion.

Sort the rest of the feedback into different types of action items. Occasionally, you'll receive feedback that is tidily presorted: a list of major requests, and some bullet points for smaller items. More likely, you'll need to do it yourself. Some things are quite small and easy to address, though keep an eye out for the note that adds "and throughout." They may have marked a problem only once, but expect you to find the other instances and correct them as well. Next, sort out the feedback that asks for more substantive changes but sets out clear expectations. You may not like it, but you understand what they are referring to, and you know how to go about addressing the point.

With those two categories separated out, see what remains. What makes for the toughest feedback? Often, it is not the harshly worded comment, but the puzzling comment. Sometimes the sentence is genuinely vague, but more often it's a challenge because you have trouble assessing how deep and comprehensive a change they're really requesting.

Personalities differ—some people understate their objections, while others are quite cavalier about indicating a drastic revision is in order. It's also possible that a small fix will do the job, regardless of how it was framed. A statement such as "This section doesn't work" *could* be a prompt to throw it out and start over. More likely, it's a sharp remark intended to make sure that area of concern wasn't lost in the shuffle. Steer a course that avoids the twin hazards of under-reacting to the input that you received and overdoing it. It might help to follow up on certain revision requests to gently encourage them to get more specific: "I was thinking of doing a and b, does that substantively address it, or should I go beyond that?"

Much earlier, you made choices about what primary sources to use. You also made decisions about starting dates, ending dates, and geographical scope. That was so long ago, you might have a little trouble even reconstructing when and why you made some of those decisions! However, reader feedback can reopen any of those matters—or all of them, leaving you revisiting issues discussed in Part Three, Part Two, and even Part One of this book. See if you can approach that input with an open mind. There are limits to how much project redesign is possible at a late stage, but sometimes it's valuable to take a few things you thought were settled, and unsettle them. At the very least, you can file those provocations away for future development, or as the focus of a promising side project.

A common concern at this stage is that the student let anecdotes pile up, but in the view of one (or more) readers, a thesis statement did not come through clearly. My approach throughout this book was to discourage storytelling and emphasize the indispensable building blocks of academic writing, but the temptation to spin a tale may have overcome you at times.

Perhaps you know perfectly well what your thesis statement was, and you believe that the narrative supported it. If you're getting pushback, though, it's a sign that something didn't work. Consider the statement "I disagree with your story"; what would such a statement mean, and how would the conversation proceed from there? Generally, we can like or dislike a story, but faced with an argument, we will agree or disagree. This is one of the best features of arguments: It is possible to disagree with them, pinpoint the precise objection, and invite an equally precise response, perhaps about amendments or clarifications, that moves the conversation forward.

For exactly this reason, if you *did* supply a discernible introduction, conclusion, lit review, and thesis statement, expect to hear a lot about them at this stage. Give the reader something clear enough that they *could* disagree with it, and there's a good chance that someone will! As uncomfortable as this can be, it's an opportunity to introduce more nuance into your claims.

Zero in on the exact objection and find a way to acknowledge it in plain language. Perhaps a reader informed you about an exception to the pattern you emphasized, or a quotation that points to a different motive for someone's action. If your overall conclusion is unchanged, then you can share both the counter-example and your reasoning for not letting it change your interpretation. You may also find yourself discriminating between serious challenges and more insignificant ones. As Pierre Vidal-Naquet once remarked, even if someone establishes that a careless astronaut "left a few grams of Roquefort" there, the thesis that the Moon is *made* of cheese is still hardly worth our notice.[6]

Some exceptions are more serious and deserve careful investigation. Perhaps that odd example comes from a visitor to the community who didn't share its values, or they are the words of someone who came from an unusual ideological or religious background. That strange quotation may date from a late (or early) period in your chronology. Perhaps the existence of this outlier serves as a reminder that your thesis statement itself would benefit from a little qualification or sharpening:

> This was the situation *in the 1680s*.
> *Unlike the neighboring colonies,* Rhode Island…

If you have a reader who doesn't see the point of your whole project, there's no simple fix. As noted in Chap. 5, entire subfields of history initially drew some puzzlement and derision because they seemingly did not connect to anything. While it's tempting to meet dismissal with dismissal, giving up on the uncomprehending reader and anyone else like them, consider the possibility that this is just someone who needs more context. After delving deeply into a

---

[6] Pierre Vidal-Naquet, *Assassins of Memory: Essays on the Denial of the Holocaust*, trans. Jeffrey Mehlman (New York: Columbia University Press, 1992), xxiv.

topic for weeks or months on end, it's easy to forget what reference points an outsider would need to appreciate the stakes of the inquiry and the potential benefits of arriving at a better grasp of this material. Even your advisor may startle you by asking a remarkably basic question. Take a deep breath and then get to work on an answer to that question. Include it in your revised version.

What about feedback that's negative, but also vague? I've learned to treat it as a gift because a reader has flagged something that didn't work for them. Sometimes the objection was ill informed and poorly expressed, but the instinct that my word choice was ambiguous—or my treatment of that theme needed work—was exactly right. You need some time to go figure out what the remedy is. Indeed, the revision process often consists of a listening stage, followed by a little while working on your own. The next section explores what you can do during this period of introspection.

Reappraise, Rework, Rebalance

Start by asking: Do you, yourself, agree with your position as stated in your latest draft? This is more of an open question than it sounds. Many writers start with one thesis and change their mind by the last page. You may even discover that in the course of your paper, you took three different positions on the same question! Take a good hard look at the beginning and the middle of your draft for these vestiges of your older thinking.

For historians, one of the trickiest balancing acts is between contingency and determinism. You may feel that this isn't an issue in your paper, but watch out for soft "contingency" claims that can creep in. *Was* that individual indispensable? *Was* this decision the crucial turning point? Perhaps, while reaching too hard for an impressive-sounding thesis statement, you implied a chain of causation that's debatable at best, or attributed motives to the historical actors when they aren't very easy to discern.[7]

To be sure, there are *two* extremes to avoid here. A narrative that resists any hint of contingency may leave readers suspicious that you are oversimplifying. Look over your paper and ask yourself whether the overall picture is a little too neat. Or do you have the opposite problem? If you didn't intervene to set clear priorities, all is a tangle, because everything and everyone was important.[8] Changing a single sentence, or even a single word, could spare you some embarrassing questions later.

Any reformulation of your thesis statement may require a new direction for portions of the manuscript. The people who gave you feedback probably didn't anticipate all those ripple effects, but you need to think those through now.

---

[7] This is a running preoccupation throughout Leo Tolstoy's novel *War and Peace*. For a short essay that captures Tolstoy's spirit neatly, see Max Fisher, "20 Years On, a Question Lingers about Iraq: Why Did the U.S. Invade?" *New York Times*, March 19, 2023.

[8] Commager, *Nature*, 86–87 offers some well-considered thoughts on this.

Whether or not your readers pointed it out, I'll hazard a guess that your lit review needs some work. For instance, your project may have grown in new directions. An environmental history project that morphed into a labor history project could well contain a strong and appropriate lit review section for the project that *was*, but not for the project *as it exists today*.

Get rid of signs that point to a road you didn't build! Relic language often persists in "sectioning, headings, subheadings, signposts and promises"; these may "reflect your original plan while the body of the text you have written in fact does something different."[9] Your paper deserves section headings and mission statements that really speak to how the project turned out.

The revision stage is a great opportunity for tidying and consolidation.[10] Patrick Dunleavy warns that many drafts contain "closely related points" that are "dissipated across different bits of the text."[11] Leaving them scattered will strain the reader's memory, or leave important content in places where it could go unnoticed. Gather up those waifs and strays and give them a new home. Reshuffling elements in this way may leave you with a shorter and stronger exposition.

The writer who wants to revise by only *adding* is missing out on a lot. If there is no deletion, I'll venture a guess that you aren't really revising. For most of us, saying something at length in a draft is the way of arriving at a better place: The shorter statement that is more elegant, clear, and true.

Zachary Schrag captures one of the reasons that deletion is a natural part of the process. "A work in progress," he observes, "is like a growing tree, sending branches in every direction that might have some sunlight."[12] However, a vining, sprouting impulse has its own internal logic, as one sentence succeeds the next. You aren't obligated to nurture every errant tendril. A little pruning or trimming may leave you—not only with a neater manuscript—but a shortened to-do list.

To be sure, cutting extensive, footnoted passages can feel drastic, like a major surgical procedure. Paste minor slices and large amputations alike into a "Cuts" document. Then carefully back that file up just like anything else, so you are at no risk of losing it. I predict that the overwhelming majority of your deletions will remain deleted. If there is something you can't bear to part with, paste the cut material into a special document with a different title. That way, you are saving it for future reference. One historian has likened this to the "starter dough" from which a new project might arise.[13]

---

[9] Dunleavy, *Authoring*, 145.
[10] Murray, *Craft*, 166-193.
[11] Dunleavy, *Authoring*, 144.
[12] Schrag, *Princeton Guide*, 375.
[13] Mara Keire, quoted in Schrag, *Princeton Guide*, 376.

Settling Your Intellectual Debts

Have you been told that you need to strike out on your own a bit more and establish which aspects of your contribution are really new? Or did someone suggest that you are not as original as your paper seems to imply, and ask you to acknowledge those who have preceded you in this area? New work or new approaches often meet with confusion, so some reactions down these lines may be a bit off the mark. Even so, the way to address that situation is to ground yourself carefully and clarify where you actually stand in relation to the historiography.

I warned you that your uneasy dialogue with your cousins would continue throughout your research and writing process. Now is the time to offer a final verdict, most likely *both agreeing and disagreeing* with those who have gone before. Avoid the temptation to vagueness here:

> This paper complicates the picture.

As Robin Briggs once dryly remarked, "one would prefer to have something more than ever-increasing complexity to claim as a result of one's efforts."[14] Revision at its best means holding a kind of debate with yourself, taking on board the toughest lessons of that process, and then expressing those results on the page.

There's a potential downside to this, though. It's not uncommon to see sentences—even in published work—that visibly bear the marks of stress and contortion, perhaps as a result of very late revisions:

> Although they disapproved of much of it, they were not unwilling or unable to change as such; rather, they were committed to the civic values and notions of public order and good government with which they were familiar.[15]

When we undertake a complex balancing act like this, it often takes the form of a long, grammatically complex sentence, perhaps piling up so many negations that it's hard to see what it affirms. If you catch yourself doing that, break it up into several shorter sentences. You can also punctuate your new, refined statement of your position with short, appropriate examples and direct quotations from the sources. A good rule of thumb: If you're introducing important new language, always slow down and give it room to breathe!

---

[14] Briggs, "'Many Reasons Why,'" 49.
[15] Judith Pollmann, "The Spirit of the Belltower: Chronicling Urban Time in an Age of Revolution," in Pollmann and te Velde, eds. *Civic Continuities*, 271–293, see 291.

> **Pivot Point: Setting Yourself Apart**
> It is likely that your project was a work of incremental scholarship in *some* respects, but innovative in *others*. If readers aren't quite spotting the innovation, now is the time to mark it off clearly.
>
> 1. *Signpost exactly where—and how—your evidence sheds light on an ongoing debate.* If there are four explanations or positions out there already in the historiography, you are under no obligation to refute one, or all, of these; nor must you tie yourself in knots to produce a fifth one. Finding evidence that gives us a better way to evaluate the validity of other scholars' claims is also a real contribution to knowledge.
> 2. *Remind your readers where your work sits in relation to its peers.* Perhaps your case study isn't the famous, or familiar, example of such-and-such. Explain how your example offers a revealing or surprising contrast.
> 3. *Add nuance to a familiar line of interpretation.* You might write: "Not as much changed in this supposedly transformative time period as some scholars would have us believe." Or you might need to argue the opposite: "The crisis ran deeper than historians thought."
> 4. *Put the spotlight on what's interesting about your findings.* Interesting findings are more common than a truly unprecedented method, or lens of analysis. Almost by definition, the unexpected result isn't one that you would have discussed in your prospectus, but maybe this is what deserves a prominent place now. Sometimes unexpected results suggest a new insight. Now would be the time to jot that down, too.
> 5. *Explain the payoff of your use of new or unusual materials, or your choice to focus on a different time period or location.* Never lose sight of the power of formulations down the lines of "I looked at *this* to get at *that*, and here's what we know now as a result."
>
> This is, quite possibly, the clarification that your advisor, or other trusted reader, hoped you would provide. Run it by them and make sure that they aren't really asking for paragraphs or pages of new language, but a well-formulated line or two can go a long way.

Whichever aspect of your project you choose to spotlight at this stage, it's often hard to draw attention to agreement and disagreement while avoiding a quarrelsome tone. One tactful approach is to offer a clinically precise description of where your project diverges from past work, while nodding to *why they didn't approach things the way that you did:*

> In keeping with the priorities of her discipline, Carrillo sought quantifiable evidence, missing the rich texture of these oral history testimonials...
> This omission is not surprising, since Hsia's priorities lay elsewhere...
> Jones published at a time when environmental history did not yet inform many scholars' investigations...

Sanchez' widely influential theory, and the scholarship it has inspired, did not contemplate a situation such as…

Next, gently but firmly signal that you are moving on:

Since this is not borne out by the evidence, we need to look elsewhere for…
This appears less credible than it did a generation ago. What are the alternatives?
How can we avoid this dilemma? The perspective of [scholar, method] offers some attractive possibilities.

Total originality is an elusive goal. We are taught to assiduously search for precedents, and we do. It is still possible to unknowingly set forth an insight or an interpretation that reads like a reprise of someone else's work. In some realms of thought, such as chess and mathematics, the universe of possible "moves" is sufficiently rule-bound that independent discoveries occur regularly. If you doubt this, an internet search for "Stigler's Law of Eponymy"—which proposes that no scientific discovery is named after its original discoverer—will turn up numerous examples.

The humanities and social sciences are not immune to this. In Chap. 11, I discussed Jonathon Glassman's book *War of Words, War of Stones*, which astutely depicted the erosion of civil society and democratic norms in mid-twentieth-century Zanzibar. Here, though, is a remarkably similar account from almost 2500 years earlier. In Thucydides' *History of the Peloponnesian War*, he describes what happened in the city of Corcyra during its civil war:

> Words had to change their ordinary meaning and to take that which was now given them. Reckless audacity came to be considered the courage of a loyal ally; prudent hesitation, specious cowardice; moderation was held to be a cloak for unmanliness; ability to see all sides of a question inaptness to act on any. Frantic violence became the attribute of manliness; cautious plotting, a justifiable means of self-defense. The advocate of extreme measures was always trustworthy; his opponent a man to be suspected.[16]

This account of corroding norms has an uncanny resonance with what Glassman elucidates in his book.

War of Words, War of Stones does not cite Thucydides. Is that really so surprising? We might expect Glassman, who writes about the mid-twentieth-century, to be conversant with African intellectuals of the era; with Hannah Arendt and George Orwell; with any number of scholars who have written about modern African politics. However, if a precondition for writing a new book was to have first read *all* the old ones, we would miss out on a lot of scholarship—if, indeed, new scholarship ever appeared at all!

While the example of Thucydides and Glassman is not as precise an overlap as the independent discovery of calculus, in some sense these two historians stood in the same spot, and the same thing caught their eye. If you discover

---

[16] Thucydides, *The History of the Peloponnesian War*, Book 3, Chapter 82, translated here by Richard Crawley (New York: Barnes and Noble Classics, 2006), 198–199.

one of your favorite insights has a distinguished predecessor, add a footnote. Modify your lit review to acknowledge your long-lost cousin. This is not an ideal situation, but if it arises, I predict your advisor will be less shocked by it than you are.

Intellectually, it's more awkward to discover, late in the game, that someone's written on your exact subject matter and cogently argued for *different* conclusions. Perhaps it's brand new—or they published under different keywords—so you are only encountering it now. Time probably doesn't permit a substantive rethink, or new research in the primary sources to fend off this challenge. In that situation, it is perfectly okay to include a footnote indicating that so-and-so's work came to your attention too late in the process for you to address here. You may have seen such footnotes in published work; they are not uncommon. Welcome to the wonderful world of academic writing.

Of the many sentences that you tinker with and improve at this late stage, it's likely that one of the very last will be somewhere in your introduction. This is fitting. You are clear, now, on what your project became. You know, now, how the paper ended up. With that in mind, you're ready to reconsider just what it is that the reader needs to hear at the very beginning.

Titles and Abstracts

In 2021, the web comic XKCD published a parody, "Types of Scientific Paper," that consisted of nothing but a list of twelve titles for imaginary articles. To give you a sense of them, one was "We put a camera somewhere new" and another was "My colleague is wrong and I can finally prove it."[17] It became an internet sensation and spawned dozens of imitations; seemingly everyone felt that their academic field, too, was ripe for parody.

Titles can actually perform a lot of work for you, if you choose them thoughtfully. In Chap. 9, I introduced you to some very hard working book and article titles, which actually managed to hint at entire thesis statements. Now is a good time to refer back to those examples. Paul Silvia remarks that "a title must balance generality and specificity," and if you skim the titles of academic publications in History, you will notice a pattern involving the frequent use of the colon, which often separates a brief, arresting phrase or couplet ("Chronicling Poverty"; "Arguing Disability") that carries thematic, emotional, or conceptual weight, and a longer subtitle that supplies details such as a place and a time.[18]

---

[17] "Types of Scientific Paper," https://xkcd.com/2456/, accessed July 22, 2023. For the parody's impact and its imitators, see Benjamin Mazer, "Scientific Publishing Is a Joke," *Atlantic*, May 6, 2021.

[18] Silvia, *How to Write*, 81; Tim Hitchcock, Peter King, and Pamela Sharpe, eds., *Chronicling Poverty: The Voices and Strategies of the English Poor, 1640–1840* (New York: St. Martin's, 1997); Geoffrey L. Hudson, "Arguing Disability: Ex-Servicemen's Own Stories in Early Modern England, 1590-1790," in *Medicine, Madness, and Social History: Essays in Honour of Roy Porter*, ed. Roberta Bivins and John V. Pickstone (New York: Palgrave Macmillan, 2007).

Historians often embed quotations in their titles. Catch one of your primary sources speaking very directly to a theme that you, also, believe was important. Then incorporate that phrase into the title. Here are some examples of this:

What Soldiers Do: Sex and the American GI in World War II France
A Hard Fight for We: Women's Transition from Slavery to Freedom in South Carolina

These are stylish titles, but also hard working titles.[19] They each gesture toward a tension or ambiguity that requires more exposition. Is "what soldiers do" a settled matter? A reference to an intercultural arena fraught with tension and misunderstanding? A term that probably meant very different things to women than it did to men? A callous catchphrase that brushes off sexual crimes? Likewise, "a hard fight for we" evokes many challenges. What sort of fight is implied here, and what were the stakes? Who exactly is the "we" in this formulation, and was that contested at the time? What are the problems and opportunities when we engage with a primary source that may contain dialect and unconventional grammar? While neither of these titles encapsulates a thesis statement, they suggest a destination and establish intellectual suspense.

In addition to crafting an effective title, you may be asked to write an abstract. There is probably a specific length limit for the abstract. Adhere to this. You can consult abstracts of earlier submissions to your own department, or the abstracts that appear with academic journal articles. Be warned, however, that abstracts are invariably written late in the writing process. Fatigued authors—perhaps wondering if anyone will ever read the abstract—rarely turn in their best performance. Some abstracts actually do a poor job of identifying the sources used, or the major conclusions. This is unfortunate, especially if prospective readers are browsing abstracts online and choosing to read further only if it catches their interest.

Let's see if you can do better. In Chap. 11, I challenged you to produce a miniature version of your entire paper in five or six paragraphs. To produce a good abstract, you can return to that and see if you can condense each paragraph into a single sentence. Kim Peters remarks that an abstract is nothing more or less than "a spoiler," and she's got a point.[20] Happily, though, for academic readers, a good abstract is not the same as learning the final score of a sporting event, or the plot twist of a famous film; we relish an elegant, pointed summary, and it may well leave us primed to read more.

Even if no one reads it, writing an effective abstract is never wasted effort, or a mere formality. It's a dry run for other tasks that could have major consequences for your professional development. All of us, sooner or later, find ourselves delivering the proverbial "elevator pitch" to a stranger about our

---

[19] *Soldiers* is by Mary Louise Roberts (Chicago: University of Chicago Press, 2013); *Hard Fight* is by Leslie A. Schwalm (Urbana: University of Illinois Press, 1997).
[20] Peters, *Your Human Geography Dissertation*, 202.

project. Perhaps that will come in the form of an invitation to write a blog post about where your scholarship fits into the wider historiography. Or you might want to obtain funding to continue your research, but for the grant application, you need to write a short overview of your work, and why people should care about it. Get the abstract right, and you'll have a running start at the task.

THE DEFENSE

The format of a final presentation varies internationally, and even within countries. How it is done at your university may differ from the way it's handled down the road, at what you consider a peer institution. Likewise, your friend or relative who went through this process—perhaps in a different discipline—may have well-meaning advice, but it won't necessarily correspond to your situation. There is no substitute for reviewing any written requirements, and checking with your advisor about expectations.

A public presentation of some kind—perhaps in front of other students who have also done similar projects—may be all that is expected. At the other extreme, which is more characteristic of the Master's and PhD levels, you will need to share your work with a group of faculty, perhaps including an outside reader, and the outcome must await their verdict. It is difficult to predict the long-term impact of artificial intelligence on higher education, but perhaps it will make these oral defenses more common everywhere, and at all academic levels.

The line of demarcation between an undergraduate defense and one conducted at the graduate level is more a matter of intensity than a profound qualitative difference. For this reason, there is no separate section here devoted just to graduate, or undergraduate, defenses.

All these varied arrangements have two distinctive elements in common. The first is that you are encountering one or more *outside questioners* (at the very least, beyond your advisor). The second distinctive element is the format, which requires you to answer *viva voce*, without the chance to compose yourself. Furthermore, you may get follow-up questions, whether from the original questioner or someone else in attendance. You can't just glide past a thorny topic; you, and your project, are the sole focus of the attention in the room. All this, of course, is a time-honored practice, perhaps dating back to the time when members of a guild quizzed a would-be initiate on the mysteries of the trade.

Some universities have a formal mechanism to draw an examiner from a different department or a different university altogether. Even if this isn't happening in your situation, you're still hearing from people who have come to your project late (additional committee members), or are hearing about it for the first time (random peers and a scattering of faculty who turned up for a less formal public presentation).

While you and your advisor share an understanding that comes from a long period of working together, it's likely that an outsider's questions will come at you from an unexpected direction. The odds are very good that your advisor wouldn't have allowed things to get this far unless they were substantially on board with you, your project, and how it turned out. On the day of the big event, the biggest challenges are likely to come from others.

The word "defense" seems to imply that someone is attacking. Whatever anxious scenarios you may spin out in your head, it is unlikely that your advisor—or anyone else—will be waiting to launch a barrage of logic puzzles or "gotcha" questions. If you have a committee, you can exercise some influence on the likelihood of the truly unexpected question, because you will have input on who at least some of the committee members will be. An effort to create a perfectly harmonious committee isn't a realistic approach, though. It is difficult to assemble three or four academics whose instincts and attitudes are in accord on absolutely everything! Inevitably, there will be differences in emphasis and priorities as they approach your work.

Perhaps the defense is better described as an exam, but if so, it's understandable to wonder: What, really, is on the test? Usually, it's not a quiz on the narrow topic or time period that you worked on. More likely, the conversation will turn—and return—to the professional norms and values that historians share. Indeed, you may get more than one question that harks back to themes covered in Chaps. 3 and 4 of this book. You'll be expected both to show mastery of the relevant debates between historians, *and* a skeptical awareness that the experts don't have all the answers. Likewise, the committee will expect you to display both a fascination with what primary sources could possibly tell us about the past *and* a sensitivity to the ways that primary sources are often slippery and self serving.

Typical questions at the outset include:

How did you become interested in this topic?
What was your research question?
What kinds of primary sources did you use?
What was your research experience like?
What did you find out?
What are your most important conclusions?

Follow-up questions will zero in on more complex issues and potential trouble spots:

Why did you choose the primary sources that you did?
Where does your work fall within the existing historiography?
This term seems important, where do you define it?
Is that term, concept, or category used appropriately here?
What is your thesis statement exactly?
How does your evidence actually align with the claims that you make?

It is also common, particularly in a formal defense, for questioners to ask about something from a particular page:

Explain this graph.
I don't understand the context for this photo from the caption you supplied here.
You offer a number here, but how was that measured? Is that your measurement, or someone else's?
What's your evidence for the claims in this paragraph?
Aren't you giving too much weight to just one example here—why should we think that this was typical?
What would you say to [a particular historian's] objection to this line of reasoning?

As I have warned throughout this book, you won't simply be judged on having *done a lot of work*. Hopefully, your diligence is already evident to the committee. However, readers familiar with Chaps. 9 and 10 of this book will not be surprised to receive questions about how you connected evidence and claims, whether the word "warrant" itself comes up or not. Having answers to such questions—indeed, *anticipating* that such questions will come up—is a sign of a student who has learned the lessons that matter most.

Peggy Hawley offers this canny suggestion:

> If you really want to impress the committee, cite some research published after your dissertation was finished. It is worth a last-minute computer search to locate a publication hot off the press. Having current information like this at your fingertips is prima facie evidence of your commitment to the field and shows you are making the transition from student to scholar.[21]

Perhaps "have you made the transition from student to scholar?" is, indeed, the *only* question on this exam. Listen to the questions at the defense with that underlying, implied question in mind.

There's no script to rely on here. However, you can take some practical steps to prepare. In many settings, the viva is—as much as anything else—a chance to meet in person and *review what you did in response to earlier feedback*. One of the best things you can do at this stage is to demonstrate that you made a thorough effort in good faith to act on the feedback you've already received.

To that end, you may wish to consider ways to help your advisor and any committee members find the changes that you made. This could take the form of a letter that you send before the defense, enumerating feedback and what was done in response, point by point. Another method might be to highlight new material throughout in some consistent color, both in your text and your

---

[21] Peggy Hawley, *Being Bright Is Not Enough: The Unwritten Rules of Doctoral Study* (Springfield, IL: Charles C. Thomas, 2003), 144.

footnotes, in the version that you share with them right before the defense. If highlighting seems inelegant, here is a sneaky way to help them spot the additions. Place most, or all, new text at the beginning or the ending of a paragraph. A reader who skims—and academic readers are sometimes very hurried readers—is likely to miss it if it's tucked away in the middle of something.

It may be possible to arrange a mock viva or another kind of dry run, whether with your advisor or with peers. Even explaining your work in depth to a relative or friend may elicit interesting reactions that will help you think differently about how to communicate your priorities, methods, and conclusions better to someone who's unfamiliar with some of the reference points you've come to take for granted. Let them run you through the generic questions and follow-ups I've provided in this section. This will give you a chance to hear yourself covering many of the standard themes in a defense. If you don't like the way you sound, you can prepare a different answer.

On the day of the big event, don't get hung up on judging what is happening. It's best to live in the moment and speak to the question that was just asked, rather than wondering what happened to the question you expected.

In a live setting, you can't excuse yourself and step outside, but taking a few seconds to compose yourself is helpful. Take notes as you go, particularly if you get multi-part questions. Consulting those notes is a way to buy yourself a few seconds here and there. It is also okay to ask for clarification. If you get a long and complex question, it may be prudent to pause and rephrase out loud what you think the essence of the question was.

Keep your replies concise. It is okay to politely check in with a questioner at the end: "Did I address everything?" Still, consider that if there are thirty minutes allotted for questions at a defense, and your first questioner goes on for a long time, eliciting an equally lengthy reply from you, then others in the room may feel crowded out.

It's possible that someone missed a fine distinction, and you need to tactfully walk them through it: "I *did* mention so-and-so position which is vigorously defended by Historian A, but my own argument is actually…" A patient, cheerful explanation can go a long way. If you misunderstood the question, a follow-up is always a possibility, but your small clarification may be exactly what was needed.

If you don't have an answer to something, it may be helpful to distinguish between "I don't know;" "we don't know enough" (perhaps there's just a single documented instance of something, and it is unwise to treat that as typical); "it is not known" (the historiography on this topic doesn't even afford a partial answer); and "unfortunately, this is not knowable because those records were destroyed during the Easter Rising of 1916."

One of the most complex and stressful aspects of a *viva voce* defense—and some public question-and-answer sessions—is the collision of different personality types, mindsets, and styles of scholarship. You may not approve of someone's tone or attitude, but a defensive reaction isn't in your best interest. Cultivate detachment. Earlier in this book, I discussed the differences between foxes and hedgehogs; between those who take incremental scholarship as the norm and those who yearn for unconventional approaches; and between academics who relish a debate with winners and losers versus those who are most comfortable with a collaborative search for better answers. You may see some, or all, of these attitudes on display at your defense or public presentation.

Never completely dismiss a question. Contriving a constructive response, in the moment, is a good test of both your intellectual flexibility and your emotional intelligence. Treat each question as if that were the most important one, because in the mind of that questioner, it really could be. If you feel that the question—and, of necessity, your reply—is getting the conversation as a whole a bit off track, you can make sure to close your response with a reminder of what you *did* look at, the questions that interested *you* the most, and your *actual* evidence and findings.

Come prepared for questions that push you all the way back to your initial choices. In particular, outside questioners have a habit of unexpectedly bringing up matters that fall outside the research framework that you adopted. They often ask about what was going on just before, or just after, the chronological period that you studied. Don't treat such questions as illegitimate. The outside questioner's mind often builds bridges from what is familiar to them. Thus, a project about Japan may suddenly elicit a line of inquiry that makes a comparison to something that happened in China.

The questioner who asks insistently about a neighboring country, a parallel development, or a slightly earlier time period *may* be misguided. Or, they could be offering you a valuable opening for further analysis. Seen in this different and wider context, your project might be more important, and your findings more interesting, than you even knew. There's no need to apologize for the project that you did; it's fine to agree that someone has suggested a useful direction that someone—maybe you—could explore next.

The good news is that you won't, ultimately, be judged on whether you had a superb answer or a witty rejoinder to every single question. Your goal in the *viva* is to be a patient listener and a tolerably good explainer, take good notes, and then—once again—retreat to a period of introspection and revision which will incorporate that final round of insight into the finished product.

Defenses often end with a verdict such as "minor revisions." As with earlier rounds of feedback, sort the input into different categories. Which are the minor fixes? Where is clarification needed? Must you (yet again) differentiate yourself from some strand of past scholarship? Is it time to modify the wording of your thesis statement, and if so, in what direction?

It's not unusual to come away from the defense with some homework. Perhaps you quoted from David Wootton's "Unbelief in Early Modern Europe." Although it is less than twenty pages long, it is a rich article that entertains many different examples and interpretations. At the defense, someone might say "you bring up this article, but doesn't Wootton argue for the opposite position?"

What's going on here? Their memory could be faulty. They may be thinking of a different page in the article. Perhaps extracting a clear thesis statement from "Unbelief" is difficult. In the case of a historian like Wootton, who had a long career, they could even be recalling a stance he took in a different publication altogether! You'll need to investigate all the possibilities.

You may have a favorite sentence in your paper which was singled out at the defense by someone who misunderstood it, or found it puzzling. It's vexing to have your pet phrase or your preferred term subjected to this kind of questioning. Worse yet, you could receive conflicting feedback: Some loved it, some hated it, some took it the wrong way.

In his *Nicomachean Ethics,* Aristotle cited a proverb, "Two of the same trade never agree," so you can take solace that this kind of situation has frustrated people for a very long time indeed.[22] Still, this is a chance to reflect on what you really hoped to get at with the language in the first place. It could, eventually, lead to a reformulation that captures it better, or communicates more clearly. If it was important content, then this will be time well spent.

Even the most thorough run-down of procedure, of course, doesn't capture what the anxious hours *before* the event will feel like. It's easy to get paralyzed with concern about how others may judge you. The academic language of thesis statements may feel forced and inauthentic. You may fixate on wondering what you should wear, or whether your voice sounds odd, or whether you can avoid that mannerism that someone told you that you have when you're nervous.

Instead of focusing exclusively on what they may say or what they may ask you, consider what *you* have to say to *them*. Donald Murray suggests that you interview your own paper and ask: "What is the one thing I wanted to say, the single, most important message I intended to deliver?"[23] Reminding yourself what it was all *for* is a great way to remember what matters most.

You might even change the tense of that sentence. Consider that what you have to say *now* may not be what you wanted, or expected, to be saying when you started the project. Your journey from your project's origins to its present configuration is a relatable and interesting story. If you respond to one of the early questions by sharing at least part of that narrative with the committee, the defense may feel less like an interrogation and more like a conversation.

It's a good idea to make a plan for where you will go and what you will do *immediately after* the defense or final presentation. Whatever happens in that room, you will need to decompress afterwards. You are the best judge of whether that means surrounding yourself with peers, friends, and family, or if it means a walk alone in the park or on the beach.

Don't be surprised if you can't quite let the project go. It's impolite to intrude at this moment, when you are taking your victory lap, but good ideas do not always come to light in orderly ways. You may mumble to yourself

---

[22] Aristotle, *Nicomachean Ethics,* Book 8, Chapter 1.
[23] Murray, *Craft,* 223.

about what you *should* have said at the defense, only to find that you've just articulated a simple explanation or deep insight that eluded you until now.

At the beginning of *War Without Mercy: Race and Power in the Pacific War*, John Dower confesses that the entire book grew from a single short remark in a draft of something else. He wrote a sentence about peacemaking, and how the US and Japan moved on after 1945. That sentence felt like it raised more questions than it answered. From there, he says, to a paragraph, a section, a chapter, and now to the book you hold in your hands.[24]

If you're feeling restless, it just might be the seeds of your next project that are stirring. Classic symptoms of this: Data that won't shut up, or quotations that refuse to be silenced. Maybe it's time to listen to them. Take some notes to capture these insistent thoughts, for later. Then please do take a real break. You've earned it.

Once you've caught your breath, though, the end of the process is a moment to take time for gratitude. You can reflect on your advisor's role, but also consider the patience and support of other people in your life. Some of them have lived with the project as long as you have. Now is also a good time to look in the mirror and acknowledge how far you have come.

Further Reading

Donald M. Murray, *The Craft of Revision*, 5th ed. (Boston: Thomson and Heinle, 2004) is superb and wide-ranging.

Peter Elbow, *Writing with Power* offers strategies on how to *solicit* feedback, and is revision-minded throughout.

Gerald Graff and Cathy Birkenstein, *They Say/I Say: The Moves That Matter in Academic Writing*, 3rd ed. (New York: W.W. Norton, 2014) offers templates and sample language that you can use for firming up exactly where you stand in relation to the existing historiography.

---

[24] (New York: Pantheon, 1986), x.

PART V

Looking Ahead

Today, it is common for even the earliest of "early career researchers" (ECRs) to think about building their academic brand by attending conferences, networking, presenting their own research, and looking for opportunities to publish. Many of the concepts we've already discussed carry over well to communicating ideas in those wider professional settings. There are, of course, unwritten norms of academic conduct that complicate the picture. Chapter 14, "Joining a Community of Scholars," identifies some common areas of trepidation for newcomers and offers practical strategies to address them.

The subject matter that interests historians has never seemed more timely, compelling, and controversial. Yet it is no secret that the academic job market is not flourishing in proportion to this demonstrable public fascination with—or fixation on—the past. This is not the place to dissect the reasons for this or to offer a forecast for the future. However, it is unconscionable to mentor students today without discussing career paths that range further afield.

Chapter 15, "Exploring Alternatives," takes as its premise that every History student should be looking into a Plan B, and probably a Plan C as well. Your particular version of this might involve academic-adjacent jobs—universities, libraries, and publishing houses employ many people in quite various roles—or the public-facing history positions at museums, archives, and heritage sites. Further afield, of course, a variety of possible careers beckons. You have probably heard of examples of people with History degrees who went on to excel in various fields, although how they initially got their foothold there may seem a little mysterious.

It's easy to feel you have no control and are at the mercy of larger forces. As you translate your credentials and work experience into a resume that will speak to potential employers, I have a surprise for you—many of the tips and tricks covered in this book will help you communicate here. We'll look at ways to express this new kind of thesis statement, and back it up with evidence and examples. Whatever your preferred version of Plan A might look like, Chap. 15 will help you appreciate your strengths, position yourself wisely, and—when possible—make your own luck.

CHAPTER 14

Joining a Community of Scholars

This whole chapter is about getting out there, presenting your work, and possibly even submitting something to a journal—and already, some of you may need a pep talk. Meeting strangers is daunting. Meeting strangers in a professional setting can be doubly so. The anxiety of presenting your work to a roomful of strangers? Even worse. Casting it on the uncertain waters of peer review? Unthinkable.

I'm going to take a contrarian position and suggest that notwithstanding some initial butterflies in the stomach, you will feel *better* if you give these activities a chance. Let's consider conferences. The unscripted interactions at conferences are often the most informative, enlightening, and career-shaping moments of all. You may think you know the trends in your area of interest and in the profession more generally. No single History Department is a reliable indicator of this, though, and even the most excellent advisor is not a perfect emissary. Conferences will allow you to connect with a wider cross-section of historians. Quite possibly, you'll also hear about approaches that haven't even shown up on your radar yet. Many of us can recall meeting people at conferences who turned out to be kindred spirits, new friends, and long-term allies. Against all expectations, you may feel truly heard and seen in ways that you haven't before.

Perhaps the scariest aspect of mingling with a wider academic community is the risk of getting caught out by the "real" historians, the people whose work you've admired, the people who seem larger than life to you right now. One of the best cures for imposter syndrome is listening to what others present at conferences and public lectures. Could you encounter a daunting master at work? You will, now and then. You'll also see plenty of examples where the level of accomplishment is well within your grasp. I guarantee that you'll see at least a few cases where you know you could do better.

The chapter concludes with a discussion of submitting your work to a peer-reviewed journal. If you have followed the steps I have outlined in this book

© The Author(s), under exclusive license to Springer Nature
Switzerland AG 2024
I. Land, *The Craft of Historical Research*,
https://doi.org/10.1007/978-3-031-68457-9_14

and taken on board the feedback of your advisor and others, you may be closer to having something submission-worthy than you're giving yourself credit for. If you are one of those people who doubt whether your research is even remotely worthy of publication, please take a good hard look at what finds its way into print! As you may recall, I'm fond of Marc Bloch's analogy: Scholarship is like a play of various searchlights roaming across a scene. No one searchlight can do it all, but each one picks up a new spot or throws something unexpectedly into sharp relief. If you add your beam to the mix, you're making it better for everyone.

Networking and Academic Small Talk

I could have entitled this section "how to talk to people at conferences," but academic small talk occurs between peers and friends, not just with strangers who have crossed paths in an unfamiliar city. Reflecting back on my own path, I first navigated these waters at parties and informal gatherings within my first few weeks of grad school.

For many people, small talk feels fake. It's useful, then, to think about the whole situation a little differently. *Listening* is an underrated activity. You may feel an implicit pressure to talk a lot in order to impress, but just listening now may give you the information you need to impress someone else down the road, when it matters most. Soak up all the tips and hints. Gossip may be a vice, but it's helpful to know where the bodies are buried.

Listening also sets you up for speaking. That means *listening for opportunities* to connect about a shared interest. You may have to be patient before you hear something that resonates, but consider these examples:

- You both undertook oral history interviews as part of your research.
- You both used legal records of some sort.
- You're both looking for news about digitization projects.
- You're both excited about so-and-so's new publication, even though neither of you work on that particular time period or country.

Any of these could spark a long, substantive conversation.

There is an Aesop's Fable that deserves to be better known. It is the story of the bat. The bat refused to help the birds in their war with the animals, because he claimed he wasn't a bird, although he flew; he also refused to help the animals, because he had wings. Then, later, when the bat needed help, both the birds and the animals had no interest in helping him.

Perhaps people who pursue advanced degrees are especially susceptible to a fascination with their own uniqueness. To be sure, we are all unique. Nevertheless, your motto should be: Build bridges, don't burn them. Like the bat in the fable, if you don't belong to a group, don't expect support; if you don't have a patron, don't expect patronage. This doesn't mean you have to be all things to all people. Just don't present yourself as so unique that you could only care about someone with your precise configuration of interests and preferences.

You can practice the art of building bridges in small ways, just by changing how you introduce yourself. It's helpful to craft your short introduction as an implied invitation to engage along different registers: You *might* have a country and time period in common, but perhaps it's around the themes, or the method, where the connection is possible. For example:

> I'm a medievalist with an interest in gender and digital humanities.
> I do animal-centered history and wet ontologies in the Arctic.
> I just finished a stint as a research assistant on a GIS project, and I'm considering whether I want to find a PhD program that would support applying those skills to the environmental history of China.

Notice that each of these statements comes with several different "handles," like a suitcase that's conveniently designed so that someone could pick it up from the top *or* from the side. Someone can seize upon the familiar ("I'm learning Chinese right now!") or ask about the unfamiliar ("Okay, I'll bite. What's wet ontology?"). If you identify yourself as *just* a medievalist, *just* someone who works on the Arctic, or *just* a historian who's learning to code, that could work. Or there may be an awkward pause as someone tries to work out where the handle is on that particular suitcase.

Beyond introductions, of course, the conversation often moves to clarifying questions. Sometimes these will prod you in directions you're not ready to go. The good news is that a simple, standard question ("how's your project going?") may be more of a polite conversational maneuver; it probably doesn't mean that you need to shoot back an itemized inventory of where the project actually *is* right now.

As in tennis, though, if they serve, you need to knock it back. There are a host of reasons why you might be uncomfortable answering. Your work may be at such an early stage compared to theirs that you feel you have little to say. You may be well along, but you're having second thoughts about your project's design and aims. Or perhaps you're worried about tipping your hand by revealing a special primary source you've identified, or your hard-won insights that you hope to publish one day.

Instead of a recitation that implies completion, certainty, and achievement, why not share a story about what got you started in the first place? Perhaps you were

- Provoked by an egregiously poor piece of scholarship
- Enraged by an injustice
- Tantalized by a newly digitized or declassified resource

Even though the people you're meeting are, perhaps, not very familiar with your area of specialization or your reference points, these kinds of responses will be very relatable and interesting.

Was your choice of project an expression of what you liked, or disliked, about where the field is today? This can be tricky; one person's villain is another's hero, and so forth. Try out tactful formulations until you know these people better. "I was frustrated by…" or "something felt missing…" are ways to express honest discontent without accidentally disparaging someone else's intellectual choices or heartfelt allegiances.

We speak from our most authentic place when we share our joy, our struggle, or our pain. Do you have a story down those lines? Here are some possibilities:

- The day you set aside your first idea for this project, and embarked on the path you're taking now
- Your most embarrassing moment in the archives
- That exciting new publication that's making you rethink things

Sharing something meaningful and memorable about yourself like this can set off a chain reaction. Someone else may reciprocate because you have just reminded them of a story of their own, or you may get an invitation to meet someone else that they know. You may be surprised how many people who *don't* align with your profile of interests *do*, somehow, know someone who would be interested in meeting you.

Do you need a networking strategy? You don't want to come across as trying too hard; the most successful networking occurs as a byproduct of something else. Being nice to everyone, in a low-key way, is actually a pretty good approach if you can pull it off. Not everyone wants to be your friend, but don't underrate the value of acquaintances. Some of these people will pop up in your professional life again, but you can't always judge just who, how, and when. Being a name they know makes you visible, and sometimes visibility is all you need.

My focus here has been on speaking to peers or near-peers. Of course, sometimes you will find yourself in conversation with those who are more senior, more established, perhaps even famous. Publications like the *Chronicle of Higher Ed*, blog posts, and social media feeds can be good sources for tips.[1] However, you might be surprised how many of my suggestions here are applicable to the daunting task of meeting the people whose names populate your footnotes, or even the scholar who wrote the book that has inspired you most of all.

---

[1] Robin Bernstein, "How to Talk to Famous Professors," *Chronicle of Higher Ed*, July 5, 2017.

Giving Your First Conference Paper

What could you possibly have to say that is worthy of a conference presentation? As a researcher who's new to this process, it's understandable to have doubts. Donald Murray suggests two simple questions for writers, but they work well for public speaking too. One is "What does somebody else need to know that I know?" and the other is "What contradicted what I know—or thought I knew?"[2] You formed your first impressions while conducting your lit review, so if your subsequent research results surprised you, they might well surprise others who have read the same historiography. Reminding yourself that your project brings something new to the table (even if it's a small thing) may dispel any reproachful inner dialogue that's sapping your confidence. After all, people at the conference will see you—not so much as an individual—but as the messenger of that interesting and new content. One might even say that conferences *exist* in order for people to share interesting and new content, so clearly you belong there. Writing papers to meet a university requirement, you mostly feel like a spectator, even when you weigh in on issues that are discussed by others. At conferences, you get to be part of the conversation yourself.

Conferences vary considerably in size and scope, so consider the right venue for the particular material you have to share, and in what setting you'd feel the most comfortable. Some are huge national conventions; others are one-off events organized around a narrow topic. The most common type of conference is an annual event run by a special association devoted to the historical study of a particular geographical area, a theme, or a time period.

If you want to be on the program as a presenter, the deadline to submit a proposal (normally, just a c.v., a title, and a short abstract) is many months in advance. Sometimes it is beneficial to submit as part of a panel; most conferences also accept proposals for a single paper. They evaluate the submissions and, in the case of single paper proposals, group them into panels that more or less cohere on a thematic or chronological basis. If you get a chance, it would be a valuable learning experience to just attend a conference, listen, and observe, without the pressure of giving a paper.

I will concede that the cost of academic conferences is too high. There are usually discounts on the registration fees themselves for students and perhaps for early career researchers. If you are enrolled in a degree program or are an employee, your university may have specially designated funds to support conference registration fees and travel expenses, especially if you are presenting a paper. To be sure, the climate crisis adds another layer of concern about what we really hope to achieve by traveling long distances for such a purpose. Despite changes in technology, the in-person conference shows no signs of dying out just yet. Delivering a conference paper remains an expected rite of passage. It is also a chance to get a reality check, and a range of input, before taking the bigger leap of exposing something to peer review.

[2] Murray, *Craft*, 9.

Let's consider what to do if you are notified that your paper is accepted, and you will have your fifteen or twenty minutes at the podium. David Evans offers a veiled warning: A presentation involves the "transformation of written work into a spoken form."[3] Starting from a single page of notes and *expanding that* to an oral presentation will be much more effective than taking your fully realized paper and attempting to cut it down. Evans quotes this statement as a kind of academic proverb: "The talk is *about* the work, but is *not* the work itself."[4]

At conferences, people shuffle in from another panel or from a conversation outside in the hallway. Perhaps a co-panelist precedes you and will leave the room thinking about a different context, a different set of priorities, and a different sort of primary source. Even a specialized conference (say, in French history) won't reliably populate a room with people who study the exact same period and themes as you do. They lack the elementary reference points; it's not so much that they think you are barking up the wrong tree, but that forests are new to them, to say nothing of squirrels and acorns.

With this in mind, it is tempting to fill up your whole presentation time with background, lit review, and your statement of the research problem. Don't do it. I will suggest that a fifteen-minute oral presentation should only spend two to four minutes on background. A quick series of slides at the start can help, perhaps a map and then a timeline in brisk succession. Share a story about a difficulty that you experienced in the archives; this offers a great excuse to put an interesting photo of a document or other primary source up on the screen. The language, provenance, and format of that document communicate a lot at a glance *and* testify to what sort of material you care about—suggesting your overall research interests and agenda. If you put up a slide showing a couple of recent books in the field, this can serve as a reminder of what sort of academic company you keep.

A successful conference paper, though, doesn't just sidle up to the subject matter and then leave off just at the moment when it might say something substantial, new, surprising, or complicated. Make sure that you are reserving most of your presentation time to discuss your *own* work: what you mainly looked at, how you approached and interpreted it, and your overall findings.

One of the delicate aspects of presenting at a conference, especially as a first-timer, is that you face a room full of question marks. You may well have things to say about the historiography—indeed, we train students to do so, and I have regularly encouraged it in this book. How to manage the possibility that Scholar A, Scholar B, or their former students will wander in? Plan beforehand on some muted language that would be safe with almost any combination of audience members. For example

> It is useful to complicate this picture...

or even

---

[3] Evans et al., *How to Write*, 203.
[4] Evans et al., *How to Write*, 204.

> This evidence complicates that picture…

This will come through loud and clear, but it is not adversarial. It even suggests that your new work *could* be construed as extending the previous scholarship, rather than negating it.

Understatement usually works well. Rather than saying Scholar A refuted Scholar B, you can indicate that

> Scholar A took a different approach, putting the emphasis on…

If there is laughter at your oblique word choice, at least you didn't make the point in a needlessly polarizing way. Nor did you bow and scrape to the senior academics who may be lurking somewhere in the back. Remember that a *respectful dissent* isn't cowardly; it's still a dissent, so your point is made.

There is no one "correct" way to approach public speaking, and each style has its own characteristic strengths and weaknesses. Reading from a prepared text is quite common. Just remember that an immaculately planned and scrupulously revised written script isn't what the audience *hears*. A listener will probably miss a paragraph break. Even a section heading, read aloud, lacks the impact it would have on the page. Make conscious choices about pacing: When is the time to speak quickly, and when should you slow down? Silence may allow something to really sink in. If that's true, then pauses may be the most important form of punctuation available to you.

Pausing also gives you a chance to make at least a little eye contact with the audience. I like to scan the room and locate one or two people who seem attentive or even appreciative. Checking in with them from time to time helps me feel as if I am communicating, rather than just reciting. Perhaps this is why my public speaking style doesn't rely much on prepared text. It naturally evolved from my need for a human connection with someone in the room.

In fact, you might think about your conference paper as a series of mini-talks, punctuated by verbal "asides." These conversational "asides" are at least as important as any slides or web content that you pop up on the screen. The aside could be a short anecdote:

> and then when I opened the first box in the archive I realized…

It could be a rhetorical question.

> What are we supposed to do with a source like this?

Deliver the aside, pause, maybe make eye contact, and move on to your next point. Hopefully, your little aside set it up for you.

If you have limited experience speaking from a loose outline or minimalist notes, rehearsal may help you get more comfortable with it. Rehearsal is also a way to get a sense of how much you can say, in your particular speaking style, in ten, fifteen, or twenty minutes. Bear in mind, though, that in the heat of the moment, some people are prone to reading much more rapidly (perhaps finishing early) or to improvised digressions (unexpectedly running over time).

Pacing isn't just about completing the talk in the allotted time. Slowing down permits you to actually explain things. Putting a typed quotation—or the primary source itself—up on the screen doesn't tell us what it means or where it fits into your argument. The same goes for vague non-explanations like "Here's a graph." The lessons of Chaps. 10 and 12 are very pertinent here.

If just looking at your plan for the presentation leaves you feeling stressed and hurried, that's probably a sign that you should cut out some examples or reduce the number of themes that you address.

Really eager to say more about one or two things? Try some version of this quick verbal gesture:

> I'd be happy to discuss the challenges of working with this type of primary source more in the Q&A if you are interested.

This will probably elicit just that sort of question in due course, but in the meantime, honor the time limit that everyone else respects. It's basic courtesy.

People will remember how your paper ended, so choose that final note with care. If public speaking is not your favorite thing, you may catch yourself wrapping up with a sentence that's more of a sigh or a whimper. Don't end by mentioning what you didn't do; the audience wants to be reminded of what you *did*. A closing could be crisp and definitive:

> Here's what we thought we knew; here's what we know now.

A closing could be forward-facing:

> What I've found raises additional questions, so here are some themes or sources I'll be looking at next.

It can feel awkward to give a progress report on an unfinished research project, but sharing it with an audience—perhaps for the first time—has a freshness and a special energy that can leave the room sympathetic and engaged.

It is customary to have someone (who's listed as "chair" or "commentator") deliver remarks on the panel after everyone has presented. In some formats, you'll have sent them a copy of your paper in advance, so respect the deadline for this; they need time to digest it. The "comment" usually consists of summaries of each paper, followed by a mix of reflection, critique, and suggestions for next steps. The panelists get a chance to reply. Afterward, there will be questions from the floor and further discussion.

The advice on how to think, and feel, about feedback in Chap. 13 should be helpful here. Taking copious notes may help you feel anchored. Even if you are a bit rattled, looking down at the notes as you begin to answer will make the situation feel more like an academic discussion than a personal confrontation. Responding point by point, based on your notes, will also keep your responses focused and on track. Questioners will notice that and appreciate it.

Perhaps, after reading this, your instinct is to wait until your own research is a little more advanced before risking an encounter with the big names in your field in a format like this. That doesn't mean you can't find academic gatherings. Your own university may host a workshop or special event about a topic that is at least somewhat relevant to your interests. Some institutions—such as the Newberry Library—run regular seminar series that have many features of an academic conference, but don't involve registration fees. You might find a spot as a presenter; undoubtedly, you can attend as an observer.

If you don't have an opportunity like that nearby, attend lots of guest lectures, even in different departments of your own university. Watch the dynamics in the room. Reflect on how questions are posed and how they are answered. Maybe make conversation with someone you met at the event. Just don't postpone your practical education in these matters. You can apply many of this chapter's lessons close to home and on a budget.

SUBMITTING YOUR WORK FOR PUBLICATION

If you ask, your advisor will have some thoughts about whether your work is ready to submit for publication. Just as a conference paper is most effective when it narrows the focus down to a very delimited set of questions and examples, don't ignore the possibility that what you'll be showcasing in your submission to a journal is just a piece of your research and writing thus far. After reading this book, you should have some sense of what it means for an article to stand neatly on an Archimedean Point; re-reading Chap. 8 now may suggest some possibilities in that vein. Solicit ideas about which elements from your work might be most suitable for a journal article. It might just be the material from one *section* of your paper.

Your advisor should also be able to shed some light on the tricky question of *where* to submit it.[5] One classic balancing act is between a journal's visibility and prestige and the likelihood of acceptance. A journal like *Past & Present* would have an extremely high rejection rate. Smaller, more specialized journals will have proportionately fewer submissions coming in and may be speedier and more responsive. If a particular journal feels like home to you—you read it regularly and you are in dialogue with scholarship that has appeared there—then even if they are known to reject many submissions, it really could make sense to give them a try first.

If you have been *invited* to submit by someone associated with a particular journal (which happens to people at conferences sometimes, especially if they

---

[5] Wendy Belcher, *Writing Your Journal Article in Twelve Weeks: A Guide to Academic Publishing Success*, 2nd ed. (Chicago: University of Chicago Press, 2019), 110–149, devotes an entire chapter to this problem alone.

gave a paper), you should consider pursuing it, although a generic encouraging remark may be that and nothing more. If someone approaches you about a special issue of a journal on a topic that's closely congruent with your work, that is a more serious invitation. You would have to meet the deadline for the special issue, and your work would still go out for peer review, but there's a real possibility that your chances of publication just improved quite a bit.

As you transition from the world of student papers to the world of academic publishing, some things will change. For example, you may have to worry a lot more about copyright, especially if you work with any visual materials at all. Please note that copyright law varies from one country to another, so you may be in for some surprises if you research (or publish) across international borders. As a starting point, I have listed some reference books on copyright in the Further Reading section for this chapter. How nice it would be if we could—through a sheer effort of will—only have clever thoughts about material that was Open Access or housed in a museum or library that happens to be generous and supportive of authors and their need for photographs and permissions! Until that day dawns, you'll have to work within the system we have.

Perhaps, as a student, you often heard people exclaim "How interesting!" when they encountered new work. Here, too, the transition to the publishing world can be disconcerting. People who won't ever have to meet you in person find it rather easy to tell you, one way or another, that they find your work *un*interesting. While journals share many of the same general standards (quality, originality, adherence to professional norms), they will interpret some standards (such as "interest and importance to a professional readership") in quite idiosyncratic ways.[6] Good scholarship that doesn't match the "interest and importance" criteria for that particular publication will probably meet with a desk reject—that is to say, it won't even get sent out for peer review.

It is hard to express in words *just how much* research is going on globally today across all academic disciplines, but here's a startling figure: There is one peer-reviewed article published every eighteen seconds or so.[7] Against such a noisy backdrop, journals—like individual scholars—struggle to stand out. What Wendy Belcher calls the "claim to significance" seems to become more important with each generation; she notes that "over the last forty years, the frequency of aggressive wording... such as *robust, novel, innovative,* and *unprecedented,* has skyrocketed" as scholars try to make their submission appear not just eligible for publication, but timely, urgent, or potentially award-winning.[8]

You have already passed a test in this regard. If your paper lacked any novelty at all, your advisor would have objected. However, submitting to a journal means you'll have to vault over a higher, and different, threshold. It is also

---

[6] Dunleavy, *Authoring*, 236–237.

[7] Belcher, *Writing*, 112, says there are about two million articles published per year (as of 2018), which is consistent with other widely reported estimates on academic publishing. I derived the eighteen seconds figure from this.

[8] Belcher, *Writing*, 192.

possible that your advisor—and others who have had input up to this point—may not be completely up to date about the newest developments. While there is no perfect guideline, the suggestion to "read abstracts of all [relevant] articles published in the last 5 years" points you in the right direction.[9]

This is especially true if you think you've caught a tiger by the tail with a new theme, new method, or new hot topic. Academic trends often swell and surge with alarming speed; yesterday's placid waters are today's tsunami of publications. That lit review you assembled a year ago could already be seriously out of date. Do the catch-up work now, before you announce to a journal editor that you have a bold and innovative take on something.

In addition to following any format and length guidelines that appear on the journal's website, you must remove your name, any academic affiliation or job title, and any similar identifying information from the manuscript that you upload to the journal's submission portal. This anonymity is part of the institution of peer review, which creates a level playing field to some degree and makes certain kinds of bias, pettiness, or retribution less likely. You, also, will not know reviewers' identities beyond some designation such as "Reviewer 2."

Peer review exists to defend the minimum standard for what should pass as scholarship in our discipline, and like other feedback, it can make good work better still. Potentially, it protects you—as well as the journal—from embarrassing errors of commission or omission. For example, the peer reviewers may direct you to

- Historiography you didn't know about
- Primary sources that complement (or contradict) your interpretation
- Unexamined errors in your reasoning
- Weak paragraphs that don't communicate well
- Outright factual errors

A full-throated defense of peer review offers the bold generalization that "published articles are always better than the first drafts" and that, as a result of incorporating peer review feedback, "published research is more focused, less confrontational, and more circumspect" than it would be otherwise.[10] Others are more ambivalent; Richard Smith, who edited a major medical journal for many years, remarks that peer review is fittingly "compared with democracy: a system full of problems but the least worst we have."[11] Smith's remarks on *why* it can be a wildly uneven process speak well to what goes on in a range of disciplines, including History:

---

[9] Belcher, *Writing*, 394.
[10] Silvia, *How to Write*, 101.
[11] Richard Smith, "Peer Review: A Flawed Process at the Heart of Science and Journals," *Journal of the Royal Society of Medicine* 99 (April 2006): 178–182; see 178.

... what is review? Somebody saying "The paper looks all right to me," which is sadly what peer review sometimes seems to be. Or somebody pouring [sic] all over the paper, asking for raw data, repeating analyses, checking all the references, and making detailed suggestions for improvement? Such a review is vanishingly rare.[12]

As a journal editor myself, I am happy to report that I have seen many examples of peer review at its best, with reviewers and authors alike participating in a thoughtful and productive exchange. I would not describe that as "rare" at all, but like Smith, I am acutely aware that there is no guarantee of this level of professionalism.

It is the scholars who are most invested, those with the most relevant expertise and interests, who are likely to receive an invitation to review your work. Often this yields excellent results, but of course, it can also create complications. I have always urged you to consider your work as in dialogue with your closest counterparts (whether we imagine them as cousins, allies, rivals, or frenemies). Occasionally, even though anonymity is maintained from start to finish, the peer review process turns into a kind of family quarrel, replete with misunderstandings and hurt feelings.

You may not encounter anything as heated as this, but rejection is common. A negative outcome with one academic journal does not mean that your work is inadequate or irredeemably flawed. Perhaps it just didn't catch their interest enough to stand out. One editor plus two (or three) peer reviewers is hardly a representative sample of the profession; even with the best of intentions, it's quite possible that this was an oddly skewed group. After a cooling-off period, go over the peer reviews carefully, perhaps in the company of someone you trust, and consider what you might do to avoid those particular reactions next time. On multiple occasions, I have been approached by an academic journal, or publishing house, about a piece I had seen before. In one case, I finally replied that I had weighed in on it so many times now that it really was someone else's turn!

The anonymity of peer review seems to encourage brief and vague characterizations of your work. Brace yourself for lines like these:

The manuscript did not make a significant contribution
(It) misinterpreted opposing theories
(It) makes unsupported claims[13]

You might well ask "on what page are the unsupported claims?" and so forth. If this were a *viva voce* defense, you would get an answer. In the case of peer review, though, you are stuck with whatever laconic remarks you got.

---

[12] Smith, "Peer Review," 178.
[13] Silvia, *How to Write*, 100. Admirably, Silvia offered these excerpts from negative peer reviews that *he himself* had received.

You can console yourself that a lack of supportive feedback may be par for the course: "Studies have demonstrated that peer reviews always have more negative comments than positive ones."[14] Even a careless misreading of your work has value because it shows where future readers, too, might go astray. Now you know that this reaction is possible, and you can take steps to guard against it.

Another common outcome is a "revise and resubmit." This is, of course, better than a rejection, though it may be challenging for different reasons. If you accept the offer, you will be in the position of working intensively with the feedback you received and perhaps asking for the editor's guidance on how to implement it. The proverb "a camel is a horse designed by a committee" comes to mind. Dutifully following all the advice from all the peer reviewers might result in a misshapen end product. You are well within your rights to offer a list of changes made while explaining—also—your rationale for the changes you *didn't* make.

As you undertake revision, never lose sight of the fact that at some point, somewhere, your work will be published. It will have your name on it. You need to be at peace with what it will look like then. Don't make so many concessions that you feel alienated from your own work.

Take the time to get the tone right, too. Sometimes a clash with a peer reviewer leaves us feeling, and sounding, defensive. You may still feel the sting from a rough treatment, but remember that those unfair remarks will be completely invisible to readers. Make the required changes, let the manuscript rest, and then do a final round of revision just focused on dialing down any signs of anger, frustration, or sarcasm. Sounding wise, nuanced, patient, and *right* is the best revenge.

I wish you luck as you embark on what is sometimes a fraught and uncertain process. I will close this section with three general principles. Look out for these, and it will improve your chances.

The first principle: Design your title itself as a miniature work of scholarship—accurate, specific, and persuasive. This could mean evoking your source material, or your conclusions, in a very explicit way. Studies suggest that articles with longer titles are cited more often, perhaps because longer titles can contain more keywords that attract the attention of search engines.[15] The importance of keywords is also an argument for leaning toward making at least part of your title "boring and factual."[16] Also, don't underestimate the degree to which your title helps the journal's editor select appropriate peer reviewers. A mismatched peer reviewer may not see the point of your project or lack the necessary background to evaluate your contribution.

The second principle: Make a well-informed decision about where to place yourself on the spectrum from bold to moderate. Some journals relish a

---

[14] Belcher, *Writing*, 362.
[15] Belcher, *Writing*, 282–283.
[16] Thompson and Kamler, *Writing*, 86.

swashbuckling style, while others avoid it.[17] I guarantee that peer reviewers will notice tentativeness or vehemence in your writing. Even one overstated claim may sour them on your whole manuscript. How do you deal with uncertainty and gray areas? How do you demarcate your original contribution while acknowledging the merit of previous work in the field? Appearing *tactful but firm* on all these matters might be ideal. If the peer reviews come back negative but infuriatingly non-specific, read between the lines. Perhaps the hidden message is "please pick a side" (if you were too vague and timid) or "you don't have to be such a jerk" (if you came across as dismissive or vain).

The third principle: Anticipate the hasty or careless reader. Eric Hayot remarks that "most people read faster than they think," and counsels you to help your points sink in by embedding repetition in your work.[18] Hayot contemplates readers who

> if you are lucky, will only occasionally skip or skim paragraphs or sections, only sometimes read while distracted by the radio, a demanding student (or colleague), their own desperate unhappiness, or an alarming rash.[19]

I sincerely hope that you never encounter a peer reviewer who passes judgment without reading the whole piece under consideration, but as an author, it has happened to me. Of course, it is a fiendishly difficult task to prepare for readers who skim or skip, because they aren't all predictably looking for the same things. Will the careless reader be satisfied if they see a string of trendy academic buzzwords? Are they scanning your footnotes for evidence that you are drawing on archival material that's not been used to shed light on this particular topic before?

You can't torture yourself with all the possibilities here, but you know your article's strengths, so at least you can do your best to showcase them upfront. Wendy Belcher offers some blunt advice: "If the worth of your article becomes apparent only on page 5, or page 25, it will fare poorly with editors or peer reviewers."[20] With that in mind, certain parts of your manuscript—the title, the abstract, the very beginning, and the very end—deserve your closest attention.

This is a necessary concession to our jittery, overwhelmed, irritable era, but it worries me to see anyone acknowledge it with a shrug. If you ever become a peer reviewer yourself, remember that authors—and, indeed, the whole system of academic publishing—deserve so much better. A world without careful readers is, ultimately, not a world where academic writing of *any* sort has a future.

---

[17] Thompson and Kamler, *Writing*, 45.
[18] Eric Hayot, *The Elements of Academic Style: Writing for the Humanities* (New York: Columbia University Press, 2014), 188.
[19] Hayot, *Elements*, 51.
[20] Belcher, *Writing*, 281.

Conclusion

Nothing in this chapter should dissuade you from sharing your work with others, whether at conferences or in a peer-reviewed journal. Donald Murray's observation is pertinent here:

> Writing and publishing is nothing more than an act of living. When we think and care and share our thoughts and our feelings, we are participating in the remaking of the world, nothing less.[21]

Think about all the everyday situations when we do speak out. We explain, we interject, we protest, we teach, we meet in dialogue. We do so because it seems called for or because silence is an unacceptable alternative. At those moments, the expectation is never that an utterance would be final, perfect, or complete, but whether it rises to the moment.

Academic discourse is more formal and moves at a slower pace, but it, too, is an ever-evolving conversation with many participants. In one sense or another, others will take up where you left off, and others will answer. When Murray writes that publishing is "an act of living," he is aware that this sets you up for a host of potential outcomes, including some that are messy or negative. If you keep to yourself, it's true that you could avoid censure. Yet you also would never get to hear the voices answering you back in validating ways. Likewise, if you stay away from academic conferences, the people who need an ally, a good listener, or a thoughtful critique might find themselves standing alone.

Some people present at conferences and receive no questions from the audience at all. Some people publish and find their work largely uncited and seemingly unread.[22] It's only human to lament outcomes like this. Consider, though, where you can exert control. For example, if *you* publish something, you can use your professional network on social media and elsewhere to spread the word and improve the odds that more people will pay attention. When you encounter good scholarship by others, even if it's not well known yet, you can take steps to amplify their signal, talking it up, sharing it with colleagues, and citing it yourself. You may witness disheartening behavior at academic conferences, but you can also spot opportunities to carry out small acts of respect and kindness. Did you notice that one person on a panel is getting no questions? Raise your hand and refocus the attention in the room on them.[23] We are all, inescapably, breathing the same atmosphere in academia, but early career researchers and senior scholars alike can shape that climate in positive ways if we make the choice to do so.

---

[21] Murray, *Craft*, 254.

[22] Rose Eveleth, "Academics Write Papers Arguing Over How Many People Read (And Cite) Their Papers," *Smithsonian Magazine*, March 25, 2014.

[23] For more practical suggestions in this vein, see Joanne Begiato et al., "Don't Be a Conference Troll: A Guide to Asking Good Questions," *Guardian Higher Ed*, November 11, 2015.

Further Reading

Pat Thomson and Barbara Kamler, *Writing for Peer Reviewed Journals* (London: Routledge, 2013): Chapter 7, "Engaging with Reviewers and Editors," is outstanding and insightful.

Wendy Belcher, *Writing Your Journal Article in Twelve Weeks*, 2nd ed. (University of Chicago Press, 2019), especially the chapter on "Revising and Resubmitting Your Article."

Michael Les Benedict, *A Historian's Guide to Copyright* (Washington, DC: American Historical Association, 2012) is a short work written for a US readership.

Tim Padfield, *Copyright for Archivists and Records Managers*, fifth edition (London: Facet Publishing, 2015) is written for a UK readership but also contains an appendix summarizing the law in a number of other countries. It is a long manual that discusses many possible situations.

CHAPTER 15

Exploring Alternatives

Watching young children play at "jobs," a quick costume change is all that it takes to assume a new role. Hold up a toy stethoscope, and you're now a nurse. Now drop the stethoscope and pop on a plastic firefighter's helmet. You've completed an abrupt, and unchallengeable, career transition. Wearing a firefighter's helmet, what else could you be?

For adults, developing a new career path is more uncertain and more laborious. We have credentials and degrees, which in some cases are appropriate for only one professional identity. Switch paths, and even our past work experience and job titles may have little relevance—and little intelligibility—to the people who will look at our resumes now. We also carry an invisible burden, the years of learned reflexes that go with a particular way of seeing and experiencing the world. Shedding this can feel like leaving a big part of our identity behind.

Switching paths can feel like a huge letdown. I anticipate that the most attentive readers of this chapter will be those who are slowly and reluctantly disentangling themselves from their dream of a university position that is centered on teaching and research. Indeed, the climate of higher education encourages people to think of the elite academic track as "a vocation" or even—in a quasi-religious sense—a calling.[1] The thought of doing something else can evoke confused feelings: embarrassment, anger, shame.

I know not everyone fits that description. Perhaps you always knew that you wanted to be a study abroad coordinator. Or the job title of your dreams was "rare books librarian." However, pandemics, budget cuts, international turmoil, demographic shifts, and other factors can destabilize almost any field, even ones that appear to be safe havens just now.[2] The technology-driven

---

[1] Christopher L. Caterine, *Leaving Academia: A Practical Guide* (Princeton: Princeton University Press, 2020), 10.
[2] Cary Carson, "The End of History Museums: What's Plan B?" *The Public Historian* 30, no. 4 (Fall 2008): 9–27.

© The Author(s), under exclusive license to Springer Nature Switzerland AG 2024
I. Land, *The Craft of Historical Research*,
https://doi.org/10.1007/978-3-031-68457-9_15

restructuring that's changing the field of education even as I write these words may reach into other corners of the employment landscape as well. Who's to say what the publishing industry will look like in a few years, for example? There are many scenarios in which any reader of this book could face genuine uncertainty, needing to drum up some ideas about where to turn next.

If you're unsatisfied with your performance on the job market as a graduate, our credential-mad society is quick to suggest yet *another* degree as the solution. To be sure, some careers require a particular paper qualification just to get your foot in the door. In the United States, for example, History students hoping for jobs in the archives are finding that a Master's degree in Library Science improves their prospects considerably. You owe it to yourself to put in the due diligence, though; for some other kinds of master's programs, the numbers really don't add up.[3] Before embarking on yet another degree, it's probably wise to ask yourself some hard questions and maybe accumulate some practical experience.

Think of a job or role that interests you a lot. Then try to formulate a sentence that matches it up with a "because" statement. Tinkering with different wording may throw up some insights. This may remind you of the exercise in Chap. 9, challenging you to write fifteen versions of your thesis statement. What you need to clarify this time is a sense of your own purpose as you approach a broader job market.

Set aside any notion of what the *correct* or *desirable* answer would be. In this case, I'm asking you to interview yourself, and the only criterion is honesty. For example, it might occur to you that you'd like to look into opportunities at museums. But what's the attraction for you, exactly?

Set down some words.

> I'm interested in museum work because my research background was with material culture, I like handling old objects, and a quiet work environment is very important to me.

Or

> I love museums because I respect how museums reach and educate a wider public. Also, I love working with kids. Bring on the chaos!

Or

> Museums are the place to be right now because they are beginning to address their elitist and colonialist past and that's going to require a lot of work to address.

---

[3] "USC Pushed a $115,000 Online Degree. Graduates Got Low Salaries, Huge Debts," *Wall Street Journal*, November 9, 2021.

What emerges from these three "because" statements is a picture of three different people who are all wondering about museums, but are driven by, chasing after, and even *thinking of* quite different things. For this reason, articulating your "because" statement can enable you to see your own skill set, but also your values, in a new light. This can have unexpected benefits: Knowing which aspects of a work environment you care about the most may suggest that you'd be almost equally fulfilled in a range of *other* jobs that carry the same key traits.

With that in mind, keep tinkering with your "because" statement. Get feedback from the people who know you best. Share your notes so far, but ask *them* what makes you tick. A career coach offers this prompt: "When do friends and family say that you're at your happiest?"[4] They may remember things that you don't—or that you never associated with career choices, until now.

Life is full of compromises, but don't signal that you're approaching a Plan B (or even Plan C) job as a consolation prize. Should you land an actual job interview, remember that the people you're meeting now come to *this* workplace every day, and they are eager to hear what sort of spirit you'll be bringing to it.[5] Describing the side of your personality that's the best match for the position is far more compelling than a wistful story about paths not taken.

Alternative careers are often lumped together, but they differ—not just from the traditional teaching and research track—but from each other. While this chapter is far from comprehensive, I discuss some of the most common subgroups within the "alternative" category: jobs that are situated "next to," or in the vicinity of, the familiar teaching positions at universities; the jobs that focus on conveying history-related content to a wider public; and the research, strategy, and leadership jobs that lie further afield, but which also offer an opportunity to put to work the kinds of skills we've discussed in this book. The most frequently asked question of all is how to express *on your resume* that you really have potential as an intrepid path changer and career jumper. I conclude the chapter with some tips on how to do that.

Academic-Adjacent Jobs

You can find many forms of employment somewhere within the orbit of university life or influenced by its powerful gravitational field. I express this as "academic-adjacent" to account, for example, for the jobs in textbook publishing. There are some roles that you've probably heard of in that industry, such as editors and sales reps. Also, because textbooks increasingly incorporate online educational materials, it is possible to work as a UX (user experience) researcher for one of these companies.[6] Meanwhile, people who work at university presses are in constant dialogue with peer reviewers and with the

---

[4] Caterine, *Leaving*, 43.
[5] Caterine, *Leaving*, 74.
[6] Caterine, *Leaving*, 22.

researchers who produce the manuscripts that they assess. Likewise, grant-awarding bodies (endowed foundations; certain government offices) aren't academic as such, but a large part of their work is to evaluate and fund what academics do.

Universities, too, employ many people other than faculty. The following is by no means an exhaustive list, but it gives a sense of the range of possibilities that might appeal to someone with a degree in History:

> associate directors of interdisciplinary centers, directors of scholarship and student-development programs, student-affairs professionals, study-abroad coordinators, career counselors, diversity trainers, academic advisers, even financial managers.[7]

There are different ways to characterize this work; one term that has caught on (and flourished as a hashtag, #alt-academy) is "alternative academic."

While many of these roles are, arguably, quite central to the life of the modern university, there is a sense of precarity about many of these positions. Free speech protections that are extended to faculty often do not apply to other staff. In "the highly stratified environment of the university," being less visible also can translate into difficulties.[8] A classic example would be in the event of an administrative reorganization or a draconian downsizing, but in other situations people report feeling unappreciated and asked to do a great deal with limited resources.

By comparison with employment in the mysterious "real world," an academic-adjacent position may sound familiar, even cozy. After all, haven't you spent a lot of time in and around universities? You studied abroad yourself, therefore you may have an instinct for what a study abroad office does, and so forth. I'll venture a guess: If you get the job, you will need to acclimate to the things about your new colleagues, the workflow, and the office culture that your liberal arts background *didn't* prepare you for.

I realize that I have just crossed the line into outright heresy. Isn't one of the magical traits of the liberal arts that it prepares you for anything? Aren't we fabled for our flexibility and eagerness to learn in new settings? Well, yes. But it's also worth owning up to the solitary habits that—in many cases—primed us to sign up for this discipline in the first place. As Carol Berkin has written, "Historians are neither natural nor trained collaborators."[9] Reflecting on her experience working on a documentary film project, she remarked:

---

[7] Anne Mitchell Whisnant, "I Am Natalie Henderson: My 'Nonacademic' Career in Academe & the #alt-ac Quest," in *#Alt-Academy: Alternative Academic Careers for Humanities Scholars*, ed. Bethany Nowviskie http://mediacommons.org/alt-ac/, 38-45; see 42.

[8] Whisnant, "I Am Natalie Henderson," 43.

[9] Carol Berkin, "So You Want To Be in Pictures? Tips from a Talking Head," *OAH Newsletter* 33, no. 1 (February 2005), 1–10, see 1.

We work alone, often in quite solitary circumstances, buried in archives or sitting at our desk surrounded by printouts or note cards... perhaps no profession in the world, except poetry writing and lighthouse keeping, allows such independence, such control over the process of creating and completing a project.[10]

She's on to something here. In contrast to a vast array of academic disciplines, co-authoring is the exception for us, not the norm. Occasionally, historians meet for lunch to discuss how their work is going, or to swap tips and gossip, but consider how different this is from the scientist who reports daily to the laboratory and works with a team on a *shared* project. Frank Furstenberg has referred to the way that a degree program (in whatever discipline) is a form of "anticipatory socialization."[11] Historians socialize students to expect that they won't need to be all that sociable!

Therein lies the problem. You have excelled on your own in the past, but success in this new setting probably means excelling at listening, excelling at articulating your strengths but ceding ground when others know more, excelling—in short—as a valuable team member. In many workplace settings, you'll find that authority, input, and skills reside in more than one place; even if you are hired for a leadership role, you may well find that what they are expecting is a skilled, shrewd, and patient *mediator*.[12]

These habits, in the aggregate, are sometimes referred to as "soft skills." Some argue that the advent of artificial intelligence will accelerate the transition from a "knowledge economy" to a "relationship economy, in which people skills and social abilities are going to become even more core to success than ever before."[13] While this is potentially good news for *some* graduates from a liberal arts background, it's a bit worrying for those who consider themselves loners, either by habit or temperament. Think about situations where you have exercised soft skills in the past. Maybe this is an area that you can strengthen. Spot opportunities to practice collaboration now, even in your academic work, should an opening present itself.[14]

Another way to smooth your transition here, and come across as more savvy in your interview, would be to seek out a relevant job while you are still a student. Try to anticipate what sort of niche might appeal to you later. Then find a job that will bring you—at least—into contact with someone who's occupying one of the roles that might interest you in the future. This is work experience that you can discuss in a job interview. Ideally, you'll also come with a letter of reference (or two) from the office that employed you.

---

[10] Berkin, "So You Want," 10.

[11] Frank F. Furstenberg, *Behind the Academic Curtain: How to Find Success and Happiness with a PhD* (Chicago: University of Chicago Press, 2013), xi.

[12] Corbett and Miller, "Shared Inquiry," 19.

[13] Aneesh Raman and Maria Flynn, "When Your Technical Skills Are Eclipsed, Your Humanity Will Matter More Than Ever," *New York Times*, February 14, 2024.

[14] Thomson and Kamler, *Writing*, Chapter 8, "Writing with Others" is instructive here.

Public-Facing History

For generations, people have complained that there aren't enough "public intellectuals."[15] It doesn't help that there are no entry-level positions in the field, and it doesn't come with anything like a steady paycheck! Next time you notice a historian writing opinion pieces for a newspaper, testifying before a legislature as an expert, or helping with *amicus* briefs in a court case, understand that such roles are usually invitation-only and go to people who are already well-established figures.

The term "public history," in contrast, emerged in the 1970s.[16] A recent textbook defines it this way:

> Public historians are individuals, usually trained historians, who work in either a professional or academic capacity and who engage in the practice of communicating the past to the public. Such individuals collaborate with various publics and communities to research and present their histories. Principally, they aim to facilitate open access of history to the public.[17]

There are some ambiguities here; as a catch-all term, public history could include some jobs—and roles—that have little in common with each other.[18] There is also controversy over whether such definitions over-emphasize the contrast between experts and the public, and privilege the role of the university-educated historian, when a shared authority approach might be more collaborative and equitable.

In this section, I will focus on what we might call public-*facing* history, which is characteristic of the work that goes on in museums and curated historic sites, but could also encompass some projects undertaken by archives, libraries, and government agencies. Why do I say public-facing? Because the public isn't monolithic. Let's imagine visitors to George Washington's mansion, Mount Vernon. A single tour group at Mount Vernon might include descendants of former slaves, white Civil War re-enactors, international visitors from six different countries, antiques enthusiasts with a lot of questions about the furniture, and more. Doing your job well would mean remaining constantly aware of all these different predispositions, expectations, and needs, even if you drew the line at times and debunked certain errors about the site and its history. However committed you are to inclusiveness, you couldn't be *of, by and for* all of those publics yourself, even if you tried.

---

[15] James M. Banner, Jr., *Being a Historian: An Introduction to the Professional World of History* (Cambridge: Cambridge University Press, 2012), 160–163.

[16] Banner, *Being a Historian*, 138–140.

[17] Faye Sayer, *Public History: A Practical Guide,* second edition (London: Bloomsbury Academic, 2019), 2.

[18] The range of articles that have appeared in the journal *The Public Historian* is illustrative of this.

Public-facing work is constantly in dialogue with various interested parties, or "stakeholders." The focus here is on accessibility, education, outreach, and building trust. I'm not suggesting that there's an expectation that you'd pander to the public's whims. Yet the work doesn't go on in a vacuum; it is always surrounded by other agendas, understandings, and priorities.[19]

It's possible to embrace a model of public-facing history that gets away from an entrenched system of gatekeepers. Shared inquiry, defined as "practitioners and stakeholders joined in give-and-take discussion to set mutually acceptable questions and to find mutually satisfying answers," opens up some exciting possibilities.[20] This is not a new concept, but social media and related technologies offer new ways to implement it. Institutions ranging from the US National Park Service to the Houston Public Library have developed initiatives that treat community members as full partners, inviting them to open-ended conversations from the project design stages onward.[21] While throwing open the digital floodgates invites a certain amount of anarchy, online platforms that invite the public to tag locations or upload images and documents of importance to them—or annotate ones already in the collection—produce a pool of subject matter knowledge that would be hard to replicate any other way.[22]

Any of these public-facing history projects, surely, would like to hire people who can carry on a skillful, tactful dialogue with potential visitors, partners, stakeholders, or contributors. You may have heard that applying for jobs requires a certain amount of bragging. It's tempting to try to establish that you are in possession of that mysterious quality, "great communication skills." However, a term like that takes on specific meaning and weight in different workplace cultures.[23] Here's an example. Suppose there are four small museums that all advertise for a new staff member. All four put something about "great communication skills" in their ad, but if you get the chance to speak to each one, what they mean by it is quite different:

- Museum A is at risk of closing and is seeking to drum up visitors from a newer, younger demographic, perhaps via a bigger social media presence.
- Museum B is mainly focused on meeting a fundraising goal so they can move into a larger building.

---

[19] Jessica Taylor, "'We're on Fire': Oral History and the Preservation, Commemoration, and Rebirth of Mississippi's Civil Rights Sites," *Oral History Review* 42, no. 2 (Summer/Fall 2015): 231–254, illustrates this well.

[20] Corbett and Miller, "Shared Inquiry," 18.

[21] Megan E. Springate, "The National Park Service LGBTQ Heritage Initiative: One Year Out," *The George Wright Forum* 34, No. 3 (2017): 394–404; Tracy B. Grimm and Chon A. Noriega, "Documenting Regional Latino Arts and Culture: Case Studies for a Collaborative, Community-Oriented Approach," *The American Archivist* 76, no. 1 (Spring/Summer 2013): 95–112.

[22] Felicity McWilliams, "A Sense of Place: Digitally Mapping Museum Collections," *Journal of Museum Ethnography* 27 (2014): 46–62.

[23] Caterine, *Leaving*, 151.

- Museum C is eligible for grants but has a disappointing track record at obtaining outside funding and hopes that hiring new staff will change that.
- Museum D has a controversy over a troubling legacy, or even over an item that is still on exhibit; they've got protesters at the door, and they're locked in indecision about what to do next.

Perhaps none of these museums would supply this information in the job listing. Yet as you research them online, or as you sit through the interview itself, you'd want to be on the lookout for hints of what's on their minds and what they would hope for from you. Of course, all this speculation may not be necessary. If you apply for a position at a museum or historic site with just a few people on the payroll, you could also find yourself asked point blank in the job interview about what solutions *you'd* propose to the problem that they are facing! Indeed, you may find that the interview is starting to feel more like a conversation.

That conversation could be quite wide-ranging. Jennifer Thomas relates how

> in the first week of my first professional museum job in a small historical museum in New York State, I suddenly found myself researching how to safely trap a raccoon in the attic... No one asks me today [about her specialized research topic as a student], but knowing how to find a raccoon trap, speak to donors, and increase staff morale has been priceless.[24]

In this spirit, don't be surprised if the interview includes questions that are meant to assess how flexible and open-minded you are.

You are allowed to ask questions, too. Keep your probing tactful, but Corbett and Miller offer "four perennial core questions" that someone could ask about any public-facing history project:

1. What are the project goals, and who set them?
2. How might the goals be met, and by whom?
3. Who are the stakeholders, and what are the relationships between the stakeholders and the target audience?
4. Can the practitioner work effectively as a historian in the setting at hand?[25]

The fourth question may leave you wondering what example they could have in mind. Serving a non-academic master may bring with it non-academic pressures and even explicit demands that would be unthinkable in a university setting.

For example, the issues around guided tours of Southern plantation houses are sufficiently fraught that there is a small, but growing academic literature

---

[24] As quoted in Sayer, *Public History*, 29–30.
[25] Corbett and Miller, "Shared Inquiry," 19.

around the practical, ethical, and political quandaries of that situation alone.[26] Martin Reuss tackled a more subtle situation when he asked: "What does it mean to be good at federal history?"[27] Historians employed in an official capacity by US government agencies ought to do more than "pick out facts that reinforce the agency self-image or policy"; they certainly should not suppress evidence because it was potentially embarrassing; yet both of these things have sometimes occurred.[28] A truly inflexible person is unlikely to flourish for long in these kinds of roles. In some workplaces, even the most pragmatic individual might need to consider what red line they would absolutely refuse to cross.

Looking Further Afield

In *The Life of the Mind*, Hannah Arendt conjured up a whimsical thought experiment, suggesting that "if a given science accidentally reached its goal, this would by no means stop the workers in that field," who'd cheerfully carry on in the expectation of fresh progress on some front.[29] In Arendt's view, this spoke to a profound human quality: We are "question-asking beings."[30] For readers of a book entitled *The Craft of Historical Research*, I suspect that such a statement feels self-evident and universal. However, don't lose sight of the fact that some people need lessons—and even worksheets—about how to be more curious and "prioritize your learning."[31]

It is striking how many books of career advice contain little pep talks about the value of curiosity. There's a lesson here for graduates who doubt they'd have any appeal to employers who operate in areas that they never studied in school. In a job market where people need to snap up new skills, catch on to new trends, and reinvent themselves every few years, your status as a "question-asking being" is, in itself, a marketable quality.

Likewise, in pursuit of your History degree, you've acquired—or enhanced—your aptitude for sleuthing. Even in today's landscape of algorithms and artificial intelligence, many employers are looking for some version of the sleuth. It could be as simple as finding something that your boss can't, or finding it faster than they would have.

---

[26] E. Arnold Modlin, Jr., "Tales Told on the Tour: Mythic Representations of Slavery by Docents at North Carolina Plantation Museums," *Southeastern Geographer* 48, no. 3 (November 2008): 265–287; Amy E. Potter, "'She Goes into Character as the Lady of the House': Tour Guides, Performance, and the Southern Plantation," *Journal of Heritage Tourism* 11, no. 3 (2016): 250–261.

[27] Martin Reuss, "Government and Professional Ethics: The Case of Federal Historians," *Public Historian* 21, no. 3 (1999): 135–142, see 141.

[28] Reuss, "Government," 137–138.

[29] Hannah Arendt, *The Life of the Mind*, vol. 1, *Thinking* (New York: Harcourt Brace Jovanovich, 1977), 55.

[30] Arendt, *Life*, 62.

[31] Helen Tupper and Sarah Ellis, *The Squiggly Career: Ditch the Ladder, Discover Opportunity, Design Your Career* (New York: Penguin, 2020), 144–149, 210.

Political campaigns conduct "opposition research." Law firms seek to uncover material to support a prosecution or bolster a defense. Marketers study what sorts of advertisements capture eyeballs, and clicks, online. Investment banks are looking for the next big thing. Investigative journalism performs an indispensable public service. Data visualization can change hearts and minds. Intelligence agencies and law enforcement employ small armies of analysts to disentangle signal from noise, on topics ranging from international espionage to human trafficking. Advocacy groups and nonprofits want real-time fact-checkers to call out slippery claims that are gaining traction on social media. Your next sleuthing assignment? Pick the version of sleuthing that appeals to your values and interests the most, and investigate it as a possible career path.

> **Pivot Point: Explaining Your Skill Set**
> As someone who has undertaken a long and demanding academic research project that was then subjected to critique and revision, you bring so much to the table. You don't have experience in a particular industry or workplace yet, but you know what it means to discuss rival explanations and weigh the validity of contested evidence, because you did it for your research paper. This is excellent preparation for other situations that call for that kind of reasoning.
>
> 1. You're aware that a big part of the task is *selecting* material, sorting out the less relevant and the less trustworthy.
> 2. You're aware that another big part of the task is *analyzing* material while remaining sensitive to other possible interpretations.
> 3. You're accustomed to discriminating between older insights and what's genuinely new.
> 4. You try to avoid making superficial statements; you attempt to speak to the heart of the problem.
> 5. You understand the need to address the most critical aspects, without oversimplifying.
> 6. You will avoid re-inventing the wheel, using the existing resources on this topic without uncritically accepting all of their assumptions, or assuming that the situation has not evolved since then.
> 7. You understand the need to summarize, and you even have experience with summarizing your summary (e.g., when you wrote your abstract).
> 8. You're prepared to make suggestions about data we *could* collect, reports we *could* commission, and questions we *hadn't thought to ask*—but should have.

Many employers are looking for people to fill management and leadership positions who are comfortable with complexity. People with a liberal arts background often excel here. One individual who started out with a specialty in ancient Rome and is now a consultant in the corporate world remarks that

> My academic work taught me to move rapidly from small details to the big picture... this skill is extremely rare: many of the professionals I work with today can only do one or the other.[32]

Beyond this, though, we come with a high tolerance for what social scientists call "wicked problems." This term was coined in a 1973 article which is still worth reading today.[33] How can we improve the performance of our schools? Law enforcement? Our health care system? Civic engagement? These are "wicked problems" for which no handbook or ready-made formula exists to supply an answer.

There is ample room to question whether a wicked problem is really just a symptom of yet another problem, setting up endless arguments over concepts and definitions. There's no laboratory where we can safely try out different approaches—every policy choice has real, and lasting, human consequences. It's likely that we never get to declare victory. Yet "we will never know" and "it can't be fixed" are not acceptable answers either. This situation creates an inexhaustible demand for new policy initiatives. Those policy ideas need strategists to devise ways to implement them, leaders to advocate for them, and researchers to monitor progress (or the lack thereof). Meanwhile, since there is lots of ambiguity over whether we even know how to measure that we are getting results, the cycle may begin anew.

The fuzziness of such situations leaves a lot of people throwing up their hands in despair. However, the very same traits that attracted you to advanced academic pursuits in the first place quite possibly mean that you are the sort of person who runs toward wicked problems instead of away from them. There's a career path here.

Perhaps you're annoyed with me now because I didn't mention an obvious wicked problem that would be at the top of your personal list of examples. May I suggest: You have your answer. Go work on that one!

WHAT GOES ON YOUR RESUME?

Whichever direction you're hoping to pursue, it's likely to be your resume that gets your foot in the door initially. It's tempting to assume that more is automatically better. As with a good graph or map, though, consider what the reader wants and needs to see, and direct them to it in short order, with a minimum of clutter and distraction. For this reason, if you are applying for three different jobs, you may well need to write up three different resumes.[34]

---

[32] Caterine, *Leaving*, 126.
[33] Horst W. J. Rittel and Melvin M. Webber, "Dilemmas in a General Theory of Planning," *Policy Sciences* 4 (1973): 155–169.
[34] For more practical tips on resume writing, including examples of complete resumes, see Susan Basalla and Maggie Debelius, *"So What Are You Going to Do with That?" Finding Careers Outside Academia*, 3rd ed. (Chicago: University of Chicago Press, 2015), 97–123.

Transitioning from an academic background to a non-academic job application requires that you learn to represent your work experience in a somewhat abstract way, as a set of skills developed and aptitudes proven. Your university should have a career center of some kind with staff who can advise you on what words will "speak" to the government, NGO, or private sector employer. Try to express your skill set in language that's abstract enough that it could survive several different career changes.

To be sure, some work experience requires little translation or reframing. An employer seeking proficiency in GIS—or intensive experience working with legal records—can scan your resume for that exact line. On the other hand, conveying the kind of detective work and creative problem-solving that you did in the archive may require a neat, short illustrative example, or a carefully chosen set of verbs. Remember that most people have never seen the inside of an archive!

Don't oversell or mislabel yourself. In the interview, anyone could ask a searching, skeptical question about a line on your resume. Step back and consider what words would capture the essence of what you really did, and what that activity has prepared you to handle well in the future. For example, "project management" isn't one size fits all. Did you deal with the workflow for a large digitization project that unfolded over two years? Did you help with local arrangements and catering for an academic conference that took place on a single hectic weekend? Each in their own way, these could set you up to hit the ground running—but in very different *kinds* of work environments.

Some employers won't be keen to hire troublemakers. I've been visited twice by FBI agents about former students who needed security clearances, and both times the emphasis was on whether that individual had ever "refused a direct order." (I had to smile, because I don't issue too many of those.) Other jobs, though, are essentially about advocacy, activism, and what is loosely called "organizing." If you're applying for something like that, you may want to include something from your past that wasn't especially relevant for other positions—but really belongs on your resume for this one.

Step back and think about what you really did in an activist setting. "Founded a working group on the graduate student housing issue" doesn't communicate that you are a coalition builder who brought a diverse, and sometimes quarrelsome, collection of international students together and kept them focused enough to pressure the university administration. It also doesn't hint that you have experience speaking to the media, because local newspapers and a TV station interviewed you about the list of demands that you posted. You might be just the troublemaker that *this* employer is looking for.

Interviewers understand if you have never had a full-time position doing a particular kind of work, but they are ready to hear about anything you've done in that direction, even briefly, even just one time. Perhaps you've never worked at a heritage site, but you did present on your research to a community group at a local library. If you have a good story about the one time you dipped your toes in those particular waters, an intelligent observation about how it went, and a "lesson learned," that could be what makes the difference.

Personality comes through, even in a brief interview. Suppose that listening is a key activity in the position. The job candidate who doesn't pick up on cues, and seems to lecture the hiring committee, is not going to get the nod. Some traits suggest rigidity; others signal you'd quickly adjust to a new environment. The list of those traits is disarmingly simple. One career coach enumerates just three that distinguish people who've transitioned well, and happily, from academia: they are "good at meeting new people, taking risks, and learning from every experience—whether good or bad."[35] We might add a fourth to that list, just being capable of sometimes saying, "I don't know."[36] That's refreshing in a world of pushy people who try to project hyper-competence at every moment. After all, admitting that you don't know something is the first step toward finding out the answers or learning the skill. And to your future co-workers, it signals that you realize you still have things to learn.

Conclusion

It's easy to obsess over what employers really want or struggle to guess the magic word that will open doors closed to others. Can you really talk about "stakeholder alignment" with a straight face, or use the word "agile" as a noun?[37] If only the transition to a new role, and new workplace culture, were that simple! Then switching career paths really could resemble the child's dress-up game.

I urge you to take a deeper look at your new possible role and the workplace culture that you'd inhabit. When possible, meet people who have relevant experience, and *listen to how they talk about their job.* Practitioners of public history, for example, remark that the work is "frequently messy" and urge flexibility: "'lay back, let it happen, try out different ideas.'"[38] They relay this advice with affection, but if you are happiest with a lot of structure and predictability in your work environment, that may not be the career path for you.

Be candid with yourself. What role in life do you feel naturally drawn to? What situations leave you cold or stressed or alienated? We can't learn the answer to what makes *us* happy from observing where *other* people flourish. Wish them well, but seek your own answers. If you bully yourself into liking things, it will backfire.

Avoid the bad, but also make a conscious effort to seek out the good. This seems obvious, but if you are still grieving the demise of your personal Plan A, it's easy to enter a period of fatalistic drift. For many people, happiness is bound

---

[35] Caterine, *Leaving Academia*, 4.
[36] Kelly Main, "Apple Secretly Looks for Candidates Who Are Willing to Say These 3 Little Words," *Inc.*, August 3, 2023.
[37] Caterine, *Leaving*, 107, 168.
[38] Corbett and Miller, "Shared Inquiry," 18.

up with helping others, feeling relevant and needed. The remark that "the world is saturated with data, yet somehow remains starving for wisdom" still resonates today.[39] As long as we have poorly understood issues and "wicked problems," the skills and talents you've cultivated in the pursuit of History set you up to make a real contribution to something bigger than yourself.

In their book *The Squiggly Career*, Helen Tupper and Sarah Ellis suggest that everyone needs three people in their life somewhere: the person who gets it, the person who asks you the hard questions, and the person who's been there.[40] Amid all the fuss about resume writing, job applications, and fretting about qualifications, don't forget to draw on—or create—a network that can support you in all of these ways. Who knows you best and understands what you want (and why you want it)? Who's always ready to talk about practical next steps and call you out on those times when you're ducking the real issue or making excuses? Who's the person in your life with real world experience that's closest to the types of jobs you are currently seeking? Each in their own way, these are people to cherish (if you've got them) or seek out (if you don't quite yet). What you are doing right now is hard. Remember that you don't have to do it alone.

Further Reading

Helen Tupper and Sarah Ellis, *The Squiggly Career: Ditch the Ladder, Discover Opportunity, Design Your Career* (New York: Penguin, 2020).

Christopher L. Caterine, *Leaving Academia: A Practical Guide* (Princeton: Princeton University Press, 2020).

Joseph Fruscione and Kelly J. Baker, eds., *Succeeding Outside the Academy: Career Paths Beyond the Humanities, Social Sciences, and STEM* (Lawrence, KS: University Press of Kansas, 2018).

Susan Cain, *Quiet: The Power of Introverts in a World That Can't Stop Talking* (New York: Crown, 2012).

Faye Sayer, *Public History: A Practical Guide*, second edition (London: Bloomsbury Academic, 2019).

Annie Duke, *Quit: The Power of Knowing When to Walk Away* (New York: Portfolio, 2022).

---

[39] Nicholas Kristof, "Starving for Wisdom," *New York Times*, April 16, 2015. He attributes the quotation originally to E.O. Wilson.

[40] Tupper and Ellis, *Squiggly Career*, 94.

Index[1]

A
Anti-library, 42, 44, 66, 67
Archimedean Point, 5, 6, 115, 133, 220, 275
Archives, 25, 61, 68, 75–77
Argument, 7, 37, 38, 52, 139–141, 144, 148, 149, 151, 153, 156, 167, 169, 171–173, 182, 192, 194, 204–206, 214, 224, 229, 232, 234, 237, 238, 242, 250

B
Bias, 13, 49, 56, 82, 104
Browsing, 13, 18–20, 22, 23, 25–27, 32, 36, 40, 67, 106, 108, 112, 257
Burnout, 91

C
Citations, 23, 67, 81, 92, 232, 233, 244
Collaboration, 44, 287
Crosschecking, 52, 54

D
Digital resources, 101
Distant reading, 109, 112
Drafts, 14, 200, 206, 220, 252, 277

E
Eyewitness, 49

F
Facts, 146, 163
Fair, 141, 144, 154, 200, 238, 242, 243, 279
Family, 8, 27, 79, 208, 263, 285
Fatigue, 220, 257
Finding aids, 10, 18, 83–85, 83n22, 92
Fonds, 80, 81, 94, 103, 105
Footnotes, 7, 8, 10, 20, 22, 36, 46, 61, 92, 194, 210, 226, 231, 232, 234, 242, 256, 261, 270, 280

---

[1] Note: Page numbers followed by 'n' refer to notes.

G
Genius, 6, 25, 67, 131

H
Honesty, 139, 200, 205, 216, 238, 284

I
Imposter syndrome, 12, 91, 267
Introductions, 7, 22, 217, 220

L
Logic, 7, 8, 37, 81, 102, 149, 164, 165, 204, 212, 221, 242

M
Mental health, 130
Metadata, 83, 84, 103, 105, 106
Metaphor, 50, 161, 193

N
Narrative, 36, 123, 133, 144, 146, 201–203, 205, 216, 219, 250, 251

O
Originality, 6, 9, 14, 63, 64, 66, 70–72, 157, 244, 255, 276
Outlining, 205, 206, 212, 214, 216, 217, 221, 245

P
Paleography, 31, 90, 93
Paraphrasing, 175, 227–229
Paywalls, 225
Privacy, 9, 55, 192
Proof, 8, 129, 146, 169, 172

Prospectus, 5, 13, 14, 47, 77, 78, 101, 111, 112, 117, 128, 130–135, 221, 254

Q
Questions, 27, 58, 63, 70, 75, 76, 81, 113, 122, 127, 129, 134, 155, 262, 264
Quotation, 8, 52, 61, 141, 149, 169, 170, 174–176, 194, 199, 218, 220, 223–232, 240, 241, 243, 250, 253, 257, 274

R
Refutation, 163, 254, 273

S
Search terms, 18, 39, 106–108
Storytelling, 148, 202–205, 250
Subscribe, *see* Paywalls

T
Thesis statement, 7, 139, 140, 143, 144, 146–150, 155–159, 161, 163–166, 204, 206, 212, 214, 215, 218, 223, 238, 249–251, 259, 262
Time management, 9, 18, 44, 95, 130
Translation, 30, 171, 172, 225, 241
Travel, 6, 29, 108, 271
Truth, 37, 54, 55, 139, 146–149

W
Warrants, 37, 140, 141, 151–153, 169–194, 206, 207
Writer's block, 9, 101, 194, 205–208, 217

Made in the USA
Monee, IL
28 April 2026